EXPLORING MICROSOFT® VISUAL BASIC®

VERSION 6.0

by *Carlotta B. Eaton*

New River Community College

Prentice Hall, Upper Saddle River, New Jersey 07458

DEDICATION

This book is warmly and affectionately dedicated to my husband, Steve, and my daughter, Cassie. This book could not have been completed without your support and encouragement.

Acquisitions Editor: Alex von Rosenburg
Assistant Editor: Lori Cardillo
Development Editor: Cecil Yarbrough
Editorial Assistant: Kyle Hannon
Executive Marketing Manager: Nancy Evans
Project Manager: Lynne Breitfeller
Senior Manufacturing Supervisor: Paul Smolenski
Manufacturing Coordinator: Dawn–Marie Reisner
Senior Manager, Manufacturing/Prepress: Vincent Scelta
Senior Designer/Interior and Cover Design: Suzanne Behnke
Composition: TSI Graphics, Inc.

ISBN 0-13-657594-3

Prentice Hall International (UK) Limited, *London*
Prentice Hall of Australia Pty. Limited, *Sydney*
Prentice Hall of Canada Inc., *Toronto*
Prentice Hall Hispanoamericano, S.A., *Mexico*
Prentice Hall of India Private Limited, *New Delhi*
Prentice Hall of Japan, Inc., *Tokyo*
Simon & Schuster Asia Pte. Ltd., *Singapore*
Editora Prentice Hall do Brasil, Ltda., *Rio de Janeiro*

Printed in the United States of America
10 9 8 7 6 5 4 3 2 1

FOREWORD

Exploring Microsoft Visual Basic 6.0, by Carlotta B. Eaton, is written with the same dedication and attention to detail as are all of the other texts in the *Exploring Windows* series. Maryann and I had always wanted to write a book on Visual Basic, but two people can only do so much. We were delighted, therefore, when Carlotta agreed to write the Visual Basic component for us. Instructors who are familiar with our series will recognize Carlotta's name from the outstanding set of Instructor Manuals she produced for Office 95 and again for Office 97. We are pleased to acknowledge her contribution to our series and to welcome her as an author in her own right.

Bob and Maryann

CONTENTS

2

Build Your First Project: A Step-by-Step Approach

3

Programming Fundamentals: Writing Code

4

Enhancing the Graphical User Interface: Multiple Forms, Controls, and Menus

5

Basics of File Input and Output: Reading, Writing, and Printing Text Files

6

Programming with Office 97: The OLE Container Control and Automation

7

Database Basics: Tables, Records, and Fields

8

Relational Databases: ActiveX Database Controls

PREFACE

Exploring Microsoft Visual Basic 6.0 can be used for an introductory programming course for both non-programming majors and majors. *Essentials of Microsoft Visual Basic 5.0* is suitable for use as a module in Visual Basic for locations that have not yet upgraded to the latest version of Visual Basic.

Both editions are part of the Prentice Hall custom binding program, enabling you to create your own text by selecting any modules in the *Exploring Windows* series (see back cover for a complete list) for a course teaching application software as well as programming. You could, for example, create a custom text consisting of the introductory (essential) chapters in Word, Excel, Internet Explorer, and Visual Basic. You get exactly the material you need, and students realize cost savings. You can also take advantage of our ValuePack program to shrink-wrap multiple books together. A ValuePack results in significant savings for the student.

Users of other volumes in the Grauer and Barber series will find the features on which they have come to rely. Like the other books in the *Exploring Windows* series, the hands-on approach and conceptual framework of this book helps students master key computing and programming concepts as well as the Visual Basic programming language. Take a look:

- This textbook can be used with both Visual Basic 6.0 and Visual Basic 5.0. This is an advantage when lab upgrades are on different schedules, or students have the previous version on home computers.
- Students learn by doing, with an average of *three hands-on exercises* in every chapter that provide just the right amount of practice time. These exercises make use of a *student data disk* that can be downloaded from the Prentice Hall Web site **http://www.prenhall.com/grauer** or the author's textbook site at **http://www.swva.net/ceaton**.
- Shortcuts and other important information are consistently highlighted in the many *boxed tips* that appear throughout the book. Boxed tips also give alternate instructions for Visual Basic 5.0 where the two versions of the software differ.
- Each chapter contains 15 *multiple-choice questions* (with answers) so that students can test themselves quickly and objectively.
- An average of *six practice exercises* per chapter provide substantial opportunity for students to master the material, while simultaneously giving instructors considerable flexibility in student assignments.
- Every chapter ends with four open-ended *case studies* that provide substantial opportunity for students to master the material.
- An *Exploring WWW icon* appears whenever the World Wide Web is referenced as a resource in conjunction with a Visual Basic exercise.

- This textbook may be ordered with a tutorial CD from CBT systems. The CDs have been certified by Microsoft to include all topics necessary to sit for the Visual Basic 5.0 certification exam.

Instructors can visit the author's textbook site at **http://www.swva.net/ceaton** or the Prentice Hall Web site at **http://www.prenhall.com/grauer** for the latest information on the available instructor resources. An excellent Supplements CD (for the series) contains every instructor resource, solutions, computerized test banks, printed version of the test bank, PowerPoint lectures, the Instructor's Resource Manual in Word 97 format—everything! Additionally, instructors can use the Prentice Hall Computerized Online Testing System to prepare customized tests for their courses.

FEATURES AND BENEFITS

Exploring Visual Basic 6.0
is written for the programming
novice and assumes no previous
programming experience. An
introductory chapter on
programming basics introduces
such general concepts as
machine language, high-level
programming language, event-
driven language, and the
specifics of the Visual
Basic environment.

An average of three in-depth
tutorials (hands-on exercises)
guide the reader at the computer.
Each tutorial is illustrated with
large, full-color screen captures
that are clear and easy to read.
Each tutorial is accompanied by
numerous tips that present
different ways to accomplish a
given task, but in a logical and
relaxed fashion.

programming with graphics in a text-based procedure-oriented language. Object-
oriented languages emphasized the objects and actions instead of procedures for
a task. For example, if you are creating a drawing application, the objects are circles, rectangles, and lines. The actions are click, drag, and release. Programs were
easier to design and understand because of the emphasis on objects instead of procedures and tasks. ***Object-oriented programming*** (or ***OOP***, pronounced to rhyme
with "hoop") was a major mind-set shift for the programming community. Examples include Smalltalk, C++, and Ada 95. Figure 1.2 displays a partial listing of an
Ada 95 program for translating the names of days of the week from English
into French.

Event-driven Languages

Today's applications usually have a ***graphical user interface*** (or ***GUI***, pronounced
"goo-ey"). The object-oriented languages helped program with graphics, but more
help was needed for programmers to keep pace. Event-driven languages were
designed to make it easier to produce GUIs. With an ***event-driven language***, the
computer spends its time responding to events rather than stepping through a pre-
arranged series of actions. Many computer programs that run under graphical user
interfaces such as the Macintosh operating system and Microsoft Windows are
event driven. Such programs respond to events such as the user choosing an item
on a menu or clicking an icon with a mouse. Visual Basic implements event-
driven programming.

Event-driven languages took object-oriented programming to another level.
The instructions were replaced with icons or symbols. Each icon represents an
object or a programming function or procedure. Actions such as clicking and dragging were already programmed into the icon, so the programmer did not need to
program nearly as many instructions. Microsoft's Visual Basic became one of the
most popular event-driven languages for end users as well as professional programmers. Figure 1.3 shows the integrated development environment for the older
Visual Basic 4.0.

FIGURE 1.2   Example of an Ada 95 Program

▶ Click the **Yes button** to save your project changes if needed.
▶ The Main form will display as shown in Figure 6.2a.

(Display the Embed form)
(Display the Paste form)
(Display the Link form)
(Display the Icon form)
(Exit the Application)

(a) Open and Save the OLE Starter Project (step 1)

FIGURE 6.2   Hands-on Exercise 1

▶ Click the **Embedding Example button** to display the Embed form. Click the
Close button to close the form.
▶ Click the **Embedding Example using Paste button** to display the Paste form.
Click the **Close button** to close the form.
▶ Click the **Linking Example button** to display the Link form. Click the **Close
button** to close the form.
▶ Click the **Linking Example using Icon button** to display the Icon form. Click
the **Close button** to close the form.
▶ Click the **Exit button** to stop execution.

STEP 2: Add the OLE Container Control to the Embed Form
▶ Double click the **Embed form** in the Project Explorer window to display
the form.
▶ Click the toolbar's **Toolbox button**.
▶ Select the **OLE Container tool** and draw the container on the form. Click the
Create from File option button to display the Insert Object dialog box as
shown in Figure 6.2b.
▶ Select the dialog box's **Create from File option button**. Click the **Browse
button** and select the **OLE Container Demo.xls file** in the *Exploring Visual
Basic 6* folder. Click the **Insert button** to return to the dialog box.
▶ Click the **OK button** to display the worksheet in the OLE Container area.
This may take a moment, so be patient.

(Click here to finish)
(Click this option)
(Click here and select the worksheet file)
(Select the OLE Container tool)

(b) Add the Container Control to the Embed Form (step 2)

FIGURE 6.2   Hands-on Exercise 1 (continued)

▶ The form will look like Figure 6.2c at this point. You may need to resize
the OLE container or form to display the worksheet contents as shown in
the figure.

(Resize the Container control if needed)

(c) The Completed Embed Form (step 2)

FIGURE 6.2   Hands-on Exercise 1 (continued)

PRACTICE WITH VISUAL BASIC

VIDEO CLIP

1. Using the OLE Container Control (Learning Edition Only) This exercise requires that you be using the Learning Edition of Visual Basic, and that you have installed the *Learn Visual Basic Now* book on your hard drive or have access to it from the CD-ROM. This demonstration illustrates using the OLE container control to display a Paint object. Run and watch the demonstration to reinforce this material from the chapter.

  a. Start *Learn Visual Basic Now.*

  b. Open the *Chapter 2* book and the *Working with Other Applications* book as shown in Figure 6.7.

  c. Open the "OLE" or "OLE Control" topic.

  d. Read the information about OLE.

  e. Scroll to the bottom of the topic pane and click the Demonstration icon.

  f. View the entire Visual Basic demonstration.

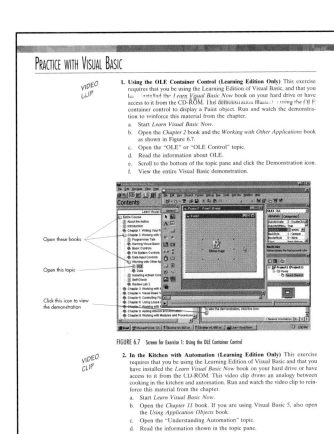

Open these books

Open this topic

Click this icon to view the demonstration

FIGURE 6.7　Screen for Exercise 1: Using the OLE Container Control

VIDEO CLIP

2. In the Kitchen with Automation (Learning Edition Only) This exercise requires that you be using the Learning Edition of Visual Basic and that you have installed the *Learn Visual Basic Now* book on your hard drive or have access to it from the CD-ROM. This video clip draws an analogy between cooking in the kitchen and automation. Run and watch the video clip to reinforce this material from the chapter.

  a. Start *Learn Visual Basic Now.*

  b. Open the *Chapter 11* book. If you are using Visual Basic 5, also open the *Using Application Objects* book.

  c. Open the "Understanding Automation" topic.

  d. Read the information shown in the topic pane.

---

  e. Click the Expert Point of View icon in the topic pane.

  f. View the entire video clip.

Open these books

Open this topic

Click this icon to view the video clip

FIGURE 6.8　Screen for Exercise 2: In the Kitchen with Automation

3. Sample Word Automation (Learning Edition Only) This exercise requires that you be using the Learning Edition of Visual Basic and that you have installed the *Learn Visual Basic Now* book on your hard drive or have access to it from the CD-ROM. This demonstration shows you have to use Word spell-check function as you did in Hands-on Exercise 2 of this chapter. You will be amazed at how quickly you can recreate the starting portion of this exercise. Run and watch the demonstration to reinforce this material from the chapter.

  a. Start *Learn Visual Basic Now.*

  b. Open the *Chapter 11* book. Open the *Controlling Microsoft Office* book, and then the *Microsoft Word* book or topic.

  c. If you are using Visual Basic 5, also open the "Sample Word Automation" topic.

  d. Click the Video Clip icon in the topic pane.

  e. View the entire demonstration.

LOCATE THE SAMPLES

You will be running several sample applications included with Visual Basic in these exercises. If you are using Visual Basic 6.0, look for them first in the default location by opening these folders: Microsoft Visual Studio, then Msdn98 (optionally 98vs, then 1033), then Samples, and finally Vb98. If you are using Visual Basic 5.0, open Microsoft Visual Studio, then Vb, then samples.

At the end of every chapter is an abundance of thought-provoking exercises that review and extend the material in different ways. The practice exercises review and extend the material in the chapter so that the student is exposed to a wide range of programming projects. Many exercises include video presentations from the Learning Edition's tutorial CD.

Every chapter also contains a number of less structured case studies that encourage the reader to further exploration and independent study. Many case studies incorporate the World Wide Web as a resource for additional up-to-date information.

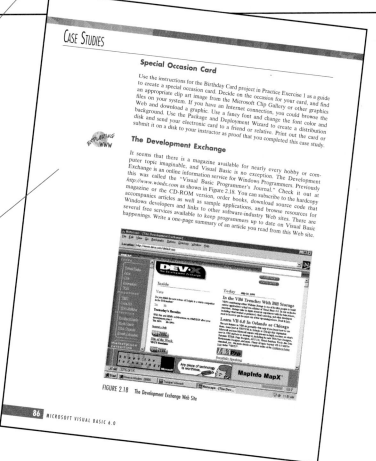

CASE STUDIES

Special Occasion Card

Use the instructions for the Birthday Card project in Practice Exercise 1 as a guide to create a special occasion card. Decide on the occasion for your card, and find an appropriate clip art image from the Microsoft Clip Gallery or other graphics files on your system. If you have an Internet connection, you could browse the Web and download a graphic. Use a fancy font and change the font color and background. Use the Package and Deployment Wizard to create a distribution disk and send your electronic card to a friend or relative. Print out the card or submit it on a disk to your instructor as proof that you completed this case study.

The Development Exchange

It seems that there is a magazine available for nearly every hobby or computer topic imaginable, and Visual Basic is no exception. The Development Exchange is an online information service for Windows Programmers. Previously this was called the "Visual Basic Programmer's Journal." Check it out at *http://www.windx.com* as shown in Figure 2.18. You can subscribe to the hardcopy magazine or the CD-ROM version, order books, download source code that accompanies articles as well as sample applications, and browse resources for Windows developers and links to other software-industry Web sites. There are several free services available to keep programmers up to date on Visual Basic happenings. Write a one-page summary of an article you read from this Web site.

FIGURE 2.18　The Development Exchange Web Site

➤ Your browser should display the page shown in Figure 1.12a. This is where you want to look for the latest updates to Visual Basic. If a Web page does not display, try *mndn.microsoft.com/vbasic/downloads* and scroll the page to see what is available. Examine the Web page carefully for any updates for Visual Basic 6.0.

➤ If you are working on your own computer, select an appropriate topic and proceed to download the update file. If you are working on a lab computer, ask your instructor before downloading or installing any updates on the machine.

(a) Free Stuff (step 1)

FIGURE 1.12   Hands-on Exercise 3

FREE STUFF USING VISUAL BASIC 5.0

If you are using Visual Basic 5 and working on your own computer, download and install the item **Visual Basic, Version 5.0, Update of BIB-LIO.MDB**. If you are working on a lab computer, ask your instructor before installing any updates on the machine. Select the topic, and specify the drive and folder in which to save the download. This file should be stored where Visual Basic is stored on your system. With the default installation, you would select the appropriate hard drive, the **Programs folder**, then the **DevStudio folder**, the **Vb folder**, the **samples folder**, the **PGuide folder**, and finally the **biblio folder**. The file will probably take several minutes to download. When the download is complete, the progress window closes.

STEP 2: Install the Update (Optional)

➤ If you are working on your own computer, click the **Start button** on the Windows 95 taskbar. Select **Programs**, then **Windows Explorer**. In the tree

---

pane of Windows Explorer, find the folder where you saved the file from Step 1 above. The default is the C drive, and you will need to open these folders in order: Program Files, Microsoft Visual Studio, Vb98.

➤ Locate the file and **double click its icon** to execute it. A DOS window or Winzip window should open. When its title bar displays the word *Finished*, **close** the window.

➤ Your update has now been installed. **Close** the Windows Explorer window.

INSTALL THE UPDATE USING VISUAL BASIC 5.0

This step is optional; proceed if you are working on your own computer. Follow the instructions given in Step 2. (The default is the C drive, and you will need to open these folders in order: Program Files, DevStudio, Vb, samples, Pguide folder, biblio.) The file you downloaded is **biblio.exe.**

STEP 3: Product News

➤ Maximize the Visual Basic window if it is not currently displayed.

➤ Pull down the **Help** menu and select **Microsoft on the Web**, then **Product News**.

➤ Your Web browser will display the screen shown in Figure 1.12b.

➤ Click any **hyperlink** that looks interesting to you. If there is information about the Visual Basic edition that you have installed on your computer, then select it. This will probably be either the Learning Edition or the Professional Edition. Read about this edition.

➤ Minimize the Web browser window.

(b) Product News (step 3)

FIGURE 1.12   Hands-on Exercise 3 (continued)

The Web icon appears throughout the book whenever the student is directed to the World Wide Web as a resource for updated and additional information. The student also learns how to access the CD help as well as the help available from the Web.

Chapter 2 covers the basics of building a Visual Basic project step by step using the methodologies used by professional real-world programmers. The student learns good programming habits from the very first exercise. Students are not just taught what to do, but are provided with the rationale for why they are doing it, and thus learn how to better design and plan programming projects for the target user.

STEP 4. Run the Program

Running a program is very simple in Visual Basic. Simply click the Start button on the toolbar.

STEP 5. Test and Debug

This is a very important step. Click the "Click Here" button and check to see that the three events listed in our plan actually occur. If they do not, we need to go back to step 3, and make needed modifications. After the first event is debugged, we test the Exit button to see that it works as planned. We repeat steps 3, 4, and 5 as many times as needed until the project works as planned. Now we can proceed to the next step.

STEP 6. Document Your Program

We have the three sheets of notebook paper from our design-and-plan step. We should also print out the forms and code from Hands-on Exercise 3 in this chapter. For a more complicated project, we would include more, but this will suffice at this time.

STEP 7. Compile and Distribute Your Program

Now we can share our program with others. To run the finished program on a computer that has Visual Basic 6.0 installed, we can simply create an *exe* file. If we want others who do not have Visual Basic to be able to run the program, we use the Package and Deployment Wizard included with Visual Basic 6.0 to create a distribution disk that will install the necessary files on their system.

LEARN BY DOING

The exercises in this chapter are linked to one another in that you perform some steps for a simple project in Exercise 1, then open the project and perform more steps in Exercise 2. The exercises are intended only as a brief introduction to building projects. You will learn more of the details on creating forms, using the Toolbox, and writing code in later chapters. Each exercise has several steps. Concentrate on completing all of the steps in order.

THERE'S ALWAYS A REASON

I would love to tell you that everything will go perfectly, that you will never be frustrated, and that the computer will always perform exactly as you expect. Unfortunately, that is not necessarily what you want it to do. There what you tell it to do, which is not going to happen, because a computer does can be a tremendous difference! There is, however, a logical reason for everything the computer does or does not do; eventually you will discover that reason, at which point everything will fall into place.

Chapter 4 explains techniques for enhancing the graphical user interface. Students learn to distinguish good from bad interface design, as well as how to design interfaces appropriate for the end user. Advanced beginner interfaces are created with multiple forms, and even advanced beginner features such as menus.

The *Explorer* is a specialized SDI style, illustrated using the Windows 95 Explorer as shown in Figure 4.1c. The Explorer-style interface uses a single, stand-alone form divided into several frames or panes. The left pane contains browsing controls such as lists of disks, folders, and files. The right pane shows a more detailed view. The Explorer-style interface is suitable for browsing folders and file structures as well as data. The Explorer-style interface was used to navigate the in Visual Basic 5 Books Online.

You can use any of the three styles to implement your projects. Use the style that best fits the application and feels most natural to the end user.

FIVE PRINCIPLES OF GUI DESIGN

With all the styles and Toolbox tools available, creating and designing forms for your graphical user interface can be a perplexing task. Remember that people usually read the manuals and instructions only when all else fails. You want to make your interface as easy and intuitive to use as possible. If you follow five basic design principles, you should have an easy-to-use Graphical User Interface (GUI).

Principle 1: Know Your End User

When you are designing your program, the first question you should answer is "Who is my audience?" Will your application be used by children, adults, or both? If your program is used by children, what will be their reading level? For preschool children, you will need to use symbols and graphics instead of words for your screens. If you are designing for retired adults, are the fonts large enough to be easily read? Write down as much as you know about your end user before you start sketching and designing your screens. Designing for the end user was discussed in more detail with the Learning to Add application in Chapter 3. This interface is shown in Figure 4.2.

FIGURE 4.2   The Learning to Add Project Designed for a Preschool Child

Acknowledgments

This book is dedicated to my husband, Steve, and daughter, Cassie. They were very supportive and patient during crunch modes. I want to thank Robert T. Grauer and Carolyn Henderson for incorporating this title into the *Exploring Windows* series, and their encouragement and advice along the way. Cecil Yarbrough did an outstanding job in checking the manuscript for technical accuracy and editing it for ease of understanding. Lynne Breitfeller was in charge of production and kept the project on target. Nancy Evans, marketing manager at Prentice Hall, developed the campaigns and provided much encouragement to help me complete this project. Kyle Hannon, editorial assistant at Prentice Hall, helped in an abundance of ways on a daily basis. I would like to thank the following reviewers, who, through their comments and constructive criticism, improved the manuscript of this book:

Lynne Band, Middlesex Community College

Stuart P. Brian, Holy Family College

Carl M. Briggs, Indiana University School of Business

Kimberly Chambers, Scottsdale Community College

Alok Charturvedi, Purdue University

Jerry Chin, Southwest Missouri State University

Dean Combellick, Scottsdale Community College

Cody Copeland, Johnson County Community College

Larry S. Corman, Fort Lewis College

Janis Cox, Tri-County Technical College

Martin Crossland, Southwest Missouri State University

Paul E. Daurelle, Western Piedmont Community College

David Douglas, University of Arkansas

Raymond Frost, Central Connecticut State University

Bill Gahnstrom, University of Kansas

James Gips, Boston College

Vernon Griffin, Austin Community College

Michael Hassett, Fort Hays State University

Wanda D. Heller, Seminole Community College

Bonnie Homan, San Francisco State University

Ernie Ivey, Polk Community College

Mike Kelly, Community College of Rhode Island

Jane King, Everett Community College

John Lesson, University of Central Florida

Curtis Meadow, University of Maine

David B. Meinert, Southwest Missouri State University

Alan Moltz, Naugatuck Valley Technical Community College

Kim Montney, Kellogg Community College

Bill Morse, DeVry Institute of Technology

Kevin Pauli, University of Nebraska

Mary McKenry Percival, University of Miami

Delores Pusins, Hillsborough Community College

Gale E. Rand, College Misericordia

Judith Rice, Santa Fe Community College

David Rinehard, Lansing Community College

Marilyn Salas, Scottsdale Community College

John Shepherd, Duquesne University

John Snider, University of Kansas

Helen Stoloff, Hudson Valley Community College

Margaret Thomas, Ohio University

Mike Thomas, Indiana University School of Business

Suzanne Tomlinson, Iowa State University

Karen Tracey, Central Connecticut State University

Sally Visci, Lorain County Community College

David Weiner, University of San Francisco

Connie Wells, Georgia State University

Wallace John Whistance-Smith, Ryerson Polytechnic University

Jack Zeller, Kirkwood Community College

A final word of thanks to current and former students at Radford University and New River Community College in Virginia. When you tell me two years after the course, "It was hard, I learned a lot, and my next computer class was easy," it makes it all worthwhile. And most of all, thanks to you, my student and instructor readers, for choosing this book. Please feel free to contact me with any comments and suggestions.

Carlotta B. Eaton
nreatoc@nr.cc.va.us
www.nr.cc.va.us/eaton
Assistant Professor, Information Systems Technology
New River Community College, Dublin, Virginia

INTRODUCTION TO VISUAL BASIC®: PROGRAMMING AND APPLICATIONS

OBJECTIVES

After reading this chapter, you will be able to:

1. Differentiate between machine language and high-level language.
2. Define and explain the differences between procedure-oriented, object-oriented, and event-driven programming languages.
3. Explain the background of the Visual Basic programming language.
4. Describe the elements of the Visual Basic integrated development environment.
5. Use the online documentation and help features available with Visual Basic.

OVERVIEW

Computers would be of very little use to us without programs. There are thousands of programs available for personal computers today, all of them written using a programming language. This introduction will acquaint you with programming languages in general and more specifically with the Visual Basic programming language. The history of programming languages will be discussed, and the advantages of using a high-level language such as Visual Basic will be explained.

You will become familiar with the Visual Basic 6.0 Integrated Development Environment. You will also learn how to use the online documentation and help features available with Visual Basic.

The hands-on exercises in this chapter enable you to apply all of the material at the computer, and are indispensable to the "learn by doing" philosophy of the text. Because Visual Basic is a programming language for Windows applications, your familiarity with the Windows 95 or Windows 98 interface (which this text assumes) will make Visual Basic even easier to learn.

Visual Basic was developed as a programming language for end users as well as professional programmers, and is considered the most popular end-user programming language in use today. Visual Basic was specifically designed to build applications for the Windows environment, and is an ideal language to use if you want to customize a Windows program for your computer. Let's look at some basic definitions.

A *program* is simply a detailed set of instructions for a computer to execute. The computer executes program instructions one by one in order to perform a task. A program must be written in a programming language, such as Visual Basic. *Application programs*, also called *applications* or simply *apps,* are a self-contained collection of programs that perform a specific task directly for the user. Examples of application programs are word processing applications such as Word and Word-Perfect; spreadsheets such as Excel and Lotus 1-2-3; and presentation programs such as PowerPoint and Freelance. These are examples of general-purpose applications used by a variety of people performing very different jobs.

A *programming language* is a formal language used to give instructions to computers. It is the tool used to write computer programs. There are probably as many programming languages in use as there are spoken languages.

HISTORY OF PROGRAMMING LANGUAGES

We communicate with computers using programs that are created using a programming language. Today programs are written using programming languages that look very much like English. This was not always the case. Historically, programs were very difficult to read.

Machine Language

Machine language is the language that the computer understands and executes directly. Machine language is mostly binary or hexadecimal (base 16) numbers. Binary uses the base 2 numbering system, where all numbers are represented by 0s and 1s. Humans count in decimal (base 10) numbers, so writing programs in machine language is a very difficult task. To further complicate matters, there are many different variations of machine language for different types of computers. Programming languages were produced to overcome the difficulties of programming in machine languages.

Procedure-oriented Languages

High-level languages that were more like English and easier to write and understand first appeared in the late 1950s. These languages had the advantage of being usable by more than one type of computer, whereas each computer had its own machine language. Programmers wrote programs as procedures in a more English-like language to solve problems. These programming languages are now classified as *procedure-oriented languages*. Each procedure was a sequence of steps to complete a task. Usually a procedure was created for each action of the task. Procedures for an accounting program might include read-account, read-transaction, post-transaction, update-account, and summary-report. After the program was completed, it was translated into machine language using a software program called a compiler.

The first procedure-oriented programming languages were FORTRAN and COBOL. **FORTRAN** (**FOR**mula **TRAN**slator), developed by IBM between 1954 and 1957, was used for scientific and engineering applications that require complex mathematical computations. **COBOL** (**CO**mmon **B**usiness **O**riented Language) was developed in 1959 and used primarily for business applications that require manipulation of large amounts of data. Today, more than half of all commercial business applications are programmed in COBOL.

A popular beginner language is *Pascal*, developed by Nicklaus Wirth in 1971. Pascal was designed for teaching structured programming in academic environments. The language is named for Blaise Pascal, a seventeenth century mathematician and philosopher who invented a calculating device.

The *C language* was developed by Dennis Ritchie at Bell Laboratories in 1972. C initially was known as the development language for the UNIX operating system. A C compiler is provided as a part of the UNIX operating system, and C was used to write most of UNIX itself. Today many new major operating systems are written in C or C++. See Figure 1.1 for a partial listing of a C program that reads input commands from the keyboard.

Ada is a programming language developed during the late 1970s and early 1980s for the U.S. Department of Defense. The language is named for Lady Augusta Ada Byron (1815–1852), Countess of Lovelace, daughter of the poet Lord Byron. Lady Ada worked with Charles Babbage and his mechanical calculators; she is generally credited as the first programmer.

If you took a beginning programming class at most universities in the 1970s, you probably studied FORTRAN or COBOL. In the 1980s, Pascal became the preferred introductory programming language at most universities.

Object-oriented Languages

With the emergence of the personal computer in the late 1970s and early 1980s, the user interface became increasingly graphical instead of text-based. Object-oriented programming languages were produced to overcome the difficulties of

```
main()
{
  int    i,j,          /*loop counters*/
         steps;        /* number of steps forward */
  char   command,      /* command input for the user */
         skip1;        /* used to read commas and returns */

  down = 0;
  intro();

  for (i=0; i<=SIZE; i++)
    for (j=0; j<=SIZE; j++) cell[i][j]=0;

  while ((command != 'q') && (command!= 'Q')) {
    printf("Enter command (Q to end input): ");
    scanf("%c%c",&command,&skip1);
    switch (command) {
    case 'U': case 'u':
      down = 0;
      break;

    case 'D': case 'd':
      down = 1;
      break;

    case 'R': case 'r':
    case 'L': case 'l':
      printf(" %c", direction);
      changedir(command);
      printf(" -> %c\n", direction);
      break;

    case 'F': case 'f':
        scanf("%d%c",&steps,&skip1);
```

FIGURE 1.1   Example of a C Program

programming with graphics in a text-based procedure-oriented language. Object-oriented languages emphasized the objects and actions instead of procedures for a task. For example, if you are creating a drawing application, the objects are circles, rectangles, and lines. The actions are click, drag, and release. Programs were easier to design and understand because of the emphasis on objects instead of procedures and tasks. ***Object-oriented programming*** (or ***OOP***, pronounced to rhyme with "hoop") was a major mind-set shift for the programming community. Examples include Smalltalk, C++, and Ada 95. Figure 1.2 displays a partial listing of an Ada 95 program for translating the names of days of the week from English into French.

Event-driven Languages

Today's applications usually have a ***graphical user interface*** (or ***GUI***, pronounced "goo-ey"). The object-oriented languages helped program with graphics, but more help was needed for programmers to keep pace. Event-driven languages were designed to make it easier to produce GUIs. With an ***event-driven language***, the computer spends its time responding to events rather than stepping through a pre-arranged series of actions. Many computer programs that run under graphical user interfaces such as the Macintosh operating system and Microsoft Windows are event driven. Such programs respond to events such as the user choosing an item on a menu or clicking an icon with a mouse. Visual Basic implements event-driven programming.

Event-driven languages took object-oriented programming to another level. The instructions were replaced with icons or symbols. Each icon represents an object or a programming function or procedure. Actions such as clicking and dragging were already programmed into the icon, so the programmer did not need to program nearly as many instructions. Microsoft's Visual Basic became one of the most popular event-driven languages for end users as well as professional programmers. Figure 1.3 shows the integrated development environment for the older Visual Basic 4.0.

```
WITH Ada.Text_IO;
WITH Ada.Integer_Text_IO;
WITH Ada.Float_Text_IO;

PROCEDURE French IS
------------------------------------------------------------------------
--| Purpose: Translates the days of the week names from English to French
|-----------------------------------------------------------------------
  TYPE English_Days IS (Monday, Tuesday, Wednesday, Thursday, Friday, Saturday, Sunday);

  TYPE French_Days IS (Lundi, Mardi, Mercredi, Jeudi, Vendredi, Samadi, Dimanche);

  PACKAGE English_Days_IO IS
     NEW Ada.Text_IO.Enumeration_IO (Enum => English_Days);

  PACKAGE French_Days_IO IS
     NEW Ada.Text_IO.Enumeration_IO (Enum => French_Days);

  English : English_Days; -- Day of week in English to Translate
  French : French_Days;  --  Translated day of week
  Position : Natural;  -- Position of day of week in enumeration
  -- I : Positive; -- Loop Counter

BEGIN -- French

  -- Information Message
  Ada.Text_IO.Put (Item => "This is the French Day of Week Translator Program.");
  Ada.Text_IO.New_Line;
  Ada.Text_IO.New_Line;

  -- Get Input
  FOR I IN 1 .. 8 LOOP

     Ada.Text_IO.Put (Item => "Please enter a day of the week in English: ");
```

FIGURE 1.2   Example of an Ada 95 Program

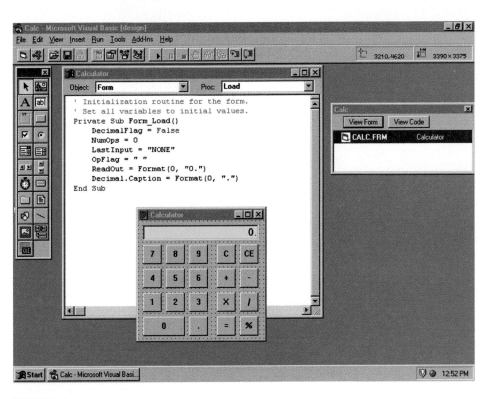

FIGURE 1.3   The Visual Basic 4.0 Integrated Development Environment

Natural Languages

Natural languages are the next step in the evolution of programming languages. A natural language will accept a user's native or natural language, such as English. The user will not have to learn a programming language but can simply type in or speak a request just as in an ordinary conversation. The state of natural languages is somewhat primitive. Researchers are working in this area and have the gigantic task of getting a computer to understand the syntax of our spoken language.

THE BACKGROUND OF VISUAL BASIC

BASIC (**B**eginner's **A**ll-purpose **S**ymbolic **I**nstruction **C**ode) is the ancestor of the Visual Basic programming language. BASIC was developed by John Kemeny and Thomas Kurtz at Dartmouth College in 1964 to teach programming to beginners. In the 1970s and 1980s, numerous software vendors, especially Microsoft, added features to BASIC. Today BASIC is one of the most popular and complex programming languages. However, it is still easy for beginners to use.

When William Gates and Paul Allen founded the Microsoft Corporation, their first product was a BASIC language interpreter, released in 1977. (An ***interpreter*** is a programming language translator that also runs the program. It reads a program statement, translates it into machine language, executes it, and then reads the next statement.) Microsoft's BASIC was the first personal computer programming language. In 1981, when IBM introduced the IBM Personal Computer, it used the DOS operating system written by Microsoft as well as Microsoft's BASIC interpreter. This first PC included a few BASIC programs, too. One program computed loan payments, and another played songs on a piano keyboard. There were a few rudimentary editing programs available at that time. However, if you wanted to have your computer do almost anything else, you needed to write your own BASIC program. The DOS command BASICA called up an interpreter for a special version of Microsoft BASIC. Because the first PC had no hard drive, this interpreter used code stored on a ROM chip inside the computer. Later PCs had greater capabilities, and starting with DOS Version 5, a new version of BASIC was distributed with the DOS operating system: *QBASIC*, a subset of Microsoft Quick BASIC. However, the Windows 95 operating system does not include a BASIC interpreter.

Visual Basic as a Language for Office Applications

The first major PC application, an electronic spreadsheet called *VisiCalc*, was released in 1978. This application was the major reason many PCs began to appear in business offices. *Lotus 1-2-3* improved on the VisiCalc design by integrating database capabilities into the spreadsheet, and, very importantly, it included a simple macro language. The first macros had been written in the mid-1940s and were called macroinstructions. PC applications borrowed the term *macro* to describe the ability to record a series of keystrokes and mouse actions. The macro could be played back with a single keystroke.

When Microsoft introduced its Windows spreadsheet application *Excel* in 1987, it included an expanded macro capability. Excel's macro language was a full-featured programming language, making it possible to program a spreadsheet. In 1990, Microsoft introduced the macro language *WordBasic*, a version of the BASIC language, in its word-processing application, Word. Then in 1992, Microsoft introduced the first version of *Visual Basic* for Windows 3 and the DOS operating system. Microsoft created Visual Basic for end users, and it remains true to its roots today. *Visual Basic 4.0* is designed for the Windows 95 32-bit operating system, and Office 95 applications. *Visual Basic 5.0* is designed for the Windows 95 operating system and Office 97 applications. Visual Basic is the language used to create macros and add programming enhancements for all of the Office applications. *Visual Basic 6.0* includes new data access and Web development features.

VISUAL BASIC EDITIONS

Visual Basic 6.0 is available as standalone products in Learning, Professional, and Enterprise editions. Visual Basic 6.0 is also a component of the Visual Studio suite of programmer products.

- The *Learning Edition* was a new edition with Visual Basic 5. It was specifically designed for people who have never programmed before, and includes all the essential elements and a self-paced, interactive CD-ROM tutorial.

- The *Professional Edition* was designed for the professional programmer who creates applications for others. It includes all the features of the Learning Edition, plus additional features such as Internet tools, report generation, and high-speed database access.

- The *Enterprise Edition* was designed for professional programmers in a team/corporate environment. It includes all the features of the Professional Edition plus the tools and support systems needed to manage, debug, and support large products.

Visual Basic is the programming language included in the Microsoft Office applications to provide programming-development capability from within them. This capability is called **Visual Basic for Applications,** or VBA, and was originally released as part of Microsoft Excel in 1993. The Visual Basic Version 5.0 family of products also included **Windows CE Toolkit for Visual Basic, Visual Basic Scripting Edition,** and Control Creation Edition. The **Control Creation Edition** assists programmers in creating controls and applications for the Internet environment. It is available as a free download from Microsoft's Web site at *www.microsoft.com/vbasic/download.* For more information about Visual Basic 6.0, see Appendix F, "What's New with Visual Basic 6.0." For the latest up-to-date information about Visual Basic, refer to Microsoft's Visual Basic Web site at *www.microsoft.com/vbasic.*

The differences among the three editions are important when you are shopping and comparing prices from different sources. Be sure to purchase the edition that is appropriate for your needs. This book was written and tested using the Visual Basic Learning Edition 5.0 and Visual Basic Enterprise Edition 6.0. If you are using another edition, your screens may look slightly different from the screens shown in this book.

TRY THE COLLEGE BOOKSTORE

Do you have Visual Basic for your personal computer? The best place to buy Microsoft products may be your college bookstore, where you can take advantage of the educational discount. Check out the prices for the retail editions of Visual Basic to find your best buy.

THE VISUAL BASIC INTEGRATED DEVELOPMENT ENVIRONMENT

You will use the Visual Basic environment to create and execute your programs. After you create a program, you need to run (or execute) it in order to use it. You can run your program within the Visual Basic environment, or you can create an executable file so that it can be run outside Visual Basic. Visual Basic uses the term *project* instead of program, so each program that you develop is known as a project.

Elements of the Visual Basic Environment

Visual Basic is started the same way as any other Windows 95 application. (This book assumes that you know basic Windows 95 procedures.) Click the Start button on the Windows taskbar, point to the Programs menu, then to the Microsoft Visual Basic 6.0 folder, and then click Visual Basic 6.0. When you start Visual Basic, the interface of the development environment is displayed. By default, the Visual Basic development environment overlays the entire desktop. (If you used Version 4, only portions of the desktop are covered with Visual Basic windows, and Visual Basic 6.0 can be set that way as well, but the default setting is clearer.)

The Visual Basic integrated development environment (IDE) consists of the following major elements: the menu bar, toolbars, the Form Designer, the Toolbox, the Project Explorer window, the Properties window, the Form Layout window, the Code Editor window, the Object Browser, and context menus. Figure 1.4a shows these elements, not all of which will be visible at once.

The ***title bar*** shown in Figure 1.4a includes (from left to right) the application icon; the name of the current project, application, and view mode; and the standard Windows Minimize, Maximize or Restore, and Close buttons. The ***application icon*** at the left end of the title bar is used to access frequently used menu items. The ***current project*** is Project 1, which is what we see in the title bar of Figure 1.4a, followed by the ***application name***, Microsoft Visual Basic. Projects are opened in the design ***view mode***, as indicated in the figure. (When you run them or debug them, as we will see later, the view mode indicator changes.) The ***Minimize button*** shrinks the window to an icon on the taskbar. The ***Maximize*** or ***Restore button*** toggles to enlarge the window to fill the entire screen or restores the screen to its original size. The ***Close button*** closes the current window and, in this case, exits Visual Basic.

The ***menu bar*** shown below the title bar in Figure 1.4a contains the menus and commands for working with Visual Basic projects. The Visual Basic menu bar contains the File, Edit, View, Format, Tools, Window, and Help commands found in most Windows applications. It also contains menus specific to programming such as Project, Debug, and Run. To open a menu and display its commands, click the menu name.

The ***Standard toolbar*** appears below the menu bar (it can also be moved to another location) and offers a quick way to execute common commands available from the menu bar. Point to a toolbar button to display the ***ToolTip*** for that button. Click a toolbar button once to carry out the action represented by that button. The Standard toolbar buttons are shown in Figure 1.4b.

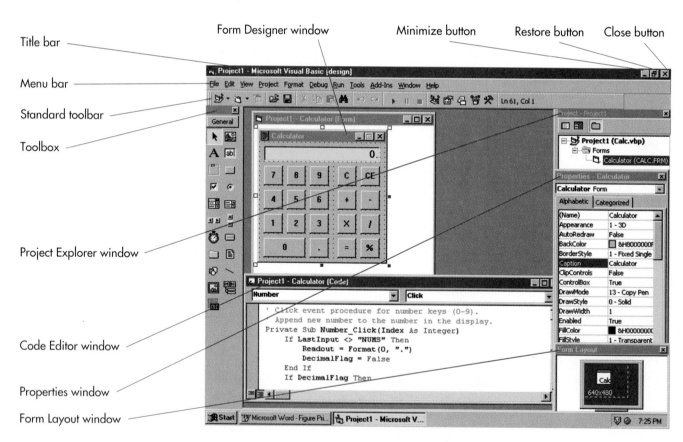

(a) Major Elements

FIGURE 1.4   The Visual Basic 6.0 Environment

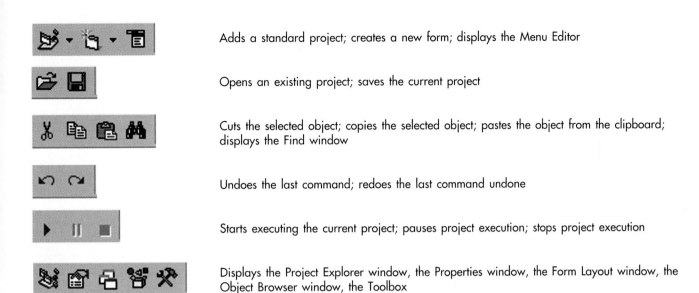

Adds a standard project; creates a new form; displays the Menu Editor

Opens an existing project; saves the current project

Cuts the selected object; copies the selected object; pastes the object from the clipboard; displays the Find window

Undoes the last command; redoes the last command undone

Starts executing the current project; pauses project execution; stops project execution

Displays the Project Explorer window, the Properties window, the Form Layout window, the Object Browser window, the Toolbox

(b) Standard Toolbar Buttons

FIGURE 1.4 The Visual Basic 6.0 Environment (continued)

The **Form Designer window**, shown in Figure 1.4a and 1.5a, is used to design and create forms. Forms are used to create the screens and windows that embody the user interface for your projects. The window is initially a gray dotted rectangle with a title bar, application icon, and Minimize, Maximize or Restore, and Close buttons. You edit this window to design a form, which becomes a Windows 95 or Windows 98 window when your project is executed. You use the tools in the Toolbox to draw buttons, input boxes, graphics, and so on (called controls) on your forms. Forms are discussed in Chapter 4.

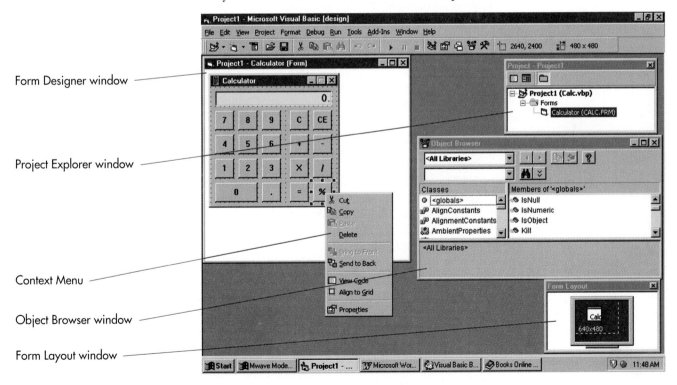

(a) More Windows

FIGURE 1.5 The Visual Basic 6.0 Environment

To create a form, pull down the Project menu and select Add Form, or click the toolbar's Add Form button. If you have created forms using Microsoft Access, you will already be familiar with forms.

The **Form Layout window** shown in Figure 1.4a and 1.5a allows you to select the placement of your forms on the Windows desktop. Notice that the Form Layout window shown in the figure depicts the lower resolution 640-by-480-pixel desktop inside a higher-resolution (800-by-600) desktop. This ensures that your entire form can be displayed even with lower resolution monitors. The open form, *Calc*, is displayed in the middle of the dotted rectangle, so this form will be displayed in the middle of the desktop at 640-by-480 resolution. If a higher resolution such as 800 by 600 is utilized, the form will be displayed in the position indicated on the full monitor in the window.

To open the Form Layout window, pull down the View menu and select Form Layout Window, or click the toolbar's Form Layout Window button.

The **Toolbox**, shown in the Figure 1.4a, contains the tools you use to place controls on your forms. (This screen displays the 21 basic tools of the Visual Basic Toolbox. Your toolbox may look different from the figure.) **Controls** are objects such as boxes, button, and labels you draw on a form to get input or to display output. They also add visual appeal to your form. Point to any tool in the Toolbox to display the ToolTip for that tool.

To open the Toolbox, pull down the View menu and select Toolbox, or click the toolbar's Toolbox button. Close the Toolbox by clicking its Close button. You will learn the details of the tools and controls in Chapter 4 of this book.

The **Project Explorer window**, shown in Figure 1.4a and 1.5a, displays a list of the files associated with the current project. Each project is stored in a file with a file extension of *vbp* (for "Visual Basic Project"). Each form is stored in a separate file with a file extension of *frm*. The Project Explorer window allows you to open any form. First, double click the Forms folder to open it. Then double click the icon of the desired form to display it.

To open the Project Explorer window, pull down the View menu and select Project Explorer, or click the toolbar's Project Explorer button. To close the Project Explorer window, click the window's Close button.

Context menus are pop-up menus containing shortcuts to frequently used commands. An example of a context menu is displayed in Figure 1.5a. To display a context menu, click the right mouse button on the object you are using. The specific list of shortcuts available from context menus varies with the item you click—which is why they are called context menus.

The **Object Browser**, also shown in Figure 1.5a, lists objects available for use in your project. An **object** is a combination of data and code that is treated as a single unit. Examples of objects you can use in Visual Basic are buttons, forms, databases, and charts. The Object Browser displays the objects in your project and gives you a quick way to navigate within it. You can use it to find and use the objects you create. You can also display objects from object libraries, as well as objects from other applications. To open the Object Browser, pull down the View menu and select Object Browser, or click the toolbar's Object Browser button.

The **Properties window**, shown in Figure 1.4a, is used to display or change how controls (buttons, images, text, etc.) look and react on a form. A **property** is a named attribute of an object, such as size, color, and screen location. Properties are set for forms and controls. To open the Properties window, pull down the View menu and select Properties, or click the toolbar's Properties button.

The most important window is the **Code Editor window**, shown in Figure 1.5b. **Code** consists of the instructions you write for your project using the Visual Basic programming language. It is in this window that you write, display, and edit Visual Basic code for your project. A separate code window is available for each form. To open a Code Editor window, right click the form or the control where

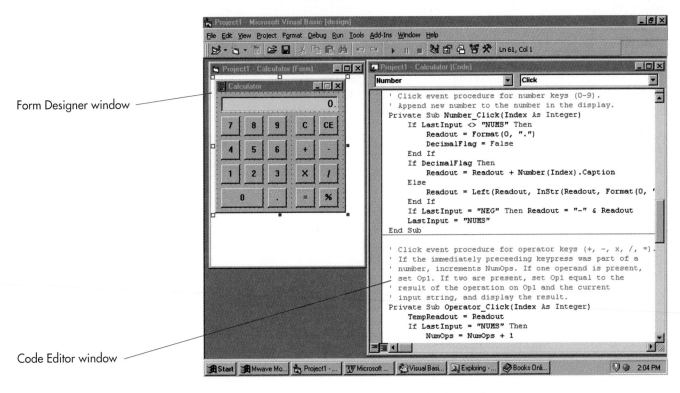

Form Designer window

Code Editor window

(b) The Code Editor Window

FIGURE 1.5 The Visual Basic 6.0 Environment (continued)

you wish to add or edit code, then click the context menu's View Code command. Alternatively, pull down the View menu and select Code.

There are also additional windows available when running and fixing bugs (programming errors) in your project. The ***Immediate***, ***Locals***, and ***Watch windows*** are only available when you are running your project. More windows, elements, and dialog boxes appear when creating a Visual Basic project. These will be discussed as appropriate in later chapters.

THE DATA DISK

The exercises throughout this book show you how to use Microsoft Visual Basic. They make use of a ***data disk*** containing a series of practice files. You will need to get the data disk before you attempt any of the hands-on exercises.

Your instructor may make the files from the data disk available to you in a variety of ways:

- The files may be on a network drive, and you can use Windows Explorer to copy them to a floppy disk.
- There may be an actual "master data disk" that you are to check out from the lab and duplicate using the Copy Disk command.
- If you have access to the Internet and the World Wide Web, you can download the files from the author's text site, *http://www.swva.net/ceaton*, or from the Prentice Hall site, *http://www.prenhall.com/grauer*. Click the icon to download the data disk, and follow the instructions.
- Ask your instructor for any additional instructions that are tailored for your location.

You now come to the first exercise in this chapter that implements the "learn by doing" philosophy of this book. The exercise shows you how to start Microsoft Visual Basic and execute a program available from the data disk that is referenced throughout the book.

HANDS-ON EXERCISE 1

Introduction to Microsoft Visual Basic

Objective: To start the Microsoft Visual Basic programming environment; to open and execute an existing project; to exit the programming environment. Use Figure 1.6 as a guide for the exercise.

STEP 1: Start Microsoft Visual Basic 6.0

➤ From the Windows desktop, click the **Start button** on the taskbar. Click (or point to) the **Programs menu**, click (or point to) **Microsoft Visual Basic 6.0** (alternatively, Microsoft Visual Studio 6.0), then click **Microsoft Visual Basic 6.0** to start the program. You should see a Microsoft Visual Basic environment screen similar to the one shown in Figure 1.6a.

STEP 2: Open the Welcome Project

➤ Select (click) the New Project dialog box's **Existing tab** as shown in Figure 1.6a.

➤ Click the **drop-down arrow** on the Look in list box. Click the letter of the drive—drive C or drive A or a network drive—where you have stored the files from your data disk.

Click the Existing tab

Click here to select the appropriate drive and folder

Click here to select the project file

Click here to open the project

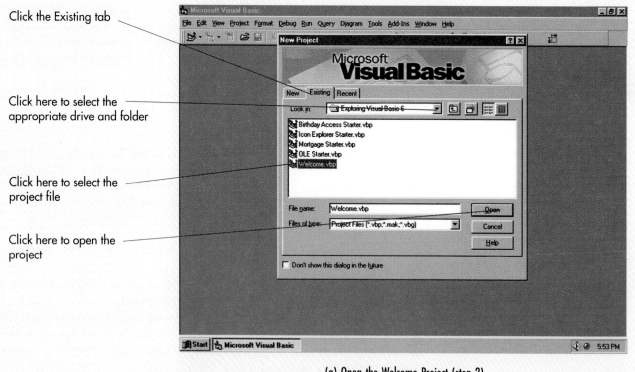

(a) Open the Welcome Project (step 2)

FIGURE 1.6   Hands-on Exercise 1

➤ Select (click) the **Exploring Visual Basic 6 folder**—where you stored the files from your data disk—to make it the active folder.

➤ Select (click) the **Welcome.vbp file**. (If file extensions are not displayed on your system, look for **Welcome**.)

➤ Click the **Open command button** to open the project. If a Source Code Control message box appears, click the **No button** to continue.

"ADD THIS PROJECT TO SOURCE CODE CONTROL?"

You may get this message box if you have installed Microsoft Visual SourceSafe (VSS). VSS is a source code control system that helps you manage large team projects. This textbook assumes that you are not using VSS, but if the message box appears, your instructor can give you specifics for your lab installation. (In most cases, you will want to click No. This will add the file to your Visual Basic project without adding it to the VSS database.)

STEP 3: Open the Welcome Form

➤ The Welcome project opens, to a screen similar to that shown in Figure 1.6b, though, depending on how a previous user has left Visual Basic set, your screen may look different. If any windows within the Visual Basic environment are open, close them before continuing.

➤ Open the Project Explorer window by clicking the toolbar's **Project Explorer** button. From the Project Explorer window, click the **plus sign** (if necessary) to open the Welcome.vbp project. Click the **plus sign** (if necessary) to open the Forms folder. Double click the **Welcome.frm** to open the Form Designer window. You should see the screen exactly as shown in Figure 1.6b.

Click here to open the Project Explorer window

Click here to open project files

Click here to open Forms folder

Double click here to open Form Designer window

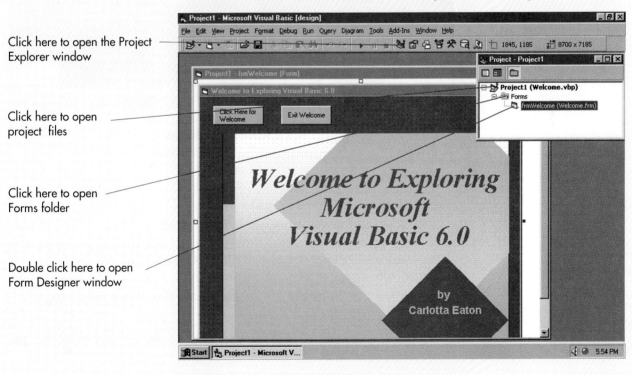

(b) Open the Welcome Form (step 3)

FIGURE 1.6   Hands-on Exercise 1 (continued)

➤ Close the Project Explorer window and Form Designer window to allow you to see the project executing better.

STEP 4: Run the Welcome Project

➤ Now start executing the Welcome project. Click the **Start button** on the Standard toolbar.

➤ You should see a purple background with two gray buttons as shown in Figure 1.6c. Your screen may look slightly different, depending on how a previous user has set the Visual Basic environment options. If other windows (such as the Immediate and Project Explorer) are open, leave them open.

➤ To continue running the project, click the command button labeled **Click Here for Welcome**.

Click this button to display the Welcome image

Project Explorer window displayed

Immediate window displayed

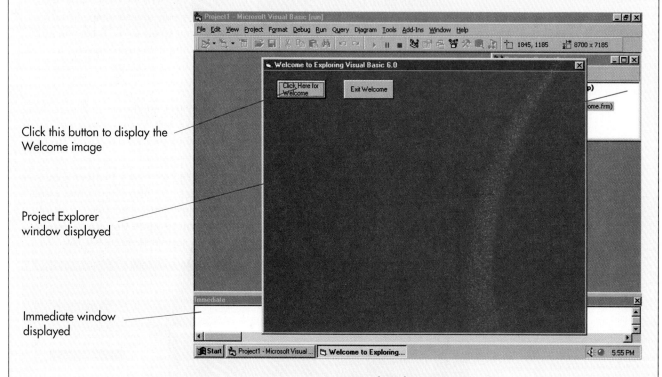

(c) Run the Welcome Project (step 4)

FIGURE 1.6   Hands-on Exercise 1 (continued)

STEP 5: End the Welcome Project

➤ You should see the screen shown in Figure 1.6d.

➤ To stop executing the project, click the command button labeled **Exit Welcome** or click the Welcome window's **Close button**. The Welcome window should disappear from the screen.

➤ Congratulations. You have just executed your first Visual Basic project.

STEP 6: Exit Visual Basic

➤ The screen shown in Figure 1.6e should be displayed. Pull down the **File** menu and select **Exit**.

➤ The Visual Basic programming environment will close, and you will return to your Windows desktop.

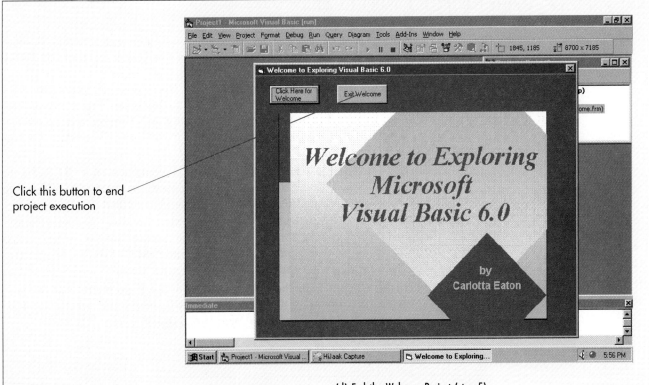

Click this button to end
project execution

(d) End the Welcome Project (step 5)

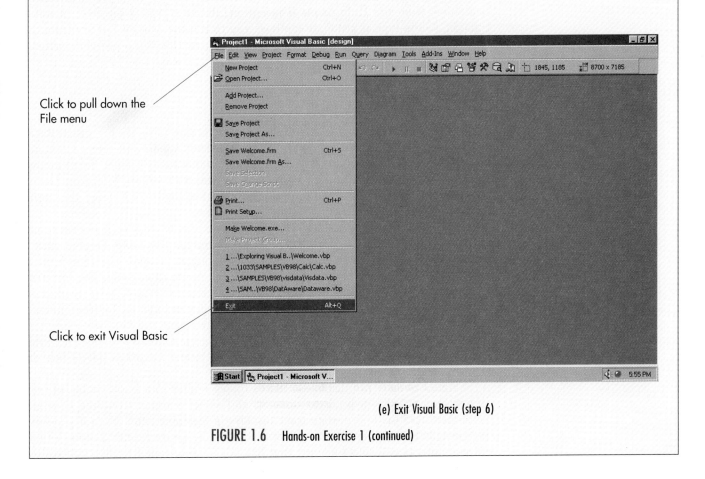

Click to pull down the
File menu

Click to exit Visual Basic

(e) Exit Visual Basic (step 6)

FIGURE 1.6   Hands-on Exercise 1 (continued)

GET HELP WHEN YOU NEED IT

The **Learning Edition of Visual Basic 6.0** includes a wealth of information designed for the novice programmer. The package includes a small book and four CD-ROMs:

- **Visual Basic 6.0 in Action**, a 218 page book, has selected chapters from three beginner books. The books are published by Microsoft Press: *Visual Basic Step by Step* by Michael Halvorson, *Visual Basic Programmer's Guide* by Microsoft Corporation, and *Visual Basic Developer's Workshop* by John Clark Craig and Jeff Webb.
- **Learn Visual Basic Now**, a multimedia tutorial contained on a CD-ROM that demonstrates key concepts and techniques. You wil be directed to this tutorial in Practice with Visual Basic exercises in future chapters of this textbook.
- **MSDN Library**, packaged on two CD-ROMs, contains the comprehensive online documentation for the entire Visual Studio suite of products. The Visual Studio suite includes Visual Basic, the MSDN Library, Visual C++, Visual FoxPro, Visual InteDev, Visual J++, and Visual SourceSafe.
- **Microsoft on the Web**, can be accessed from the Help menu. For the latest up-to-date information, visit *msdn.microsoft.com/vbasic* for Visual Basic help on the Web at Microsoft's Web site.

HELP FROM THE CD-ROMS

Let's start by looking at help available from the MSDN Library. Depending on how Visual Basic has been set up on your system, most of these features will be accessible from the Help menu. The entire Library is over a gigabyte of information, so the typical installation allows you to run the MSDN Library from the two CDs. If you cannot access Help, you need to run the setup program again or have your network administrator do so.

MSDN Library

The *MSDN Library* provides a virtual reference library of books for Visual Basic. To display the MSDN Library, pull down the Help menu and select Contents, Index, or Search. Alternatively, you can access this feature from the Windows desktop. Click the Start button on the taskbar, select Programs, Microsoft Developer Network, then MSDN Library Visual Studio. Figure 1.7 shows the entire table of contents for the MSDN Library.

Notice that the MSDN Library window is displayed like a browser, and divided into three panes. The left pane is the *navigation pane*. Double click a book to open it, and then double click the chapter and topic. The right pane is the *topic pane*. The page you select is displayed in the topic pane. The top pane contains the *toolbar* which contains the Hide, Locate, Previous, Next, Back, Forward, Stop, Refresh, Home, and Print buttons. If you have an Internet connection, you can also view Web pages in this window, using the Go menu.

In the figure, the navigation area is displayed in Contents mode. The Navigation pane contains the Contents, Index, Search, and Favorites tabs. Click the appropriate tab to change the displayed mode.

The *Contents tab* displays a list of topics similar to a book's table of contents. Double click a book to open it, and select a topic. Continue to select subtopics until the appropriate topic displays in the topic pane. Even if you have not installed the entire library, you will still see the entire MSDN Library's table of contents. If you select a topic that has not been installed locally, you will be prompted to insert the appropriate MSDN Library CD.

Toolbar

Contents tab

Index tab

Search tab

Favorites tab

Navigation pane

Topic pane

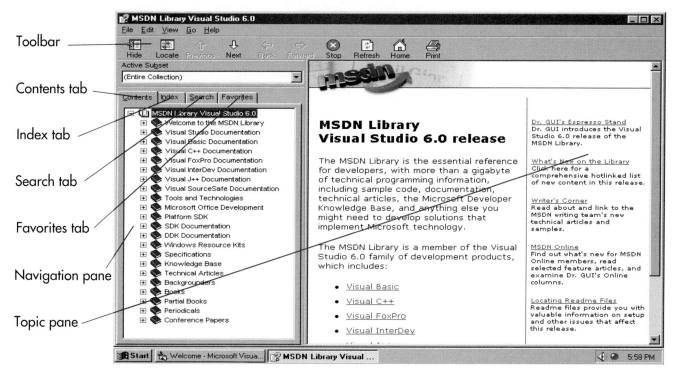

FIGURE 1.7   The MSDN Library

The *Index tab* displays a list of help topics in alphabetical order. Scroll through the list, or, better, type the first word of the topic you are interested in, and select from the shorter list to display the information in the topic pane.

The *Search tab* employs a full text search mode. Type in a search word, and a list of topics containing the word will appear. Select the appropriate topic to view the information in the topic pane.

The *Favorites tab* displays a list of previously marked topics. This is similar to creating bookmarks with a Web browser. You can add topics to and delete topics from the Favorites list and access the previous list here. This feature replaces the Notebook tool available in Visual Basic 5.0.

MIGRATING FROM VISUAL BASIC 5.0

If you are using Visual Basic 5.0 with this textbook, read Appendix F, "What's New in Visual Basic 6.0." One of the major differences between the two versions is the online help system. The MSDN Library is new to Visual Basic 6.0. Visual Basic 5.0 included several online help books: Programmer's Guide, Visual Basic Help, and Visual Basic Technical Support.

Visual Basic Documentation

The best place to start reading the MSDN Library is with the Visual Basic Documentation books. To display the Visual Basic online books, select the Visual Basic Documentation book from the Contents tab of the MSDN Library. As shown in Figure 1.8, the Visual Basic documentation includes a Documentation Map, What's New, Programmer's Guide, Samples, and Reference Guidebooks for all editions of Visual Basic. The Professional Edition and Enterprise editions include additional books such as the Component Tools Guide and the Data Access Guide.

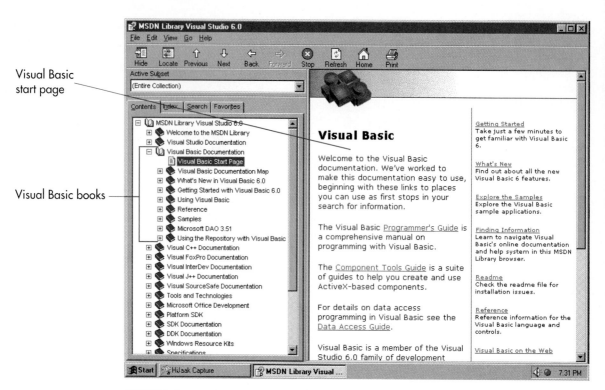

Visual Basic
start page

Visual Basic books

FIGURE 1.8   Visual Basic 6.0 Online Documentation

ABOUT VISUAL BASIC

Pull down the Help menu and click About Microsoft Visual Basic to display version and other licensing information, including the product serial number. This help screen also contains a useful command button, System Info. System Info displays information about the hardware installed on your computer system, including the amount of memory and available space on the hard drive. The System Info window may not be available depending upon your Windows operating system setup.

Learn Visual Basic Now

Learn Visual Basic Now is an online book contained on a CD-ROM that comes with the Learning Edition of Visual Basic. To access it, insert the *Learn Visual Basic Now* CD-ROM into the drive. If the online book has been installed to your hard drive, from the desktop, click the Start button on the taskbar, then the Programs menu, the Learn Visual Basic Now folder, and the Learn Visual Basic Now program icon. The initial screen for this online book is displayed in Figure 1.9. This book can be used to learn more about Visual Basic. It also contains video clips that demonstrate programming techniques. You will be directed to this tutorial in *Practice with Visual Basic* exercises in future chapters of this textbook.

FIGURE 1.9   Learn Visual Basic 6.0 Now—The Learning Edition's Tutorial

HANDS-ON EXERCISE 2

Get Help from the Visual Basic CD

Objective: Use the CD's online documentation: run a sample application; get help from Help Topics; read from Visual Basic Online documentation. Use Figure 1.10 as a guide for the exercise.

STEP 1: Open the Calc Sample Application

➤ Start Visual Basic.

➤ Click the New Project dialog box's **Existing tab**, as shown in Figure 1.10a.

➤ If necessary, click the arrow in the Look in list box to select the drive and folder where Visual Basic is stored on your system. (The default installation is in the **Vb98 folder**.)

➤ Click the **Up One Level** button to move up one level. Double click the **MSDN98 folder**, then the **Samples folder** (alternatively click 98VS, then 1033, then Samples). Double click the **Vb98 folder** as shown in Figure 1.10a. Open the **Calc folder**. Select the **calc.vbp file name** in the list box. Click the **Open command button** to open the project.

➤ The screen should be blank at this point, though, depending on how a previous user has left Visual Basic set, your screen may look different. If any windows within the Visual Basic environment are open, close them before continuing.

WHERE ARE THE SAMPLES LOCATED?

If you are using Visual Basic 5.0, the default location for Visual Basic should be displayed (Vb). First click the Vb folder, then the samples folder, then the Pguide folder to display the list of sample applications.

If you are using Visual Basic 6.0, and did not install the samples, they are located on the MSDN Library CD. Locate the Samples folder and then select the Vb98 folder to display the list of sample applications. The Visual Basic Documentation also contains a book called Samples that contains descriptions of the sample applications.

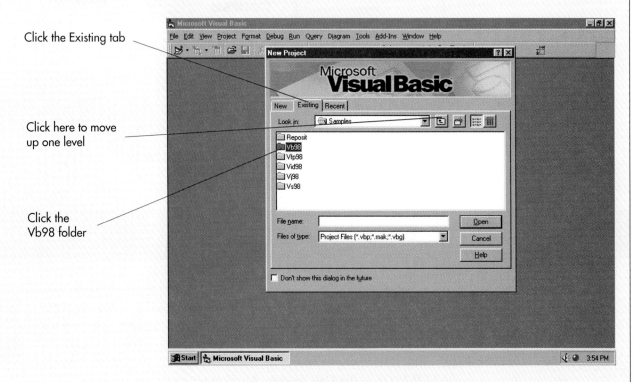

Click the Existing tab

Click here to move up one level

Click the Vb98 folder

(a) Open the Calc Sample Application (step 1)

FIGURE 1.10   Hands-on Exercise 2

STEP 2: Run the Calc Sample Application

➤ Click the toolbar's **Start button** to display the calculator as shown in Figure 1.10b. Notice that the title bar now displays the mode indicator **[run]** to indicate that the program is in that mode.

➤ Click buttons on the calculator to test the application. Results of your calculations are displayed in the yellow box.

➤ When finished, click the toolbar's **End button** to stop running the application. The application disappears from the screen, and the title bar displays **[design]** to indicate the program mode.

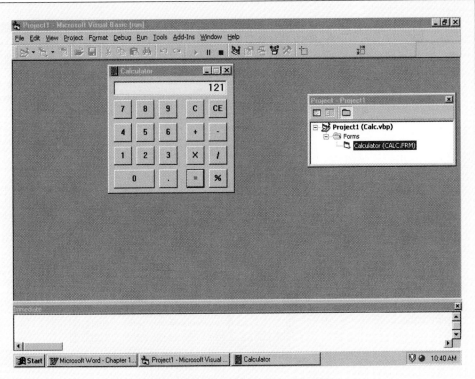

(b) Run the Calc Sample Application (step 2)

FIGURE 1.10 Hands-on Exercise 2 (continued)

STEP 3: Get Help from the MSDN Library

➤ Pull down the **Help menu** and select **Contents**. If necessary, click the **plus sign** to open the MSDN Library Visual Studio 6.0 book. Double click the **Visual Basic Documentation book** in the navigation pane (the left pane) as shown in Figure 1.10c.

➤ Double click the **Using Visual Basic book** and then the **Programmer's Guide**.

➤ Double click the **Part 1: Visual Basic Basics book**, and then **Developing an Application in Visual Basic**.

GET HELP USING VISUAL BASIC 5.0

If you are using Visual Basic 5.0, here's how to get help. Pull down the **Help menu** and select **Books Online**. Click **Start Here** in the Navigation pane, and select **Visual Basic Basics** in the Topic pane. Double click **Part 1: Visual Basic Basics** and continue as instructed in Step 3.

➤ Finally, double click the **Elements of the Integrated Development Environment book** to display the screen in the topic pane (right pane) as shown in the figure.

➤ Click the **Integrated Development Environment Elements topic** and read to review the information learned in this chapter. **Scroll** and continue reading until you reach the end of the topic.

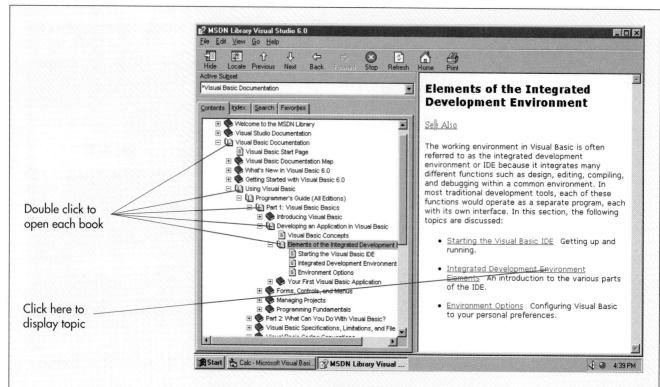

Double click to
open each book

Click here to
display topic

(c) Get Help from the MSDN Library (step 3)

FIGURE 1.10   Hands-on Exercise 2 (continued)

STEP 4: Add a Topic to the Favorites List

➤ Click the **Favorites tab** in the Navigation pane.

➤ Click the toolbar's **Locate button** to locate the current topic in the table of contents.

➤ Click the **Favorites tab** again to return to it.

➤ Notice that the topic heading, "Integrated Development Environment Elements," is displayed in the Current topic text box. If you want to rename the topic, change the topic name now.

➤ Click the **Add button** to add the current topic to the Favorites list.

ADD A TOPIC USING VISUAL BASIC 5.0

If you are using Visual Basic 5.0, here's how to add a topic using the Notebook feature. Click the toolbar's **Notebook button** to display the Notebook window. Click the **Add to Notebook button** on the Notebook's toolbar. Click in the Notes pane on the right and enter *Explains the VB environment elements* to remind you where to find this information in the future. Click the Notebook window's **Close button** to close the Notebook. Visual Basic 6.0 replaced the Notebook feature with the Favorites tab.

STEP 5: Search for a Definition

➤ Click the **Index tab**.

➤ Enter the term *event* in the keyword text box. Select the item **event (defined)** in the list and click the **Display button**.

➤ The definition for *event* will display in the Topic pane as shown in Figure 1.10e. Look up other definitions while you are here. When finished, continue to the next step.

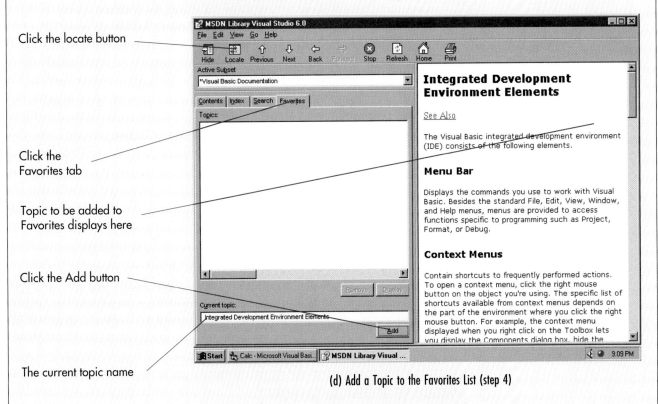

Click the locate button

Click the Favorites tab

Topic to be added to Favorites displays here

Click the Add button

The current topic name

(d) Add a Topic to the Favorites List (step 4)

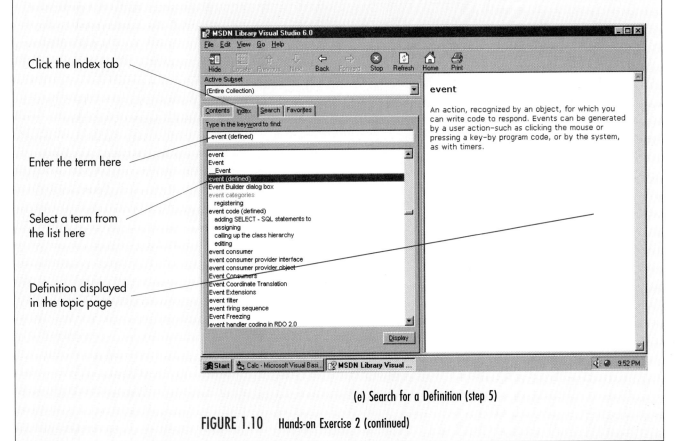

Click the Index tab

Enter the term here

Select a term from the list here

Definition displayed in the topic page

(e) Search for a Definition (step 5)

FIGURE 1.10   Hands-on Exercise 2 (continued)

STEP 6: Exit Help and Visual Basic

➤ Click the window's **Exit button** to close the MSDN Library.

➤ Pull down the **File menu** and select **Exit**.

HELP FROM THE WEB

Microsoft offers a wealth of information at its Web site. The ***Microsoft on the Web*** command on the Help menu enables you to get to the page you need quickly, as illustrated in Figure 1.11. Select a topic, and your default Web browser will display the appropriate page. Several of these pages will be explored in the next hands-on exercise.

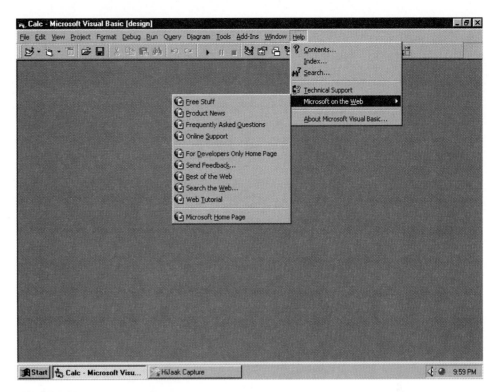

FIGURE 1.11   Microsoft on the Web

HANDS-ON EXERCISE 3

Get Help from the Web

Objective: Use the Visual Basic online documentation available on the World Wide Web. This exercise requires a connection to the Internet and an installed Web browser such as Netscape Navigator or Microsoft Internet Explorer. Use Figure 1.12 as a guide for the exercise.

STEP 1: Use the Free Stuff Page to Update Visual Basic

➤ Remember that you must have an Internet connection and an installed Web browser to complete this exercise. Remember, too, that one of the advantages of the Web is the ease of updating Web pages. The Web pages you visit in this exercise will probably have been updated from the ones shown in Figure 1.12.

➤ Start your Web browser. Minimize the browser window.

➤ Start Visual Basic. Click the New Project dialog box's **New tab**. Click the **Standard Exe icon**. Click the **Open command button**.

➤ Usually the Form Designer window opens when starting a new project. Click the **Close button** for the Form Designer window (not just the form) to close it. Depending on how a previous user has left Visual Basic set, none or more windows in the Visual Basic environment may be open. In any case, close all the open windows within Visual Basic. Closing the open windows will give you an uncluttered environment to work in.

➤ Pull down the **Help menu** and select **Microsoft on the Web**, then select **Free Stuff**.

➤ Your browser should display the page shown in Figure 1.12a. This is where you want to look for the latest updates to Visual Basic. If a Web page does not display, try *mndn.microsoft.com/vbasic/downloads* and scroll the page to see what is available. Examine the Web page carefully for any updates for Visual Basic 6.0.

➤ If you are working on your own computer, select an appropriate topic and proceed to download the update file. If you are working on a lab computer, ask your instructor before downloading or installing any updates on the machine.

(a) Free Stuff (step 1)

FIGURE 1.12   Hands-on Exercise 3

FREE STUFF USING VISUAL BASIC 5.0

If you are using Visual Basic 5 and working on your own computer, download and install the item **Visual Basic, Version 5.0, Update of BIB-LIO.MDB**. If you are working on a lab computer, ask your instructor before installing any updates on the machine. Select the topic, and specify the drive and folder in which to save the download. This file should be stored where Visual Basic is stored on your system. With the default installation, you would select the appropriate hard drive, the **Programs folder**, then the **DevStudio folde**r, the **Vb folder**, the **samples folder**, the **PGuide folder**, and finally the **biblio folder**. The file will probably take several minutes to download. When the download is complete, the progress window closes.

STEP 2: Install the Update (Optional)

➤ If you are working on your own computer, click the **Start button** on the Windows 95 taskbar. Select **Programs,** then **Windows Explorer.** In the tree pane of Windows Explorer, find the folder where you saved the file from Step 1 above. The default is the C drive, and you will need to open these folders in order: Program Files, Microsoft Visual Studio, Vb98.

➤ Locate the file and **double click its icon** to execute it. A DOS window or Winzip window should open. When its title bar displays the word *Finished,* **close** the window.

➤ Your update has now been installed. **Close** the Windows Explorer window.

INSTALL THE UPDATE USING VISUAL BASIC 5.0

This step is optional; proceed if you are working on your own computer. Follow the instructions given in Step 2. (The default is the C drive, and you will need to open these folders in order: Program Files, DevStudio, Vb, samples, Pguide folder, biblio.) The file you downloaded is **biblio.exe.**

STEP 3: Product News

➤ Maximize the Visual Basic window if it is not currently displayed.

➤ Pull down the **Help menu** and select **Microsoft on the Web**, then **Product News**.

➤ Your Web browser will display the screen shown in Figure 1.12b.

➤ Click any **hyperlink** that looks interesting to you. If there is information about the Visual Basic edition that you have installed on your computer, then select it. This will probably be either the Learning Edition or the Professional Edition. Read about this edition.

➤ Minimize the Web browser window.

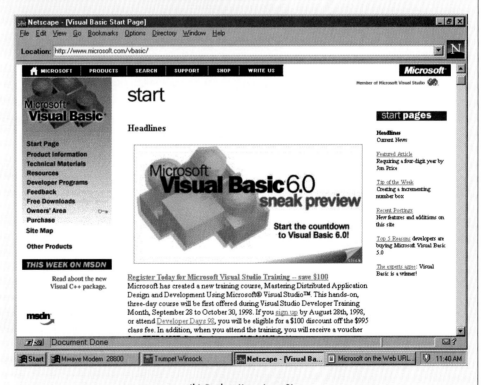

(b) Product News (step 3)

FIGURE 1.12   Hands-on Exercise 3 (continued)

GOOD HOUSEKEEPING PRACTICE

After installing an update to your computer, you can delete the original downloaded zipped file(s). In this case, the downloaded file is biblio.exe (if using Visual Basic 5.0). This file only needs to be executed once to install the update. After installation, you can delete this file to save hard drive

STEP 4: Frequently Asked Questions

➤ Maximize the Visual Basic window if it is not currently displayed.

➤ Pull down the **Help menu** and select **Microsoft on the Web,** then **Frequently Asked Questions**. Your Web browser will display the screen shown in Figure 1.12c after you register for support.

➤ Select any item that seems interesting. Read several questions and answers. Minimize the browser window.

MICROSOFT SUPPORT ONLINE REGISTRATION

When your computer visits the Microsoft Support Web pages the first time, the Support Online Registration page will open. If you are working on your own computer, complete the online form and follow the instructions to register.

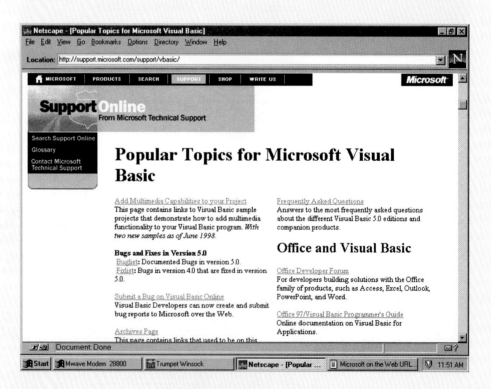

(c) Frequently Asked Questions (step 4)

FIGURE 1.12   Hands-on Exercise 3 (continued)

STEP 5: Online Support

➤ Maximize the Visual Basic window if it is not currently displayed. Pull down the **Help menu** and select **Microsoft on the Web**, then **Online Support**.

➤ Your Web browser will display the screen shown in Figure 1.12d. Select the topic **Visual Basic Support Resources**. Read and scroll down the page and select any other topic that seems interesting. Read the topic information.

➤ When finished, close the Web browser window.

➤ Close any open windows in Visual Basic; then click the **Close button** on the title bar to exit Visual Basic.

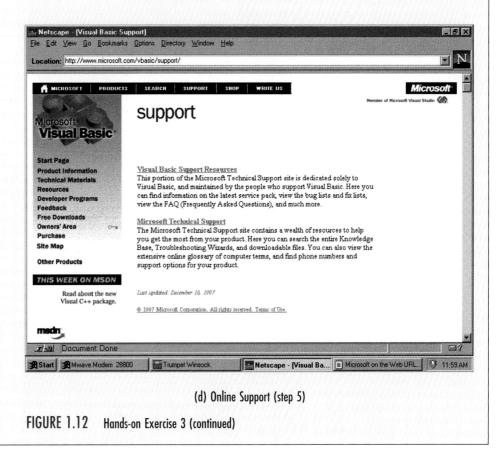

(d) Online Support (step 5)

FIGURE 1.12   Hands-on Exercise 3 (continued)

USE THE RIGHT TOOL FOR THE JOB

Applications for the personal computer were first introduced in 1978, with VisiCalc as the first spreadsheet. Today application programs abound. Internet applications include programs such as those used for electronic mail and Web browsing. *Microsoft Office* is a suite of application products including Word (word processing), Excel (spreadsheet), PowerPoint (presentations), and Access (database).

While the Office applications are good tools for end users, you still need to choose the right tool for the job. You need to understand the strengths and capabilities of the different applications to decide which tool to use. You may have heard the old saying, "When the only tool you have is a hammer, every problem looks like a nail." If you are familiar with only a single application, you will fall into the trap of using that tool for every problem you encounter.

During his summer break, a friend once wrote a program for a business to generate invoices for its customers. He wrote the program in Pascal (a beginning programming language), and it took him several weeks of nights and weekends

TABLE 1.1 Tools for the Task					
Task	Visual Basic	Word	Excel	Power Point	Access
Create a letter or document		✔			
Write a form letter with many recipients		✔			
Store an address list		✔	✔		✔
Publish reports and documents		✔			
Financial calculations, accounting			✔		
Data entry for any database	✔				✔
User interface for any application	✔				
Computer training system	✔			✔	
Forms for data entry, editing, and viewing	✔		✔		✔
Store and retrieve data and information			✔		✔
Slide show and presentations				✔	
Automated, graphical slide shows (kiosks)				✔	
Statistical analysis			✔		
Reports generated from data			✔		✔
Financial models			✔		
Wide variety of custom applications	✔				

to complete. He was familiar with the Pascal programming language, but not with the Microsoft Office application tools. A faster tool for this job would have been Microsoft Excel or Access. Excel is a spreadsheet application that "excels" at number-crunching tasks. The invoice could have been started using a template. In fact, Excel comes with several invoice templates. Each invoice could have been saved in its own file, and the invoice summary information could have been saved in a summary worksheet file.

Another option would have been to use Access, the Microsoft Office database application. Each invoice could have been saved as a record in an Invoice table. Each customer could have been saved as a record in a Customer table. Access could generate a summary report for monthly billing. This problem could have been solved using Excel or Access in a few hours, instead of several weeks of programming from scratch.

With such a multitude of applications available for personal computer users, why would we need a programming language like Visual Basic? The answer is customization. You need to program your own application when you need a very specialized, customized program.

One of the major benefits of programming using Visual Basic is the ability to integrate objects from Office applications and other Windows programs. Microsoft Windows programs share information through a technology known as **object linking and embedding**, commonly called **OLE** (pronounced "ol-é"). OLE is a technology used by Microsoft's Windows products to integrate the output from one program as data into another (for example, a drawing into a word processing document). You may be familiar with using OLE with Word and Excel. You can create a **compound document** consisting of OLE objects with the Office applications.

You really want to avoid "reinventing the wheel." To help you in deciding the appropriate tool for the problem at hand, here is a list of tasks, shown in Table 1.1 (see page 30), with check marks next to the applications that are suitable for performing them. Many times an Office application is naturally suited to the task, and building a Visual Basic program is inefficient. There are many more tasks. This is merely a starting list to consider.

You can of course use another tool for the task at hand. For instance, you can write a simple report in Excel. Excel is not a writer's tool; it is an accountant's tool. If you are using Excel to write, you are making the job harder for yourself. Remember to work smart, and choose and use the right tool for the job.

Visual Basic Applications Edition (VBA) is included in the Microsoft Office 97 and Office 2000 applications. If you need to customize any Office application, you will use the same programming language—Visual Basic. Visual Basic can be thought of as the "glue" that binds all these Windows objects together.

SUMMARY

There are many programming languages available. Programming languages have improved over time to the event-driven programming languages that are optimized for the Windows graphical environment of today. Programming languages such as Visual Basic are used to build application programs. We started with the history of programming languages in general, and continued to Microsoft's history with its first BASIC programming language product. Microsoft distributes three major editions of Visual Basic 6.0: Learning Edition, Professional Edition, and Enterprise Edition.

The Visual Basic programming environment includes the title bar, menu bar, toolbar, Toolbox, and context menus. The windows that form the environment include the Form Designer, Form Layout, Code Editor, Project Explorer, Properties, and Object browser. These tools and windows are introduced in this chapter and will be explored in later chapters.

CD-ROM Online documentation includes the MSDN Library and for the Learning Edition, *Learn Visual Basic Now*. Sample programs are also available with Visual Basic. World Wide Web documentation is accessible from the Help menu's Microsoft on the Web command.

Choose the right tool for the job when creating and using programs. Visual Basic is the glue that binds objects together when creating custom Windows applications. OLE technology allows Windows programs to share information. There may be a Microsoft Office application, or another Windows program that is suitable for your task. If there is not, then writing your own custom Visual Basic program may be the best route.

About Microsoft Visual Basic

Application program

Code Editor window

Context menu

Event-driven programming language

Form Designer window

Form Layout window

Graphical User Interface (GUI)

Machine language

Menu bar

Microsoft on the Web

Object Browser window

Object Linking and Embedding (OLE)

Object-oriented language

Procedure-oriented language

Program

Programming language

Project

Project Explorer window

Properties window

Technical Support

Title bar

Toolbar

Toolbox

Visual Basic Control Creation Edition

Visual Basic Enterprise Edition

Visual Basic for Applications (VBA)

Visual Basic Learning Edition

Visual Basic Professional Edition

Visual Basic Scripting Edition

Windows CE Toolkit for Visual Basic

MULTIPLE CHOICE

1. The language that the computer understands and executes is called:
   (a) Binary
   (b) Hexadecimal
   (c) Machine language
   (d) High-level language

2. All of the following are major categories of high-level programming languages except:
   (a) Machine
   (b) Procedure-oriented
   (c) Object-oriented
   (d) Event-driven

3. Visual Basic may be classified as a member of the following type of language:
   (a) Machine
   (b) Procedure-oriented
   (c) Object-oriented
   (d) Event-driven

4. All of the following are major editions of Visual Basic 6.0 except:
   (a) Learning Edition
   (b) Basic Edition
   (c) Programming Edition
   (d) Enterprise Edition

5. The Visual Basic title bar displays all of the following information except:
   (a) The date the project was last updated
   (b) Name of the current project
   (c) View mode (design or run)
   (d) Minimize button, Maximize/Restore button, Close button

6. The Visual Basic menu bar contains all of the following menus except:
   (a) Project
   (b) Debug
   (c) Run
   (d) Design

7. The Visual Basic Standard toolbar contains command buttons to display all the following windows except:
   (a) Form Designer
   (b) Project Explorer
   (c) Properties
   (d) Toolbox

8. Which window is used to create the screens and windows that embody the user interface for your projects?
   (a) Form Layout
   (b) Toolbox
   (c) Form Designer
   (d) Code Editor

9. Which window is used to write the Visual Basic instructions using the programming language?
   (a) Form Layout
   (b) Toolbox
   (c) Form Designer
   (d) Code Editor

10. All of the following windows are only displayed when running your project except:
    (a) Immediate
    (b) Locals
    (c) Watch
    (d) Form Designer

11. Which help feature would you utilize first to look up a definition of a Visual Basic term?
    (a) Contents tab
    (b) Index tab
    (c) Search tab
    (d) Favorites tab

12. Which help feature would you use to save a note about information found in the MSDN Library?
    (a) Contents tab
    (b) Index tab
    (c) Search tab
    (d) Favorites tab

13. If you have a question about Visual Basic, what should you do before calling Microsoft Technical Support?

(a) Read this textbook

(b) Use the online help tools available from the Visual Basic CDs and the Web

(c) Ask a classmate or your instructor

(d) All of the above methods should be utilized first

14. All of the following information is available from the Microsoft on the Web menu except:

(a) Product News

(b) Frequently Asked Questions

(c) MSDN Library

(d) Online Support

15. There is a multitude of applications available for the personal computer. When would your best option be to write a Visual Basic program?

(a) You are unaware of an application available for your task

(b) You need a very specialized, customized program

(c) You don't have time to buy a program

(d) You want to create a letter or document

ANSWERS

1. c	**6.** d	**11.** b
2. a	**7.** a	**12.** d
3. d	**8.** c	**13.** d
4. b	**9.** d	**14.** c
5. a	**10.** d	**15.** b

PRACTICE WITH VISUAL BASIC

1. **Automated Teller Machine.** There are several interesting sample projects included with Visual Basic. You ran a sample project in Hands-on Exercise 2. Follow the same steps, and run the ATM sample project as shown in Figure 1.13. Select the Microsoft Visual Studio folder, then Msdn98, (optionally 98vs, 1033), then Samples, Vb98, and finally ATM. Open the ATM.vbp project, do not add the project to SourceSafe. Run the project.

USING VISUAL BASIC 5.0

The default location for the sample projects folder is DevStudio, then Vb, then Samples, and finally Pguide.

FIGURE 1.13 Automated Teller Machine Sample Project

This project has a sound component. If your PC has a sound card and speakers, you should be able to hear a voice response at the end of each transaction. Try the project in more than one language, to hear the voice responses in different languages. Do not change or save the project when you exit Visual Basic.

2. **Personal News Service.** Microsoft on the Web includes a Best of the Web topic. This topic has a special feature where you can create your own start page for reading the news from the Web. You can also personalize the Web newspaper so that it displays the news that is interesting to you. From the Microsoft on the Web help feature, select Best of the Web, and then Your Start Page. Follow the instructions on the Web to create your own personal news service. Print out a customized page to turn in to your instructor to demonstrate that you completed this exercise.

PERSONAL NEWS SERVICE ALTERNATIVES

The updated Microsoft Personal News Service requires a HotMail account. There are several other personalized news services alternatives available on the Web. Free news services include InfoBeat News at *www.infobeat.com*, PointCast at *www.pointcast.com*, and My Yahoo at *my.yahoo.com*. Other services require a monthly fee such as NewsEdge at *www.newsedge.com* and Inquisit at *www.inquisit.com*.

---

3. **Getting Assistance While You Work.** This chapter highlighted some of the help features available with Visual Basic. Use the MSDN Library and read all the topics in the MSDN Library Help book. Also open the Visual Basic Documentation books and read the Visual Basic Start Page topic. Write a short summary (one-half to one page) using the Windows WordPad accessory or your favorite word processor. Print the page to submit to your instructor.

GETTING ASSISTANCE USING VISUAL BASIC 5.0

If you are using Visual Basic 5.0, use the Books Online and read the *Welcome to Visual Basic* topic. Continue reading the *Getting Assistance While You Work* topic. Write a short summary to submit to your instructor.

---

4. **Pricing Information.** Use the Microsoft on the Web help feature to find the current retail prices for the different editions of Visual Basic. Start your search with the Product News topic. You should be able to find current prices for the Learning Edition, Professional Edition, and Enterprise Edition. Now go to your college bookstore and get the academic price for the three editions as well. Which edition is most applicable for a beginning Visual Basic programmer? Which edition is the best value at your local bookstore? Are any editions packaged with an edition of Microsoft Office? Write a short summary of your findings to submit to your instructor.

I Wish I Could

Visual Basic can be used to implement many tasks for your computer. Make a list of tasks that you would like to do using your computer that you don't know how to do at this point. After writing down your list, compare it against Table 1.1 (in this chapter) to determine if it would be best to use an Office application (or another product) or build it using Visual Basic. Bring your wish list and your suggested method of implementation to class and compare to your classmates' lists.

Visual Basic Help on the Web

Search the World Wide Web for information available on using Visual Basic. Use a search engine to search for Visual Basic. Look for newsgroups as well as Web pages. Write a short summary of the Visual Basic information you found on the Web and submit it to your instructor.

Quick Reference Manual

Use the online Visual Basic documentation to browse the information available. Select five topics that you think will be good references for you in this class. Use the Print command button to print each screen, and create a cover page using the Windows WordPad accessory or your word processor. Submit the six pages to your instructor. A good place to start your reference manual would be the **Visual Basic Start Page** (Visual Basic 6.0) or the **Welcome to Visual Basic** section (Visual Basic 5.0), using the Contents tab. You may want to include information on the toolbar, the Toolbox, and forms in your printout.

Planning for Disaster

This case has nothing to do with Visual Basic per se, but it is perhaps the most important case of all, as it deals with the question of backup. Do you know what a backup strategy is? Do you have a backup strategy? As my father always says, "You're not going to learn any younger." Now it a good time to learn to prevent losing several hours of hard work in the future. The problem usually occurs the night before a major project is due. The ultimate disaster is the disappearance of your computer, by theft or natural disasters. Describe in a page or less the backup strategy you plan to implement in connection with your work in this class. You could also share "I wish I had had a backup" horror stories with your classmates and your instructor.

BUILD YOUR FIRST PROJECT: A STEP-BY-STEP APPROACH

2

OBJECTIVES

After reading this chapter, you will be able to:

1. Describe compilers, interpreters, source code files, pseudo code files, native code files, and executable files.
2. Describe the steps in building an application program.
3. Describe the steps in building a project with Visual Basic.
4. Create a Visual Basic project following the step-by-step approach.

OVERVIEW

Programming is the way to solve problems by writing programs for a computer. This chapter covers the fundamentals of problem solving by creating projects using Visual Basic. (Visual Basic uses the term *project* rather than *program*.) In this chapter, you will watch the steps in developing a Visual Basic programming project, learning thereby how to plan your own project. For a real-world analogy, we will observe the steps in building a deck.

The hands-on exercises in the chapter enable you to apply all of the material at the computer, and are indispensable to the learn-by-doing philosophy of the text. You will build your first project while doing the hands-on exercises in the chapter.

PROGRAMMER'S LINGO

A ***program*** is a detailed set of instructions for a computer. Programs are written to solve problems and perform tasks using a computer; they range in size from a few instructions to millions of instructions. A ***programming language*** is the tool used to create a program. It is the formal language used to write computer programs. A programming language, like any other language, is defined by both ***semantics*** (the meaning of the words used in the language) and *syntax* (the rules for combining the various symbols of the language). The program that you write using the programming language is usually called *code*, or more specifically *source code*.

After you write your program, you need to translate it so that you can execute it. Programs can be translated and executed using a compiler or an interpreter. Visual Basic 6.0 contains both. The *interpreter* translates the source code and executes it statement by statement without ever producing a separate executable file, as shown in Figure 2.1a. Interpreters make it easier to examine and change the program while it is running, and they store the program in a more compact form than a compiled program. When you run your projects within the Visual Basic environment, you are using the interpreter.

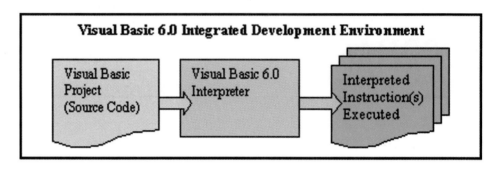

(a) The Visual Basic 6.0 Interpreter Process

FIGURE 2.1   Visual Basic's Interpreter and Compiler

Another way to translate and run source code is to use the compiler. Compilers can create a stand-alone *executable file*. You can easily create an executable file by pulling down the File menu, and selecting Make project exe. To create the file, the Visual Basic compiler produces a pseudo code file, as shown in Figure 2.1b. *Pseudo code* (also called P-code) is an intermediate step between the high-level instructions in your program and the low-level native code. You can create an executable file with the Learning, Professional, or Enterprise editions. In the Windows operating systems, an executable file has the file extension *exe*. Executable files are used to distribute most Windows applications.

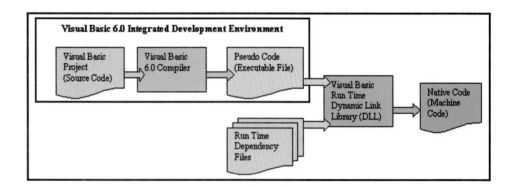

(b) The Visual Basic 6.0 Compiler Creates an Executable File

FIGURE 2.1   Visual Basic's Interpreter and Compiler (continued)

The advantage of an executable file is that it allows your program to be executed outside of the Visual Basic programming environment. At run time, the instructions in the executable file are translated by a runtime *Dynamic-Link*

Library (*DLL*) as shown in the figure. Windows 95 and Windows 98 are comprised of DLLs and applications. If Visual Basic is installed on your computer, these runtime files and DLLs are already available to the operating system.

If you want to run the executable file on a computer without Visual Basic, you need to create a distribution disk. This is easy to do using the *Package and Deployment Wizard* (formerly called the *Application Setup Wizard*). The wizard creates a disk that includes a setup program, the executable file, and the necessary runtime support files. The runtime files include the dependency files and the DLL as shown in the figure.

One of the new features starting with Visual Basic 5.0 is the ability to create a native code file. If you have the Professional or Enterprise edition, you can compile your source code directly to native code. *Native code* (also called machine language) consists of instructions that a computer can execute directly and is binary. When you compile directly to native code, you eliminate the intermediate pseudo code step, as shown in Figure 2.1c.

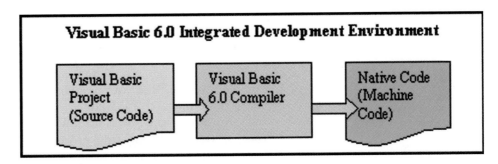

(c) The Visual Basic 6.0 Compiler Creates a Native Code File

FIGURE 2.1   Visual Basic's Interpreter and Compiler (continued)

To help you remember the types of code files, remember that *source code* is written and read by humans. *Pseudo code* and *native code* can only be read by computers. Source code is written in a computer language using English words. (Programmers all over the world usually need to understand English, which has become the international language of programmers.) If you try to open a pseudo code or native code file using a text editor such as Notepad, it will look like gibberish because it can only be read by a computer.

You will be using the Visual Basic interpreter and the Visual Basic compiler in the hands-on exercises for this chapter.

STEPS IN BUILDING A PROJECT

You have looked at the alternatives, and have decided that you really need to build your own custom software program. To get you started in the right direction, here is a step-by-step approach to building a program. The following steps are used by many professional programmers.

1. **Define the Problem.** Decide exactly what problem you wish to solve or what task you want to perform. Be sure that you understand what needs to be done. The detail of your needs is called the *specification*.

2. **Design and Plan.** This is the most important step of the process. If you spend more time at this step, you will spend much less time during the succeeding steps. First, find a step-by-step solution to your problem. A step-by-step solution to a problem is called an *algorithm*. If your problem involves math, figure out an equation. You will also need to design your *user interface* at this step.

Draw some sketches of the screens and windows you will need. Do a storyboard of your interface with sheets of paper to see if it makes sense. Add buttons, text, and the graphics needed for the input and output of your program.

3. **Build the Program.** Translate your problem or task solution into the programming language. In this case, you will be using Visual Basic. *Coding* is the term used for writing the program in a programming language. During this step, you will create the user interface, set properties, and write code for commands and instructions. You will also save your project in this step.

PLAN, PLAN, PLAN

This step-by-step plan for creating a programming project is often called the *software development life cycle*. Many software development companies employ different planning methods that may have different steps. The main point is to plan your project before you touch the computer, and then to follow your step-by-step plan.

---

4. **Run the Program.** Run your program in the Visual Basic environment—the Visual Basic Interactive Development Environment, or IDE, to use the formal term. Simply click the Start button to execute your project.

5. **Test and Debug.** *Testing* is the process of running your program looking for errors, to ensure that it executes as you intended in your design. *Debugging* is the process of removing errors from your program. (An error in your program is called a *bug*.) Steps 4 and 5 will be repeated until your program solves the problem or completes the task from your specification in step 1.

6. **Document Your Program.** This is the most often skipped step, but very important if the program will be updated in the future or used for any length of time. *Documentation* consists of notes to help you remember the hows and whys of your program. These notes will be invaluable if you need to change your program a year later. In a professional program, documentation consists of all the material that describes the program in all the steps. It allows another programmer to modify your program later if needed. Keep all your sketches, notes, and printouts in a notebook or a binder and organize them in case you need them later.

7. **Compile and Distribute your Program.** Once you have removed all the bugs from your program, it is ready to be distributed to the end user. The *end user* is the person that will be using your program to accomplish the tasks or solve the problems listed in your specification.

STEPS IN BUILDING A DECK: AN ANALOGY

To give you an idea of the importance of the steps involved in building a program, let's use the analogy of building a deck for a house, and go through the steps involved in our seven-step plan.

1. **Define the Problem.** You need a deck outside the back door of your house. It needs to be big enough to grill out, and hold a table with four chairs so that you can eat outside. You need to check the local building and zoning codes and include them in your design. You may need approval from your local homeowners association if you live in a subdivision or planned urban housing development of a city. You need to include time to get any approvals or inspections needed in your plan.

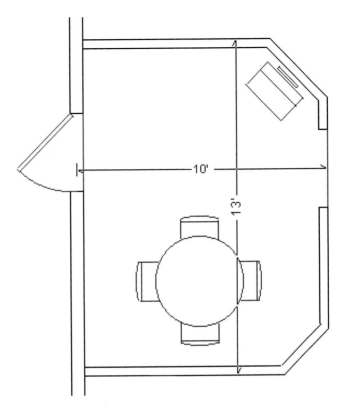

FIGURE 2.2   Floor Plan for a Deck

2. **Design and Plan.** You will probably make sketches at this point so that you can visualize the finished deck. See Figure 2.2 for an example of a floor-plan sketch. (This sketch was created using a popular floor-planning computer program, but an accurate pencil sketch would suffice.) Notice that the table, chairs, and grill are drawn to scale on the deck to be sure that the deck is large enough. Notice also that the corners are diagonal. The house is a contemporary style, and the diagonal corners will match it. The diagonal corners are more expensive than square corners, so this was a cost decision tradeoff. You also need to create a materials list. You may want to investigate deck kits, which include all the necessary materials. From your materials list, create a financial budget. Your simple algorithm to build this deck may look something like this:

(a) Stake out dimensions of deck.

(b) Dig postholes and set posts.

(c) Install floor joists.

(d) Install decking boards.

(e) Install railings.

(f) Install railing-top boards.

(g) Stain deck.

(h) Clean up and return tools.

3. **Build the Deck.** This step is analogous to building the computer program. You will use your plan and implement your algorithm. Do you have a hammer, nails, a drill, posthole digger, and other needed tools? Purchase all materials, supplies, and tools needed. Consider renting any expensive tools or borrowing them from a friend or relative. You will now implement your building algorithm to build the deck. You will add more details as you work.

(a) Stake out dimensions of deck using string and stakes.

(b) Determine positions of posts. Dig postholes. Set posts with cement.

(c) Measure and cut floor joists. Put floor joists in place and nail.

(d) Measure, cut, and install decking boards.

(e) ***OOPS, we forgot stairs in our plan!*** We need a decision here. We decide to add more money to the budget and include stairs for access to the ground from the deck. Purchase materials, and install stair stringers and stair boards.

(f) Measure, cut, and install railings.

(g) Measure, cut, and install wide railing-top boards. We just realized that it would be great to have railing-top boards wide enough to hold a drink. Check the first board cut to ensure that it is wide enough to hold a drink before continuing.

(h) Stain deck with deck-protector finish.

(i) Clean up, discard scrap materials, and store leftover materials and tools. Return tools to rental store, friends, or neighbors.

4-5. Run, Test, and Debug. We really were doing these steps as we built the deck. You will be programming in Visual Basic using this iterative process as well. We realized that we forgot to include stairs as we were building the deck. This means more money and another trip to the hardware store. We made the decision to include stairs. We also added the additional specification of making the railing-top boards wide enough to hold a drink.

6. Document the Work. For the deck, you will probably want to keep all your receipts in a single file folder. (For one thing, you will need proof of the amount you have spent on capital improvements for tax purposes when you sell your house.) Include your drawings and materials list from step 2 as well.

7. Compile and Distribute. Put your table and chairs and grill on your new deck. Invite some friends over for a cookout to share and enjoy your new deck.

Critique the Process

You really need to think of creating a Visual Basic program as a building process. In your first step, you need to write down as much about the problem or task as you can think of. In your design-and-plan step, you need to sketch out ideas for your screens, and write down the steps in the algorithm in the correct order to solve your problem.

For our deck project, we also considered a deck kit as opposed to building from scratch. This decision is often called a ***make-or-buy decision***. It is analogous to your decision in buying an application or programming your own. Remember to build your program a little at a time. Code a little and then test it. Then add a little more code and test it. This iterative process works successfully when programming with Visual Basic.

Show your plan to some friends, and ask them to find any flaws. Many times a friend can see things that you did not. In our deck example, we left out the stairs. The missing stairs are not as obvious in the two-dimensional floor plan as in the three-dimensional plan shown in Figure 2.3. We had to make a decision at this point. We did not have stairs in the budget. We could have left out the stairs for a more secure deck or found more money and time and included the stairs.

In any case, if we had included the stairs in the original plan we would have saved time and money. (When we added the stairs, we ended up with more railings than we needed, and they will be wasted.) It would have been more intelligent to include the stairs in the beginning plan. Also, remember that every

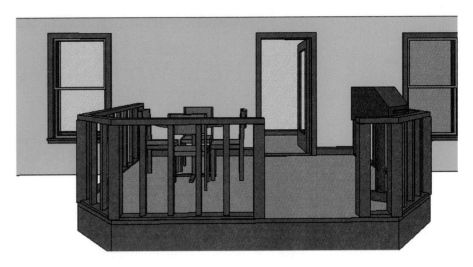

FIGURE 2.3   3-D View of a Deck

time you change the plan after the building process has begun, the costs are much higher. This is true in programming as well. It is much easier and cheaper to change a decision in the specification (step 1) than it is after the building has begun.

The documentation step is also important. This is a step needed for the future, so many times it is ignored. I personally believe in working smarter instead of harder, so I try to document as I go, and simply gather it all together in a single file folder when my project is finished.

The last step of distributing will be enjoyable if you have built and tested correctly. Nothing is more disastrous than having friends over and the deck falls down. This happened to a colleague. He saved some money on his deck by putting in smaller posts, but he now had a useless deck and a problem of potential lawsuits. Software manufacturers have been through litigation as well because they distributed an application with known problems. Testing and debugging before distributing is very important to prevent dissatisfied customers and lawsuits.

BUILD A VISUAL BASIC APPLICATION

Let's create a very simple application to demonstrate the steps in programming an application. This is a classic programming example known as "Hello World." We'll use it to execute the step-by-step plan.

STEP 1. Define the Problem

This is a very simple task. We want to display the words "Hello World!" on a screen. To make the screen more interesting, we will add an image of a world to the screen.

STEP 2. Design and Plan

Next, we need to sit down with a pencil and paper and come up with the design. You may want to bring out your colored pencils for this step. We need to design the *graphical user interface* that consists of the screens and windows. Use your paper in landscape mode because screens are oriented that way. If you are not

(a) Design for the Hello World Project's Initial Screen

FIGURE 2.4   Planning the Hello World Project

using colored pencils, make notes about color on your page. We design the initial screen as shown in Figure 2.4a. Notice the light blue background, and a single button on the screen.

Next, we design the final screen as shown in Figure 2.4b. We have used the same light blue background. "Hello World" is displayed in a 36-point Arial font in black. We found a clip-art globe in the Microsoft Clip Gallery. (We could have searched the Internet for a clip-art file instead.)

Finally, we need to decide the order of events. Remember that Visual Basic is an event-driven programming language. An **event** is an action recognized by an object, such as clicking the mouse or pressing a key, and for which you can write code to respond. We need to plan the events needed for this project, as shown in Figure 2.4c. These events are very simple. The user clicks the "Click Here" button on the initial screen. Then the user clicks the "Exit" button on the final screen. We have also written down exactly what should happen when an event occurs. We need to plan this before our hands touch the computer.

STEP 3. Build the Program

Now we will use Visual Basic to build our program. First, we will use the Form Designer window and the Toolbox to create the screens and controls. Second, we will set properties such as the color of the background and the text font and color. Next, we will write code for the events. In this case, the user will be clicking two buttons, so we need to write code only for these buttons. Finally, we will save our project to disk. You will build the program in Hands-on Exercise 1, and add code in Hands-on Exercise 2, in this chapter.

(b) Design for the Hello World Project's Final Screen

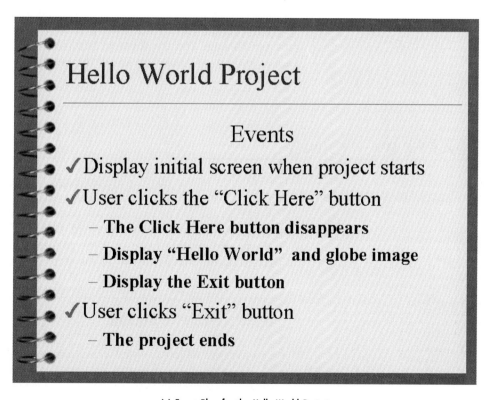

(c) Event Plan for the Hello World Project

FIGURE 2.4   Planning the Hello World Project (continued)

STEP 4. Run the Program

Running a program is very simple in Visual Basic. Simply click the Start button on the toolbar.

STEP 5. Test and Debug

This is a very important step. Click the "Click Here" button and check to see that the three events listed in our plan actually occur. If they do not, we need to go back to step 3, and make needed modifications. After the first event is debugged, we test the Exit button to see that it works as planned. We repeat steps 3, 4, and 5 as many times as needed until the project works as planned. Now we can proceed to the next step.

STEP 6. Document Your Program

We have the three sheets of notebook paper from our design-and-plan step. We should also print out the forms and code from Visual Basic to add to our documentation. You will document the program in Hands-on Exercise 3 in this chapter. For a more complicated project, we would include more, but this will suffice at this time.

STEP 7. Compile and Distribute Your Program

Now we can share our program with others. To run the finished program on a computer that has Visual Basic 6.0 installed, we can simply create an *exe* file. If we want others who do not have Visual Basic to be able to run the program, we use the Package and Deployment Wizard included with Visual Basic 6.0 to create a distribution disk that will install the necessary files on their system.

LEARN BY DOING

The exercises in this chapter are linked to one another in that you perform some steps for a simple project in Exercise 1, then open the project and perform more steps in Exercise 2. The exercises are intended only as a brief introduction to building projects. You will learn more of the details on creating forms, using the Toolbox, and writing code in later chapters. Each exercise has several steps. Concentrate on completing all of the steps in order.

THERE'S ALWAYS A REASON

I would love to tell you that everything will go perfectly, that you will never be frustrated, and that the computer will always perform exactly as you expect. Unfortunately, that is not going to happen, because a computer does what you tell it to do, which is not necessarily what you want it to do. There can be a tremendous difference! There is, however, a logical reason for everything the computer does or does not do; eventually you will discover that reason, at which point everything will fall into place.

Build Your First Application

Objective: Start building your first Visual Basic application by creating the Hello World project. Use Figure 2.5 as a guide in the exercise.

STEP 1: Create a New Project
➤ Start Visual Basic.
➤ Click the New Project dialog box's **New tab**, as shown in Figure 2.5a.
➤ Click the **Standard EXE icon**. Click the **Open button** to open a new project window.

Click the New tab

Click this icon

Click here to open the project

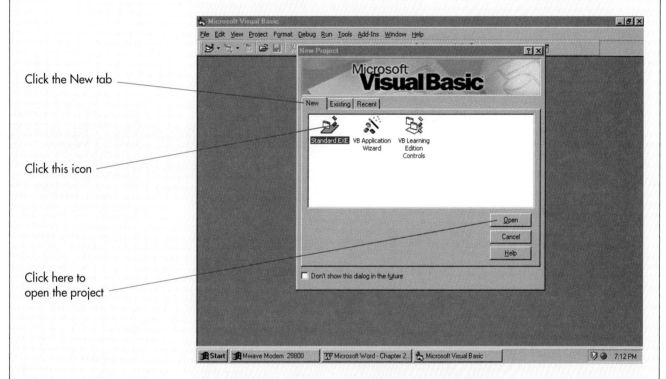

(a) Create a New Project (step 1)

FIGURE 2.5 Hands-on Exercise 1

STEP 2: Set Visual Basic Options
➤ To ensure that future steps looks as much like the figures as possible, set your Visual Basic options to match ours. Pull down the **Tools** menu, and select **Options**.
➤ The Options dialog box is displayed, as shown in Figure 2.5b. Click the **Editor tab**. In the Code Settings section, click to select or clear the options until they match the figure. If necessary, click in the Tab Width box and change the width to 4. In the Window Settings frame, select all of the options.
➤ Click the **Editor Format tab** to display Figure 2.5c, and make your settings match those in the figure. Under Code Colors, click Normal Text. Change the Foreground, Background, and Indicators color to Auto. Change the Font to Courier New, and the Size to 10. If necessary, click to select the Margin Indicator Bar.

Click the Editor tab ──────

Select this option ──────

Click to change the
settings as needed ──────

Change the tab
width if needed ──────

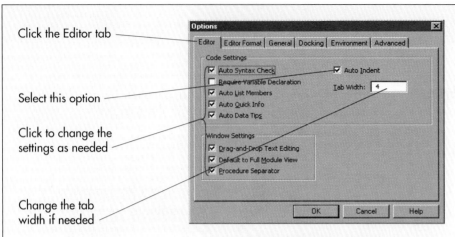

(b) Set Editor Options (step 2)

Click the Editor Format tab ──────

Set the font ──────

Select Normal Text ──────

Set the font size ──────

Select this option ──────

Change colors if needed ──────

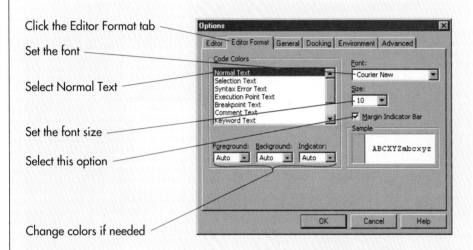

(c) Set Editor Format Options (step 2)

FIGURE 2.5   Hands-on Exercise 1 (continued)

➤ Click the **General tab** to display Figure 2.5d, and make your settings match the figure's. In the Form Grid Settings frame, click to select the **Show Grid** option. Change the Width and Height to 100. Click to select the **Align Controls to Grid** option. In the Error Trapping frame, select the **Break in Class Module** option. Click to select both Compile options. Click to select the **Show ToolTips** and **Collapse Proj. Hides Windows** options.

➤ Click the **Docking tab** to display Figure 2.5e. Under Dockable, select all options except Object Browser.

➤ Click the **Environment tab** to display Figure 2.5f. Set the options as shown in the figure. Change your templates directory only if needed. If you are using a lab PC, ask your instructor for the correct location. The default is shown in the figure.

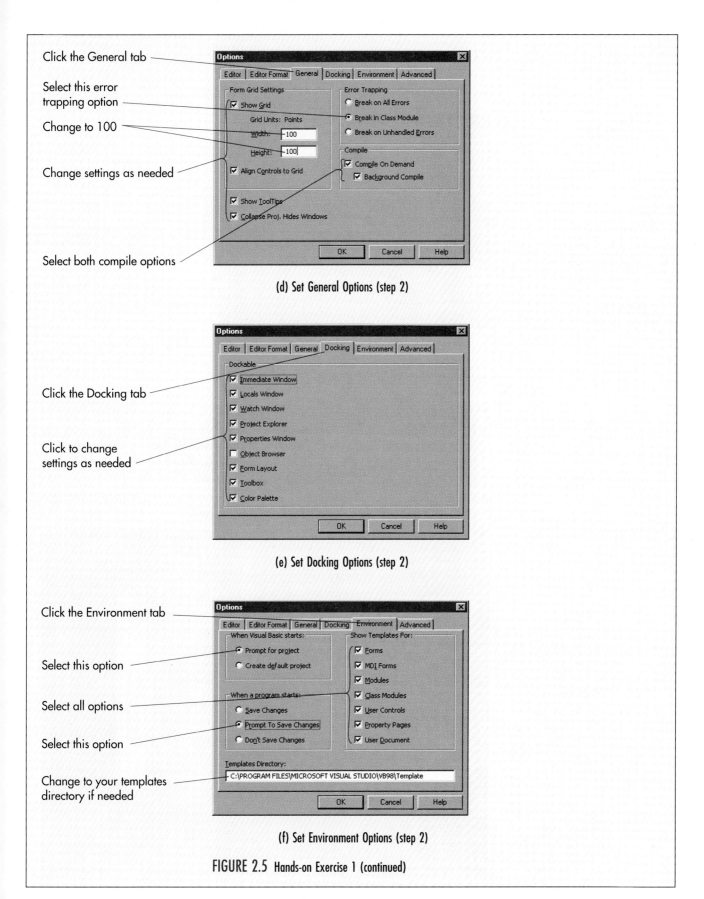

Click the General tab

Select this error trapping option

Change to 100

Change settings as needed

Select both compile options

(d) Set General Options (step 2)

Click the Docking tab

Click to change settings as needed

(e) Set Docking Options (step 2)

Click the Environment tab

Select this option

Select all options

Select this option

Change to your templates directory if needed

(f) Set Environment Options (step 2)

FIGURE 2.5 Hands-on Exercise 1 (continued)

➤ Click the **Advanced tab** to display Figure 2.5g, and set the options as shown in the figure.

➤ Click the **OK button** to save your option changes.

Click the
Advanced tab

Click to change
settings as needed

Click here to save
option changes

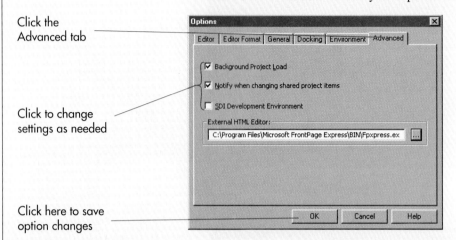

(g) Set Advanced Options (step 2)

FIGURE 2.5 Hands-on Exercise 1 (continued)

STEP 3: Restart Visual Basic (If Prompted)

➤ If you changed the Advanced options from a previous setting, you may see the message displayed in Figure 2.5h. Click the OK button to remove the message. You may see other messages as well. Read any messages before closing to ensure that your options have been set correctly.

➤ If the message appeared as shown in the figure, then exit Visual Basic and restart it. Repeat Step 1, and then jump to step 4.

Click here to
remove message

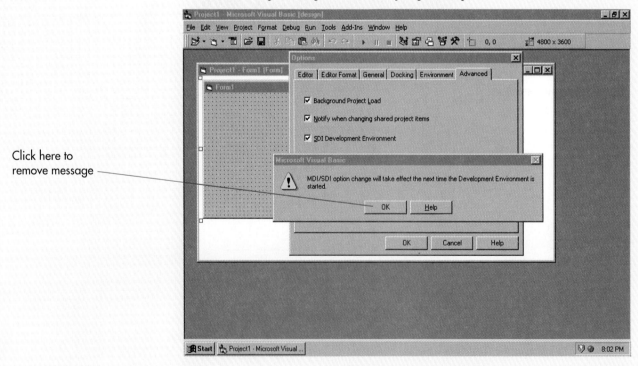

(h) Change Message Displayed (step 3)

FIGURE 2.5 Hands-on Exercise 1 (continued)

STEP 4: Create the Initial Screen

➤ Now that you have your design on paper (from Figure 2.4), you can start to build your project by creating the interface or form. Use Figure 2.5i as a guide in setting up your screen display. The Form Designer window should already be displayed.

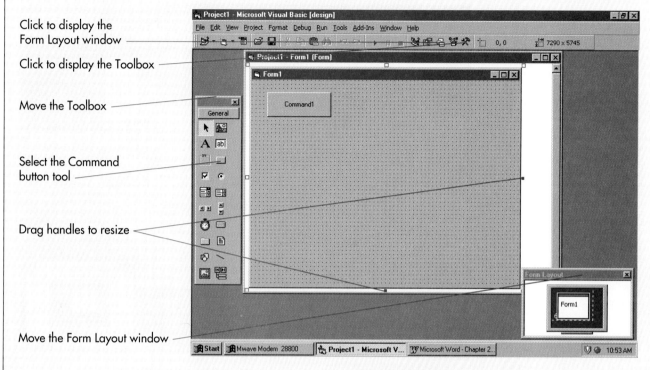

Click to display the Form Layout window

Click to display the Toolbox

Move the Toolbox

Select the Command button tool

Drag handles to resize

Move the Form Layout window

(i) Create the Initial Screen (step 4)

FIGURE 2.5   Hands-on Exercise 1 (continued)

➤ Click the **Toolbox button** on the toolbar. Grab the Toolbox by its title bar and move it to the location shown in the figure.

➤ Click the **Form Layout button** on the toolbar. Grab the Form Layout window by its title bar and move it to the location shown in the figure.

➤ Grab the **Form Designer window** by its title bar and move it to the location shown in the figure. If necessary, point to its borders and resize it to match the figure. Select the gray form, and resize it to the size shown in the figure. The bottom edge of the window should reach to the bottom of the 640-by-480 dotted rectangle shown in the Form Layout window. If the resolution of your screen is 640 by 480, you will not see the dotted rectangle. (Otherwise, if the dotted rectangle isn't displayed, right click inside the Form Layout window and select the context menu's Resolution Guides option.)

➤ Now move to the Toolbox and click the **Command Button tool** (it looks like a 3-D rectangle.) We will use this tool to place a command button control on our form.

➤ Move to the form, and, using Figure 2.5i as a guide, click to place the upper left corner of your button, then drag to the lower right corner and release. A 3-D rectangle will be displayed as shown in the figure.

➤ Now we will set the properties for the form. Click the **Properties Window button** on the toolbar to display the window. Click the **Categorized tab** in the Properties window as shown in Figure 2.5j. If necessary, resize the window to match the figure. If the Properties window does not currently display Form1, click the **drop-down arrow** in the Properties window's Object box and select **Form1**.

Click to display the
Properties window

Object box

Click this tab

Click this arrow

Click this tab

Choose light blue

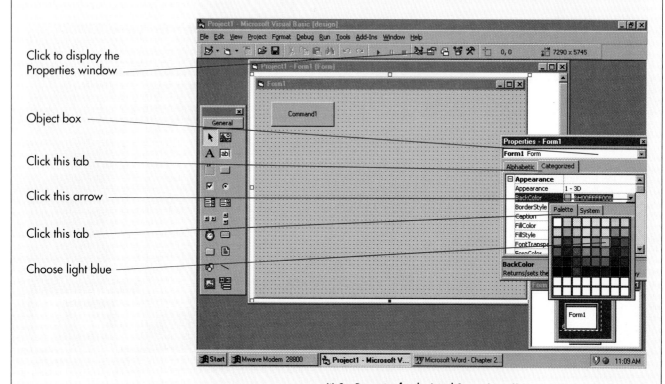

(j) Set Properties for the Initial Screen (step 4)

FIGURE 2.5   Hands-on Exercise 1 (continued)

➤ Click in the **BackColor property setting**, and a drop-down arrow is displayed. Click the arrow and then click the **Palette tab**. Select the **light blue color** in the third row. The form's background will change to light blue.

➤ Next, we will set the properties for the command button control. In the Form Designer window, click the **Command1 button** to select it. The Properties window's Object box changes to show that the command button is now selected. Click in the Caption setting and drag to highlight the default setting, Command1. Type over it to change it to **Click Here**. Change the Style setting to **1 – Graphical**. Change the BackColor setting to **light blue** as described in the previous bullet. You have completed the initial screen.

STEP 5: Create the Final Screen

➤ Now you are ready to create the final screen. The only differences between the initial screen and the final screen are the objects they display. So we will add objects to the current form, and display or hide them using the Visible property.

➤ First we will add a label, "Hello World!" to the form. Move back to the Toolbox and click the **Label tool** (it looks like an A) to select it.

➤ Now refer to Figure 2.5k for placement of the label control. Move to the form, and click to place the upper left corner where the words "Hello World" will be displayed. Drag to the lower right corner and release. A large rectangle with no dots will be displayed with the word *Label1* in the upper left corner.

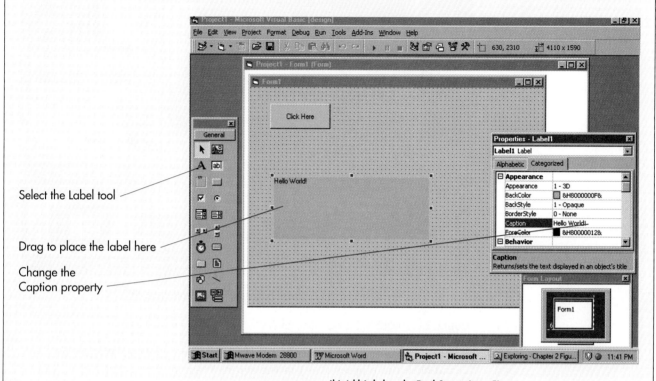

Select the Label tool

Drag to place the label here

Change the
Caption property

(k) Add Label to the Final Screen (step 5)

FIGURE 2.5   Hands-on Exercise 1 (continued)

➤ Set properties for the label control. Move to the Properties window, and change the Caption setting to **Hello World!** Change the BackColor setting to **light blue**. Scroll down to the Font property and select it. Click the ellipses (. . .) in its setting column to display the Font dialog box. Change the Font setting to **Arial**, **Bold** with a size of **36**. Now look back at the form and check how the label fits. If necessary, select the control and resize it. Back in the Properties window, scroll up to Behavior properties. Change the Visible setting to **False**. This will hide the label in the initial screen when we run the project.

➤ Move back to the Toolbox, and click the **Command Button tool** again. Use Figure 2.5l as a guide in placing the Exit command button. Move to the form and click to place the upper left corner for the Exit button. Drag to the lower right corner and release.

➤ Set properties for the command button. Move to the Properties window, and change the Caption setting to **Exit**. Change the Style setting to **1 – Graphical**. Change the BackColor setting to **light blue**. Change the Visible setting to **False**.

STEP 6: Add an Image to the Final Screen

➤ Add the image of the globe to your form. Move to the Toolbox and click the **Image tool** (it looks like a picture of mountains and sun).

➤ Move to the form, and click to place the upper left corner of the image control to the right of *Hello World*, then drag to the lower right corner and release.

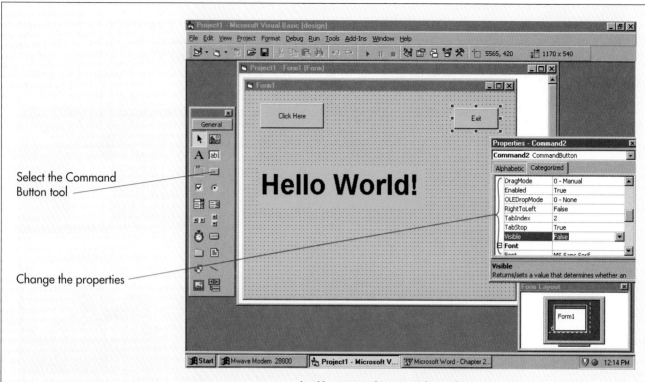

Select the Command Button tool

Change the properties

(l) Add a Command Button to the Final Screen (step 5)

FIGURE 2.5   Hands-on Exercise 1 (continued)

➤ Move to the Properties window, scroll down and click the **Picture property** and click the ellipses (. . .) in the setting column. The Load Picture dialog box as shown in Figure 2.5m is displayed.

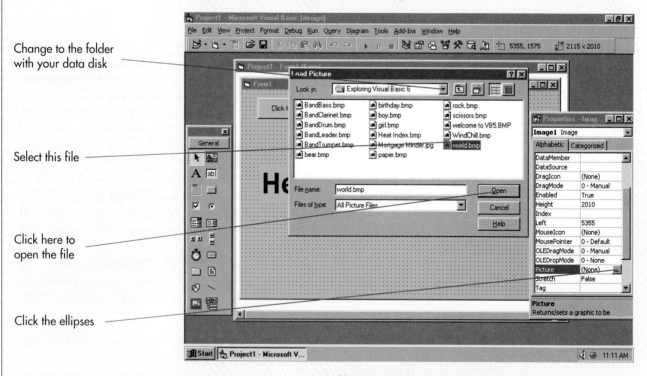

Change to the folder with your data disk

Select this file

Click here to open the file

Click the ellipses

(m) Add an Image to the Final Screen (step 6)

FIGURE 2.5   Hands-on Exercise 1 (continued)

➤ Select the disk and directory that contains your data disk, as described in Hands-on Exercise 1 in Chapter 1 (*Exploring Visual Basic 6*).

➤ Select the **world.bmp** file. Click the **Open button**. The world image will appear in the image control you placed on the form.

➤ Move back to the Properties window, and change the Visible setting to **False**.

➤ You have finished creating the form. Your form will look like previous Figure 2.4b (page 45) when you complete this step.

STEP 7: Save Your Project

➤ Pull down the **File** menu and select **Save Project** to save your project. Because you have created a form, you must save this form file first.

➤ The Save File As dialog box shown in Figure 2.5n is displayed. Select the drive and folder where you stored your data disk. Enter **Hello World** in the File name text box. Click the **Save button** to save the file and close the dialog box.

Change to the folder with your data disk

Enter the file name

Click here to save the form

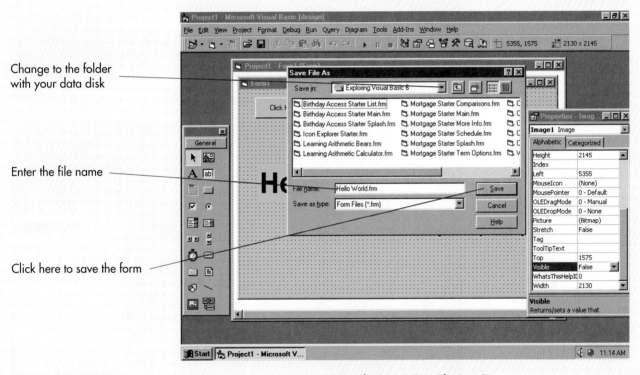

(n) Save the Project's Form Files (step 7)

FIGURE 2.5   Hands-on Exercise 1 (continued)

➤ The Save Project As dialog box is now displayed as shown in Figure 2.5o. Notice that it is set to the folder in which you saved the form. Enter **Hello World** in the File name text box. Click the **Save button** to save the project files and close the dialog box.

Change to the folder
with your data disk

Enter the file name

Click here to
save the project

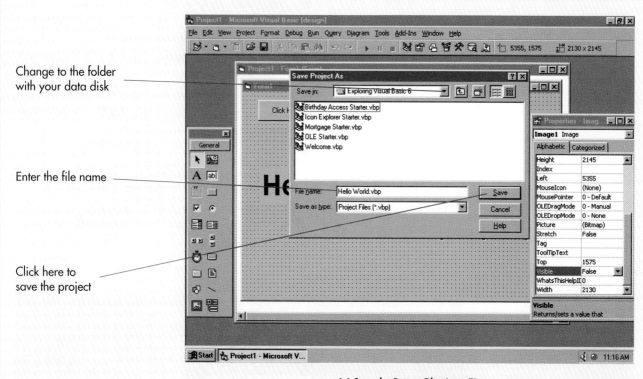

(o) Save the Project Files (step 7)

Click to exit the project

The form's first screen

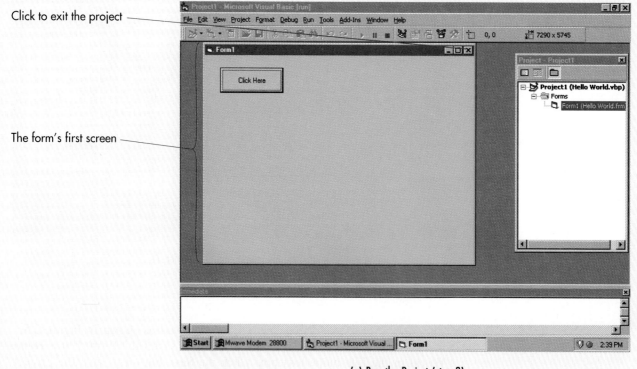

(p) Run the Project (step 8)

FIGURE 2.5   Hands-on Exercise 1 (continued)

STEP 8: Run Your Project

➤ Click the **Start button** on the toolbar. (If you see a message asking whether you want to save files, click Yes.) The form's initial screen should display, as shown in Figure 2.5p.

➤ Click the form's **Click Here** command button. Notice that nothing happens. You need to add code to your project to activate the command buttons. You will add code for this project in the next hands-on exercise.

STEP 9: Close the Project and Exit Visual Basic

➤ Click the **Close button** at the top right corner of the form. Pull down the **File menu** and select **Exit** to exit Visual Basic. (If you see any message asking whether you want to save files, click Yes.)

PROJECT FILES

A Visual Basic project consists of several files. Figure 2.6 shows the files for the Hello World project as they appear in the My Computer window. Every project contains:

- One *project file* that keeps track of all the project's components. This file is called Hello World.vbp. All Visual Basic projects are stored using the *vbp* file extension.
- One *form file* for each form. This file is called Hello World.frm. All forms are stored using the *frm* (form) file extension.
- One *binary form file*, automatically generated for each form containing data. Our file is called Hello World.frx. All binary forms are stored using the *frx* (form in hex) file extension.
- One *workspace file* that is automatically generated when you start a new project. Our file is called Hello World.vbw. All workspace files are stored using the *vbw* (Visual Basic workspace) file extension.

You can also access your project files from the Project Explorer window in Visual Basic. Figure 2.7 shows the Project Explorer window for the Hello World project. Notice that the binary files and workspace files are not shown. You can edit any of the files shown in Project Explorer. The binary files are automatically generated; because you cannot directly edit the binary files, they are not displayed in the Project Explorer window.

Other file types will be created for more advanced projects. Some of these files are class modules, standard modules, and resource files.

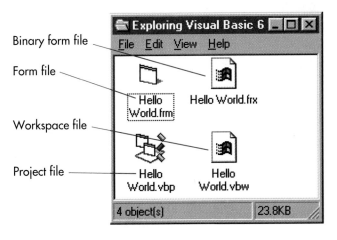

FIGURE 2.6 Hello World Project Files Viewed in My Computer

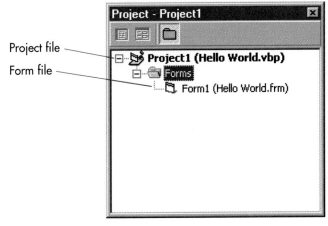

FIGURE 2.7 Hello World Project Files Viewed in a Project Explorer Window

Organizing and Naming Your Projects

When you save a project for the first time, you are prompted to save any forms that have been created for your project. If you have only one form for your project, it is a good practice to save it with the same file name as your project. If you have several forms for your project, you will need to save them with different descriptive names. File names for Visual Basic files may contain spaces and other punctuation. Periods are discouraged, since they are so easily confused with DOS file extensions.

You must specify the drive and folder in which to save your files. If you are working on your own computer, you may want to save the projects that you create in a new folder under the Documents folder. This makes it easier to distinguish your own projects from the projects included on the Visual Basic CD-ROM. Notice that in step 7 of the preceding hands-on exercise, we saved the files in a folder called *Exploring Visual Basic 6.*

THE FILE MENU

The most basic project commands are contained on the *File menu* as shown in Figure 2.8. This is a critically important menu in virtually every Windows application. The File menu contains the commands to start, open, save, and print projects. It contains the commands to make an executable project file or group of files. This menu also contains the commands to save an individual component file such as a form to disk. It displays a list of the most recently accessed project files and allows you to exit Visual Basic.

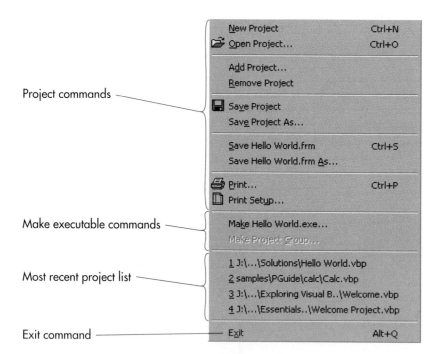

FIGURE 2.8 The File Menu

New Projects

When you select the *New Project command* from the File menu, the dialog box shown in Figure 2.9 is displayed. The options it offers vary with the edition of Visual Basic and with the program elements you have installed on your system.

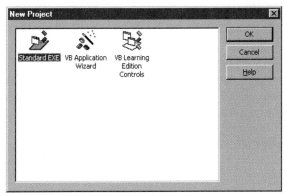

(a) Learning Edition	(b) Enterprise Edition

FIGURE 2.9   The New Project Dialog Box

You can select **Standard EXE** to create simple projects or the **VB Application Wizard** for projects that contain menus. Figure 2.9a shows one more option, **VB Learning Edition Controls**. Figure 2.9b shows several templates that are available with the Enterprise Edition.

A **template** is a particular pattern for a project or project element that has been stored on disk so that it can be reused. Using the template saves you from having to retype or recreate the specifications and code for the project element each time. Your computer may not have templates installed. You can choose whether to display them in the New Project dialog box by using the Environment tab of the Options dialog box.

Open Projects

The **Open Project command** brings a copy of a previously saved project from disk into memory, enabling you to work with that project. The Open Project command displays the Open Project dialog box where you specify the project file to retrieve. You can select the **Existing tab** to display the dialog box shown in Figure 2.10a. This tab displays projects included with Visual Basic. You can also change to other folders to display and open more projects.

Select the **Recent tab** (shown in Figure 2.10b) to display the projects that you have recently accessed. (This is similar to the Windows Start menu's Documents folder.) Notice that the Hello World project is at the top of the list because it is the last project we worked with in the previous hands-on exercise.

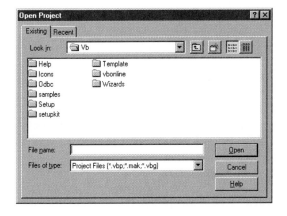

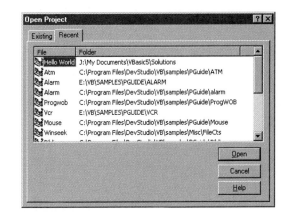

(a) The Existing Tab	(b) The Recent Tab

FIGURE 2.10   The Open Project Dialog Box

Project Groups

As a beginning programmer, you will be working on simple projects. As your projects become more complicated, you may want to combine projects together and work with them simultaneously in a Visual Basic session. This can be achieved with a ***project group***. A project group is simply a collection of multiple projects.

The ***Add Project command*** adds the selected project to the current project group. You can add an existing project or a new project to the project group. The ***Remove Project command*** removes the selected project from the current project group.

Save Projects

The ***Save Project command*** copies the project that is currently being edited (the project in memory) to disk. The first time a project is saved, you are prompted to save any component files such as forms that have not been previously saved. After saving the forms, then the Save Project As dialog box appears, so that you can specify the project file name. Subsequent executions of the Save Project command save the project under the assigned name, replacing the previously saved version with the new version.

The ***Save Project As command*** saves another copy of a project under a different name, and is useful when you want to retain a copy of the original project. The original project is kept on disk under its original name. A copy of the project is saved on disk under a new name. You will also need to copy any component files such as forms associated with the project with a new name using the Save As command.

Save Forms

The ***Save command*** copies the component file that is currently being edited to disk. Generally, you are saving a form with this command. This command saves a component (form) independently of the project file. The project file contains a list of references to the component files. When the component file is updated, the project will automatically reflect the changes. The first time a component file is saved, the Save As dialog box appears so that you can specify the file name. Subsequent executions of the Save command save the component under the assigned name, replacing the previously saved version with the new version.

The ***Save As command*** saves another copy of a component (form) under a different name, and is useful when you want to retain a copy of the original component. The original component is kept on disk under its original name. A copy of the component is saved on disk under a new name. You can add and remove components from a project using the ***Project menu***.

SAVE YOUR PROJECTS AND FORMS

I cannot overemphasize the importance of periodically saving your project, so that if something does go wrong, you won't lose all of your work. Nothing is more frustrating than to lose hours of work due to an unexpected problem in Windows or a temporary loss of power. Save your work frequently, at least once every 15 minutes. Pull down the File menu and click Save Project, or click the Save Project button on the toolbar. Just do it!

Print Projects

The **Print command** allows you to print a complete project or a component of the current project. For example, you can print the code, the forms in text format, the forms in graphical format, or any combination. You will be printing your project in Hands-on Exercise 3 in this chapter.

The **Print Setup command** allows you to select the printer, paper size, and print orientation for subsequent print operations.

Make Executable Projects

When you have finished testing your project, you can create a stand-alone **executable file** for your project. The **Make command** compiles your project and creates an executable file. The advantage of an executable file is that it allows your program to be executed outside of the Visual Basic programming environment. Refer to previous Figure 2.1b (page 38) to review the compiling process.

The **Make Project Group command** compiles your project group and creates an executable file for each project in the group. If you want to run the executable file on a computer without Visual Basic, you need to create a distribution disk. This is easy to do using the **Package and Deployment Wizard**. In the Windows operating systems, an executable file has the file extension **exe**. Executable files are used to distribute most Windows applications.

Exit Command

The **Exit command** closes the current project and exits Visual Basic. If you have not saved changes to your work, you will be prompted to save any component files or projects.

QUIT WITHOUT SAVING

There will be times when you do not want to save the changes to a project or component, such as when you have changed it so much that you wish you had never started. Pull down the File menu and click the Exit command, then click No in response to the message asking whether you want to save the changes to the form and project files. Pull down the File menu and reopen the file, then start over from the beginning.

USING THE CODE EDITOR

Let's continue the Hello World project, beginning with a review of what you have done so far.

First, you have completed the form you need for your project. When you create forms using the Form Designer window, you are creating the screens and windows that the user will see. Forms are the elements that make up the **graphical user interface** (**GUI**, pronounced "goo-ey") in applications created using Visual Basic. The GUI gives us the "visual" in Visual Basic. Chapter 4 discusses GUIs and forms in depth.

After you designed and created your form, you used the Properties window to set properties for the form and its controls (the command buttons, label, and image). A *property* is a characteristic or attribute of an object that determines how the object looks and behaves. Each control in a form has its own set of properties. An example of a property is the background color of blue. The property is background color, and the setting is blue. There are properties associated with the form itself, as well as with each button, graphic, and input box on the form. The advantage of setting properties is that Visual Basic does some coding for you.

Having created the interface and set properties, you are ready to proceed to *writing the code*. The coding portion of the building step is where you write the instructions (commands) using the Visual Basic programming language. Visual Basic is easier to learn than many conventional languages because you only need to write code for events. An *event* is a user action, such as clicking a button. You write the code to make your project respond to the user's actions. For the Hello World project, we need to add code for the click events associated with the two command buttons on the form.

You will write Visual Basic code for your project in the *Code Editor window*, shown in Figure 2.11. You can view and edit any code in your project using the Code Editor window. The Code Editor window is a word processor specialized for writing Visual Basic code statements. It makes writing code much easier. It has features that can automatically fill in statements, properties, and other items for you. As you enter code, the editor displays a list of appropriate choices. You simply select an item from the list. Many times your code is simply changing a property of a control.

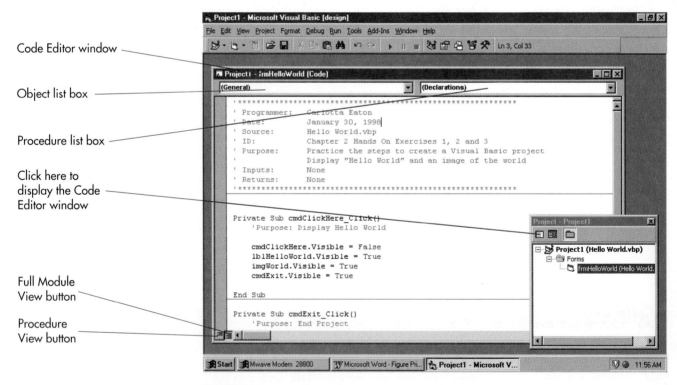

FIGURE 2.11   Code Editor Window

The code must be perfect if it is to execute as detailed in the specification, and humans beings make mistakes. You are virtually certain to make mistakes when you write code for a project. To test your project, you simply run it as a user would. If the project does not run, or runs incorrectly, you need a way to correct these mistakes. When Visual Basic encounters an error during the execution of a project, it displays as much information as it can to help you determine the reason for the error and assist you in *debugging* your program.

DEBUGGING: THE FIRST BUG

A bug is a mistake in a computer program; hence debugging refers to the process of correcting program errors. Grace Hopper told this story as now has become legend, the first bug was an unlucky moth crushed to death on one of the relays of the electromechanical Mark II computer, bringing the machine's operation to a halt. The cause of the failure was discovered by the operator, who promptly taped the moth to her logbook, noting, "First actual case of bug being found." You can read more about this amazing lady at

http://www.norfolk.navy.mil/chips/grace_hopper

from the U.S. Navy's memory Web pages.

Continue your first project, Hello World, with the following hands-on exercise. You will add code using the Code Editor window, then test your project, and debug it if necessary. This exercise is intended only as a brief introduction to coding projects. You will learn more of the details for writing code in the next chapter.

HANDS-ON EXERCISE 2

Code, Test, and Debug Your First Application

Objective: Continue building your first Visual Basic application following the project steps. Code your program, then save and run it. Test your program. Debug it if necessary. Use Figure 2.12 as a guide in the exercise.

STEP 1: Open the Hello World Project

➤ Start Visual Basic. Click the **Recent tab** in the New Project dialog box. Click the **Hello World project** from the previous hands-on exercise. Click the **Open command button** to open the project.

➤ If the Project Explorer window is not open, click the **Project Explorer button** on the toolbar to open it. If necessary, double click the **Forms folder** in the Project Explorer window to expand it and show its contents. Double click the **Hello World form**. The Form Designer window will display the form as you left off from the previous exercise, as shown in Figure 2.12a.

Project Explorer window

Double click here to open
the form

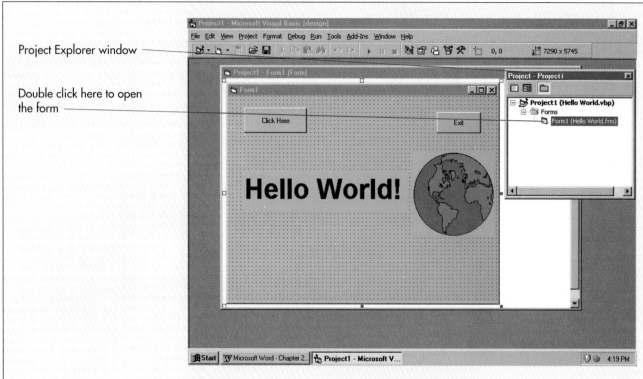

(a) Open the Hello World Project (step 1)

FIGURE 2.12   Hands-on Exercise 2

THE MOST RECENTLY OPENED PROJECT LIST

Another way to open a recently used project is to select the project directly
from the File menu. Pull down the File menu, but do not click the Open
Project command. Instead, check to see if the project appears on the list
of the most recently open projects located at the bottom of the menu. If it
does, you can click the project name rather than having to make the appropriate selections through the Open Project dialog box.

STEP 2: Change the Form's Name and Caption Properties

➤ Click the **Properties button** on the toolbar to open the Properties window. Resize
and move windows as needed so that they match those shown in Figure 2.12b.

➤ Select the form by clicking its **title bar** in the Form Designer window. Move
to the Properties window, and click the **Alphabetic tab**. Click in the **Caption
property**, which controls the title bar of the form. In the property setting column, click and drag over the word Form1 and replace it with **Hello World**.
The title bar of the form displays the change, as shown in Figure 2.12b.

➤ The Name property is the first property listed in the alphabetic list, and it should
be at the top of the Properties window. Click and drag over the setting Form1
and replace it with **frmHelloWorld**. Notice that there are no spaces allowed in
the name of a form. You are using the standard prefix *frm* to denote that this
is a form. The name *HelloWorld* describes the form to aid your memory later.
The title bar in the Form Designer window displays the name change. The
Object box at the top of the Properties window will also change. Figure 2.12b
displays the results of changing the properties for the form.

Select the form

Change the form's Name
property

Change the Caption
property

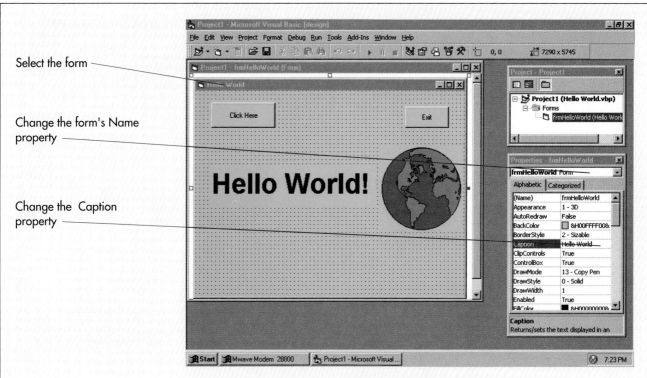

(b) Change the Form's Properties

FIGURE 2.12   Hands-on Exercise 2 (continued)

NAMING FORMS AND CONTROLS

Every form and control on a form must have a name. It is much easier to work with forms and controls if the names help remind you of what they do. The computer doesn't care what you call the controls, but it makes using programs easier for humans if you use descriptive names and prefixes. See Appendix B, "Object-Naming Conventions for Visual Basic," for more information.

STEP 3: Change the Name Property for the Command Buttons

➤ In the Form Designer window, select the **Click Here command button**. Move to the Properties window. The Name property should be at the top of the list. Type over Command1 and replace it with **cmdClickHere**. Notice that there are no spaces allowed in the name of a button. You are using the standard prefix *cmd* to denote that this is a command button. Figure 2.12c displays the results of setting the properties for the command button.

➤ In the Form Designer window, select the **Exit command button**. Move to the Properties window. The Name property should be at the top of the list. Type over Command2 and replace it with **cmdExit**.

STEP 4: Change the Label's Name Property

➤ In the Form Designer window, select the **Hello World label control** as shown in Figure 2.12d. Sizing handles appear around the label control to show it is selected, and the Properties window's Object list box changes to read "Label1 Label."

Select this command button

Change the Name property

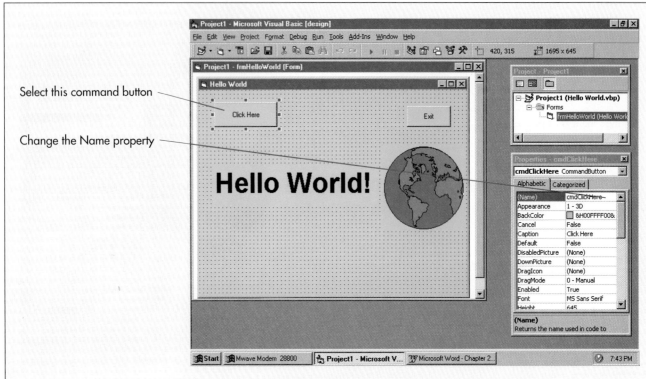

(c) Change the Name Property for the Command Button (step 3)

Select the label

Change the Name property

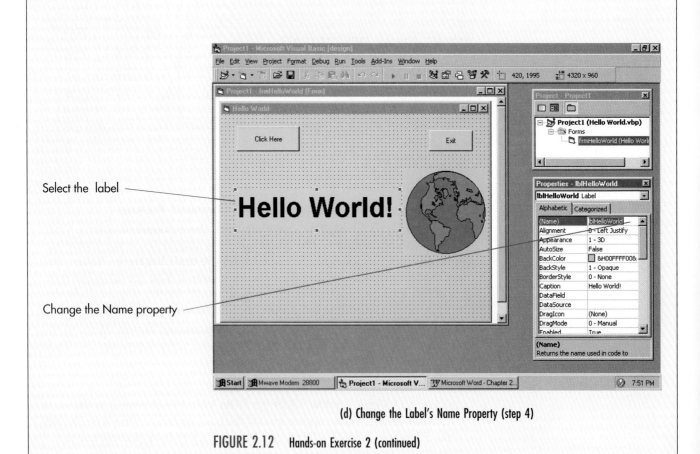

(d) Change the Label's Name Property (step 4)

FIGURE 2.12   Hands-on Exercise 2 (continued)

➤ Move to the Properties window. Change the Name property from Label1 to **lblHelloWorld**. You are using the standard prefix *lbl* to denote that this is a label.

STEP 5: Change the Image's Name Property

➤ In the Form Designer window, select the **World image** as shown in Figure 2.12e. Sizing handles appear around the image to show it is selected.

➤ Move to the Properties window. Change the Name property from Image1 to **imgWorld**. You are using the standard prefix *img* to denote that this is an image.

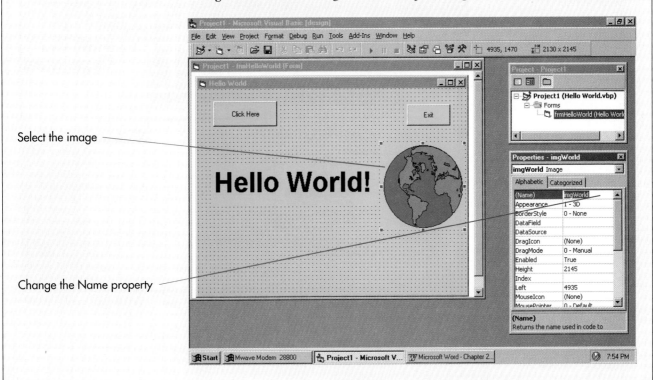

Select the image

Change the Name property

(e) Change the Image's Name Property (step 5)

FIGURE 2.12   Hands-on Exercise 2 (continued)

MOVING, DOCKING, AND RESIZING WINDOWS

The Visual Basic environment can be a crowded place. You can rearrange the tools and windows to your personal preferences. You can open, close, move, dock, undock, and resize any of the programming tools and windows.

To make a window dockable, right click anywhere inside the window except the title bar. Click the context menu's *Dockable* option. The advantage of docking windows is that they will not be hidden behind other tools or windows. The toolbars, Toolbox, Form Layout window, Project Explorer, Properties window, Object Browser, color palette, and debugging windows can be docked.

To dock a window (attach it to an edge), click the title bar and drag the window to the right, top, left, or bottom of the Visual Basic environment window. Docked windows will automatically link (attach to each other) if you align one along the edge of another.

To undock or move a window, simply click the title bar and drag the window to a new location.

STEP 6: Add Code for the Click Here Button

➤ In the Form Designer window, select the **Click Here command button**. Move to the Project Explorer window and click the **View Code button**. The Code Editor window will open, as shown in Figure 2.12f.

1) Select the command button

2) Click here to view code

3) Enter the code statement

4) Select the Visible property

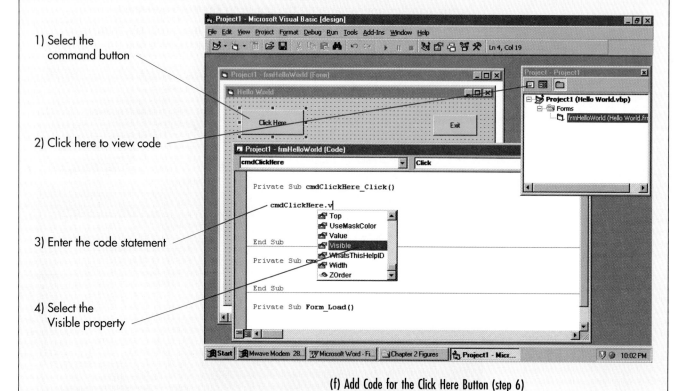

(f) Add Code for the Click Here Button (step 6)

FIGURE 2.12 Hands-on Exercise 2 (continued)

➤ Move to the Code Editor window. At the top are two list boxes: the Object list box at the left, and the Procedure list box at the right. The Object list box should display **cmdClickHere**, and the Procedure list box should display **Click**. If they display something else, click the drop-down arrow in the Object list box to select cmdClickHere. You will be adding lines of code that will be executed when the user clicks the Click Here command button.

➤ The first and last lines shown below should already be displayed in the Code Editor window. Insert the middle line exactly as shown below, using the Tab key to indent the line.

```
Private Sub cmdClickHere_Click()
  cmdClickHere.
End Sub
```

➤ As soon as you type the period, Visual Basic's Auto List Members feature will display the list of available properties, as shown in Figure 2.12f. Scroll and select the Visible property (or type a *V* to go straight to that letter). After choosing the Visible property, type an **equal sign (=)**. The Auto List Members feature will display the available settings for the Visible property. Select **False**. When this line of code is executed when the project is run, it will hide the Click Here button.

➤ Add the remaining lines of code exactly as shown below, using the Auto List Members feature to save time:

```
Private Sub cmdClickHere_Click()
  cmdClickHere.Visible = False
  lblHelloWorld.Visible = True
  imgWorld.Visible = True
  cmdExit.Visible = True
End Sub
```

➤ These lines display the Hello World label, the World image, and the Exit command button on the form. You have completed the code for the Click Here button.

STEP 7: Add Code for the Exit Button

➤ Click the **Object list box arrow** in the Code Editor window and select **cmdExit**, as shown in Figure 2.12g.

➤ The first and last lines shown below should already be displayed in the Code Editor window. Insert the only new line exactly as shown below.

```
Private Sub cmdExit_Click()
  End
End Sub
```

➤ This code stops the execution of the Hello World project.

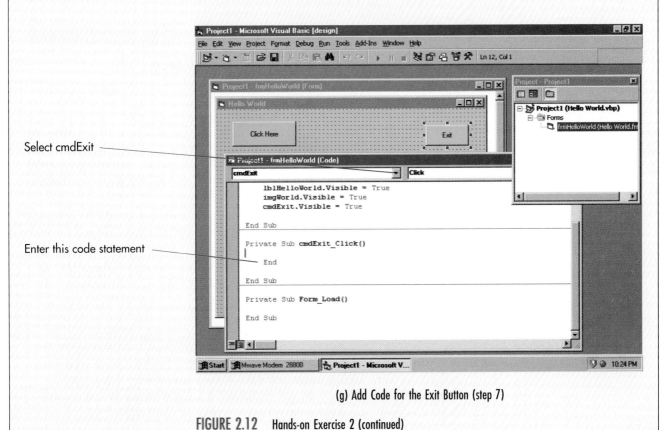

Select cmdExit

Enter this code statement

(g) Add Code for the Exit Button (step 7)

FIGURE 2.12   Hands-on Exercise 2 (continued)

STEP 8: Save and Run Your Project

➤ Click the **Save Project button** on the toolbar. Close the Code Editor window, Project Explorer window, Properties window, and the Form Designer window. Click the **Start button** on the toolbar.

STEP 9: Test and Debug Your Project

➤ The screen shown in Figure 2.12h will appear. Click the **Click Here button**.

Click to display the final screen —

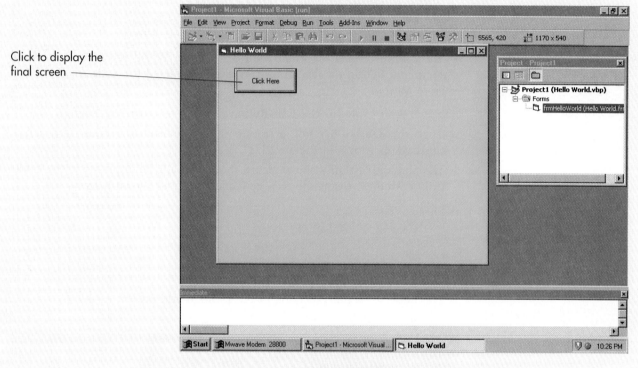

(h) Testing the Click Here Button's Code (step 9)

FIGURE 2.12   Hands-on Exercise 2 (continued)

➤ The final screen, shown in Figure 2.12i, will appear. Check to see that the Click Here button disappeared. The Hello World label, world image, and Exit button should be displayed. If this did not occur, retrace your steps beginning at step 2 to ensure that you entered everything correctly. Repeat steps 6 and 9 as needed.

➤ Click the **Exit button**. The project should end, and you should be returned to the Visual Basic environment. If this did not occur, repeat steps 7 through 9 as needed.

➤ If you made an error, you may receive a warning message. Read the message, and repeat any previous steps as needed to debug your project.

TESTING IS IMPORTANT

One of the most common mistakes that beginning programming students make is to skip testing their program before submitting it for grading. Remember to allow time in your schedule for a day or so of testing and debugging to ensure that your program works as planned.

Click here to exit the project —

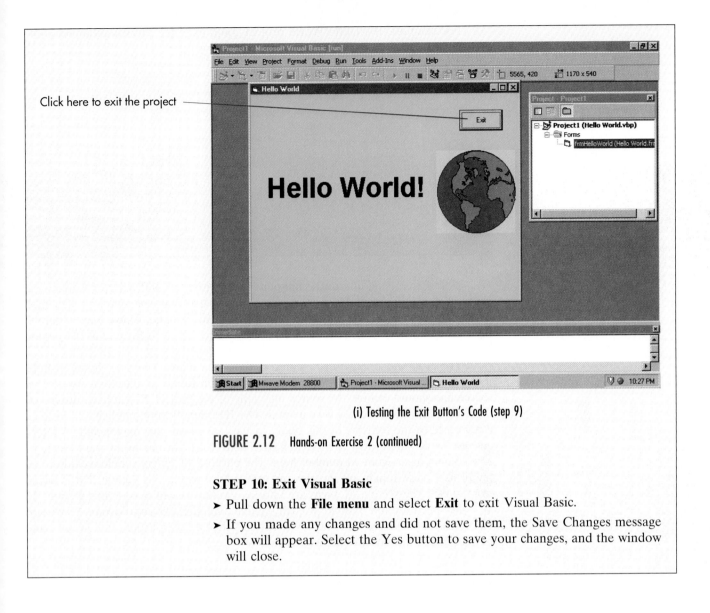

(i) Testing the Exit Button's Code (step 9)

FIGURE 2.12   Hands-on Exercise 2 (continued)

STEP 10: Exit Visual Basic
➤ Pull down the **File menu** and select **Exit** to exit Visual Basic.
➤ If you made any changes and did not save them, the Save Changes message box will appear. Select the Yes button to save your changes, and the window will close.

DOCUMENTING YOUR PROJECT

After debugging your project, the final steps in building a program are documenting and distributing it. Documentation becomes very important when you need to modify or update your program in the future. After just a few weeks, you may forget details such as a property setting for a control. Make it a practice to document your program as you go along, as illustrated in the next exercise.

Insert Banner Comments in Your Code

Documentation consists of the pages created during the planning steps, comments, and code printouts. The easiest way to document your code is to insert comments where an explanation is needed. This is known as "commenting your code." A *comment* is a coding statement read by humans, but not interpreted nor executed by the compiler. All projects should begin with a brief description and overview. The description should not include implementation details but provide an overview for human readers of the project. Each section of the code should also have at a minimum a comment explaining the purpose of the section.

For example, the Hello World project could have the following banner comment for the project:

```
' ******************************************************************
' Programmer:  Carlotta Eaton
' Date:        June 30, 1998
' Source:      Hello World.vbp
' ID:          Chapter 2 Hands-on Exercises 1, 2, and 3
' Purpose:     Practice the steps to create a Visual Basic project
'              Display "Hello World" and an image of a world
' Inputs:      None
' Returns:     None
' ******************************************************************
```

Notice that each line in the banner comment begins with an apostrophe ('). This apostrophe must be the first character in any line that is a comment. The first line and last lines are a row of asterisks after the apostrophe. These lines separate the banner comment from the rest of the code. The banner is located at the beginning of your project code.

The programmer statement should include your name. The date should include the date you started the project. It may also contain future modification dates. The source line should include the source file name of the project. If you have dozens of these files, this line becomes very helpful. The ID (identification line) should include a reference to the exercise in this book. In the real world, this may include a reference to the actual product or module name. Your instructor may want you to include a programming assignment number here. The purpose statement should include what the project does. Inputs are information that is used within this section that is taken from outside the section. Returns are information that is sent outside this section.

For each section of code, we can include comments as appropriate. Since our Hello World project is very short, we will only include the purpose line in our banner comments for the procedure sections.

Follow Code Conventions, and Print Your Code

The main reason for using a consistent set of coding conventions such as banner comments is to standardize the coding style of a project so that you and others can easily read and understand the code. You want to make your projects easy to read without cramping your creativity. This book shows the block indenting style that is used by many professional programmers. Your instructor may have other coding conventions to follow in this class.

You can easily print your code to place in your documentation folder as well. Pull down the File menu, select the Print command, and in the Print dialog box select the Print Code option. You can print the entire project, a single module, and even forms.

DISTRIBUTING YOUR PROJECT

After you have removed all the bugs from your program, and it works as you planned, you can distribute your programs to your friends. (You could even continue to learn more about Visual Basic and create programs and be paid as a professional programmer for your efforts.) One way to distribute the project is to create an executable file. Executable files are stored with the *exe* file extension. To compile your project and create an executable file that will run on any computer that has Visual

Basic 6.0 installed, simply pull down the File menu and select the Make Project,exe command. You can also use the Visual Basic's Package and Deployment Wizard to create your own setup executable file that will install and run independently of Visual Basic.

Continue your first project, Hello World, with the following hands-on exercise. You will add comments as documentation using the Code Editor window. Then you will make an executable file that can be run outside the Visual Basic environment on computers that have Visual Basic installed.

NEW PACKAGE AND DEPLOYMENT WIZARD

If you want to distribute your project to friends who do not have Visual Basic installed on their computers, use the **Package and Deployment Wizard**. This wizard replaces Version 5.0's **Setup Wizard**. Either wizard allows you to easily create a distribution disk with your executable project file along with all the necessary runtime files. Start the appropriate wizard from the Visual Basic Start menu. See Appendix F, *What's New with Visual Basic 6.0*, for more information.

HANDS-ON EXERCISE 3

Document and Distribute Your First Application

Objective: Finish your first Visual Basic application. Document your application by adding comments. Print your project. Create an executable file to distribute your application. Use Figure 2.13 as a guide in the exercise.

STEP 1: Open the Hello World Project

➤ Start Visual Basic. Click the New Project dialog box's **Recent tab**. Open the **Hello World project** from the previous exercise.

➤ The project opens as you left it at the end of the previous exercise. Click the **Project Explorer button** on the toolbar. If necessary, double click the **Forms folder** in the Project Explorer window to expand it and show its contents. Click the **Hello World form** to select it. Click the **View Code button** to open the Code Editor.

DOCUMENT YOUR PROGRAMS

To help those who use your program, you document it with comments directly in the program code. Begin each comment line with an apostrophe (ʼ) so that Visual Basic will ignore it when compiling your program. Comments are needed by the humans using the program, not by the computer.

STEP 2: Add Banner Comments

➤ In the Code Editor window, click the **Procedure View button** at the bottom left corner. Then click the **Object list box arrow** and select **General**.

➤ Click the **Procedure list box arrow** and select **Declarations**.

➤ Enter the following program documentation in the Code Editor window. Substitute your name and the current date. (Use tabs after the colons to align the items.) When you finish the banner comments, your screen should look like the one in Figure 2.13a.

```
'******************************************************************************
' Programmer:  Carlotta Eaton
' Date:        June 30, 1998
' Source:      Hello World.vbp
' ID:          Chapter 2 Hands-On Exercises 1, 2, and 3
' Purpose:     Practice the steps to create a Visual Basic project
'              Display "Hello World" and an image of a world
' Inputs:      None
' Returns:     None
'******************************************************************************
```

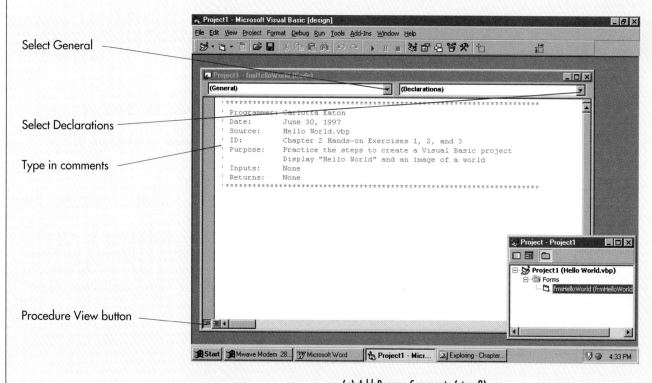

(a) Add Banner Comments (step 2)

FIGURE 2.13   Hands-on Exercise 3

STEP 3: Add Procedure Comments

➤ In the Code Editor window, click the **Object list box arrow** and select **cmdClickHere**. Ensure that Click is displayed in the Procedure list box, as shown in Figure 2.13b.

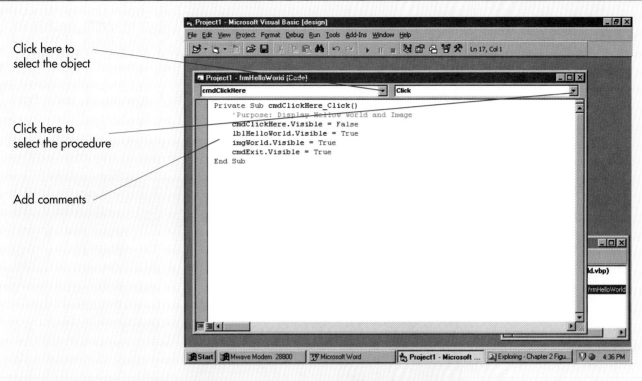

Click here to
select the object

Click here to
select the procedure

Add comments

(b) Add Procedure Comments (step 3)

FIGURE 2.13 Hands-on Exercise 3 (continued)

➤ Insert the following line after Private Sub cmdClickHere_Click. Ensure that all statements are indented by one tab as shown in the figure.

```
' Purpose: Display Hello World and Image
```

➤ Click the **Object list box arrow** and select **cmdExit**. Ensure that Click is displayed in the Procedure list box.
➤ Insert the following line after Private Sub cmdExit_Click:

```
' Purpose: End the Project
```

COLOR-CODED CODE EDITOR

The Code Editor automatically assigns different colors to different types of statements. Comments appear in green. Any Visual Basic statement containing key words appears in blue. Any statement containing a syntactical error appears in red.

STEP 4: Save and Run the Project
➤ Click the **Save Project button** on the toolbar to save your changes.
➤ Close the Project Explorer window and the Code Editor window.

➤ Click the **Start button** on the toolbar. Run your project to ensure that you did not introduce bugs when you added comments to your project. If you find errors, correct them before continuing to the next step. Click the **Exit button**.

STEP 5: Print the Project

➤ Make a printout of your program. Pull down the **File menu** and select **Print** to display the Print dialog box shown in Figure 2.13c.

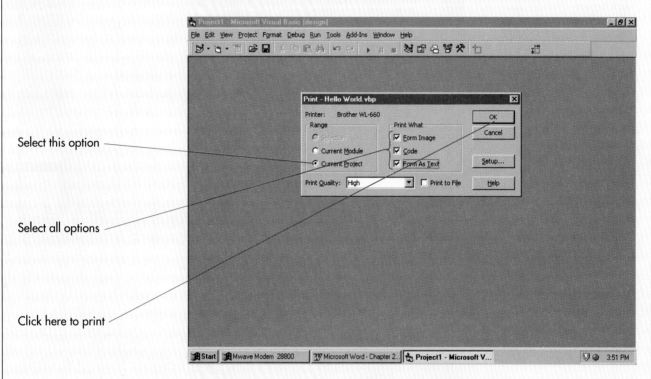

Select this option

Select all options

Click here to print

(c) Print the Project (step 5)

FIGURE 2.13   Hands-on Exercise 3 (continued)

➤ Under Range, select **Current Project**. Under Print What, select all three options. If a printer is attached to your computer, click the **OK button** to start printing.

➤ The first printed page contains the project's code. The second and third pages should contain the form as an image and again as text with all the property settings listed. Staple these together with any other notes and diagrams that you made while completing this project. This completes your documentation step.

STEP 6: Make an EXE File to Distribute Your Project

➤ Pull down the **File menu** and select **Make Hello World.exe** to display the dialog box shown in Figure 2.13d.

➤ Choose a drive and folder in which to save your project.

➤ **Hello World.exe** will be automatically entered in the File name text box. Click the **OK** button to create and save your executable project.

STEP 7: Test Your Executable Project

➤ Exit Visual Basic.

➤ From the Windows desktop, double click **My Computer**. Open successive My Computer windows until you can display the executable file you just saved, as shown in Figure 2.13e.

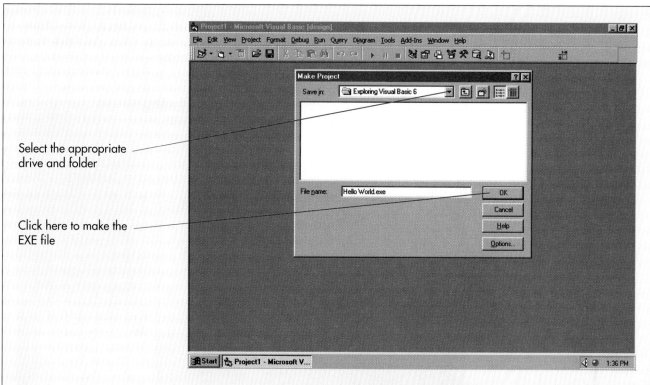

Select the appropriate
drive and folder

Click here to make the
EXE file

(d) Make an EXE File (step 6)

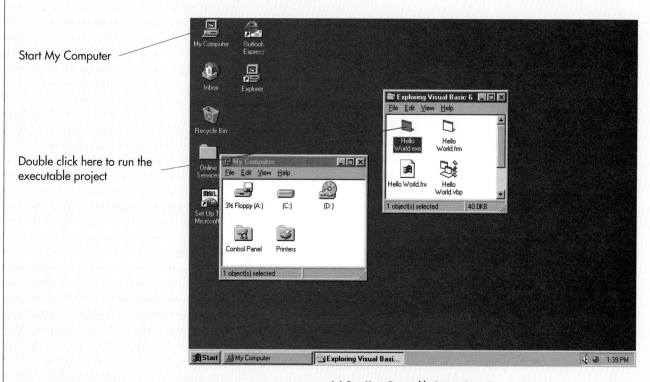

Start My Computer

Double click here to run the
executable project

(e) Run Your Executable Project (step 7)

FIGURE 2.13   Hands-on Exercise 3 (continued)

> Double click the **Hello World.exe** file as shown in the figure. Your Hello World project should execute directly on the desktop. Click the **Click Here button** to display the screen shown in Figure 2.13f.

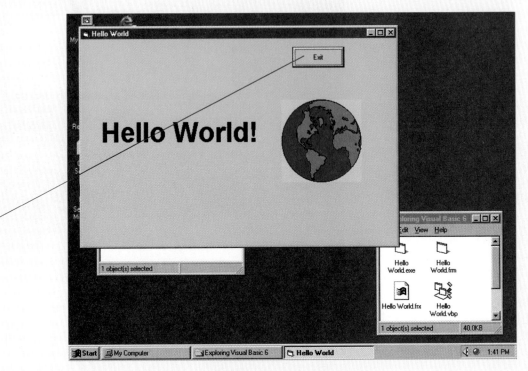

Click button to end execution

(f) Test Your Executable Project (step 7)

FIGURE 2.13   Hands-on Exercise 3 (continued)

> Click the **Exit button** to stop execution and close the project window.
> Congratulations! You have completed your first Visual Basic project. Remember: the first time you do anything takes a long time. The second time you create a project, it will go faster, and you will get even faster with practice.

SUMMARY

The chapter showed you how to create a Visual Basic project by following a systematic process. First you define the problem you are trying to solve, then design and plan your solution. Next you create the graphical user interface with forms, set properties, and write the code. Test and debug your program to ensure that it works as you planned. Document your program to make it easier to read and modify. After all of the bugs have been removed, create an executable file and distribute your project. A compiler translates the program that you built into pseudo code or native code. Visual Basic uses an interpreter to run your program in the programming environment. Building a program is analogous to most home building projects. When you spend time planning, designing, and drawing sketches for your project before you touch the computer, you will spend much less time in the computer lab.

Algorithm	Event	Project file
Bug	Executable file	Property
Code	Form file	Pseudo code
Code Editor window	Graphical user interface (GUI)	Semantics
Comment	Interpreter	Source code
Compiler	Native code	Specification
Debug	Package and Deployment Wizard	Syntax
Documentation	Program	Testing
End user	Programming language	Workspace file

MULTIPLE CHOICE

1. When following the step-by-step plan in building your project, a specification is
   - (a) The definition of your problem or task
   - (b) Your design and plan
   - (c) The debugging phase
   - (d) Documentation of your entire project

2. A detailed set of instructions for a computer is called a
   - (a) Program
   - (b) Compiler
   - (c) Programming language
   - (d) Syntax

3. Code that can be read and written by humans is called
   - (a) Source code
   - (b) Pseudo code
   - (c) Native code
   - (d) Machine language

4. Code that is created by a compiler and cannot be read by humans is called
   - (a) Pseudo code
   - (c) Native code
   - (d) Machine language
   - (d) All of the above

5. The details of the problem you are solving or the task you are performing with your program is called a(n)
   - (a) Algorithm
   - (b) User interface
   - (c) Specification
   - (d) Code

6. A step-by-step solution for the problem you are solving or the task you are performing is called a(n)
   (a) Algorithm
   (b) User interface
   (c) Specification
   (d) Code

7. Writing your program in a language such as Visual Basic is called
   (a) Specifying
   (b) Coding
   (c) Testing
   (d) Debugging

8. The process of running your program to ensure that it works as intended is called
   (a) Specifying
   (b) Coding
   (c) Testing
   (d) Debugging

9. The process of removing errors from your program is called
   (a) Specifying
   (b) Coding
   (c) Testing
   (d) Debugging

10. The notes that you keep and comments included in your program to help with future updates and to improve readability are called
    (a) Specification
    (b) Algorithm
    (c) Program
    (d) Documentation

11. The intended audience of your completed program is called a(n)
    (a) Programmer
    (b) End user
    (c) Administrator
    (d) Decision maker

12. To save a copy of your project with a different project file name use the
    (a) Save command
    (b) Save As command
    (c) Save Project command
    (d) Save Project As command

13. The command to print your project is located under the following menu:
    (a) File
    (b) View
    (c) Insert
    (d) Run

14. The most important step of your project that helps you spend less time coding and testing is
(a) The specification
(b) Design and plan
(c) Debugging
(d) Documentation

15. The Open Project command brings a copy of a project
(a) From disk to memory
(b) From memory to disk
(c) From disk to disk
(d) From memory to memory

ANSWERS

1. a	**6.** a	**11.** b
2. a	**7.** b	**12.** d
3. a	**8.** c	**13.** a
4. d	**9.** d	**14.** b
5. c	**10.** d	**15.** a

PRACTICE WITH VISUAL BASIC

1. Birthday Card. Modify the Hello World project you created in the hands-on exercises for the chapter to create a birthday card for a friend. You can use the design shown in Figure 2.14 or, even better, create your own design for this exercise.

a. Open the Hello World project as completed in the three hands-on exercises for this chapter. Save your form to your disk with a new file name. Open the Form Designer window to display the form. Pull down the **File menu** and select **Save As**. Select the appropriate disk drive and folder. Enter the file name **Birthday Card** for the form.

b. Save your project to your disk with a new file name. Pull down the **File menu** and select **Save Project As**. Select the appropriate disk drive and folder. Enter the file name **Birthday Card** for the project.

c. Resize the Form Designer window to full screen size. Change the properties to the following:

Object	Property	Setting
Form	BackColor	Light blue or choose another
Form	Caption	Happy Birthday
Form	Name	frmHappyBirthday
Image	Name	imgGolf
Label	Caption	Happy Birthday Steve! *or another birthday message*
Label	Name	lblHappyBirthday

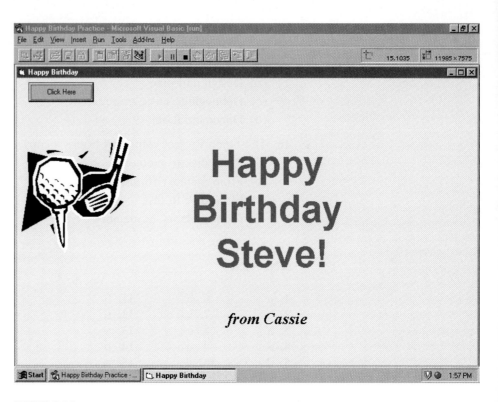

FIGURE 2.14 Screen for Practice Exercise 1: Birthday Card

    d. Click the **image control** to select it, and move it to the desired located on the card. In the Properties window, change the Picture property for the image to the desired image. The image shown is called *golf.wmf* and is located in the Microsoft Clip Gallery. Change the Name property to **imgGolf** or another descriptive name.

    e. Open the Toolbox. Click the **Label tool** and add a label to contain your signature message. Change the Caption property to the desired message or **from Cassie**. Change the Name property to **lblFromMessage**.

    f. Pull down the **View menu** and select **Code** to open the Code Editor window. In the ClickHere procedure, insert the following lines of code:

```
lblHappyBirthday.Visible = True
imgGolf.Visible = True
lblFromMessage.Visible = True
```

    g. Save your project. Run and test the project. Fix bugs if needed. Make an exe project file to give the birthday card to your friend. The friend will need to have Visual Basic installed on his machine, or use the Package and Deployment Wizard to create a distribution disk.

VIDEO CLIP

2. **Moving, Docking, and Resizing Windows: Video Demonstration (Learning Edition Only).** This exercise requires that you be using the Learning Edition of Visual Basic, and that you have installed the *Learn Visual Basic Now* book on your hard drive or have access to it from the CD-ROM. This video clip, one of several included on the Learn Visual Basic Now CD, shows details of moving, docking, and resizing windows, a topic we discussed in the hands-on exercises. Run and watch the video clip to reinforce this material from the chapter.

   a. Start *Learn Visual Basic Now*.

   b. Open the books from Chapter 1 as shown in Figure 2.15.

   c. In the Topic pane, scroll to the bottom and click the Video icon.

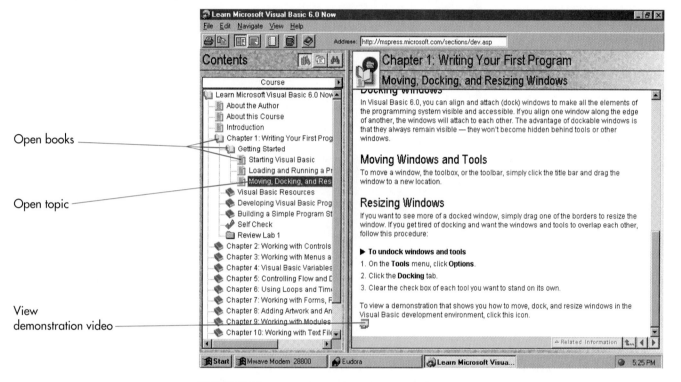

Open books

Open topic

View demonstration video

FIGURE 2.15 Screen for Practice Exercise 2: Moving, Docking, and Resizing Windows

3. **Package and Deployment Wizard.** The Visual Basic Package and Deployment Wizard makes it easy for you to create a setup program for your application. When you create an EXE file, the executable file will run only on computers with the same version of Visual Basic installed. To share your projects with others, you must create distribution diskettes using the wizard. Create a distribution diskette for the Hello World project or the Birthday Card project from Exercise 1. This wizard was called the Application Setup Wizard in Visual Basic 5.0, so use this wizard if using Version 5.0.

   a. Start the Package and Deployment Wizard from the Windows Start menu. Select the Programs menu, optionally Microsoft Visual Studio 6.0, then Microsoft Visual Basic 6.0 Tools (alternatively Microsoft Visual Studio 6.0 Tools), then Package and Deployment Wizard. Select the project file, then click the Package button.

b. Each screen of the wizard, such as the one shown in Figure 2.16, will prompt you for information about your project and let you choose options for distribution.

c. As you progress through each screen, click the Help button if you need more information.

d. Submit your setup diskette(s) to your instructor as proof that you completed this exercise.

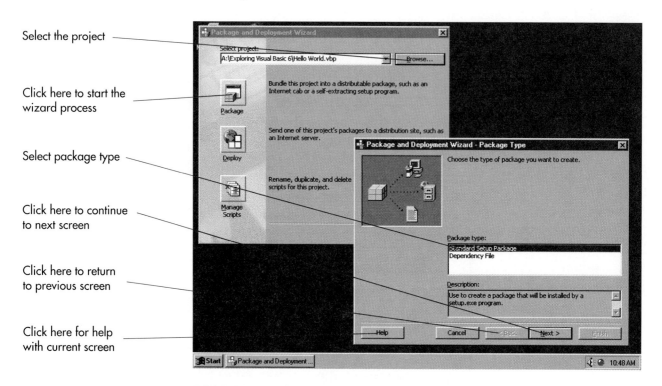

Select the project ──────────

Click here to start the wizard process ──────────

Select package type ──────────

Click here to continue to next screen ──────────

Click here to return to previous screen ──────────

Click here for help with current screen ──────────

FIGURE 2.16   Screen for Practice Exercise 3: Package and Development Wizard

VIDEO CLIP

4. **Building a Simple Program Step by Step: Video Demonstration (Learning Edition Only).** This exercise requires that you be using the Learning Edition of Visual Basic, and that you have installed the *Learn Visual Basic Now* book on your hard drive or have access to it from the CD-ROM. This video clip, one of several included on the CD, shows the step-by-step process for creating a form, setting properties, and writing code. The official Visual Basic 6.0 has several CDs. Version 5.0 had only two CDs. The project is called Lucky Seven. Run and watch the video clips and animation to reinforce this material from the chapter.

a. Start *Learn Visual Basic Now*.

b. Open the books from Chapter 1 as shown in Figure 2.17a.

c. Open the "Planning Lucky Seven" topic. In the Topic pane, scroll to the bottom and click the Video icon.

d. There are several video clips in this demonstration. Open the next topic, called "Creating the Lucky Seven Interface." In the Topic pane, click the Video icon, as shown in Figure 2.17b.

e. Open the next topic. Click its Video icon. Repeat until you have finished viewing the entire virtual chapter.

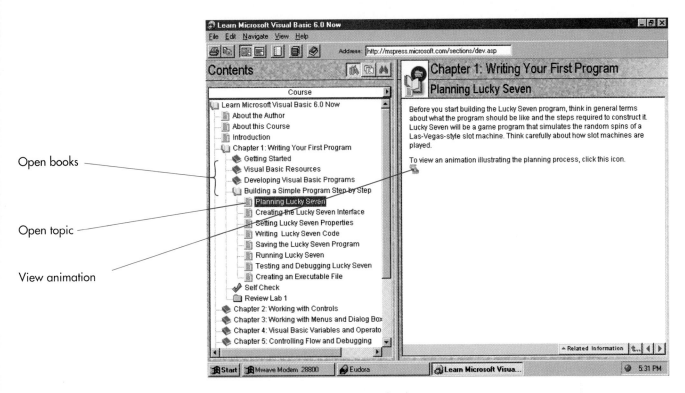

Open books

Open topic

View animation

(a) The Planning Process Animation

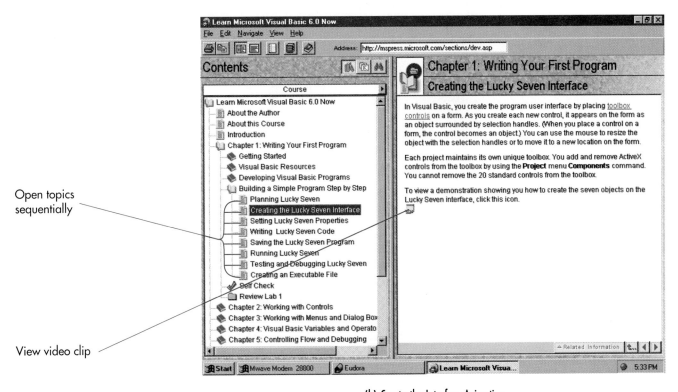

Open topics
sequentially

View video clip

(b) Create the Interface Animation

FIGURE 2.17   Screen for Practice Exercise 4

Special Occasion Card

Use the instructions for the Birthday Card project in Practice Exercise 1 as a guide to create a special occasion card. Decide on the occasion for your card, and find an appropriate clip art image from the Microsoft Clip Gallery or other graphics files on your system. If you have an Internet connection, you could browse the Web and download a graphic. Use a fancy font and change the font color and background. Use the Package and Deployment Wizard to create a distribution disk and send your electronic card to a friend or relative. Print out the card or submit it on a disk to your instructor as proof that you completed this case study.

The Development Exchange

It seems that there is a magazine available for nearly every hobby or computer topic imaginable, and Visual Basic is no exception. The Development Exchange is an online information service for Windows Programmers. Previously this was called the "Visual Basic Programmer's Journal." Check it out at *http://www.windx.com* as shown in Figure 2.18. You can subscribe to the hardcopy magazine or the CD-ROM version, order books, download source code that accompanies articles as well as sample applications, and browse resources for Windows developers and links to other software-industry Web sites. There are several free services available to keep programmers up to date on Visual Basic happenings. Write a one-page summary of an article you read from this Web site.

FIGURE 2.18   The Development Exchange Web Site

Visual Basic Newsgroups

There are several newsgroups available with Visual Basic as the primary topic. Use your favorite news reader program, and link to one of the following newsgroups. Check out the FAQ (Frequently Asked Questions) for the newsgroup. Read the postings for a week or more before posting a message to any newsgroup. Remember that the whole world can read your message, so you don't want to ask a silly question or one that has already been answered in the same newsgroup. You are not required to post a message to the newsgroups; instead, write a one-page summary of an article you read.

An easy way to search for additional newsgroups it to use the Deja News service at *http://www.dejanews.com*. Enter Visual Basic in the interest box and click the Find button. Here is a partial listing of newsgroups that discuss Visual Basic. Be sure to check your news server for additional groups.

Newsgroup Site	Description
Microsoft.public.vb.bugs	Bug reports
Microsoft.public.vb.controls	Control usage and programming
Microsoft.public.vb.controls.databound	Database programming controls
Microsoft.public.vb.controls.Internet	Internet aware controls
Microsoft.public.vb.database	Database issues
Microsoft.public.vb.installation	Installation, setup issues
Microsoft.public.vb.ole	General OLE issues
Microsoft.public.vb.setupwiz	Setup wizard kit
Microsoft.public.vb.syntax	General language issues
comp.lang.basic.visual	Visual Basic programming language

Visual Basic Coding Conventions

We discussed the importance of documenting your programs using banner comments and comments in general. Commenting is only one of the many things that you can do to make your code easier to read, understand, and maintain. The MSDN Library contains an appendix on Coding Conventions. Pull down the Help menu, and select Contents. Open the *Visual Basic Documentation* book, then *Using Visual Basic Programmer's Guide*, and then open the *Visual Basic Coding Conventions*. Read this appendix, and write a one-page summary of the importance of coding conventions using your favorite word processing application.

FIND CODING CONVENTIONS USING VISUAL BASIC 5.0

Pull down the Help menu, and select Books Online. From the Table of Contents, open the *Programmer's Guide* book, and then open the *Visual Basic Coding Conventions* book.

PROGRAMMING FUNDAMENTALS: WRITING CODE

3

OBJECTIVES

After reading this chapter, you will be able to:

1. Understand the use of and create event procedures and general procedures using the Sub command.
2. Understand and use variables in your project; differentiate between the various data types and understand which data types are appropriate for your project.
3. Differentiate between a variable and a constant and understand their appropriate uses.
4. Differentiate between the Dim and Static statements for declaring variables and constants, and understand the scope and lifetime of each.
5. Utilize a Visual Basic predefined function; use help to find the available predefined functions; create your own function when an appropriate predefined function is not available.
6. Write a program that calculates using a formula; convert an algebraic formula to a Visual Basic statement.
7. Write code statements that make a decision, using the If … Then or Select Case statement.
8. Write code statements that repeat, using the Do … Loop, For … Next, or For Each … Next looping statement.

OVERVIEW

This chapter introduces the essential programming fundamentals of the Visual Basic 6.0 programming language. In the previous chapters, we studied the Visual Basic 6.0 Integrated Development Environment and the steps to create an application. In this chapter, we will study the fundamentals of coding using an event-driven programming language. We can develop applications that are more complex with our code by adding variables and procedures and the ability to do mathematical operations, formulas, and functions.

89

We will add the capability of making decisions using code with the If … Then statement and Select … Case statement. We can repeat segments of code using the Do … Loop, For … Next, or For Each … Next looping statements.

We will apply these new programming skills with the hands-on exercises. You will create an application to calculate the wind chill temperature using a formula. You will create the Learning to Add game that makes simple decisions. Finally you will create a simple animation using a repeating loop.

MODULES AND PROCEDURES

Code is simply a set of instructions written in a programming language. Code enables the graphical user interface. The user can point to and click objects on the form, or type input. Without code, the GUI would look great, but it could not do very much.

CODE: THE MAN BEHIND THE CURTAIN

I like to think of code as the *man behind the curtain.* One of my favorite movies is *The Wizard of Oz.* I particularly like the scene where Dorothy and her friends return to the wizard's chambers and see a large head that speaks to them through a ring of fire. Dorothy's dog Toto moves the curtain aside, and they see the *man behind the curtain* causing the head to move and speak. Of course, when we are running an application we *"pay no attention to the man behind the curtain."* The code for your project is analogous to the "man behind the curtain." We want the code to be in the background, so that the user is not conscious of it.

Modules

Visual Basic is developed in large units called *modules*. A simple application project may consist of a single module, whereas a complex application may consist of dozens of modules. Every form in a Visual Basic project has its own module, known as a *form module*, which contains a form as well as the code for the form. Form modules (*.frm* file extension) are the basis for most Visual Basic projects.

Advanced projects may contain *standard modules*, which hold code that is typically accessed by many different modules in an application. Standard modules (file extension *.bas*) were called code modules in previous versions of Visual Basic. The projects contained in this textbook consist of form modules and standard modules. You can also create new objects by writing *class modules* (*.cls* file extension) in more complex projects. Class modules are beyond the scope of this book.

Procedures

Every module consists of smaller units called *procedures*. A procedure can be activated in two ways. An *event procedure* is automatically invoked by an event. Recall from previous chapters that an event is an action recognized by an object, such as clicking the mouse or pressing a key. In contrast, a *general procedure* must be explicitly called by another procedure. All *procedures* (event and general) are a set of statements executed as a unit and stored in a module. A procedure is either public or private. A *private procedure* is accessible only from within the module where it is contained. A *public procedure* is accessible from anywhere.

EVENT-DRIVEN VERSUS PROCEDURE-ORIENTED PROGRAMMING

Remember from Chapter 1 that Visual Basic is an ***event-driven programming language***. This is an ideal type of language for programming an application with a graphical user interface, where the user, not the programmer, controls the order of events. This methodology differs from that of ***procedure-oriented programming languages*** such as FORTRAN, COBOL, Pascal, and C, where the programmer writes procedures and determines the order of their execution.

THE CODE EDITOR WINDOW

Code is viewed and edited using the Code Editor window. This window is a specialized word processor for writing Visual Basic code. There are several features available that make writing Visual Basic code much easier. Let's take a detailed look at the Code Editor window.

View Selection Buttons

You can view all the procedures in a module in the Code Editor window as a single scrollable list using ***Full Module View*** (as shown in Figure 3.1a). Each procedure is separated from the next by a ***procedure separator line***, as shown in the figure.

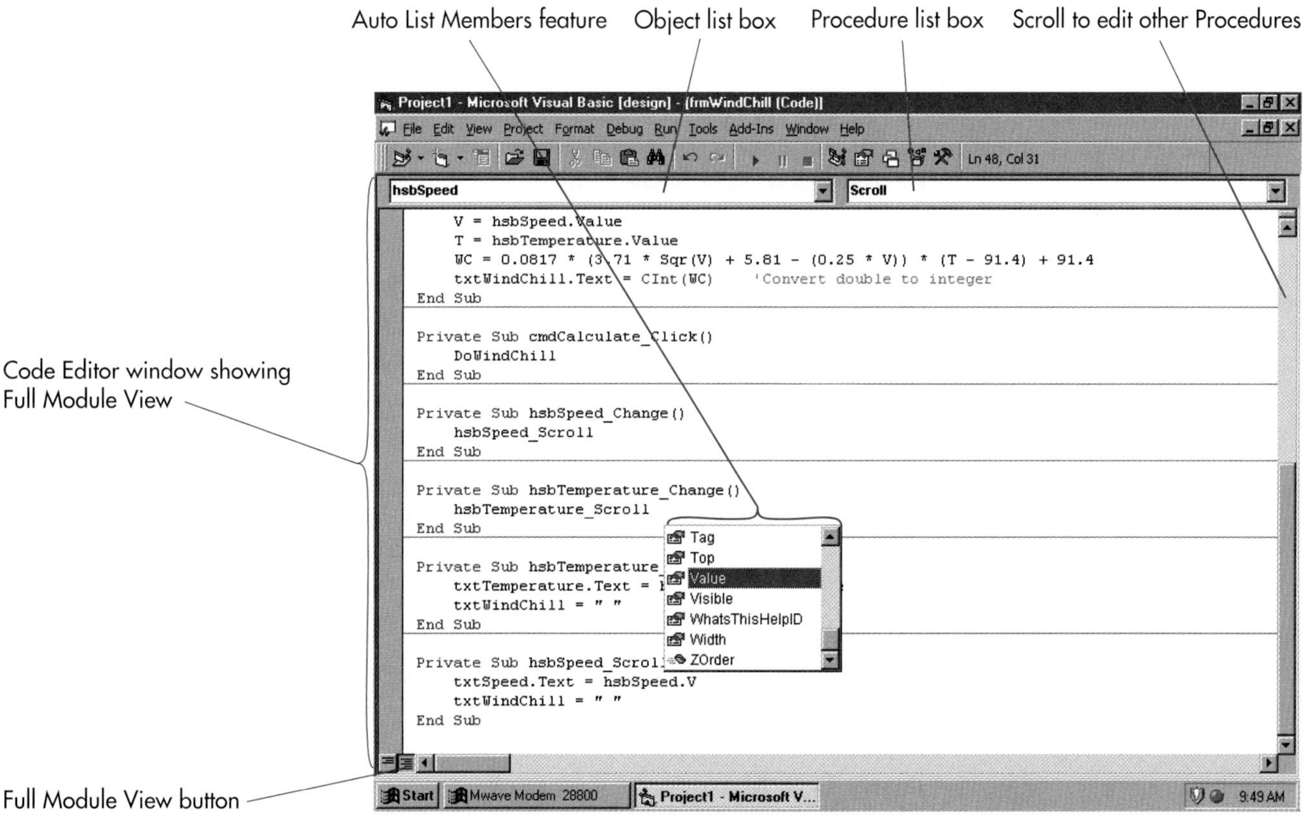

(a) Full Module View

FIGURE 3.1 Code Editor Window Views

Object list box

Procedure list box

Auto Quick Info Feature

Procedure View button

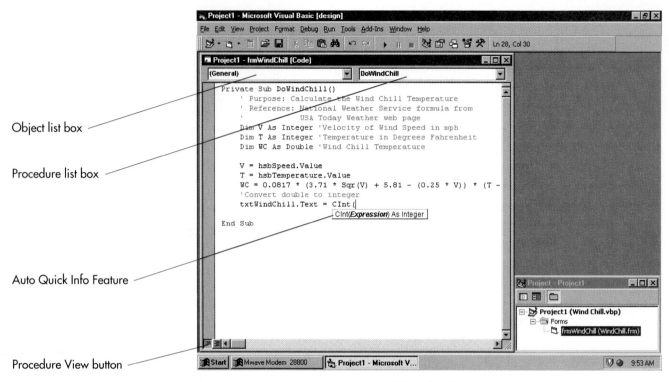

(b) Procedure View

FIGURE 3.1   Code Editor Window Views (continued)

You can also view one procedure at a time using **Procedure View** (as shown in Figure 3.1b). You can switch between the two views using the two View Selection buttons at the bottom left corner of the window.

Procedure List Box

Event procedures and general procedures are accessed using the **Procedure list box** at the top right corner of the window. The Scroll event procedure for a horizontal scroll bar is shown in Figure 3.1a. Other examples of event procedures are Click, MouseDown, and DragDrop, to name a few. A general procedure called DoWindChill is shown in Figure 3.1b.

Object List Box

The objects on a form are accessed using the **Object list box** at the top left corner of the window. Examples of objects on a form are text boxes, images, and command buttons. A horizontal scroll bar object named hsbSpeed is selected in Figure 3.1a. In a form module, the object list also includes the form itself as well as a general section as shown in Figure 3.1b. The general section of a program also includes the declarations of a program. Declarations will be discussed in more detail later in this chapter.

Auto List Members Feature

Visual Basic automatically helps you write your code. As you enter your code, the editor displays a list of choices and options where appropriate. For example, when you enter the name of a form control, the **Auto List Members feature** displays a list of properties available for that control, as shown in Figure 3.1a. In the figure, the current line of code is the third line from the bottom of the window. Enter the first few letters of a property (V in the figure) to select it from the list. Then, simply press the Tab key and the editor will automatically complete the typing for you. You can also display the Auto List Members feature at any time with the Ctrl+J key combination.

Auto Quick Info Feature

When you enter a Visual Basic statement or keyword, the syntax is shown with the *Auto Quick Info feature*, as shown in Figure 3.1b. In this example, the current line of code is the next to last line. The Cint function has been started, and the Auto Quick Info feature displays the valid syntax for the function. You will learn more about functions later in this chapter. The Auto Quick Info feature keeps the Visual Basic reference manual at your fingertips at all times. You can display the Auto Quick Info feature at any time with the Ctrl+I key combination.

Auto Syntax Check

When you enter a code statement incorrectly, you will be given a message such as the one shown in Figure 3.2 In this example, the ending parenthesis was omitted. The message box gives us a compile error message indicating the problem. If you need more information, click the help button to display a help window as shown in the figure. This feature helps you correct problems as you are entering code instead of waiting until you attempt to compile and run the project.

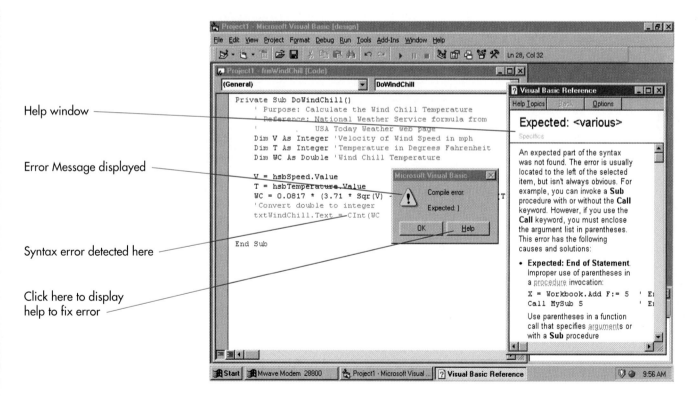

Help window

Error Message displayed

Syntax error detected here

Click here to display
help to fix error

FIGURE 3.2   Code Editor Window Auto Syntax Check

Turn On Special Features

Some of these features may be disabled for your Visual Basic installation. To enable any of the Code Editor features, pull down the Tools menu and select Options. Next, click the Editor Tab. Select the feature option boxes as shown in previous Figure 2.5b (page 48) and described in the first hands-on exercise in Chapter 2.

THE SUB STATEMENT

A *statement* is a syntactically complete sentence written in a programming language. A statement is also called a line of code. All procedures in Visual Basic are coded using the *Sub statement*. The Sub statement contains the name of the procedure as well as the code for the procedure. All Sub procedure statements employ the same syntax. We'll illustrate it with a procedure for calculating the area of a triangle, which you may remember from high school math is equal to half the product of the triangle's base times its height.

SYNTAX BOXES

The syntax for Visual Basic statements is shown in syntax boxes. The words shown in *italics* are programmer named, and will be different for every procedure. The words shown in **bold** are reserved words and cannot be changed.

Sub procedures begin and end with the Sub and End Sub statements, respectively. The *Sub statement* contains the name of the procedure. Notice that no spaces are allowed in the name of a procedure. The procedure name is composed of the object name, an underscore, and the event followed by a set of parentheses.

The simple syntax for the Sub statement is shown in the following box:

Private Sub *controlname_eventname* **()**
  statements
End Sub
where
  Private is the default procedure type for all procedures in Visual Basic; it indicates that variables within the procedure are accessible only within this procedure—they are private to the procedure
  Sub is required and indicates the beginning of a procedure
  controlname is the name of the associated control
  _ (an underscore) is required between the controlname and the eventname
  eventname is the name of the corresponding event
  ( ) set of parentheses is required
  statements are the statements to perform actions needed for this event
End Sub is required and indicates the end of a procedure
Example:
Private Sub cmdCalcTriangle_Click
  Dim Base As Single   'Base of the Triangle
  Dim Height As Single   'Height of the Triangle
  Dim Area As Single   'Area of the Triangle
  Area = 1/2 * (Base * Height)
End Sub

Sub statements to code procedures consist of:

- The Sub statement, or procedure-name header line (the first line in the example)
- A declaration section, a list of the variables used in the Sub procedure: the Base, Height, and Area of the triangle in the example. (We will learn about variables and how they are declared later in this chapter.)
- Statements to complete the task: the single line giving the formula for calculating the area of the triangle in the example
- The End Sub statement: the last line in the example

You can write your Sub procedure code from scratch, but it is much easier to use the code procedures provided in the Code Editor. The correct event procedure names for all controls on a form are automatically included in the Code Editor window. An event procedure waits until needed to respond to an event caused by the user or triggered by the system. Each time the corresponding event occurs, the event procedure is called, and the statements between Sub and End Sub are executed in order. A general procedure is called directly by another statement in the module.

DECLARATIONS, VARIABLES, AND CONSTANTS

A *variable* is a uniquely named storage location that contains data that changes during program execution. A *constant* remains constant during program execution. Before a statement can utilize a variable or constant, it must be declared using a declaration statement.

Variables

You are probably familiar with variables from your math classes. You probably used *A, B, C, X,* etc., as variable names in equations and formulas. In Visual Basic, a **variable** is a named storage location that can contain data that can be modified during program execution. You can store numbers, names, dates, and even property values in variables. Each variable has a unique name within a procedure. Variables are useful because they let you assign a short, easy-to-remember name to the data you are working with. To make your program easy to read and modify, choose variable names suitable to the data.

Variable names in Visual Basic must conform to the following rules:

- Must begin with an alphabetic character
- Can't contain an embedded period or type-declaration characters such as %, &, !, #, @, $
- Must be unique within the same scope (for Private procedures, this means inside the procedure)
- Must be no longer than 255 characters
- Should not be Visual Basic reserved words (see Appendix A for a list of reserved words)

In the example for calculating the area of a triangle, above, we used names for the variables that help us to remember what data is stored in them. We chose *Base, Height,* and *Area* for our variable names. In math classes, you probably used *B, H,* and *A,* but the entire words are much more descriptive.

STATIC KEYWORD FOR SUB STATEMENTS

The static keyword indicates that the variables declared inside the procedure are saved between calls. If the static keyword is omitted, the variables are not saved between calls.

Declaring Variables

A **declaration** statement is nonexecutable code that sets aside storage locations for future use. Variables can be declared in the general section of a module or within a procedure. Variables are called **local** when they are declared within a procedure or function, and **global** when they are declared in the general section.

DECLARE YOUR VARIABLES

Visual Basic doesn't require that you explicitly declare variables; however, it is a very good programming practice that can save you hours of debugging time.

As we name our variables, we need to decide what information they will store and declare them. We do this with the **Dim statement,** where "Dim" is short for "dimension." Each variable will have a name and a data type. The data type determines what type of data can be stored in the variable.

DIM VERSUS STATIC VARIABLES

Variables can be declared with the Dim or the Static statements. Variables declared with the Static statement preserve the value for the entire time the program is running. Use the Static statement to declare variables inside non-static procedures. Variables declared with the Dim statement are preserved only until the procedure ends. See the Online Help for more information on the differences between the Dim and Static statements.

The syntax for the Dim statement is shown in the following box:

Dim *variablename* **As** *datatype*
where
    Dim is required
    variablename should be a descriptive name
    As is required
    datatype is the type of data the variable will contain

Examples:
```
Dim Number1 As Integer
Dim FirstName As String
Dim LoanAmount As Currency
Dim Length As Single
```

When variables are declared, they must be assigned a data type. You can choose from the following data types:

Boolean – Stores either True or False.

Byte – Short numbers between 0 and 255.

Date – Dates from January 1, 100 to December 31, 9999.

Integer – Numbers without a decimal point. The number must be between –32768 and 32767.

Long – Long Integer. Numbers without a decimal point that are too long to fit in an Integer type. The number can range from –2,147,483,648 to 2,147,483,647.

Single – Numbers that contain a decimal point. Numbers with 38 digits can be stored with this data type.

Double – Numbers that contain a decimal point that are too long to fit in a Single type. Numbers with 308 digits can be stored with this data type.

Currency – Numbers that are dollar amounts from –$922,337,203,685,477.5808 to $922,337,203,685,477.5807. The numbers are stored with 4 decimal place accuracy.

String – Characters and alphanumeric data. Strings may also contain special characters such as % and @.

Object – Any object reference such as a Word document or an Excel spreadsheet.

Variant – The variant data type is the default data type for any variable that is not explicitly declared using the Dim statement. It is a special data type used to store data in controls (located on your forms), and date and time values. Variant is an all-purpose data type because it can store numeric values as large as Double as well as String data. Visual Basic stores each control on a form as the Variant data type.

Assigning Values to Variables

An *assignment* statement assigns a value or a property to a variable. The syntax for an assignment statement is shown in the following box:

variablename = *value*
   where
         variablename is the descriptive name of the variable
         = is the assignment operator
         value is the value the variable will contain

Examples:
```
Number1 = 5
FirstName = "Steve"
LoanAmount = 67.38
Length = 17.8
```

Remember to match the data type with the data. For example, you cannot store 17.275 as an Integer data type because it contains a decimal point. Instead, you need to use a Single or Double data type. If the number represented a monetary amount, you should use the Currency data type.

ORDER IS IMPORTANT

In algebra,

   Number1 = 5 is equivalent to *5 = Number1*

This is not the case in Visual Basic and most programming languages. The variable name must be on the left side of the equal sign and the assigned value on the right. Otherwise, you will get an error message or unexpected results.

Constants

Often when you are writing a program, you will find the same number appearing as a value many times. Instead of using a variable and assigning it a value, you can use a constant. A constant contains a value that does not change during the execution of a program. The rules for naming constants are the same as for naming variables. When you use a constant in your program, you declare it and assign it using the same statement.

The syntax for declaring and assigning a constant is shown in the following box:

Const *constantname* **As** *datatype* = *value*
   where
        Const is required
        constantname should be a descriptive name
        As is required
        datatype is the type of data the constant will contain
        = is required
        value is the value of the constant

Examples:

```
Const Pi As Single = 3.14159265358979
Const MaxNumber As Integer = 100
Const VB As String = "Visual Basic 6.0"
```

THE WIND CHILL PROJECT

In this exercise, you write a program that calculates the wind chill temperature. This winter was a cold winter: on January 10, the temperature was 4 degrees Fahrenheit, and the wind was blowing gusts of 25 miles per hour. Your program should calculate the wind chill for this day, as well as for other temperatures and wind speeds.

First, we need a formula for calculating the wind chill temperature. You can search the library or the Web for this information. The National Weather Service uses the following formula (taken from the USA Today Weather Web site, as shown in Figure 3.3a):

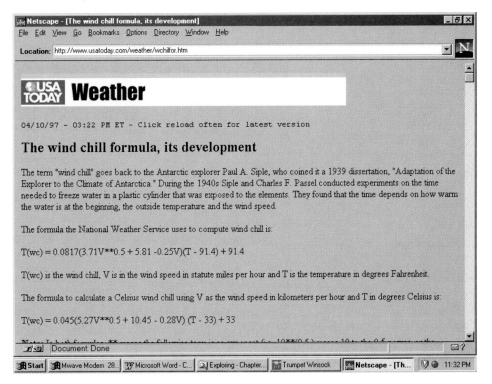

(a) The Wind Chill Formula Web Page (*www.usatoday.com/weather/wchilfor.htm*)

FIGURE 3.3   The Wind Chill Project

$$WC = 0.0817(3.71(V ** 0.5) + 5.81 - 0.25V)(T - 91.4) + 91.4$$

where

    WC is the wind chill
    V is the wind speed in miles per hour
    T is the temperature in degrees Fahrenheit
    In this formula, ** 0.5 means the square root of V and the standard
    rules of algebra apply. Note: The formula is appropriate for wind speeds
    between 4 and 45, and temperatures between –35 and 35 degrees.

Now we have a formula, and we know that we need to know the wind speed and temperature before we can calculate the wind chill. Therefore, the wind speed and temperature are the inputs to our program, and the wind chill is the output. The graphical user interface to gather the inputs and display the output is shown in Figure 3.3b. Now let's name the objects on the form and the variables needed to calculate the wind chill. For the Temperature input, we have three objects: a label, a horizontal scroll bar, and a text box. Using our naming conventions from Chapter 2, we will call these *lblTemperature, hsbTemperature*, and *txtTemperature*, respectively. For the Wind Speed input, we also have three objects. We will call these *lblSpeed, hsbSpeed,* and *txtSpeed.* (We could have called these objects *Wind-Speed,* but that could be easily confused with the output, *WindChill,* so we used simply *Speed* instead.) Next we have two output objects: a label and a text box, called *lblWindChill* and *txtWindChill,* respectively. Next we have a command button, called *cmdCalculate.* Last, we have the image, which is called *imgWindChill.*

So far, we have named all the objects on the form. Now let's look at the variables needed for our calculation. To keep our program as close to the original formula as possible, let's use *V* for the wind speed velocity, *T* for the temperature, and *WC* for the wind chill calculation. Next, let's convert our wind chill formula into a Visual Basic statement.

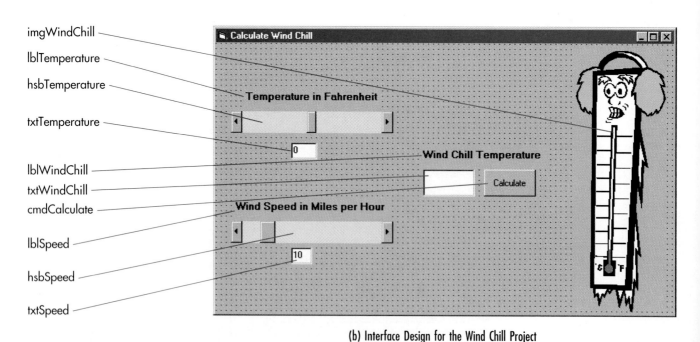

(b) Interface Design for the Wind Chill Project

FIGURE 3.3   The Wind Chill Project (continued)

Arithmetic Operators

When performing calculations in Visual Basic, the following symbols are used for arithmetic operations:

+ for addition
– for subtraction
* for multiplication
/ for division
Sqr(x) for the square root of x
x ^ y to raise x to the power of y

Notice that this differs from the way you write formulas in math class. Now let's rewrite the formula in Visual Basic.

$$WC = 0.0817 * (3.71 * Sqr(V) + 5.81 – (0.25 * V)) * (T – 91.4) + 91.4$$

Notice that you need to add an asterisk (*) between all elements that are multiplied together. Thus, where in algebra you would write **0.25V**, in Visual Basic you must write **0.25 * V**. You may also need to add parentheses to keep the order of operations correct for many formulas and equations. Notice that you need to use the Sqr function to calculate the square root. Let's look at functions in more detail.

FUNCTIONS

A function is very similar to a procedure. A ***function*** is a unit of code that returns a value, whereas a procedure does not. Some functions are built into Visual Basic, and you can create your own function using the ***Function statement***.

Built-in Functions

In the first hands-on exercise for this chapter, you will use the Sqr function built into Visual Basic. The ***Sqr*** function returns the square root of a number. If you have worked with Excel or another spreadsheet application, you are probably familiar with other built-in functions. In this exercise, you will also use the ***Cint*** function that converts any valid expression to an integer. In the second hands-on exercise, you will be using three functions: the ***Rnd*** function, which generates a random number between zero and one; the ***Int*** function, which returns the integer portion of a number; and the ***Val*** function, which converts a string to a value (for example, the string "5" is converted to the numeric value 5).

There are many mathematical and financial functions built into Visual Basic. These include the trigonometric functions such as cosine and tangent, and statistical functions such as ***Stdev*** (standard deviation).

Locating Built-in Functions

To locate a function in Visual Basic, pull down the Help menu and select Contents. Open the Reference book, then Language Reference. Next, open the Functions book. The functions are listed alphabetically, as shown in Figure 3.4a.

Many times you do not know if a function you need exists. In this case, click the MSDN Library window's Search tab and enter a search term such as **square+root**. Choose a topic from the research results and click the Display button to display it in the topic pane.

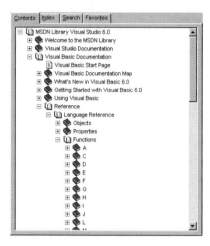

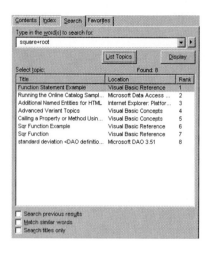

(a) Locating Functions Using Contents

(b) Locating Functions Using Search

FIGURE 3.4   Locating Built-in Functions

Programmer-written Functions

You can also write your own functions by means of a Function statement. The simple syntax for the Function statement in shown in the box below:

> **Private Function** *function-name (argument1, argument2 . . .)*
>   *statements*
> **End Function**
> where
>   **Private** is one of the types for a function. Private indicates that this function
>   is accessible only within the module. Other types are public and static.
>   **Function** is required and indicates the beginning of a function
>   *Function-name* is the name that will be used to call the function
>   **( )** parentheses are required around the argument list
>   *argument1*, *argument2* are the variables that are needed before the func-
>   tion can be calculated. Arguments are optional.
>   *statements* are the statements to perform the calculations or actions
>   needed for the function
>   **End Function** is required and indicates the end of the function

To calculate the area of a triangle, you could write the following function:

```
Function TriangleArea (Base As Integer, Height As Integer)
    TriangleArea = (Base * Height) /2
End Function
```

You call a function the same way you call any of the built-in functions in Visual Basic:

```
Area = TriangleArea(B,H)
```

In the first hands on exercise, you will create the following function to calculate the wind chill temperature. The WindChill function is called from the Calculate command button event procedure.

```
Private Function WindChill( )
' Purpose: Calculate the Wind Chill Temperature
' Reference: National Weather Service formula from
'        USA Today Weather Web page
 Dim V As Integer 'Velocity of Wind Speed in mph
 Dim T As Integer 'Temperature in Degrees Fahrenheit
 V = hsbSpeed.Value
 T = hsbTemperature.Value
 WindChill = 0.0817 * (3.71 * Sqr(V)+ 5.81 - (0.25 * V)) * (T - 91.4) + 91.4
End Function


Private Sub cmdCalculate_Click()
    WC = WindChill( )
    txtWindChill.Text = CInt(WC) 'Convert Double to Integer
End Sub
```

Now we are ready to create the Wind Chill program using the step-by-step process. Let's create event procedures, a function, and use variables in this hands-on exercise.

HANDS-ON EXERCISE 1

The Wind Chill Project Using Functions and Procedures

Objective: Create a program to calculate the wind chill using event procedures, variables, and the formula. Use Figure 3.5 as a guide for the exercise.

STEP 1: Create a New Project

➤ Start Visual Basic. Click the New Project dialog box's **New tab**.

➤ Click the **Standard EXE icon**. Click the **Open button** to open a new project window. Set your Visual Basic options as shown in Chapter 2, Hands-on Exercise 1, Step 2 (see page 47) if you want to ensure that the following steps look as much like the figures shown as possible.

➤ Pull down the **File menu** and select **Save Form1 As** to display the Save File As dialog box. Select the drive and folder where you stored your data disk (*Exploring Visual Basic 6*). Enter **Wind Chill** in the File name text box. Click the **Save button** to save the form file and close the dialog box.

➤ Pull down the **File menu** again and select **Save Project As** to display the Save Project As dialog box. Notice that the Save in list box is set to the folder in which you saved the form. Enter **Wind Chill** in the File name text box. Click the **Save button** to save the project files and close the dialog box.

➤ Open the Project Explorer, Form Designer, and the Form Layout windows. Use Figure 3.5a as a guide in setting up your screen display. Move and resize the windows as appropriate so you can work with the form.

➤ Select the form, then move and resize it to the size shown in the figure.

➤ Move to the Form Layout window and select the form. Move the form to the position shown in the figure. Close the Form Layout window.

➤ Click to select the form. Open the Properties window. Change the Caption property to **Calculate Wind Chill**.

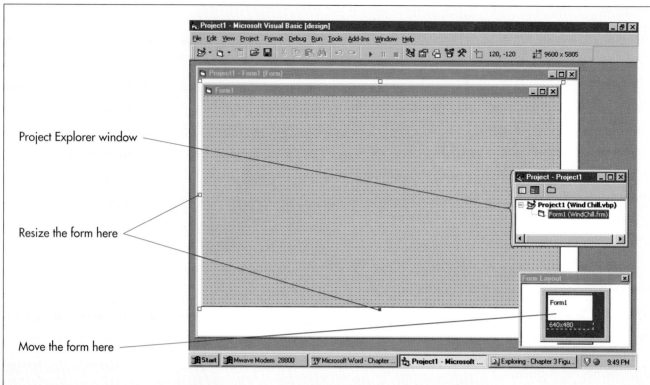

Project Explorer window

Resize the form here

Move the form here

(a) Create a New Project (step 1)

FIGURE 3.5   Hands-on Exercise 1

STEP 2: Create the Controls for the Temperature Input

➤ Open the Toolbox. Move to it and select the **Label tool**. Move to the form and, using Figure 3.5b as a guide, drag and drop to place the Temperature label.

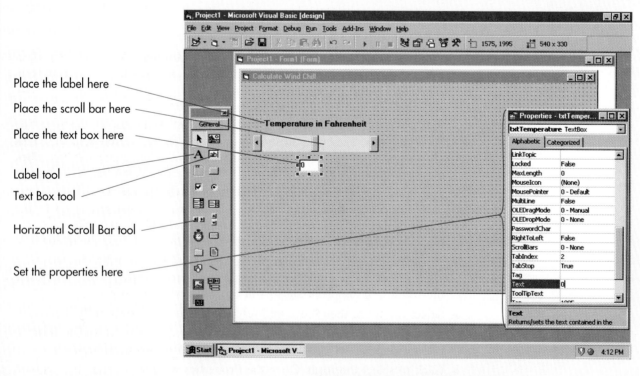

Place the label here

Place the scroll bar here

Place the text box here

Label tool

Text Box tool

Horizontal Scroll Bar tool

Set the properties here

(b) Controls for the Temperature Input (step 2)

FIGURE 3.5   Hands-on Exercise 1 (continued)

➤ Move to the Properties window, and set the following properties for the label:

Property	Setting
Name	lblTemperature
Caption	Temperature in Fahrenheit
Font	MS Sans Serif, Size 10, Bold

➤ Move to the Toolbox and select the **Horizontal Scroll Bar tool**. Move to the form and, using the figure as a guide, drag and drop to place the Temperature scroll bar. Set the following properties for the scroll bar:

Property	Setting
Name	hsbTemperature
LargeChange	5
Max	35
Min	–35
SmallChange	1
Value	0

➤ Move to the Toolbox and select the **Text Box tool**. Move to the form and, using the figure as a guide, drag and drop to place the Temperature text box. Set the following properties for the text box:

Property	Setting
Name	txtTemperature
Enabled	False
Text	0

STEP 3: Create the Controls for the Speed Input

➤ Move to the Toolbox and select the **Label tool**. Move to the form and, using Figure 3.5c as a guide, drag and drop to place the Speed label.

➤ Move to the Properties window, and set the following properties for the label:

Property	Setting
Name	lblSpeed
Caption	Wind Speed in Miles per Hour
Font	MS Sans Serif, Size 10, Bold

➤ Move to the Toolbox and select the **Horizontal Scroll Bar tool**. Move to the form and, using the figure as a guide, drag and drop to place the Speed scroll bar. Set the following properties for the scroll bar:

Property	Setting
Name	hsbSpeed
LargeChange	5
Max	45
Min	4
SmallChange	1
Value	10

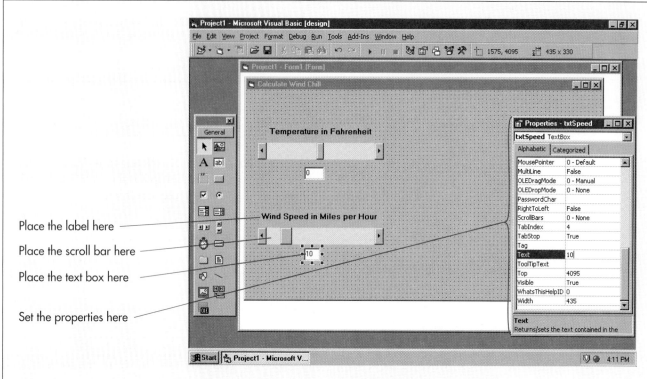

Place the label here

Place the scroll bar here

Place the text box here

Set the properties here

(c) Controls for the Speed Input (step 3)

FIGURE 3.5   Hands-on Exercise 1 (continued)

➤ Move to the Toolbox and select the **Text Box tool**. Move to the form and, using the figure as a guide, drag and drop to place the Speed text box. Set the following properties for the text box:

Property	Setting
Name	txtSpeed
Enabled	False
Text	10

STEP 4: Create the Controls for the Wind Chill Output

➤ Move to the Toolbox and select the **Label tool**. Move to the form and, using Figure 3.5d as a guide, drag and drop to place the Wind Chill label.

➤ Move to the Properties window, and set the following properties for the label:

Property	Setting
Name	lblWindChill
Caption	Wind Chill Temperature
Font	MS Sans Serif, Size 10, Bold

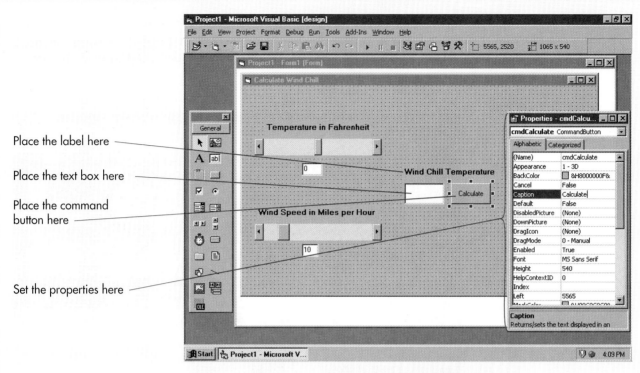

Place the label here

Place the text box here

Place the command button here

Set the properties here

(d) Controls for the Wind Chill Output (step 4)

FIGURE 3.5   Hands-on Exercise 1 (continued)

➤ Move to the Toolbox and select the **Text Box tool**. Move to the form and, using the figure as a guide, drag and drop to place the Wind Chill text box. Set the following properties for the text box:

Property	Setting
Name	txtWindChill
Enabled	False
Text	

➤ Move to the Toolbox and select the **Command button tool**. Move to the form and, using the figure as a guide, drag and drop to place the Calculate command button. Set the following properties for the command button:

Property	Setting
Name	cmdCalculate
Caption	Calculate

STEP 5: Create the Image Control

➤ Move to the Toolbox and select the **Image tool**. Move to the form and, using Figure 3.5e and Figure 3.5f as a guide, drag and drop to place the image control.

Place the image here ———

Select the WindChill image here ———

Image tool ———

Click here to open the image ———

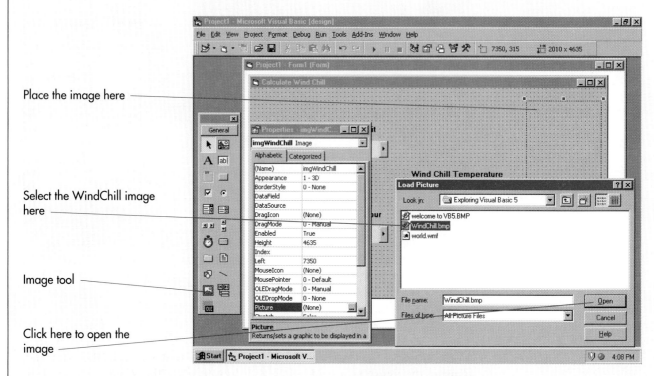

(e) Add the Image Control (step 5)

FIGURE 3.5   Hands-on Exercise 1 (continued)

➤ Move to the Properties window, click the **Picture property**, and click the ellipses (...) in the setting column. The Load Picture dialog box as shown in the figure is displayed.

➤ Select the drive and folder that contains your data disk.

➤ Select the **WindChill.bmp** file. Click the **Open button**. The wind chill image will appear in the image control you placed on the form.

➤ Move back to the Properties window and change the Name setting to **imgWindChill**.

STEP 6: Add Banner Comments

➤ Close the Properties window. Pull down the **View menu** and select **Code** to display the Code Editor window.

➤ In the Code Editor window, click the **Full Module View button** at the bottom left corner. Then click the **Object list box arrow** and select **General**.

➤ Click the **Procedure list box arrow** and select **Declarations**.

➤ Enter the following program documentation in the Code Editor window. Substitute your name and the current date. (Use tabs after the colons to align the items.) When you finish the banner comments, your screen will look like the one in Figure 3.5f.

```
'**********************************************************
'   Programmer:      Carlotta Eaton
'   Date:            June 30, 1998
'   Source:          Wind Chill.vbp
'   ID:              Chapter 3 Hands-on Exercise 1
'   Purpose:         Practice coding skills
'                    Calculate the Wind Chill Temperature
'   Inputs:          Wind Speed in Miles per Hour
'                    Temperature in Degrees Fahrenheit
'   Outputs:         Wind Chill Temperature
'   Reference:       The National Weather Service wind chill
'                    formula from USA Today Weather Web page
'**********************************************************
```

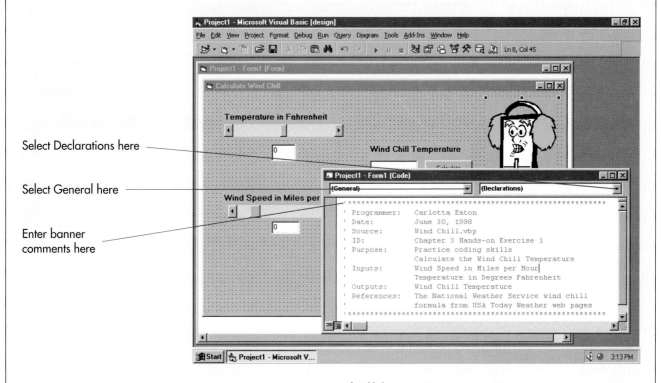

Select Declarations here

Select General here

Enter banner comments here

(f) Add the Banner Comments (step 6)

FIGURE 3.5   Hands-on Exercise 1 (continued)

STEP 7: Add the Wind Chill Function

➤ In the Code Editor window, ensure that the Object list box still displays **General**. We are now going to create a function in the General section of the module.

➤ Position the cursor directly under the banner comment section, and enter the first line of the **WindChill function**. The Code Editor will automatically add the End Function line for the last line of the function.

➤ Move above the End Function line and enter the remaining code to calculate the Wind Chill as shown below in the Code Editor window. When you finish the procedure, your screen will look like the one in Figure 3.5g.

```
Private Function WindChill( )
   ' Purpose: Calculate the Wind Chill Temperature
   ' Reference: National Weather Service formula from
   '        USA Today Weather Web page
   Dim V As Integer 'Velocity of Wind Speed in mph
   Dim T As Integer 'Temperature in Degrees Fahrenheit
   V = hsbSpeed.Value
   T = hsbTemperature.Value
   WindChill = 0.0817 * (3.71 * Sqr(V) + 5.81 - (0.25 * V)) * (T - 91.4) + 91.4
End Function
```

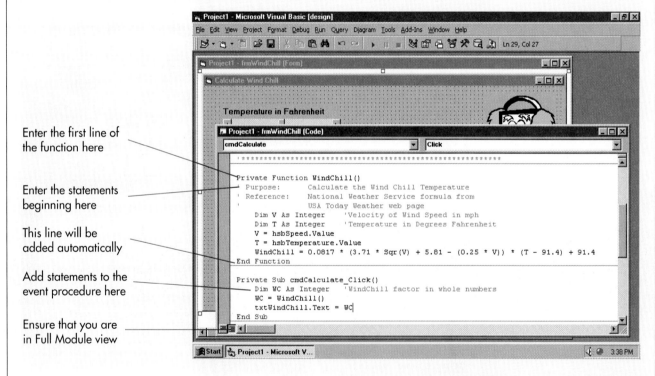

Enter the first line of the function here

Enter the statements beginning here

This line will be added automatically

Add statements to the event procedure here

Ensure that you are in Full Module view

(g) Add the Wind Chill Function (step 7)

FIGURE 3.5   Hands-on Exercise 1 (continued)

➤ In the Code Editor window, click the **Object list box arrow** and select **cmdCalculate**. Ensure that you are still in Full Module View.

➤ Click the **Procedure list box arrow** and select **Click**.

➤ Enter the statement shown below between the Sub and End Sub statements already in the program.

```
Private Sub cmdCalculate_Click()
    Dim WC As Integer 'Wind Chill factor in whole numbers
    WC = WindChill()
    txtWindChill.Text = WC
End Sub
```

➤ When the user clicks the Calculate command button, the WindChill function will be executed and return the answer into the WC variable.

➤ When you finish the event procedure, your screen will look like the one in Figure 3.5g.

STEP 8: Add the Temperature and Speed Event Procedures

➤ In the Code Editor window, click the **Object list box arrow** and select **hsbSpeed**. Click the **Procedure list box arrow** and select **Scroll**. This event procedure is executed with ongoing changes for a scroll bar. This happens when the user moves the scroll box, clicks the scroll arrows, or clicks the scroll bar itself. The first line displays the value of the scroll bar in the associated text box. The second statement blanks out the calculated wind chill value until the user clicks the Calculate command button. Add the statements as shown below to the procedure.

```
Private Sub hsbSpeed_Scroll()
    txtSpeed.Text = hsbSpeed.Value
    txtWindChill.Text = " "
End Sub
```

➤ In the Code Editor window, click the **Object list box arrow** and select **hsbSpeed**. Click the **Procedure list box arrow** and select **Change**. The Change event procedure is used to update only once after a scroll bar change. Add the statement as shown below to the procedure, which executes the preceding Scroll event procedure.

```
Private Sub hsbSpeed_Change()
    hsbSpeed_Scroll
End Sub
```

➤ In the Code Editor window, click the **Object list box arrow** and select **hsbTemperature**. Click the **Procedure list box arrow** and select **Scroll**. The first line displays the value of the scroll bar in the associated text box. The second statement blanks out the calculated wind chill value until the user clicks the Calculate command button. Add the statements as shown below to the procedure.

```
Private Sub hsbTemperature_Scroll()
    txtTemperature.Text = hsbTemperature.Value
    txtWindChill.Text = " "
End Sub
```

> In the Code Editor window, click the **Object list box arrow** and select **hsbTemperature**. Click the **Procedure list box arrow** and select **Change**. Add the statement as shown below to the procedure, which executes the preceding Scroll event procedure.

```
Private Sub hsbTemperature_Change()
    hsbTemperature_Scroll
End Sub
```

> When you finish the four event procedures, your screen will look like the one in Figure 3.5h.

Add event procedure statements

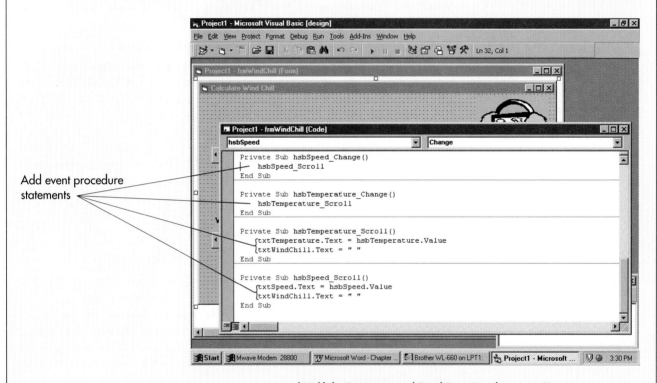

(h) Add the Temperature and Speed Event Procedures (step 8)

FIGURE 3.5   Hands-on Exercise 1 (continued)

STEP 9: Save and Run Your Project

> Open the Properties window. Click the form in the Form Designer window to select it. Move to the Properties window and change the Name property to **frmWindChill**.

> Click the **Save Project button** on the toolbar. Close the Code Editor window, Form Designer window, Properties window, and any other open windows within the development environment.

> Click the **Start button** on the toolbar. If asked whether to save changes to the form and the project, click **Yes**.

STEP 10: Test Your Project

> The form will appear on your screen.

> The Temperature text box should read 0, and the Speed text box should display 10.

➤ Click the **Calculate command button**.

➤ Verify that (**–21**) appears in the Wind Chill text box.

➤ The specification for this project was to calculate the wind chill for January 10 when the temperature was 4 degrees Fahrenheit, and the wind speed was 25 mph. Move the Temperature scroll box until the text box displays **4**. Move the Speed scroll box until the text box displays **25**.

➤ Click the **Calculate command button**. The wind chill text box should display **–38**, as shown in Figure 3.5i.

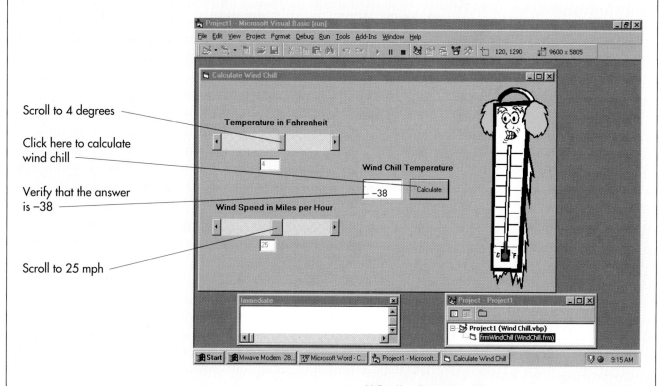

Scroll to 4 degrees

Click here to calculate wind chill

Verify that the answer is –38

Scroll to 25 mph

(i) Test Your Project (step 10)

FIGURE 3.5   Hands-on Exercise 1 (continued)

➤ Move the scroll box in the Temperature scroll bar and verify that the minimum temperature is –35, and the maximum is 35.

➤ Click the scroll bar arrows and verify that the temperature increments and decrements by 1 degree for each click.

➤ Click in the scroll bar on either side of the scroll box and verify that the temperature increases and decreases by 5 degrees for each click.

➤ Move the scroll box in the Speed scroll bar and verify that the minimum speed is 4, and the maximum is 45.

➤ Click the scroll bar arrows and verify that the speed increases and decreases by 1 mph for each click.

➤ Click in the scroll bar on either side of the scroll box and verify that the speed increases and decreases by 5 mph for each click.

➤ Using Figure 3.5j, test several combinations of temperature and speed and verify that your program calculates the correct wind chill. Due to rounding error, your calculation may be off by 1 degree. If the calculations are off by more than 1 degree, check your calculation statement.

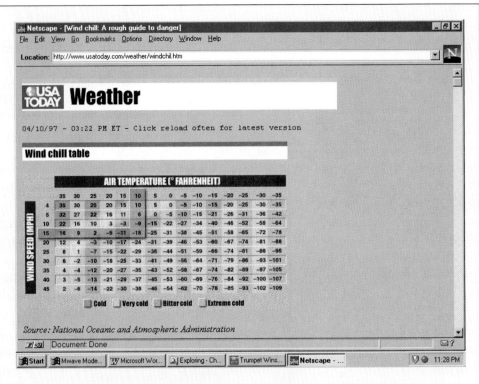

(j) Check Your Calculations (step 10) *(www.usatoday.com/weather/windchil.htm)*

FIGURE 3.5   Hands-on Exercise 1 (continued)

➤ Test the temperature and speed combinations for the four corners of the table to test the boundaries of your program.

➤ If you made any errors, you may receive a warning message, your calculations may be incorrect, or a scroll bar may not work properly. Repeat any previous steps as needed to debug your project.

STEP 11: Exit Visual Basic

➤ Pull down the **File menu** and select **Exit** to Exit Visual Basic.

➤ If you made any changes and did not save them, the Save Changes message box will appear. Click the **Yes button** to save your changes, and the window will close.

CONTROLLING YOUR APPLICATION: SEQUENCE, SELECTION, AND REPETITION

Functions and procedures are used to control the execution of your program. The real power of a program comes from the ability to change the order of execution using control structures. There are three types of control structures in most programming languages: *sequence*, *selection*, and *repetition*. We have already seen how functions and procedures allow us to control the sequence of a program. In the last section of this chapter, we will see how to repeat actions with loop statements. Now let's see how we decide among a selection of alternatives in a program—enabling our program to make decisions.

There are two statement structures available in Visual Basic for making decisions in your programs. The first is the If ... Then ... Else statement. This is useful when making a true/false type of decision. The second is the Select Case statement structure. This is best used for a multiple-choice type of decision.

The If Statement

The If ... Then ... Else statement (commonly referred to as the If statement) executes a statement (or group of statements) when a statement condition is true. The statement executes another statement (or group of statements) when the condition is false. The syntax for the If ... Then ... Else statement is shown in the following box:

> **If** *condition* **Then** *statement(s)* **Else** *statement(s)* **End If**
>   where
>   The **If** condition is evaluated as either true or false. If the condition is true, the statements following **Then** are executed. Otherwise the statements following **Else** are executed. Either way, execution continues with the statement following **End If**.
>
> The **Else** keyword and statements are optional.

In the next hands-on exercise, if the student enters the correct answer, then the Smiling image is displayed. On the other hand, if the user enters the wrong answer, then the Frowning image is displayed. The code decides which image to display based on the student's answer.

```
If UserAnswer = CorrectAnswer Then
    imgSmile.Visible = True
Else
    imgFrown.Visible = True
End If
```

The Select Case Statement

The Select Case statement evaluates a condition at the beginning of the statement. The result of this evaluation is compared with the values for each Case; when a match is found, the statements associated with it are executed. The syntax for the Select Case is shown in the following box:

> **Select Case** *condition* **Case** *expression1 statement(s)* **Case** *expression2 statement(s)* **Case Else** *statement(s)* **End Select**
>   where
>   The **Select Case** condition is evaluated. Each **Case** expression is evaluated in turn and if the expression is true, the statements following are executed. If none of the Case statements are true, the statements following the **Case Else** are executed. Execution continues with the statement following **End Select**.
>
> The **Case Else** keyword and statements are optional.

For example, if you were writing a program to play the childhood Rock, Paper, Scissors game, the code would look something like the box below:

```
Select Case Weapon
  Case "Rock"
    txtMessage = "Rock crushes scissors."
  Case "Scissors"
    txtMessage = "Scissors cut paper."
  Case "Paper"
    txtMessage = "Paper covers rock."
End Select
```

THE LEARNING TO ADD PROJECT

Let's apply the decision statements to build a simple project. First, we need to define the problem. Many children have trouble learning math. In kindergarten and first grade, children are just learning to write, so they are really working on two new skills simultaneously, and this can further compound the problem of learning math skills.

If learning math can be made fun in kindergarten and first grade, then these skills can be developed further in the later grades, and students will not have the "mathphobia" that so many of them develop.

Specification for the Game

Going back to our step-by-step plan from Chapter 2, our basic problem definition is to create a math game that kindergartners and first graders can use to practice their addition skills. The specifications for this math game include:

- purpose of the game is to practice addition skills
- numbers used will be between 0 and 9
- user is a child of pre-school age, in kindergarten, or in first grade
- user may not yet know how to read
- game should give visual feedback in the form of fun pictures indicating a correct or incorrect answer

Design the User Interface

Now that we have our specifications, let's concentrate on the user interface design. This step should be written down using pencil and paper. After trying many designs, let's go with the screens shown in Figure 3.6. Notice that we are assuming that the child may not be able to read, so we are using graphical icons instead of text command buttons. Figure 3.6a shows the screen the child will see when the game starts.

The child enters an answer to the math problem as shown in Figure 3.6b. Next, the child clicks the Check Mark icon to check the answer. If the answer is correct, the screen shown in Figure 3.6c is displayed. If the answer is wrong, the screen shown in Figure 3.6d is displayed. To continue playing the game, the child clicks the Arrow Sign icon, and the initial screen is displayed again, with a new math question. To quit playing the game, the child clicks the standard Windows Close button in the top right corner of the screen.

Child enters answer here —

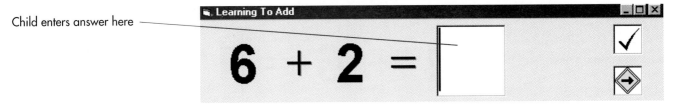

(a) Initial Screen

Child clicks here to
check answer —

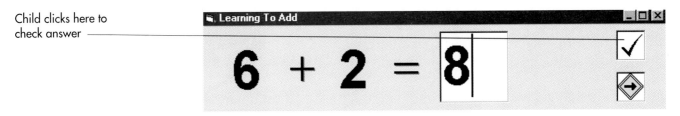

(b) Next Screen

If correct answer is given,
display smiling girl

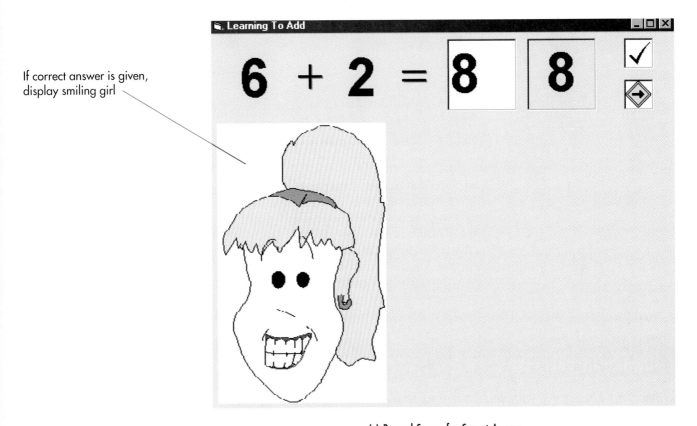

(c) Reward Screen for Correct Answer

FIGURE 3.6   Screens for the Learning to Add Game

Now that we have the design on paper, we can go to the computer and actually create the form using Visual Basic. Before you add the code to a project, you
will have completed the prototype of the math game. A **prototype** is a partially
completed version of an application that demonstrates the "look and feel" of the
finished application. The advantage of a prototype is that the end user or client
can test out the design of your user interface. This type of testing is called
usability testing. The user can provide immediate feedback on the portion of the

If wrong answer is given, display frowning boy

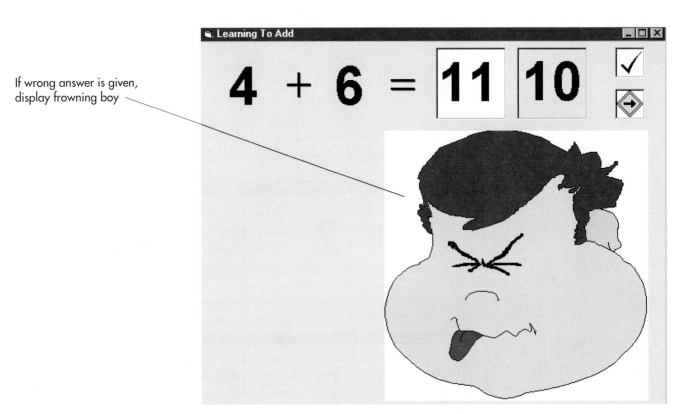

(d) Screen for Wrong Answer

FIGURE 3.6 Screens for the Learning to Add Game (continued)

application that has been completed. He or she may request changes in the user interface. The sooner the user or client communicates the needed changes, the easier it is for you to make those corrections. Once the prototype has been approved by the client (or child in this case), the rest of the application can be built by coding. My eight-year-old daughter actually designed the screens for this exercise, so it has been kid tested. This program decides which image to display based on the child's answer. Now let's create the Learning to Add program using the step-by-step process.

HANDS-ON EXERCISE 2

Making Decisions with the Learning to Add Game

Objective: Create a program to help primary children practice addition using If ... Then decision statements and built-in functions. Use Figure 3.7 as a guide for the exercise.

STEP 1: Create the Learning to Add Project

➤ Start Visual Basic. Click the New Project dialog box's **New tab**.

➤ Click the **Standard EXE icon**. Click the **Open button** to open a new project window. Set your Visual Basic options as shown in Chapter 2, Hands-on Exercise 1, Step 2 (page 47) if you want to ensure that the following steps look as much like the figures shown as possible.

➤ Pull down the **File menu** and select **Save Project As** to display the Save File As dialog box. Select the drive and folder where you stored your data disk (*Exploring Visual Basic 6*). Enter **Learning to Add** in the File name text box. Click the **Save button** to save the form file and close the dialog box.

➤ The **Save Project As** dialog box displays with the Save in list box set to the folder in which you saved the form. Enter **Learning to Add** in the File name text box. Click the **Save button** to save the project files and close the dialog box.

➤ Open the Project Explorer, Form Designer, and the Form Layout windows. Use Figure 3.7a as a guide in setting up your screen display. (The Properties window is not yet open.) Move and resize the windows as appropriate so you can work with the form.

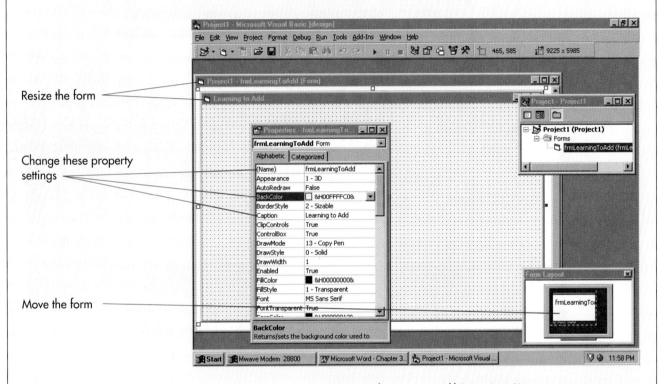

Resize the form

Change these property settings

Move the form

(a) Create the Learning to Add Project (step 1)

FIGURE 3.7   Hands-on Exercise 2

➤ Grab the form by its title bar, and move and resize it to the location and size shown in the figure. Move to the Form Layout window and position the form as shown in the figure. Close the Form Layout window.

➤ Click the form to select it. Open the Properties window, and set the following properties for the form:

Property	Setting
Name	frmLearnToAdd
BackColor	Lightest blue color in the top row of the color palette
Caption	Learning to Add

STEP 2: Add Controls to Display the Problem

➤ Close the Project Explorer window.

➤ Right click in the Properties window to display a context menu, then click the menu's **Dockable command** to deselect it. The Properties window now acquires Restore and Minimize buttons. Click the **Minimize button** to minimize the window and give you more room on the form. Open the Toolbox.

➤ You will be adding the numbers and symbols to the form. Use Figure 3.7b as a guide in placing the controls.

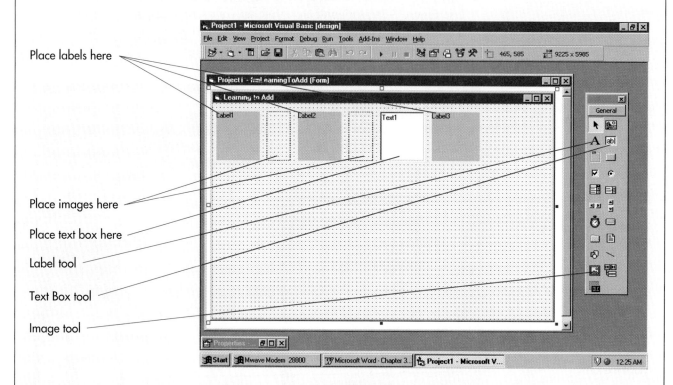

(b) Add Controls to Display the Problem (step 2)

FIGURE 3.7   Hands-on Exercise 2 (continued)

➤ Select the **Label tool** from the Toolbox. Move to the form, and drag and drop to place a label control below the "Learning to Add" title, making it 12×12 grid units in size. The first number of the problem will be displayed here.

➤ Move to the Toolbox and select the **Image tool**, then move to the form and drag and drop to add an image control 12×6 grid units to the right of the previous control. The plus sign will be displayed here.

➤ Move to the Toolbox and select the **Label tool** again, move to the form, and add another 12×12-size label control to the right of the image control. The second number of the problem will be displayed here.

➤ Move to the Toolbox and select the **Image tool** again, move to the form, and add another 12×6-size image control to the right of the label control. The equal sign will be displayed here.

➤ Move to the Toolbox and select the **Text Box tool**, move to the form, and add a 12×12-size text box control to the right of the last box. The child will enter an answer here.

➤ Back in the Toolbox, click the **Label tool** again, and add the final control to the right of the text box. The correct answer will be displayed here.

➤ Save the project.

CONTROLS VERSUS OBJECTS

An *object* is a combination of code and data that can be treated as a unit. Examples of objects in Visual Basic are controls, forms, and other application components. A *control* is an object you can place on a form that has its own properties and events. So a control is also an object, and you will see the terms used interchangeably in many Visual Basic textbooks.

STEP 3: Set Common Properties

➤ Click the Label1 box, hold down the Ctrl key, then click the Label2, the Text1, and the Label3 boxes to select all of them. Release the Ctrl key, then right click to display a context menu. Choose **Properties** to open the Properties window. Set the following properties common to these controls, as shown in Figure 3.7c.

Property	Setting
Alignment	2 – Center
BackColor	Light Blue in top row
Font	Arial, Bold, 48

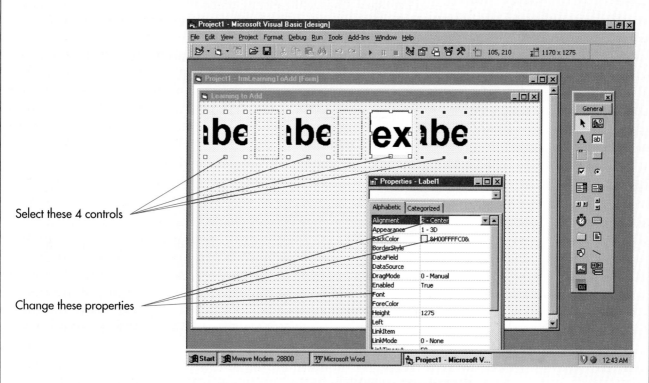

(c) Set Common Properties (step 3)

FIGURE 3.7   Hands-on Exercise 2 (continued)

MULTIPLE CONTROLS AND PROPERTIES

Press and hold the Ctrl key as you click one control after another to select multiple controls. To view or change the properties for the selected controls, click the right mouse button to display the context menu, then click Properties to display the Properties window. If the value of a property is the same for all selected controls, that value will appear in the Properties window; otherwise, the box for that property will not be displayed. Changing a property when multiple controls are selected changes that property for all the selected controls.

STEP 4: Set Individual Control Properties

➤ Click anywhere on the blank section of the form to deselect the controls. We will now set properties for each of the controls individually, starting at the left of the form. Move to the left most control (a label) and select it. Change its Name property to **lblNumber1**.

➤ Select the second control from the left (an image). Changes its Name property to **imgPlus**. Change the Picture property to **\Vb\Graphics\Icons\Misc\Misc18**. See the tip box if you cannot find the image. The image, a plus sign, will display in the control. Reposition the control if necessary to align the sign.

➤ Move to the third control (a label), and select it. Change its Name property to **lblNumber2**.

➤ Move to the fourth control (an image) and select it. Change its Name property to **imgEqual**. Change the Picture property to **\Vb \Graphics \Icons \Misc \Misc22**. The image, an equal sign, will display in the control. Reposition the control if necessary to align the sign.

➤ Move to the fifth control (the text box) and select it. Set the following properties for Text1.

Property	Setting
Name	textUserAnswer
Back Color	White
Text	

FIND THE ICON LIBRARY FILES

An Icon Library is included with both Visual Basic 5.0 and 6.0. You can find the icon files at \Vb\Graphics\Icons, or alternatively at Microsoft Visual Studio\Common\Graphics\Icons. If you cannot find the icon files, they are available on the data disk. The plus sign icon file is called plus.ico, and the equal sign is called equal.ico. You'll add more icons in step 6. The Checkmark is available as Chckmrk.ico, and the Traffic right arrow is available as RightArrow.ico.

> Move to the rightmost control (a label) and select it. Change the following properties for Label3.

Property	Setting
Name	lblCorrectAnswer
Visible	False

> The form will now look like Figure 3.7d.
> Save the project.

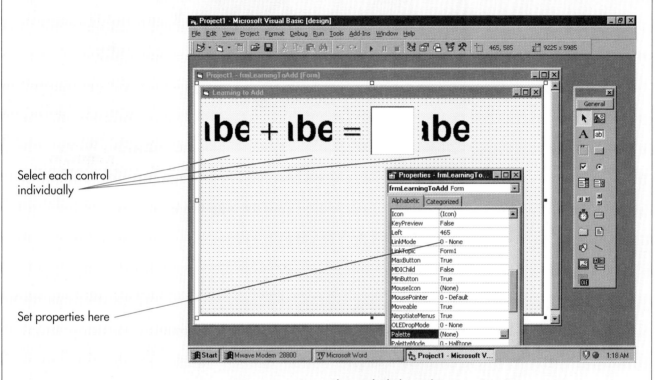

Select each control individually

Set properties here

(d) Set Individual Control Properties (step 4)

FIGURE 3.7 Hands-on Exercise 2 (continued)

STEP 5: Add More Images and Set Properties

> Minimize or close the Properties window to give you more room on the form. You will be adding the images of the boy and girl to give the student feedback. Use Figure 3.7e as a guide in placing the images on the form. Open the Toolbox and click the **Image tool**. Drag to place an image control at the left, below the row of controls you have already placed on the form.

> Right click the control to display a context menu. Select **Properties** to display the Properties window. In the Properties window, change the Name property to **imgGirl**.

> In the Properties window, scroll down, click the **Picture property**, and click the ellipses (...) in the setting column to display the Load Picture dialog box. Select the disk and folder that contains your data disk.

> Select the **girl.bmp** file. Click the **Open button** to display the smiling girl image in the image control you created. Resize the control and the form if necessary to display the entire image.

Place images here

Set properties here

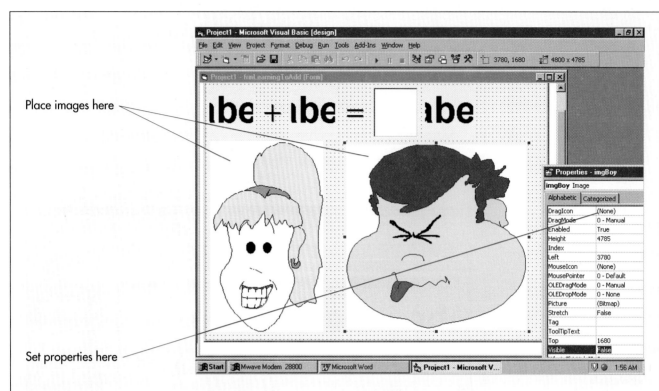

(e) Add More Images (step 5)

FIGURE 3.7   Hands-on Exercise 2 (continued)

➤ Move back to the Properties window. Change the Visible property setting to **False**. The image will not be displayed on the form until the child answers a problem correctly.

➤ Repeat this process and create another image control to the right of the previous image. Right click on the image box, and change the properties to the following settings:

Property	Setting
Name	imgBoy
Picture	Boy.bmp
Visible	False

SIZING OR MOVING A CONTROL

To move a control after you have created it, simply click the Toolbox's Pointer tool, and then click a control to select it and drag the control to a new location. To change the size of the control, click the control to display the sizing handles. Drag the control by any of the sizing handles to resize the control.

STEP 6: Add Picture Box Controls for Icon Buttons

➤ Use Figure 3.7f as a guide in placing the picture box controls.

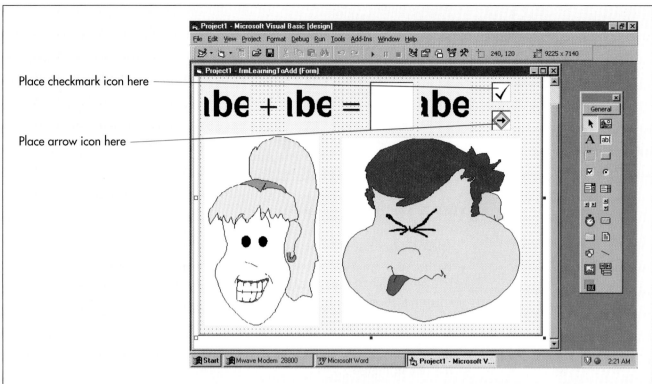

Place checkmark icon here

Place arrow icon here

(f) Add Pictures for Icon Buttons (step 6)

FIGURE 3.7   Hands-on Exercise 2 (continued)

➤ Move to the Toolbox and select the **Picture Box tool**. Move to the form to the right of the row of labels and boxes, and drag a picture box control about 5×5 grid units in size.

➤ Right click and select **Properties**. Change the following property settings:

Property	Setting
Name	picCheck
BackColor	white
Picture	\DevStudio\Vb\Graphics\Icons\Misc\Checkmrk

➤ Double click the **Checkmrk.ico** file name to open it and display it in the picture box control.

➤ Move back to the Toolbox and click the **Picture Box tool** again. Move to the form and drag a picture box control about 5×5 grid units in size just below the check mark. Change the following properties:

Property	Setting
Name	picNext
BackColor	white
Picture	\DevStudio\VB\Graphics\Icons\Traffic\Trffc02

➤ Double click the **Trffc02.ico** file name to open it and display it in the picture box control.

➤ Pull down the **File menu** and select **Save Learning to Add.frm** to save your work on the form so far.

STEP 7: Add Banner Comments

➤ Close the Properties window and the Toolbox. Pull down the **View menu** and select **Code** to display the Code Editor window.

➤ In the Code Editor window, click the **Procedure View button** at the bottom left corner. Then click the **Object list box arrow** and select **General**.

➤ Click the **Procedure list box arrow** and select **Declarations**.

➤ Enter the following program documentation in the Code Editor window. Substitute your name and the current date. (Use tabs after the colons to align the items.) When you finish the banner comments, your screen will look like the one in Figure 3.7g.

```
'***********************************************************
' Programmer:     Carlotta Eaton
' Date:           June 30, 1998
' Source:         Learning To Add.vbp
' ID:             Chapter 3 Hands-on Exercise 2
' Purpose:        Practice adding decisions to a program
'                 Math game for first grade students
'                 to practice addition skills
' Inputs:         2 random numbers between 0 and 9, and
'                 User answer
' Outputs:        The correct sum and a picture feedback
'***********************************************************
```

STEP 8: Add the Load Form Procedure

➤ In the Code Editor window, click the **Object list box arrow** and select **Form**. The Procedure list box will display **Load**.

Select the Declarations procedure

Select the General object

Enter code here

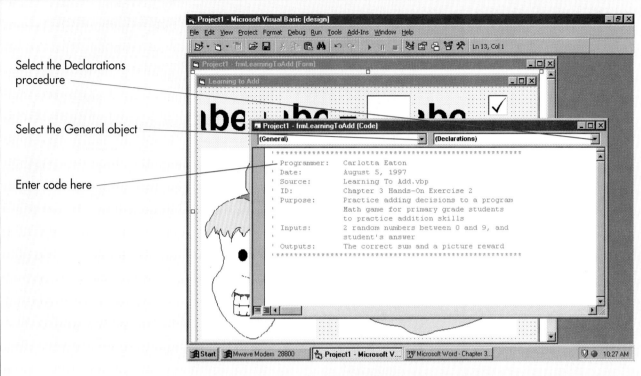

(g) Add the Banner Comments (step 7)

FIGURE 3.7 Hands-on Exercise 2 (continued)

➤ Position the cursor below the Sub statement line, and enter the following block of code. When you finish the procedure, your screen will look like the one in Figure 3.7h.

```
Private Sub Form_Load()
' Purpose: Load the initial screen and display the first problem
    txtUserAnswer.Text = " "
    lblCorrectAnswer.Visible = False
    Randomize 'start random number generator
    lblNumber1.Caption = Int(Rnd * 10) 'choose number1
    lblNumber2.Caption = Int(Rnd * 10) 'choose number2
End Sub
```

STEP 9: Add the Checkmark Picture Procedure

➤ In the Code Editor window, click the **Object list box arrow** and select **picCheck**. The Procedure list box will display **Click**.

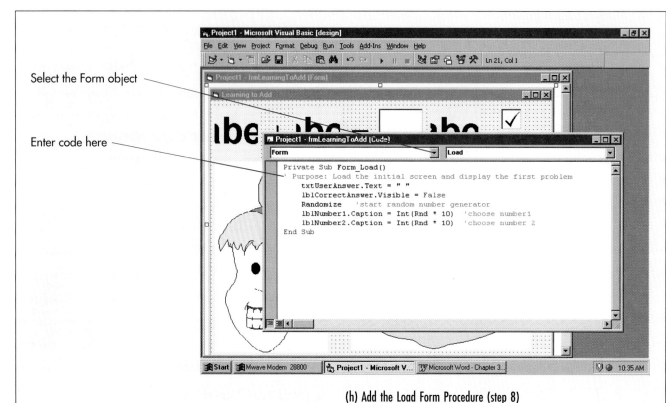

Select the Form object

Enter code here

(h) Add the Load Form Procedure (step 8)

FIGURE 3.7   Hands-on Exercise 2 (continued)

➤ Position the cursor below the Sub statement line, and enter the following
block of code.

```
Private Sub picCheck_Click()
' Purpose: Calculate correct answer and display appropriate face
    imgBoy.Visible = False
    imgGirl.Visible = False
    lblCorrectAnswer.Visible = False
    'Check to see if student gave answer
    If txtUserAnswer.Text = " " Then
        Beep
        picNext.SetFocus
        Exit Sub
    End If
    ' Calculate correct answer
    lblCorrectAnswer = Val(lblNumber1.Caption) + Val(lblNumber2.Caption)
    lblCorrectAnswer.Visible = True
    ' Display image based on right or wrong answer
    If (Val(lblCorrectAnswer)) = (Val(txtUserAnswer)) Then
        imgGirl.Visible = True
     Else
        imgBoy.Visible = True
    End If
    picNext.SetFocus ' move mouse pointer to User Answer
End Sub
```

STEP 10: Add the Arrow Picture Procedure

➤ In the Code Editor window, click the **Object list box arrow** and select **picNext**. The Procedure list box will display **Click**.

➤ Position the cursor below the Sub statement line, and enter the following block of code.

```
Private Sub picNext_Click()
'Purpose: Hides images and displays the next problem
    imgGirl.Visible = False
    imgBoy.Visible = False
    lblCorrectAnswer.Visible = False
    txtUserAnswer.Text = " "
    lblNumber1.Caption = Int(Rnd * 10) 'reset number1
    lblNumber2.Caption = Int(Rnd * 10) 'reset number2
    txtUserAnswer.SetFocus 'move pointer to user answer
End Sub
```

STEP 11: Run and Save Your Project

➤ Close the Form Designer and the Code Editor windows. Click the toolbar's **Start button**.

➤ If the save message box shown in Figure 3.7i asks whether you want to save changes, click **Yes** to continue and save your coding changes.

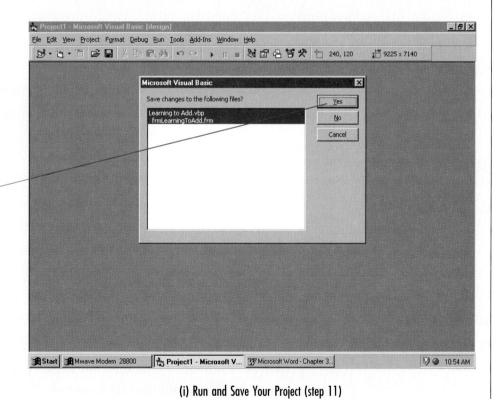

Click here to save changes

(i) Run and Save Your Project (step 11)

FIGURE 3.7   Hands-on Exercise 2 (continued)

STEP 12: Test and Debug Your Project

➤ The initial screen will display an addition problem. Remember that the numbers used in the problem are created by the Rnd function multiplied by 10, to result in an integer between 0 and 9. Enter the **correct answer** in the text box.

➤ Click the **checkmark button**. The image of the girl will display.

➤ Click the **arrow button**. The girl image and previous answer should disappear. A new problem should display.

➤ Before entering the answer, click the **checkmark button**. You should hear a beep indicating that you need to do more before checking the answer.

➤ Enter an **incorrect answer**. Click the **checkmark button**. The image of the boy will display as shown in Figure 3.7j.

Correct answer will display here —

Enter wrong answer here —

Click here to display new problem —

Boy image will display here —

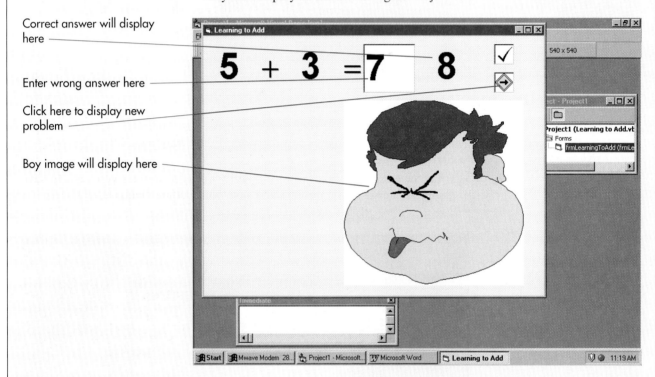

(j) Test and Debug Your Project (step 12)

FIGURE 3.7   Hands-on Exercise 2 (continued)

➤ Check more problems to ensure that random numbers are generated and that the numbers are in the range of 0–9.

➤ Verify that both digits of a two-digit answer are displayed. If there is a problem, go back to the Form Designer window and make adjustments in the size of the label control. If you change the size of this control, you may need to move other controls. If you made any errors, you may receive a warning message, or images may not display correctly, or the numbers may not display correctly. Repeat any previous steps as needed to debug your project.

➤ Click the Learning to Add window's **Close button**.

STEP 13: Print Your Project Code and Exit

➤ Pull down the **File menu** and select **Print** to display the Print dialog box.

➤ Select **Current Module** from the Range options.

➤ Select **Code** from the "Print What" options. Click the **OK button** to print the code for the project.

> ➤ Read the code for the entire project to make sure you understand it.
>
> ➤ Close any open windows in the Visual Basic environment.
>
> ➤ Pull down the **File menu** and select **Exit**. The Save Changes dialog box will display if you have not saved modifications made while debugging your project. Click **Yes** to save your changes and exit.

STATEMENTS THAT REPEAT

We have said that there are three types of control structures in most programming languages: sequence, selection, and repetition. Functions and procedures allow us to control the sequence of a program. If ... Then ... Else and Select Case statement structures provide the ability to make selections and decisions in our programs. Many times, we need to repeat blocks of code in our programs. Repetition is supported with the Do ... Loop, For ... Next, and For Each ... Next statement structures in Visual Basic.

The For ... Next Statement Structure

When you know exactly how many times you need to repeat a block of code, the **For loop** is the best choice. For a simple example, suppose you want to calculate the factorial number for 10 (10!). This is simply the product of all the numbers between 1 and 10. This can be written in a For loop as follows:

```
Private Function TenFactorial ()
'Purpose: Calculate 10 factorial
Dim I As Integer                    'Loop counter
Dim X As Double                     'Intermediate calculation
    X = 1
    For I = 1 to 10
        X = X * I
    Next I
    TenFactorial = X
End Function
```

The X variable is used to store the intermediate numbers, and function returns the final number. I is used as a counter variable for the For loop. Notice that it appears both in the For statement and in the ending Next statement. Usually we increment the counter variable by 1. The For statement can also be changed to increment differently. Suppose we want to add the odd numbers between 1 and 50. This can be written in a For loop as follows:

```
'  Sum odd numbers between 1 and 50
Dim Sum As Integer                  'Sum calculation
Dim I As Integer                    'Loop counter
Sum = 0
For I = 1 to 50 Step 2
    Sum = Sum + I
Next I
```

In general, the syntax for the *For... Next statement* structure is:

For *counter* = *start* **To** *end* **Step** *increment*
  statements
Next *counter*
  where

> The counter is set equal to start. The counter is tested to see if it is less than end. If so, the statements within the loop are executed. If not, the loop is exited, and execution continues at the statement following the Next counter statement. If the loop is executed, the counter is incremented by 1 or by the optional specified increment. Then the counter is tested again and the statements within the loop are repeated. This continues until the counter is greater than end.

The **Step** keyword and increment are optional. If the increment is negative, the counter is tested to see if it is more than end. If so, Visual Basic exits the loop.

The For Each ... Next Statement Structure

The *For Each loop* is similar to the For loop except it repeats the statements for each element in a collection of objects or in an array instead of repeating a specified number of times. This loop is commonly used for elements in a database or an array but is not used as often as the For loop in general programming. An *array* is a set of variables with the same name and an index to locate each element stored in the array. For more information and examples of this statement, refer to the Visual Basic online help.

AVOID ENDLESS LOOPS

The glossary in a popular database programmer's guide contains the following definitions:

> **Endless loop:** See *Loop, endless*
> **Loop, endless:** See *Endless loop*

We don't know whether these entries were deliberate or not, but the point is made either way. Endless loops are a common and frustrating bug.

The Do Statement

The Do statement repeats a block of statements until a condition becomes true or false. Do loops are useful when you do not know in advance how many times the loop should be executed. A condition is used to determine the number of times the loop executes. There are several variations of the Do loop. The *Do While* loop executes as long as the condition is true. The *Do Until* loop executes as long as the condition is false. When the Do Until condition becomes true, the loop exits. Both of these Do loops test the condition at the top of the loop. For example:

```
' Calculate the factorial of a number given by user
Dim Factorial As Double
Dim I As Integer
I = 1
Factorial = 1
'User enters a value in a text box called txtAnswer
Do While I <= Val (txtAnswer.text)
    Factorial = Factorial * I
    I = I + 1
Loop
```

This code calculates the factorial for a number provided by the user in a text box. If the user inputs 10, then the loop executes 10 times. If the user inputs 16, then the loop executes 16 times or while I <= 16. This same loop could be written differently using the Do Until statement. In this case, the loop executes as long as the condition is false, so we need to change our condition at the top of the loop as shown below.

```
' Calculate the factorial of a number given by user
Dim Factorial As Double
Dim I As Integer
I = 1
Factorial = 1
'User enters a value in a text box called txtAnswer
Do Until I > Val(txtAnswer.text)
    Factorial = Factorial * I
    I = I + 1
Loop
```

There is no advantage to using a *Do While* statement instead of a *Do Until* statement. Use the one that seems more logical in your situation. The general syntax for the Do While loop is:

Do While *condition*
   statements
Loop
   where
   The condition is tested, and the statements continued to execute as long as the condition is true. When the condition is false, the statements are skipped and the statement following the Loop statement is executed.

The general syntax for the Do Until loop is:

Do Until *condition*
    statements
Loop
    where
    The condition is tested, and the statements continued to execute as long as the condition is false. When the condition is true, the statements are skipped and the statement following the Loop statement is executed.

Other variations of the Do loop execute the statements first and then test the condition at the bottom of the loop. These variations guarantee that the loop executes at least once. The syntax for these variations is:

Do	**Do**
statements	*statements*
Loop Until *condition*	**Loop While** *condition*

Now let's practice loops with the next hands-on exercise. This exercise also demonstrates how to use the timer control to show simple screen animation.

HANDS-ON EXERCISE 3

Loops with the Marching Band Project

Objective: Create a program to practice For loops. This project also demonstrates simple animation using the timer control and the use of a picture array. Use Figure 3.8 as a guide for the exercise.

STEP 1: Create the Marching Band Project

➤ Start Visual Basic. Click the New Project dialog box's **New tab**.

➤ Click the **Standard EXE icon**. Click the **Open button** to open a new project window. Set your Visual Basic options as shown in Chapter 2, Hands-on Exercise 1, Step 2 (see page 47) if you want to ensure that the following steps look as much like the figures shown as possible.

➤ Pull down the **File menu** and select **Save Project As** to display the Save File As dialog box. Select the drive and folder where you stored your data disk (*Exploring Visual Basic 6*). Enter **Marching Band** in the File name text box. Click the **Save button** to save the form file and close the dialog box.

➤ The Save Project As dialog box displays. Notice that the Save in list box is set to the folder in which you saved the form. Enter **Marching Band** in the File name text box. Click the **Save button** to save the project file and close the dialog box.

➤ Open the Project Explorer, Form Designer, and the Form Layout windows. Use Figure 3.8a as a guide in setting up your screen display. Move and resize the windows as appropriate so you can work with the form.

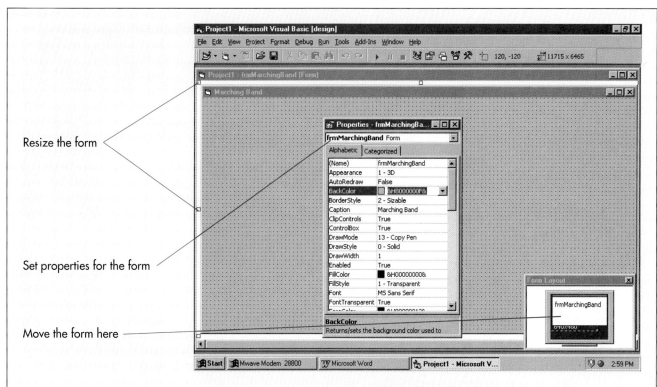

Resize the form

Set properties for the form

Move the form here

(a) Create the Marching Band Project (step 1)

FIGURE 3.8   Hands-on Exercise 3

➤ Maximize the Form Designer window. Select the form and resize it to cover most of the screen as shown in the figure.

➤ Move to the Form Layout window and position the form to the top of the screen. Close the Form Layout window.

➤ Click the form to select it. Open the Properties window, and set the following properties for the form:

Property	Setting
Name	frmMarchingBand
BackColor	white
Caption	Marching Band

STEP 2: Add Command Buttons and a Timer

➤ Close the Project Explorer window. Reduce the size of the Properties window to give you more room to work with the form. Open the Toolbox.

➤ You will be adding two command buttons and the timer to the form. Use Figure 3.8b as a guide in placing the controls.

➤ Move to the Toolbox and select the **Command Button tool**. Move to the top left corner of the form and place the button.

➤ Click the button to select it, then right click and select **Properties**. Set the following properties for the command button.

Property	Setting
Name	cmdStart
Caption	Start

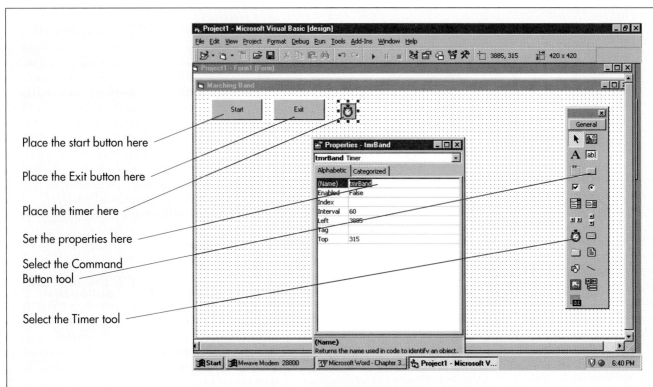

Place the start button here

Place the Exit button here

Place the timer here

Set the properties here

Select the Command Button tool

Select the Timer tool

(b) Add Command Buttons and a Timer (step 2)

FIGURE 3.8 Hands-on Exercise 3 (continued)

➤ Select the **Command Button tool** from the toolbox. Move to the right of the Start button and place the button.

➤ Move to the Properties window and set the following properties for the command button.

Property	Setting
Name	cmdExit
Caption	Exit

➤ Move to the Toolbox and select the **Timer tool** (it looks like a stopwatch). Move to the right of the two command buttons and place the timer control. The position is not important because this control will not be displayed while the program is running.

➤ Click the timer control to select it. Change the following properties for the timer control.

Property	Setting
Name	tmrBand
Enabled	False
Interval	60

➤ Reduce the size of the Properties window.

STEP 3: Add Controls to Display the Band

➤ Move to the Toolbox and select the **Image tool**. Place an image control to the bottom left of the form as shown in Figure 3.8c.

➤ Click the image control to select it. Right click and select **Properties**. Set the following properties for the image.

Property	Setting
Name	imgBand
Picture	BandLeader.bmp
	(in the folder for your data disk)
Visible	False

➤ The image of the band leader will be displayed in the image control. Do not be concerned if the entire bottom portion of the image does not display. This will work well when we add the animation.

➤ Move to the Toolbox and select the **Image tool**. Place the image control to the right and above the band leader, as shown in the figure.

➤ Click the image control to select it. Right click and select **Properties**. Change the Name property to **imgBand** for this image—the same name you used for the image of the band leader.

➤ The message box shown in Figure 3.8c will ask whether you want to create an array of the images. Click **Yes** to continue, and Visual Basic will create the array for you.

Click here to continue and create an array of images

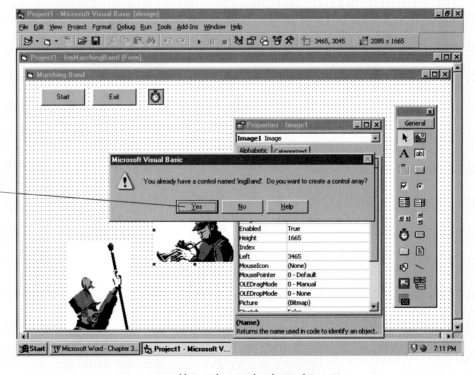

(c) Add Controls to Display the Band (step 3)

FIGURE 3.8   Hands-on Exercise 3 (continued)

➤ Change the Picture property to **BandTrumpet.bmp** located in the current folder (or where your data disk is stored). The image of the band member playing the trumpet will be displayed.

➤ Repeat this process for the other band members. Place the **BandClarinet** image below and to the right of the trumpet player. Place the **BandBass** image above and to the right of the clarinet player. Place the **BandDrum** image in the bottom right corner of the screen. Remember to change the Name property of all the images to **imgBand** and the Visible property to **False**.

➤ Move any images as needed so that they do not overlap. Do not be concerned if the entire BandDrum image is not displayed. You will see the entire image when we add animation using the timer control. Your form should look like Figure 3.8d at this point.

➤ Close the Toolbox.

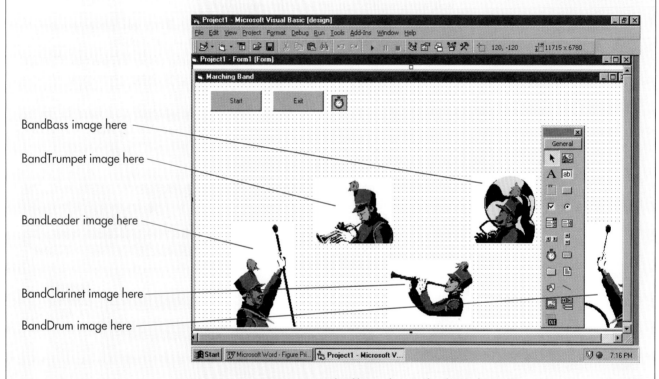

(d) Add Controls to Display the Band (step 3)

FIGURE 3.8   Hands-on Exercise 3 (continued)

STEP 4: Add Banner Comments

➤ Right click anywhere on the form and then select **View Code** from the context menu.

➤ In the Code Editor window, click the **Procedure View button** at the bottom left corner. Then click the **Object list box arrow** and select **General**.

➤ Click the **Procedure list box arrow** and select **Declarations**.

➤ Enter the following program documentation in the Code Editor window. Substitute your name and the current date. (Use tabs after the colons to align the items.) When you finish the banner comments, your screen will look like the one in Figure 3.8e.

```
'*****************************************************
' Programmer:   Carlotta Eaton
' Date:         June 30, 1998
' Source:       Marching Band.vbp
' ID:           Chapter 3 Hands-On Exercise 3
' Purpose:      Practice For loops
'               Display a marching band using
'               a timer control for simple animation
' Inputs:       None
' Outputs:      None
'*****************************************************
```

Select the Declarations procedure

Select the General object

Enter banner comments here

Click Procedure View here

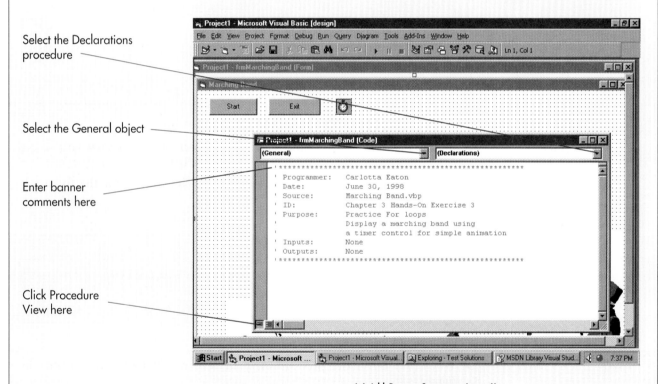

(e) Add Banner Comments (step 4)

FIGURE 3.8   Hands-on Exercise 3 (continued)

STEP 5: Add Code for Buttons and the Form

➤ Click the **Full Module View button** at the bottom left corner of the Code Editor window. Click the **Object list box arrow** and select **cmdStart**. The Procedure list box will display **Click**.

➤ Position the cursor below the Sub statement line, and enter the following block of code.

```
Private Sub cmdStart_Click()
'Purpose: Display the band and start the timer
    For I = 0 To 4
            imgBand(I).Visible = True
    Next I
    tmrBand.Enabled = True
End Sub
```

➤ In the Code Editor window, click the **Object list box arrow** and select **Form**. The Procedure list box will display **Load**.

➤ Position the cursor below the Sub statement line, and enter the following block of code.

```
Private Sub Form_Load()
'Purpose: Display the Band Leader
    imgBand(0).Visible = True
End Sub
```

➤ In the Code Editor window, click the **Object list box arrow** and select **cmdExit**. The Procedure list box will display **Click**.

➤ Position the cursor below the Sub statement line, and enter the following block of code.

```
Private Sub cmdExit_Click()
'Purpose: Exit the program
    End
End Sub
```

➤ When you finish the procedures, your screen will look like the one in Figure 3.8f.

STEP 6: Add Code to Add Animation

➤ In the Code Editor window, click the **Object list box arrow** and select **tmrBand**. The Procedure list box will display **Timer**.

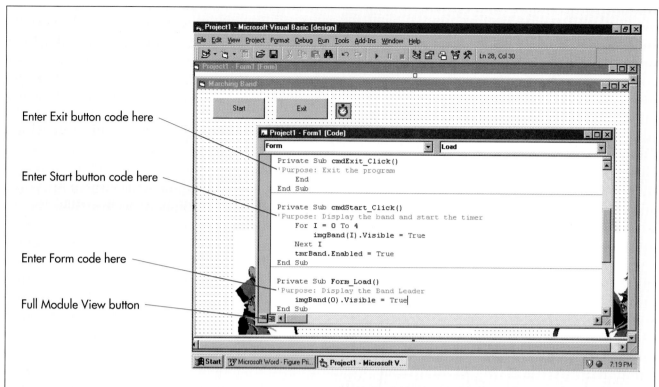

Enter Exit button code here

Enter Start button code here

Enter Form code here

Full Module View button

(f) Add Code for Buttons and Form (step 5)

FIGURE 3.8   Hands-on Exercise 3 (continued)

➤ Position the cursor below the Sub statement line, and enter the following block of code.

```
Private Sub tmrBand_Timer()
'Purpose: Move band images to top and left
'        Images disappear when an edge is reached
    Dim I As Integer
    For I = 0 To 4
        If (imgBand(I).Top > 0 And imgBand(I).Left > 0) Then
            imgBand(I).Move imgBand(I).Left — 150, _
            imgBand(I).Top — 75
        Else
            imgBand(I).Visible = False
        End If
    Next I
End Sub
```

BREAK A STATEMENT INTO TWO LINES

Sometimes a line of code is very long and is hard to fit on a single line. You can break a long statement into multiple lines using the line continuation character (a space followed by an underscore). The statement can continue onto the next line as usual.

STEP 7: Run and Save Your Project

➤ Close the Form Designer and the Code Editor windows. Click the toolbar's **Start button**.

➤ Click **Yes** if a message box asks whether you want to save changes.

STEP 8: Test and Debug Your Project

➤ The initial screen will display with the command buttons and the band leader image as shown in Figure 3.8g.

Click here to start animation ——

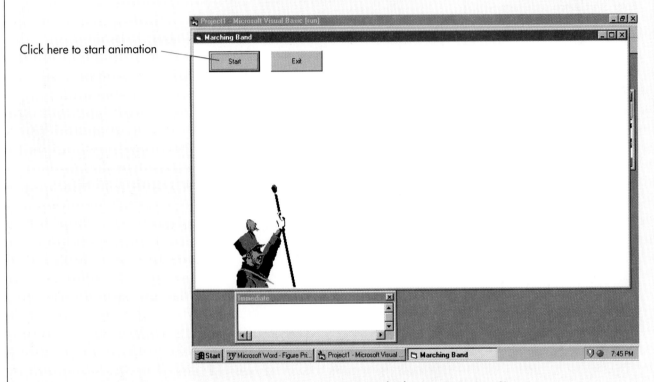

(g) Test and Debug Your Project (step 8)

FIGURE 3.8   Hands-on Exercise 3 (continued)

➤ Click the **Start button**. The 4 band member images will appear and, together with the leader, will move across the screen, as shown in Figure 3.8h.

➤ Click the **Exit button** to exit the Marching Band program.

➤ If you made any errors, you may receive a warning message, or images may not display correctly, or the button may not work correctly. Repeat any previous steps as needed to debug your project.

STEP 9: Create a Copy of the Project

➤ Pull down the **File menu**, and select **Save Marching Band As** to display the Save File As dialog box. Select the drive and folder where you stored your data disk (*Exploring Visual Basic 6*). Enter **Marching Band Again** in the File name text box. Click the **Save button** to save the form file and close the dialog box.

Images move together off the screen

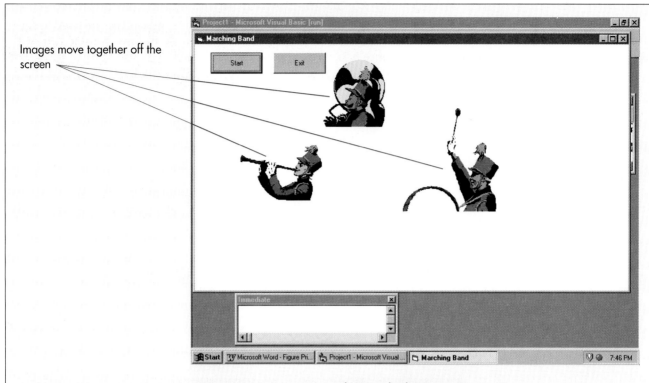

(h) Test and Debug Your Project (step 8)

FIGURE 3.8 Hands-on Exercise 3 (continued)

➤ Pull down the File menu again, and select **Save Project As** to display the Save Project As dialog box. Notice that the Save in list box is set to the folder in which you saved the form. Enter **Marching Band Again** in the File name text box. Click the **Save button** to save the project file and close the dialog box.

➤ Open the **Properties window**, and set the following properties for the form:

Property	Setting
Name	frmMarchingBandAgain
Caption	Marching Band Again

STEP 10: Change Animation Code

➤ Open the Code Editor window, and click the **Full Module View button** at the bottom left corner. Click the **Object list box arrow** and select **tmrBand**. The Procedure list box will display **Timer**.

➤ Position the cursor below the Sub statement line, and change the code to the code block shown below. When you finish the procedure, your screen will look like Figure 3.8i.

```
Private Sub tmrBand_Timer()
'Purpose: Move band members individually
'          Images move faster to top and left
'          Images disappear when an edge is reached
    Static I As Integer
    ' I defaults to 0 at start of first timer
    If (imgBand(I).Top > 0 And imgBand(I).Left > 0) Then
        imgBand(I).Move imgBand(I).Left — 500, _
        imgBand(I).Top — 350
    Else
        imgBand(I).Visible = False
        tmrBand.Enabled = False ' turn off timer
        If I < 4 Then I = I + 1 ' pick next image
        tmrBand.Enabled = True ' turn timer back on
    End If
End Sub
```

Select the timer procedure

Select tmr Band object

Change code here

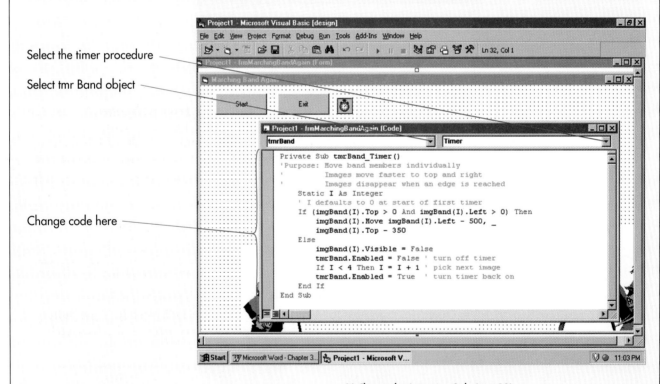

(i) Change the Animation Code (step 10)

FIGURE 3.8   Hands-on Exercise 3 (continued)

STEP 11: Update the Banner Comment, Run, Save, Test, and Debug

➤ Click the **Object list box arrow** and select **General**. Click the **Procedure list box arrow** and select **Declarations**. In the banner comments, change Source to **Marching Band Again**.

➤ Close the Form Designer and the Code Editor windows. Click the toolbar's **Start button**.

➤ When the save message box is displayed, click **Yes**.

➤ The initial screen will display with the command buttons and the band-leader image.

➤ Click the **Start button**. The 4 band member images will appear. The band-leader will move across the screen. After he disappears, the next band member will move. This will continue until all members have moved across the screen. The animation is considerably faster than the previous version of this program.

➤ Click the **Exit button** to exit the Marching Band Again program.

➤ If you made any errors, you may receive a warning message, or images may not display correctly, or the button may not work correctly. Repeat any previous steps as needed to debug your project.

STEP 12: Exit Visual Basic

➤ Pull down the **File menu** and select **Exit** to exit Visual Basic.

➤ If you made any changes and did not save them, the Save Changes message box will appear. Click **Yes** to save your changes, and the window will close.

SUMMARY

This chapter demonstrated the fundamental programming concepts and statements needed to write programs with Visual Basic. To work with formulas and equations, you need variables and constants. Variables change during the execution of a program; constants do not. Variables and constants should be declared with a name and a data type such as Integer, String, or Double. The data stored in the variable will determine the most appropriate data type. The Variant data type is a special data type that can store all types of data. Visual Basic uses the Variant data type as the default and stores all the controls on a form as the Variant data type.

You could use the Variant data type for all your variables, but this would not be efficient. Variables declared with the Dim statement exist only while the procedure is executing. Variables declared with the Static statement preserve the value even when the procedure has ended. Variables are called local when they are declared within a procedure or function. Variables are called global when they are declared in the general section outside procedures and functions.

There are three types of control structures in most programming languages: sequence, selection, and repetition. The sequence of a program can be changed by using procedures and functions. A function is a unit of code that returns a value, whereas a procedure does not. Both can be called from other parts of the code. The selection control structures available in Visual Basic are the If ... Then ... Else and Select Case statements. These statements allow us to make decisions in our programs. The repetition control structures available in Visual Basic are the For ... Next, For Each ... Next, and the variations of the Do statement. These statements allow us to repeat blocks of statements that are commonly called loops. When writing code, we want to avoid endless loops.

Boolean data type
Built-in functions
Byte data type
Constant
Currency data type
Date data type
Dim statement
Do statement
Double data type
Event-driven program-
    ming language
Event procedure
For Each ... Next
    statement

For ... Next statement
Function
Function statement
General procedure
If ... Then ... Else
    statement
Integer data type
Long data type
Object data type
Operator
Private procedure
Procedural program-
    ming language
Procedure

Prototype
Public procedure
Select Case statement
Single data type
String data type
Sub statement
Usability testing
Variable
Variant data type

MULTIPLE CHOICE

1. A unit of code that executes due to an event is called a(n)
   (a) General procedure
   (b) Event procedure
   (c) Pre-defined function
   (d) Function

2. If you had a number that did not change during your program, the best way to store this would be to use a
   (a) Variable
   (b) Constant
   (c) Variant data type
   (d) Any of the above would be equally appropriate

3. Visual Basic uses which of the following data type by default
   (a) Integer
   (b) Single
   (c) Variant
   (d) String

4. If you had a value that you wanted to preserve after a procedure has ended, you would declare this variable with the following Visual Basic statement
   (a) Dim
   (b) Constant
   (c) Static
   (d) Local

5. All of the following statements are examples of sequential control except
   (a) Sub
   (b) Function
   (c) Sqr(x)
   (d) Do

6. All of the following statements are examples of selection control except
   (a) If … Then
   (b) Select Case
   (c) For
   (d) If … Then … Else

7. All of the following statements are examples of repetition control except
   (a) If … Then
   (b) For
   (c) Do
   (d) For Each

8. When writing loops, you want to avoid the following:
   (a) Loops that may never execute
   (b) Loops that never end
   (c) Loops that execute a varying number of times
   (d) Loops that always execute the same number of times

9. The Sub statement is used to indicate
   (a) The beginning of a procedure
   (b) The beginning of a function
   (c) The beginning of a general subroutine
   (d) None of the above

10. All the following statements require a matching End statement except
    (a) Sub
    (b) Function
    (c) If
    (d) Do

11. All the following are data types supported by Visual Basic except
    (a) Boolean
    (b) Real
    (c) Integer
    (d) Date

12. Before a variable can be used in a calculation in Visual Basic, it must
    (a) Be declared
    (b) Be declared and initialized
    (c) Be initialized and optionally declared
    (d) Be initialized

13. All of the following are valid names for Visual Basic Variables except
    (a) Number1
    (b) FirstName
    (c) Interest%
    (d) LoanType

14. When assigning the value 10 to the variable Number1, the following is a valid statement:
    (a) 10 = Number1
    (b) Number1 = 10
    (c) Either of the above is equally appropriate
    (d) Neither of the above

15. All of the following are built-in functions except

(a) Sqr

(b) Rnd

(c) Int

(d) Random

ANSWERS

1. b	**6.** c	**11.** b
2. b	**7.** a	**12.** c
3. c	**8.** b	**13.** c
4. c	**9.** a	**14.** b
5. d	**10.** d	**15.** d

PRACTICE WITH VISUAL BASIC

1. **Learning to Subtract Game.** Modify the Learning to Add game created in Hands-on Exercise 2 to help a student practice subtraction instead of addition. Remember to put the larger of the two randomly generated numbers in the first number position. This can be accomplished with a simple If statement in your code. This is an important requirement because we do not expect primary grade children to be able to deal with negative numbers. Save your form and project as *Learning to Subtract*. Print out your form and code, or turn in your project and form files on disk to your instructor.

2. **Wind Chill in Celsius.** Modify the Wind Chill project created in Hands-on Exercise 1 to calculate the wind chill temperature in Celsius instead of Fahrenheit. This formula uses the wind speed in kilometers per hour and temperature in degrees Celsius as inputs as follows:

   WC = 0.045 (5.27*Sqr(V) + 10.45 – 0.28V) (T – 33) + 33

   If the temperature is 0 degrees Celsius and the wind speed is 10 kph, then the wind chill temperature is –3 degrees Celsius. Use the screen shown in Figure 3.9 as a guide in creating your form. Save your form and project as *Wind Chill in Celsius*. Print out your form and code, or turn in your project and form files on disk to your instructor.

3. **Heat Index.** Modify the Wind Chill project created in Hands-on Exercise 1 to calculate the Heat Index. The Heat Index is used to measure the amount of discomfort during the summer months when heat and humidity make it feel hotter than the temperature indicates. This is a long formula with 9 terms. The formula and a sample calculation are given at the USA Today Weather pages located at ***www.usatoday.com/weather/whumcalc.htm***.

   An appropriate graphic is available on the data disk as ***Heat Index.bmp***, as shown in Figure 3.10. Save your form and project as *Heat Index*. Print out your form and code, or turn in your project and form files on disk to your instructor.

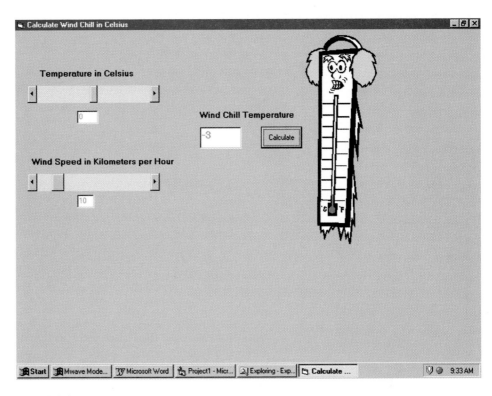

FIGURE 3.9   Screen for Exercise 2: Wind Chill in Celsius

Graphic file available as
Heat Index.bmp

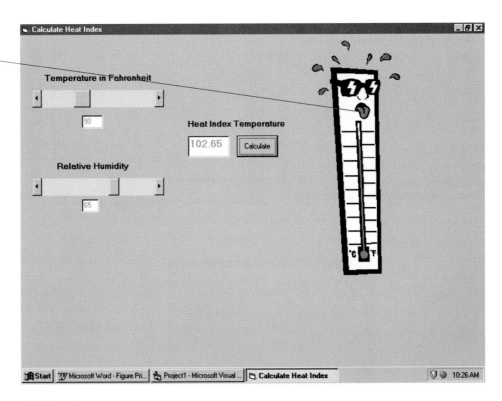

FIGURE 3.10   Screen for Exercise 3: Heat Index

4. Rock, Paper, Scissors Game. You probably played the rock, paper, scissors game as a child. Create a program that plays this game with two players. Your game should accept input for Player 1. Player 2 will be the computer. The rules are: (a) Rock crushes scissors, (b) scissors cut paper, and (c) paper covers rock. This makes nine possible combinations, and each needs to be tested for the game.

Player 1	Player 2	Outcome
Rock	Rock	Tie
Rock	Paper	Player 1 loses
Rock	Scissors	Player 1 wins
Paper	Rock	Player 1 wins
Paper	Paper	Tie
Paper	Scissors	Player 1 loses
Scissors	Rock	Player 1 loses
Scissors	Paper	Player 1 wins
Scissors	Scissors	Tie

This game is harder to code than it appears at first glance. This is an opportunity to use the Select Case statement to make your decision to determine the winner of each game. A plan for this project is shown in Figure 3.11. Graphic files for **Rock**, **Paper**, and **Scissors** are available as bmp files on the data disk. You may also use other graphics.

The player should be able to play several games with your program before quitting. Save your form and project as *Rock Paper Scissors*. Print out your form and code, or turn in your project and form files on disk to your instructor.

(a)

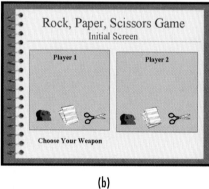

(b)

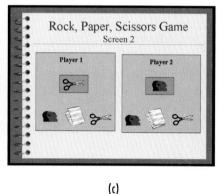

(c)

(d)

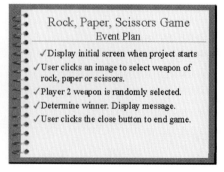

(e)

FIGURE 3.11 Screens for Exercise 4: Rock, Paper, Scissors Game

VIDEO CLIP

5. Creating Variables: Video Clip (Learning Edition Only). This exercise requires that you be using the Learning Edition of Visual Basic, and that you have installed the *Learn Visual Basic Now* book on your hard drive or have access to it from the CD-ROM. This video clip, one of several included on the *Learn Visual Basic Now* CD, shows the differences between data types and storage space. Run and watch the video clip demonstration to reinforce this material from the chapter. This demonstration includes much more than Visual Basic screens, so watch and learn.

a. Start *Learn Visual Basic Now*.

b. Open the books from Chapter 4 as shown in Figure 3.12.

c. Open the "Creating Variables" book. In the Topic pane, click the Video clip icon.

d. View the entire video clip.

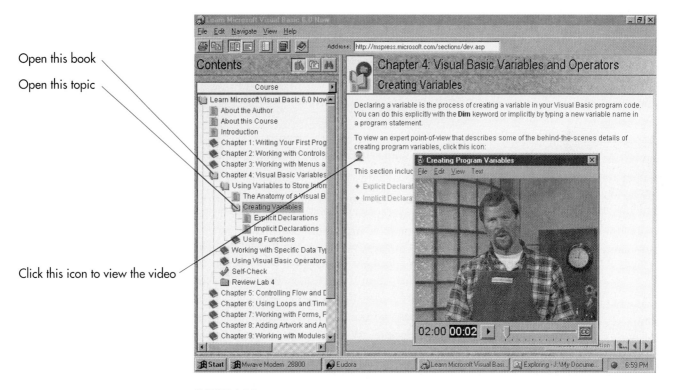

FIGURE 3.12 Screen for Exercise 5: Creating Variables

VIDEO CLIP

6. Event-driven Programming: Video Demonstration (Learning Edition Only). This exercise requires that you be using the Learning Edition of Visual Basic, and that you have installed the *Learn Visual Basic Now* book on your hard drive or have access to it from the CD-ROM. This video demonstration illustrates event-driven programming with an animated example. Run and watch the video demonstration to reinforce this material from the chapter.

a. Start *Learn Visual Basic Now*.

b. Open the books from Chapter 5 as shown in Figure 3.13.

c. Open the "Event-driven Programming" topic. In the Topic pane, click the Demonstration icon.

d. View the entire animated demonstration.

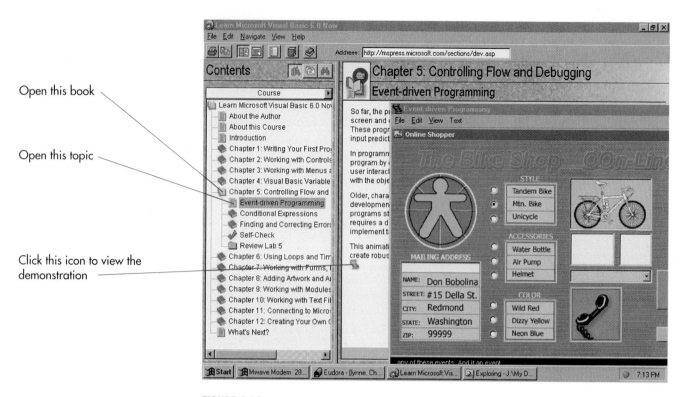

Open this book

Open this topic

Click this icon to view the demonstration

FIGURE 3.13   Screen for Exercise 6: Event-driven Programming

VIDEO CLIP

7. **For ... Next Loop: Video Demonstration (Learning Edition Only).** This exercise requires that you be using the Learning Edition of Visual Basic, and that you have installed the *Learn Visual Basic Now* book on your hard drive or have access to it from the CD-ROM. This video demonstration illustrates the For loop to change the text size on a form. Run and watch the video demonstration to reinforce this material from the chapter.

   a. Start *Learn Visual Basic Now*.

   b. Open the books from Chapter 6 as shown in Figure 3.14.

   c. Open the "Writing For ... Next loops" book.

   d. Open the "Changing Properties With a Loop" topic. In the Topic pane, click the Video icon.

   e. View the entire video demonstration.

VIDEO CLIP

8. **Digital Clock: Video Demonstration (Learning Edition Only).** This exercise requires that you be using the Learning Edition of Visual Basic, and that you have installed the *Learn Visual Basic Now* book on your hard drive or have access to it from the CD-ROM. This video demonstration illustrates how to create a digital clock in only a few minutes.

   a. Start *Learn Visual Basic Now*.

   b. Open the books from Chapter 6 as shown in Figure 3.15.

   c. Open the "Using the Timer Control" book.

   d. Open the "Creating a Digital Clock" topic. In the Topic pane, click the Video icon.

   e. View the entire video demonstration.

   f. Run and watch the video demonstration, and take notes.

   g. Create a program that displays a digital clock as shown in the demonstration. Save your form and project as *Digital Clock*.

   h. Print out your form and code, or turn in your project and form files on disk to your instructor.

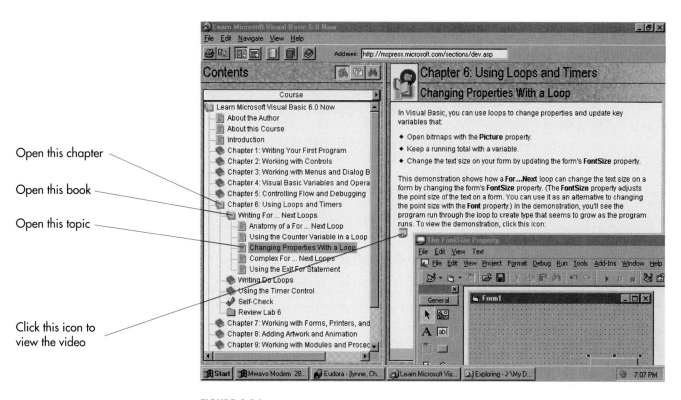

Open this chapter

Open this book

Open this topic

Click this icon to
view the video

FIGURE 3.14   Screen for Exercise 7: For ... Next Loop Demonstration

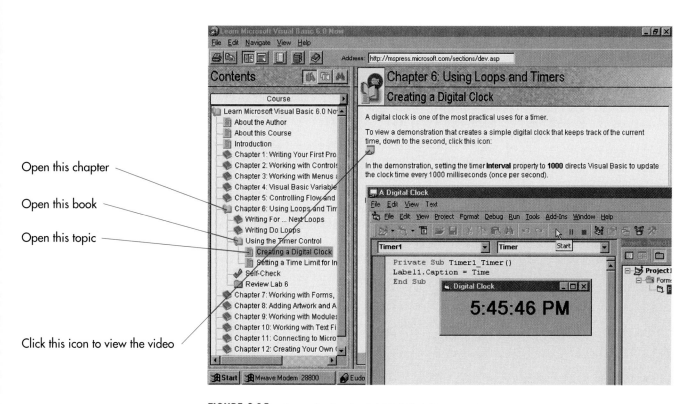

Open this chapter

Open this book

Open this topic

Click this icon to view the video

FIGURE 3.15   Screen for Exercise 8: Digital Clock Demonstration

Calculate a Formula

Pick a mathematical, statistical, financial, or scientific formula and write a program to do the calculation. You might want to start with something very simple such as the quadratic equation. You could create a homework checker program to use in another class you are currently taking. Save your form and project as *Formula Case Study*. Print out your form and code, or turn in your project and form files on disk to your instructor.

Weather Calculations

You created a program that calculated the wind chill temperature in Hands-on Exercise 1 for this chapter, calculated it again in Celsius in Practice Exercise 2, and calculated the Heat Index in Practice Exercise 3. There are many weather calculation formulas available from the USA Today Weather Web site at *www.usatoday.com/weather/wcalc0.htm*. Choose another weather calculation and write a program to implement it. Save your form and project as *Weather Case Study*. Print out your form and code, or turn in your project and form files on disk to your instructor.

More Fun and Games

You created the Learning to Add game in Hands-on Exercise 2, and modified it in Practice Exercise 1. Create a program that implements another game or learning activity. Save your form and project as *Game Case Study*. Print out your form and code, or turn in your project and form files on disk to your instructor.

More Web Resources for Visual Basic

Information about Visual Basic abounds on the Web. Here are some recommended sites for you:

- Carl and Gary's Home Page at *www.cgvb.com* has everything from a Beginner's page to The Jobs Page. A search engine is available to help you find topics of interest.
- Gary Beene's Visual Basic World at *web2.airmail.net/gbeene/visual.html* is an entire community of Visual Basic, with material for everyone from beginners to hardcore programmers, with links to over 260 sites.
- VB Online Magazine and Catalog at *www.vbonline.com* is a free source of VB programming articles, tips, tricks, source code, questions and answers, and product reviews. You can also order books and Visual Basic add-on software here.

Write a one-page summary of an article or information you read from one of these Web sites.

ENHANCING THE GRAPHICAL USER INTERFACE: MULTIPLE FORMS, CONTROLS, AND MENUS

4

OBJECTIVES

After reading this chapter, you will be able to:

1. Describe in general terms how to design a good user interface; discuss guidelines you can use in the design process.
2. Use the Toolbox tools to create a form; modify existing forms; add and delete controls in an existing form.
3. Distinguish between a Multiple Document Interface (MDI), Single Document Interface (SDI), and Explorer-style interface.
4. Create a form to include input features such as text boxes, labels, and command button controls.
5. Create a form to include graphics using the picture box or image controls.
6. Create a Graphical User Interface with menus using the VB Application Wizard, tools from the Toolbox, and the Menu Editor.
7. Create a form that includes file management features with controls such as drive list boxes, directory list boxes, and file list boxes.
8. Demonstrate a form that includes input features such as frames, check boxes, option buttons, combo boxes, and list boxes.

OVERVIEW

This chapter looks at forms and the Toolbox in detail. We start with a conceptual discussion of the importance of proper design and develop guidelines that you will find useful in anything you program. We then turn our attention to implementing the design in Visual Basic. You will see how the VB Application Wizard can be used to create a Multiple Document Interface (MDI), Single Document Interface (SDI), or Explorer-style interface.

You will refine the interface design by creating controls using the Toolbox. The appearance of the controls is controlled by changing properties. You will apply your new designing skills with the hands-on exercises. You will create a *Learning Arithmetic* game with a Calculator model interface. Next, you will create the *Icon Explorer* application using file system controls. Finally, you will add menus and the code to enable the menus. After you complete the exercises in this chapter, you will be well on your way toward creating useful projects using Visual Basic.

DESIGNING THE GUI

So far, all the projects you have created consisted of a single form. Most real-life projects consist of many forms. There are three basic interface styles provided in Visual Basic: Multiple Document Interface (MDI), Single Document Interface (SDI), and Explorer-style.

Interface Styles

The Microsoft Office applications Word, Excel, PowerPoint, and Access use a multiple document interface. The ***Multiple Document Interface (MDI)*** consists of a large parent form covering the entire desktop. This parent form contains the documents or items being edited, which are called child forms. An example is shown of the Word 97 interface in Figure 4.1a. (In the figure, the parent form is the Word application window, and the child forms are three open document windows, two of them displayed at restored size and the third minimized.) The ***Single Document Interface (SDI)*** may consist of multiple forms as well, but each form floats on its own at the same level and there is no large parent form. This style is suitable for utilities such as the Windows Media Player or any program that is oriented to a single purpose. An example of a SDI using the Calculator accessory is shown in Figure 4.1b.

Child forms

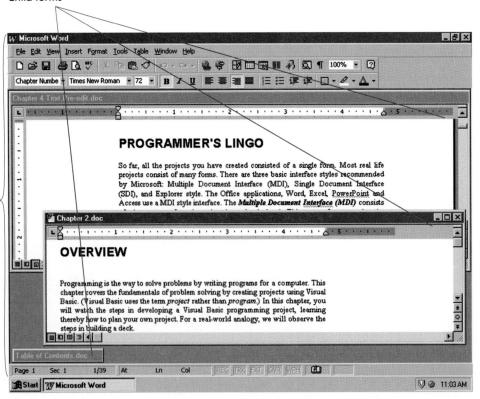

Parent form

(a) Multiple Document Interface (MDI)

FIGURE 4.1   Interface Styles

Independent form 1

Independent form 2

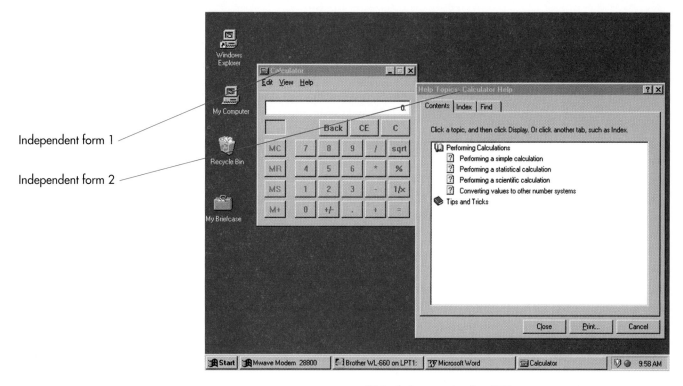

(b) Single Document Interface (SDI)

Left pane browsing controls

Right pane detailed view

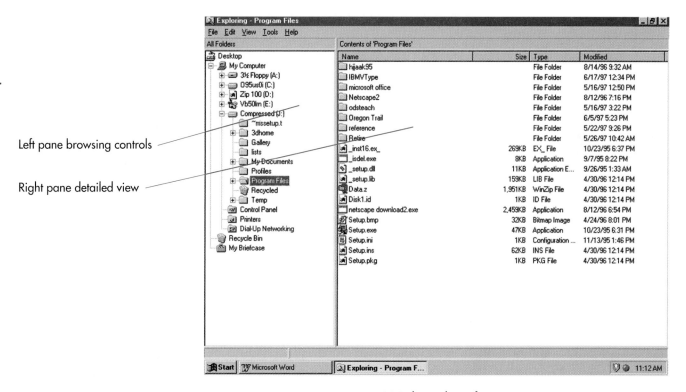

(c) Explorer-style Interface

FIGURE 4.1   Interface Styles (continued)

The **Explorer** is a specialized SDI style, illustrated using the Windows 95 Explorer as shown in Figure 4.1c. The Explorer-style interface uses a single, stand-alone form divided into several frames or panes. The left pane contains browsing controls such as lists of disks, folders, and files. The right pane shows a more detailed view. The Explorer-style interface is suitable for browsing folders and file structures as well as data. The Explorer-style interface was used to navigate the Books Online in Visual Basic 5.0.

You can use any of the three styles to implement your projects. Use the style that best fits the application and feels most natural to the end user.

FIVE PRINCIPLES OF GUI DESIGN

With all the styles and Toolbox tools available, creating and designing forms for your Graphical User Interface can be a perplexing task. Remember that people usually read the manuals and instructions only when all else fails. You want to make your interface as easy and intuitive to use as possible. If you follow five basic design principles, you should have an easy-to-use Graphical User Interface (GUI).

Principle 1: Know Your End User

When you are designing your program, the first question you should answer is "Who is my audience?" Will your application be used by children, adults, or both? If your program is used by children, what will be their reading level? For preschool children, you will need to use symbols and graphics instead of words for your screens. If you are designing for retired adults, are the fonts large enough to be easily read? Write down as much as you know about your end user before you start sketching and designing your screens. Designing for the end user was discussed in more detail with the Learning to Add application in Chapter 3. This interface is shown in Figure 4.2.

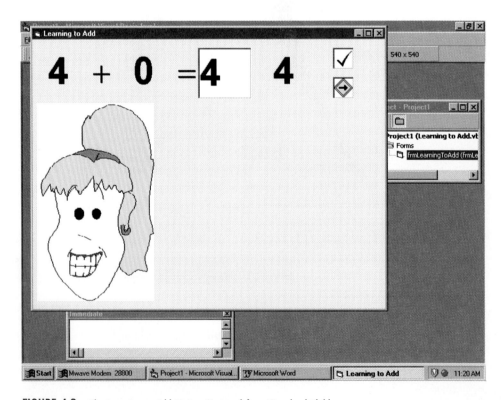

FIGURE 4.2   The Learning to Add Project Designed for a Preschool Child

Principle 2: Be Consistent

You know how frustrating it can be to learn a new program. Make it easy on your user and use the Windows guidelines that the user already knows and understands. For example, use the Close button available at the top of the window instead of creating another exit button on your forms. Use the Windows standard fonts of Arial, Times New Roman, and MS Sans Serif. These fonts were designed to be easy to read on the screen. Establish a font color and size, grouping of controls, background color, and foreground color. Pick an overall style and stick to it throughout your application.

Whichever style you use, you will want to follow the **Windows Interface Guidelines** whenever possible. A primary advantage of the Windows environment is that contains many uniform elements. Learning one Windows application makes it easier to learn another. If your user interface deviates too far from the Windows interface guidelines, your users will have trouble learning your application. Use your knowledge of Windows and follow its interface guidelines.

Menus are a good example of interface guidelines. Microsoft assigned standard menu positions to many commands. Most Windows applications have File as the leftmost menu and Help as the rightmost. Optional menus such as Edit, Format, and Tools go in the middle. Users expect to find Cut, Copy, and Paste commands in the Edit menu. If you are using menus in your application, put your commands in the expected locations.

Many applications also include toolbars, dialog boxes, and message boxes. In general, users expect to be able to do tasks in three different ways: with the menus, keyboard commands, or toolbar buttons. Providing options will provide alternatives for the preferences of your users.

More information on the Windows Interface Guidelines and creating user interfaces is available online. Pull down the Help menu and select Contents. Now open the *Visual Basic Documentation* and *Using Visual Basic* books. Open the *Programmer's Guide* then the *Part 2* book, and then the *Creating a User Interface* book. Finally, open the *Designing with the User in Mind* book.

Principle 3: Show and Use Informative Graphics and Messages

Show the user instead of telling whenever possible. Make sure your graphics are informative instead of merely creative. Sometimes programmers who want to be creative forget about helping the end user. An excellent example of the use of graphics is the File Copy window, shown in Figure 4.3, that is used in Windows Explorer and My Computer. The File Copy window shows papers flying from a folder on the left to the folder on the right. This animated graphic shows the user that a file is being copied from one folder to another. The user doesn't mind waiting because it is obvious what is going on inside the computer.

Using graphics instead of text and labels is especially useful if your program will be used internationally. Usually a picture does not need translating as words do. The GUI has often been compared to the dashboard and controls in a car, and the analogy is especially apt here. The dashboard controls of most foreign-made cars use symbols instead of words. This saves the manufacturer time and money because the same button on the dashboard can be used no matter where the car will be shipped.

Principle 4: Keep It Simple

The KISS ("Keep it simple, sweetie") principle is particularly applicable to user interfaces. If an interface looks difficult, it will probably be hard to use. If the interface appears simple, then it will be simple for your users. It is usually better to create several forms than to have a single cluttered form. Try to group items together logically. The tabbed format shown in Figure 4.4 is appropriate when you have to present a multitude of options. Many times, you will also want to set default properties to automatically select the most often chosen option.

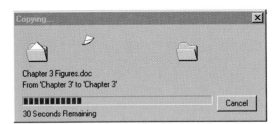

FIGURE 4.3   Good Use of Graphics Showing Copy Process

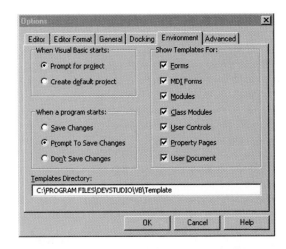

FIGURE 4.4   Logical Grouping Using Tabbed Dialog Box

Principle 5: Let the User Control the Application

Think of your application program as a conversation between the computer and the end user. You need to let the user ask the questions and decide what tasks to accomplish. As the programmer, you are controlling the computer's responses to the user by building your program. The reactions of the computer will be shown to the user by creating forms. Because Visual Basic is an event-driven programming language, this principle is easy to achieve.

THE FORM DESIGNER GRID

The Form Designer window initially displays with a grid of dots. This grid uses a screen-independent unit of measurement called *twips*. Usually screens are measured in screen-dependent units called *pixels*. See Appendix C, "The Toolbox, Toolbars, and Controls," for more information on the grid, twips, and pixels.

THE LEARNING ARITHMETIC PROJECT

Let's apply the building steps from Chapter 2 and the GUI design rules we've just learned to another project. First, we define the problem. Let's create another game to practice arithmetic skills. In the Learning to Add project from Chapter 3, the only arithmetic operation used was addition. In this project, let's extend it to the subtraction, multiplication, and division operations. We will create multiple forms using the Single Document Interface.

Specification for the Learning Arithmetic Game

The problem definition is to create a math game for school children (grades 3–5) to practice their arithmetic skills. The specifications of this game include:

- This project is a game to practice addition, subtraction, multiplication, and division skills.
- The numbers for the problems are between 0 and 9.
- The user is a child in grade 3, 4, or 5.
- The game gives visual feedback to the child to indicate a correct or wrong answer.

START WITH A PROTOTYPE

A *prototype* is a partially completed version of an application that demonstrates the "look and feel" of the finished application. It may contain only the forms with no written code. The advantage of a prototype is that the end user or client can test out the design of your user interface.

Design the User Interface

Now that we have our specification, let's design the user interface. This step should be written down using pencil and paper. Many children at this grade level enjoy using a calculator to do arithmetic or to check their homework. Let's start with the calculator model as used in the Windows Calculator accessory as shown in Figure 4.5.

Let's modify the calculator model to display arithmetic problems. After trying many designs, let's go with the screens shown in the figure. Figure 4.6a shows the screen the child will see when the game starts. The child clicks the number buttons to enter an answer to the arithmetic problem as shown in Figure 4.6b. The child can click the CE (Clear Entry) button to erase the answer and enter a new one. Next the child clicks the equal button to check the answer. The problem with the correct answer is shown in Figure 4.6c.

To continue playing the game, the child clicks the C (Clear) button, and the initial screen is displayed again with a new math question. To quit playing the game, the child clicks the screen's Close button.

FIGURE 4.5   Calculator Accessory Application

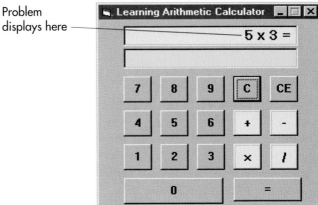

(a) Learning Arithmetic Initial Screen

FIGURE 4.6   Designing the User Interface

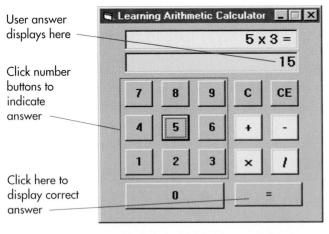

(b) Learning Arithmetic Second Screen

(c) Learning Arithmetic Third Screen

FIGURE 4.6   Designing the User Interface (continued)

GUI Enhancement with the Learning Arithmetic Project

Objective: Create a program to practice arithmetic for children. Implement the GUI design principles; create several forms, and add code to display the forms. Use Figure 4.7 as a guide for the exercise.

STEP 1: Use the Application Wizard

➤ Start Visual Basic. Click the New Project dialog box's **New tab**. Select the **VB Application Wizard icon** and click the **Open button**.

➤ On the Introduction screen, do not select a profile, and click the **Next button**.

➤ On the Interface Type screen, click the **Single Document Interface (SDI)**. Enter **Learning_Arithmetic** in the text box to name the project. Click the **Next button**.

➤ On the Menus screen, leave the **&File** and **&Help** check boxes selected, and clear the other menu check boxes as shown in Figure 4.7a.

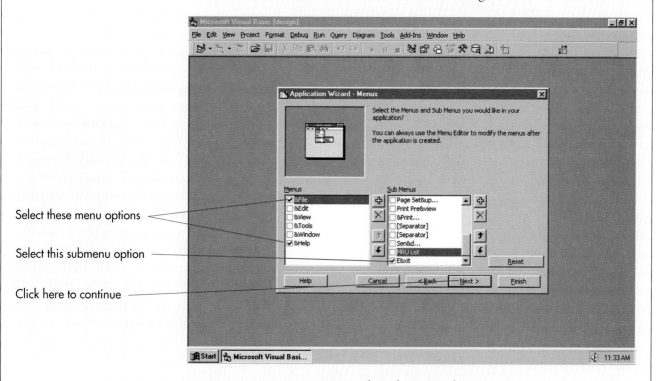

Select these menu options

Select this submenu option

Click here to continue

(a) Use the Application Wizard (step 1)

FIGURE 4.7   Hands-on Exercise 1

➤ Select **&File** in the left pane. In the right pane, clear all of the submenu items except **E&xit**. You will need to scroll the list to view all the items.

➤ Select **&Help** in the left pane. In the right pane, clear all of the submenu items except **&About**. Click the **Next button**.

➤ On the Customize Toolbar screen, click the double arrow button to delete all the buttons from the toolbar. Click the **Next button**.

➤ On the Resources screen, select the **No option**, then click the **Next button**.

➤ If you get an Internet Connectivity screen, click the **No option** and then the **Next button**.

➤ On the Standard Forms screen, select the **Splash screen** and **About Box** options, as shown in Figure 4.7b. Click the **Next button** to continue.

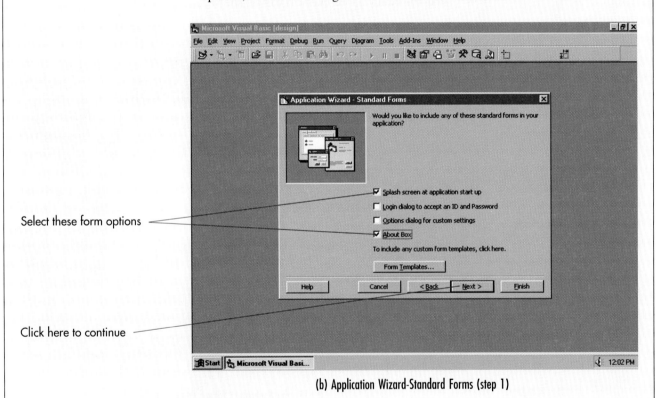

Select these form options

Click here to continue

(b) Application Wizard-Standard Forms (step 1)

FIGURE 4.7   Hands-on Exercise 1 (continued)

➤ The Data Access Forms screen will be displayed. Click the **Next button** to continue.

➤ On the Finished screen, do not select a profile, and click the **View Report** button. Read the Summary Report window as shown in Figure 4.7c. When finished, click the **Close button** to continue.

➤ On the Finished screen, click the **Finish button**. Click the **OK button** on the Application Wizard's message box.

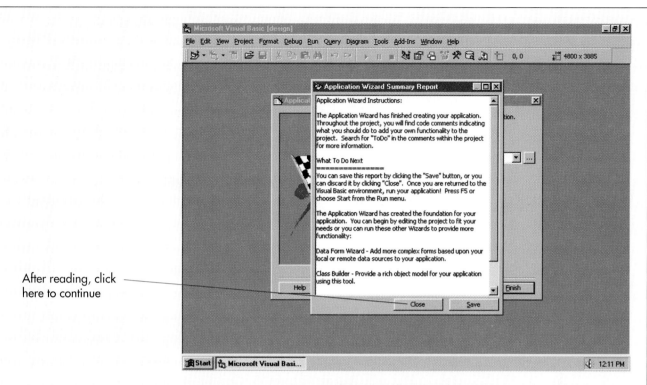

After reading, click here to continue

(c) Application Wizard Summary Report (step 1)

FIGURE 4.7 Hands-on Exercise 1 (continued)

➤ Several forms and windows will appear and disappear from your screen while the wizard creates forms and code for you. When the wizard is finished, the Application Created screen will be displayed. Click the **OK button** to complete the process.

STEP 2: Save Your Form and Project Files

➤ Set your Visual Basic options as shown in Chapter 2, Hands-on Exercise 1, Step 2 (page 47), if you want to ensure that the following steps look as much like the figures shown as possible. Pull down the **Tools menu**, and select **Options**. Select the **Docking Tab** in the Options dialog box. Uncheck the **Properties window**, and **the Project Explorer** boxes. Click the **OK button** to apply the new options.

➤ Pull down the File menu, and select **Save Project As**. Select the drive and folder where you stored your data disk (*Exploring Visual Basic 6*). Enter **Learning Arithmetic About** (was frmAbout) in the File name text box. Click the **Save button** to save the form file. Repeat this process and save the **Learning Arithmetic Splash** (was frmSplash) form, and the **frmMain** (do not change the name) **form files**.

➤ Enter **Learning Arithmetic Module** (was Module1). Click the **Save button** to save the module file with the bas file extension. Enter **Learning Arithmetic** (remove the underscore) on the Save Project As dialog box. Click the **Save button**. Open the Project Explorer window.

➤ We will be creating a new Main form, so we will delete the one created by the wizard. Click the **frmMain form's title bar** to select it. Pull down the **Project menu** and select **Remove frmMain**, as shown in Figure 4.7d. If a Save Changes message box is displayed, click **No**.

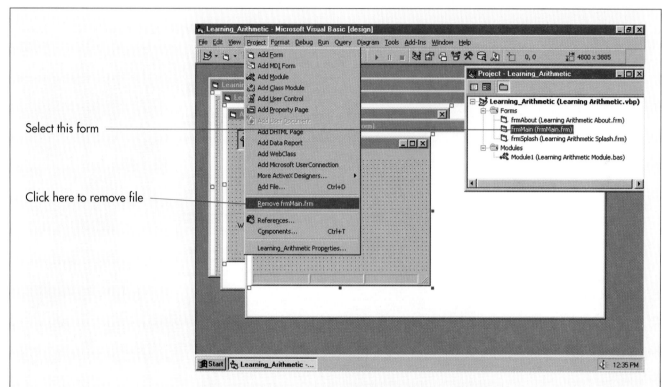

Select this form

Click here to remove file

(d) Delete the Main Form (step 2)

FIGURE 4.7   Hands-on Exercise 1 (continued)

START WITH A SPLASH SCREEN

A *splash screen* is the first form that appears when your application starts. It usually contains such information as the name of the application, the software company and copyright information, and a simple image. For example, the screen that displays when you start Visual Basic is a splash screen.

STEP 3: Modify the Splash Form

➤ The Splash form should still be displayed. If it is not, double click the **frmSplash form** in the Project Explorer window.

➤ Click the toolbar's **Properties Window button** to display the Properties window. Use Figure 4.7e as a guide in setting up your window so you can work with the form.

➤ Modify the form as shown in Figure 4.7e. First, click the **License To label** to select it. Press the **Delete key** on your keyboard to delete the label.

➤ Select the **Company Product** label. Move to the Properties window and change the Caption property to **Exploring Visual Basic 6.0**.

➤ Click the **Product label** to select it in the Form Designer window. Move to the Properties window and change the Caption property to **Learning Arithmetic**. The words will not fit the form, so resize the form and the frame control. The frame control is the large box directly inside the form.

➤ Click the **Platform label** to select it. Move to the Properties window and change the Caption property to **For Windows 95 and 98**.

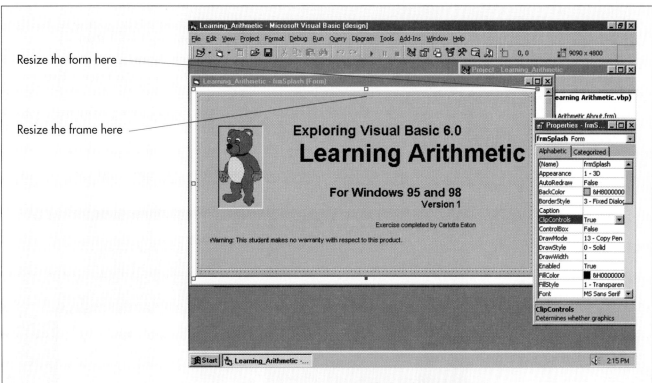

Resize the form here

Resize the frame here

(e) Modify the Splash Form (step 3)

FIGURE 4.7   Hands-on Exercise 1 (continued)

➤ Click the **Version label** to select it. In the Properties window, change the Caption property to **Version 1**.

➤ Click the **Copyright label** to select it. You are not the originator of this application, so press the **Delete key** on your keyboard to delete the label.

➤ Click the **Company label** to select it. Change the Caption property to **Exercise completed by** and add your name. If necessary, resize the control to display the whole caption.

➤ Click the **Warning label** to select it. Modify the label's Caption property to read **Warning: This student makes no warranty with respect to this product.**

➤ In the Form Designer window, click the **picture box control** to select it. Move to the Properties window and select the Picture property setting to display the Load Picture dialog box.

➤ Select the drive and folder where you stored your data disk *(Exploring Visual Basic 6)*. Select the **bear.bmp** file to display the image of a bear. Change the AutoSize property to **True**. The picture box will resize to display the bear image.

➤ Your Splash form should look like the screen shown in Figure 4.7e.

➤ Pull down the **File menu** and select **Save Learning Arithmetic Splash.frm** to save your changes to the form.

STEP 4: Add the Calculator Form

➤ Close the Properties window. Close the Splash form and the About form.

➤ Pull down the **Project menu** and select **Add Form** to display the Add Form dialog box. Click the **Existing tab**.

> If the Look in text box does not display the folder where your data disk is stored, select the correct drive and folder (*Exploring Visual Basic 6*).

> Click to select the **Learning Arithmetic Calculator form**. Click the **Open button**. The form will be added to the list displayed in the Project Explorer window.

> In the Project Explorer window, double click the **Learning Arithmetic Calculator form** to display it, as shown in Figure 4.7f.

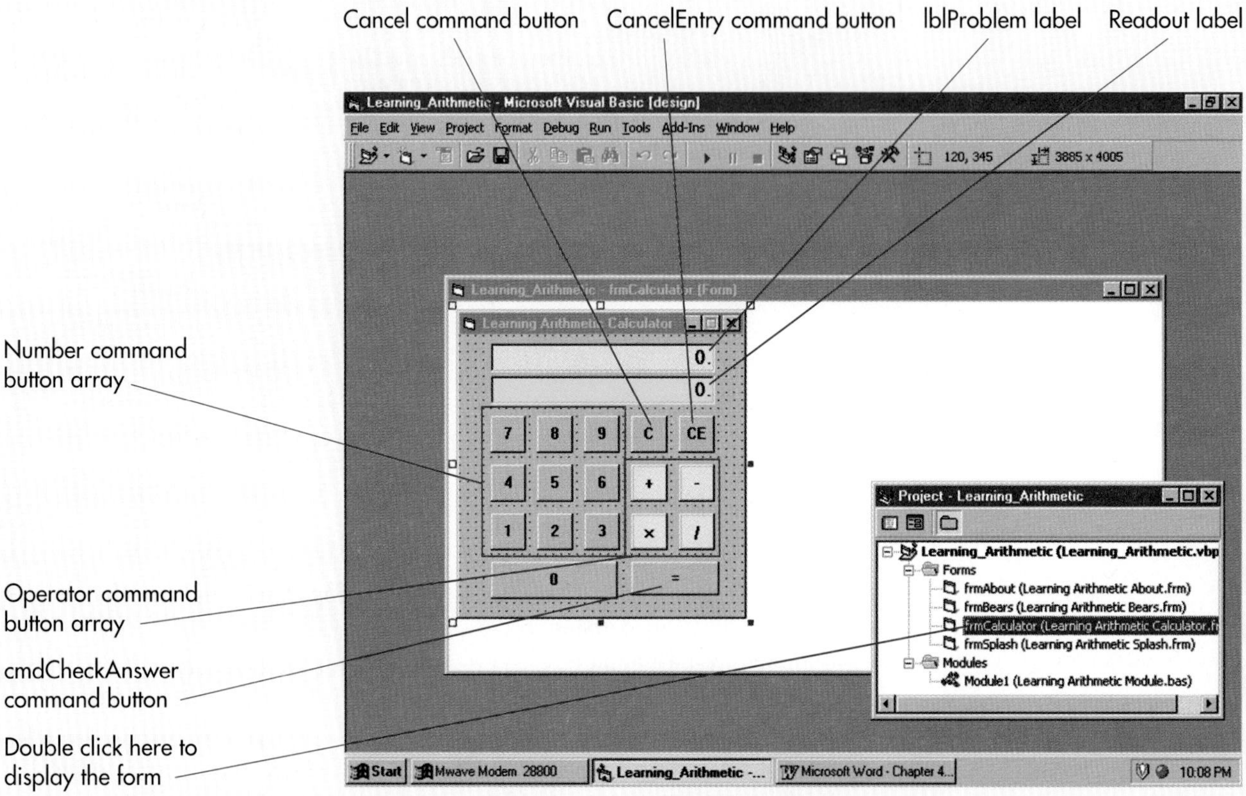

Cancel command button   CancelEntry command button   lblProblem label   Readout label

Number command button array

Operator command button array

cmdCheckAnswer command button

Double click here to display the form

(f) Add the Calculator Form (step 4)

FIGURE 4.7   Hands-on Exercise 1 (continued)

> Notice the names of the objects on the form as shown in the figure. In the Project Explorer window, click the **View Code button** to display the Code Editor window.

> In the Code Editor window, select the **General object** and the **Declarations procedure**. Change the **Programmer** name to your name. Change the **Date** to the current date. Add any other information required by your instructor.

> Read the other procedures in the project to understand the code that has been written for you.

> Click the toolbar's **Save button** to save the project. Close the Code Editor window. Close the Calculator form window.

STEP 5: Add the Bears Form

> Pull down the **Project menu** again and select **Add Form** to display the Add Form dialog box. Click the **Existing tab**.

➤ The Look in text box should display the folder where your data disk is stored. If it does not, select the correct drive and folder.

➤ Click to select the **Learning Arithmetic Bears** form. Click the **Open button**. The form will be added to the list displayed in the Project Explorer window.

➤ In the Project Explorer window, double click the **Learning Arithmetic Bears form**. Click the **Maximize button** to display the form as shown in Figure 4.7g. Notice the names of the objects on the form as shown in the figure.

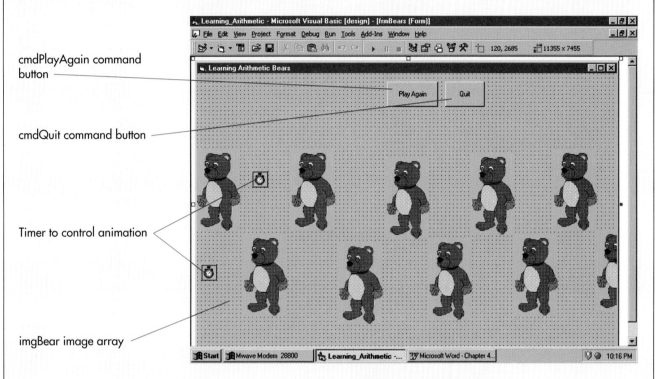

cmdPlayAgain command button

cmdQuit command button

Timer to control animation

imgBear image array

(g) Add the Bears Form (step 5)

FIGURE 4.7   Hands-on Exercise 1 (continued)

➤ Click the toolbar's **Project Explorer button** to display the window. Click the Project Explorer's **Restore button**. Click the **View Code button** to display the Code Editor window.

➤ In the Code Editor window, select the **General object** and the **Declarations procedure**. Change the **Programmer** name to your name. Change the **Date** to the current date. Add any other information required by your instructor.

➤ Read the other procedures in the project to understand the code that has been written for you.

➤ Click the toolbar's **Save button** to save the project. Close the Code Editor window. Close the Bears form window.

STEP 6: Write the Module Code

➤ In the Project Explorer window, double click the **Modules folder** to open it. Double click the **Module1 (Learning Arithmetic Module)** to open the Code Editor window.

➤ The procedure will be started for you as shown below:

```
Sub Main()
  frmSplash.Show
  frmSplash.Refresh
  Set fMainForm = New frmMain
  Load fMainForm
  Unload frmSplash

  fMainForm.Show
End Sub
```

➤ Modify the procedure as shown below:

```
Sub Main()
'Purpose: Start the Learning Arithmetic project.
'         Display the Splash form briefly.
  frmSplash.Show
  frmSplash.Refresh

'Load the Calculator form
  Set frmMainForm = New frmCalculator
  Load frmMainForm

'Unload Splash form and display Calculator form
  Unload frmSplash
  frmMainForm.Show
End Sub
```

➤ Now let's add the banner comments and declarations to our code. In the Code Editor window, select the **Declarations procedure**. The following line of code will be displayed as shown below:

```
Public fMainForm As frmMainForm
```

➤ Modify the line of code as shown below:

```
Public frmMainForm As frmCalculator
```

➤ Click before the first character of **Public**. Instead of typing the banner comments from scratch, let's use the copy and paste operations.
➤ Move to the Project Explorer window and double click the **Bears form** to select it. Click the **View Code button** to display the form's code.
➤ In the Code Editor window for the Bears form, select the **General object** and the **Declarations procedure**. Click at the first character and drag the mouse to select the banner comment section as shown in Figure 4.7h.

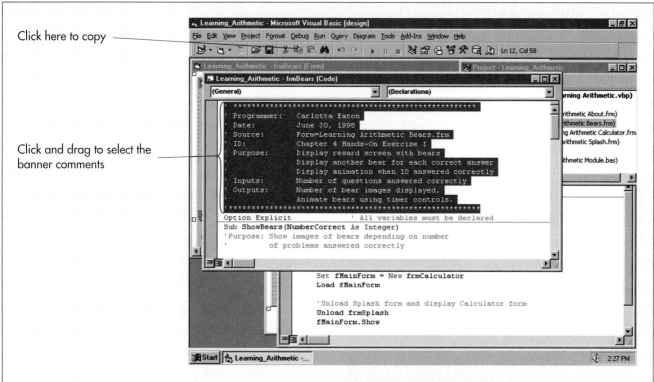

Click here to copy

Click and drag to select the banner comments

(h) Write the Module Code (step 6)

FIGURE 4.7   Hands-on Exercise 1 (continued)

➤ Right click to display the context menu and click the **Copy command**. This action places a copy of the banner comments to the Windows clipboard. Close the Bear form's Code Editor window.

➤ Move to the Code Editor window for Module 1 and select the **General object** and the **Declarations procedure**.

➤ Click at the top of the window before the line of code you previously modified. Right click to display the context menu and click the **Paste command**. This will place a copy of the Bear form's banner comments into the Module1 code.

➤ Modify the banner comments as shown below.

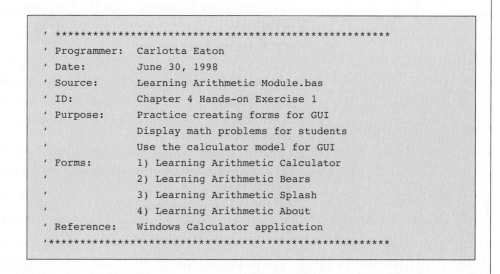

```
' ***********************************************************
' Programmer:    Carlotta Eaton
' Date:          June 30, 1998
' Source:        Learning Arithmetic Module.bas
' ID:            Chapter 4 Hands-on Exercise 1
' Purpose:       Practice creating forms for GUI
'                Display math problems for students
'                Use the calculator model for GUI
' Forms:         1) Learning Arithmetic Calculator
'                2) Learning Arithmetic Bears
'                3) Learning Arithmetic Splash
'                4) Learning Arithmetic About
' Reference:     Windows Calculator application
' ***********************************************************
```

STEP 7: Run and Test the Project

➤ Close the Project Explorer, the Code Editor, and the Form Designer windows.

➤ Click the toolbar's **Start button** to run the project.

➤ If you made any errors, you may receive a compiler message. Fix any compiler errors in your code before continuing.

➤ If the Save Changes message box is displayed, click **Yes** to continue and save changes to your forms and code.

➤ The Splash form will be displayed briefly, then the Calculator form will be displayed, and finally the blank Bears form.

➤ An arithmetic problem will be displayed in the blue label box on the Calculator form. Click the calculator's **number command buttons** to enter the correct answer. The numbers you click will be displayed in the yellow label box.

➤ Click the calculator's **equal command button** (=) to check the answer. The blue label box will be updated to display the correct answer. A bear will be appear in the blank Bears form as another indication of a correct response.

➤ Click the calculator's **Clear command button** (C) to display a new problem in the blue label box. Deliberately click number buttons for a wrong answer.

➤ Click the calculator's **equal command button** (=). The blue label box will be updated to display the correct answer. In the Bears form, the bear disappears to indicate a wrong response.

➤ Click the calculator's **plus command button** (+) to change to addition problems. Continue clicking command buttons until you have answered 3 problems correctly.

➤ Click the calculator's **subtract command button** (–) to change to subtraction problems. Continue clicking command buttons until you have answered 6 problems correctly.

➤ Click the calculator's **divide command button** (/) to change to division problems. Answer 3 more problems.

➤ After you have correctly answered 9 problems, the screen shown in Figure 4.7i will be displayed. Immediately after you answer the tenth problem correctly, the bottom row of bears will begin to move up. The top row of bears will begin to move up and to the left of the screen, as shown in Figure 4.7j. The calculator form will disappear.

➤ Command buttons will appear on the Bears form. After the bears have moved off the screen, click the **Play Again button** to continue testing the game.

STEP 8: Debug Your Project

➤ If you made any errors, you may receive a warning message, forms or images may not display correctly, or the number or operator keys may not react correctly. Repeat any previous steps as needed to debug your project.

➤ After you click the Play Again button, the calculator form will reappear. The blank Bears form will appear.

➤ Click the **divide command button** to display division problems. Keep displaying division problems until you are dividing by 0. What happens when you try to divide by 0?

➤ Click the **subtract command button** to change to subtraction problems. Notice that the larger number always displays first, so the student will not have to deal with negative numbers.

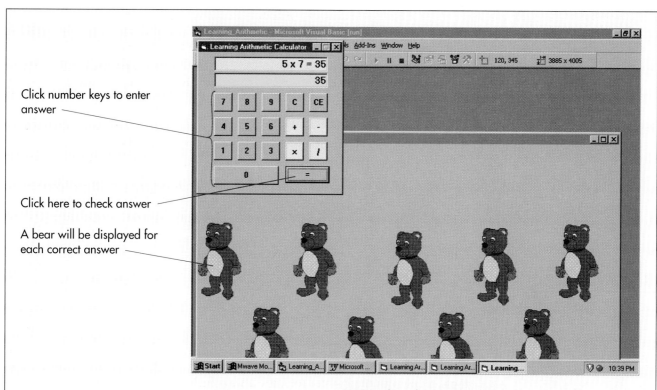

Click number keys to enter answer

Click here to check answer

A bear will be displayed for each correct answer

(i) Run and Test the Project (step 7)

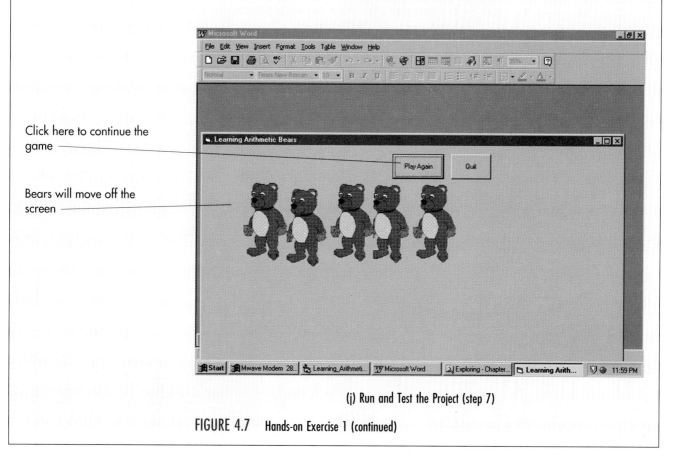

Click here to continue the game

Bears will move off the screen

(j) Run and Test the Project (step 7)

FIGURE 4.7   Hands-on Exercise 1 (continued)

➤ Click the **Clear command button** to display a new problem. Click the **equal command button** before entering an answer. What happens?

➤ Continue until you have answered 10 problems correctly. After the bears have moved off the screen, click the **Quit command button** to end the program.

STEP 9: Print Your Project and Exit

➤ Pull down the **File menu** and select **Print** to display the Print dialog box.

➤ Select **Current Project** from the Range options.

➤ Select **Form Image** from the Print What options. Click the **OK button** to print the forms for this project. A page for each of the 4 forms should print.

➤ Close any open windows in the Visual Basic environment.

➤ Pull down the **File menu** and select **Exit**. The Save Changes message box will be displayed if you have not saved modifications made while debugging your project. Click **Yes** to save your changes and exit.

THE TOOLBOX

The Visual Basic 6.0 Toolbox contains tools to create 20 ***intrinsic controls***. These tools, along with the Pointer tool, are always included in the Toolbox and are contained inside the Visual Basic exe file. They cannot be removed from the Toolbox. There are two other broad categories of controls available in Visual Basic: ActiveX controls and Insertable Objects. The later categories can be added and removed from the Toolbox.

ActiveX controls exist as separate files with the *.ocx* file extension (*vbx* in earlier versions of Visual Basic). ActiveX controls include familiar controls such as the toolbar, common dialog box, and tabbed dialog box. To add an ActiveX control to your Toolbox, pull down the Project menu and select Components. Click the Control tab and locate the desired control (as shown in Figure 4.8a). After selecting the desired control(s), click the OK button to add the controls to the toolbox. ActiveX Controls are available in all editions of Visual Basic 6.0.

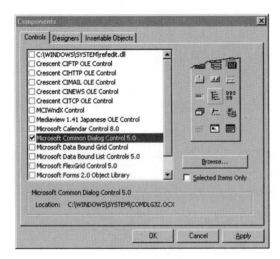

(a) Active X Controls

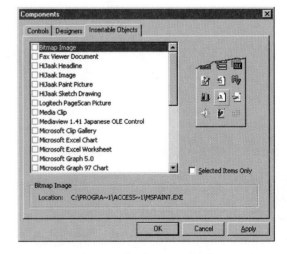

(b) Insertable Objects as Controls

FIGURE 4.8   Adding Controls to the Toolbox

Insertable objects are objects from another application such as an Excel worksheet. To add an Insertable Object to your Toolbox, pull down the Project menu and select Components. Click the Insertable Object tab, then locate the desired object(s) (as shown in Figure 4.8b). After selecting the object(s), click the OK button to add the objects to the toolbox. Insertable Objects are available in all editions of Visual Basic 6.0.

INTRINSIC CONTROLS

Let's look in more detail at the intrinsic controls, as shown in Figure 4.9, and at a few other controls that perform similar functions. The intrinsic controls include controls to display text, display graphics, present choices, execute commands, access data, and access the Windows file system. The first tool is the *Pointer*, the only tool that does not draw a control. Use the Pointer tool to move or resize any control on the form.

A TOOL OR A CONTROL?

Except for the Pointer tool, which is used to size or move a control once it has been drawn, all of the tools in the Toolbox are used to draw controls on a form. Technically, therefore, you use the Label tool to draw a label control on your form. Since the names of the tools are the same as the names of the controls they draw, the terms *control* and *tool* are often used interchangeably, and you will see them used that way in Visual Basic Documentation.

Text Controls

There are several ways to display text on a form. Use a *label* when you are displaying text to the user. The user cannot modify a label. Use a *text box* when the user needs to input text. The user can modify a text box. Use a *command button* to display text on a button. The user can click the button to carry out a command.

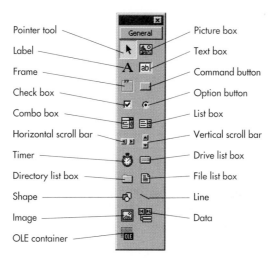

FIGURE 4.9   The Visual Basic Toolbox's Intrinsic Controls

Get Input

You can use a **text box** to get input from the user. You can also use the **horizontal and vertical scroll bars** as a way to limit the user's input. You used horizontal scroll bars in the Wind Chill project in the last chapter. It was impossible for the user to give invalid input numbers because input was limited by the horizontal scroll bars. This is a very useful way to guarantee valid input. Scroll bars are also handy tools for quickly navigating through a long list of items or a large amount of information.

You can also present choices to the user to gather input. Use a **check box** where more than one choice is allowed. Use **option buttons** within a frame to display mutually exclusive alternatives. Use a **list box** to present a list of items where only one choice is allowed. The user merely clicks an item from the list. Use a **combo box** when you want the user to choose from a list or type in a selection. A combo box automatically combines a text box with a list box.

There are other ways to get input besides using the intrinsic controls. The **tabbed dialog** Active X control is used to present several options to the user in a tabbed-style dialog box such as shown in Figure 4.8 (on page 174). For more information on this control, see "Using the Tabbed Dialog Control" in Visual Basic Documentation.

Dialog boxes can also be used to prompt the user for input. The **MsgBox** and **InputBox functions** can be used to present predefined dialog boxes that contain code. You can create a **customized dialog box** by creating a standard form and displaying it when appropriate with code. You can use the **common dialog ActiveX control** to present standard dialog boxes such as opening and saving files, setting print options, and selecting colors and fonts. This code is already written and included in Microsoft Windows. You can use this code by including the common dialog ActiveX control in your form and setting its properties. The common dialog control is invisible when you run the project, but the dialog box opens at the appropriate time using code. The common dialog control will be discussed and utilized in Chapter 5.

Display Graphics

There are four intrinsic controls available to display graphics. Use an **image** when you need to create a graphical command button or toolbar button icon or to display an image. You can stretch an image control to fit to size. Images displayed in an image control can only be decorative and use fewer resources than a picture box. Use a **picture box** when you need to create a toolbar that contains other images. A picture box acts as a visual container for other controls as well as displaying a picture. You cannot stretch or reduce a picture box, but you can autosize it so that it expands or contracts to fit the picture it contains.

If you want to display rudimentary graphics, use a **line** to draw a straight-line segment. Use a **shape** to draw a rectangle, rounded rectangle, square, rounded square, ellipse, or circle.

Besides using these four intrinsic controls, you can display graphics in other ways. You can set the **background property** of a form to display an image. This is similar to the backgrounds used in PowerPoint presentations and Web pages. Visual Basic can display bitmap (*bmp*) files, icon (*ico*) files, Windows metafiles (*wmf*), as well as GIF and JPEG files. You can use the Windows Paint or Paintbrush accessory programs to create bitmap images. You can download GIF and JPEG files from the Web.

The **LoadPicture function** can be used while you are running a project to add an image or a picture to a form. You will be using this function in the next hands-on exercise to display the icons available with Visual Basic.

File System Controls

Use a *drive list box* to display valid disk drives. Use a *directory list box* to display directories (folders) and paths. Use a *file list box* to display a list of files.

Miscellaneous Controls

Use a *frame* to group other controls together such as option buttons. (The Splash form in the Learning Arithmetic project uses a frame.) To group controls together, draw the frame first and then draw controls inside the frame. Use the *timer* like a stopwatch. You can use the timer to trigger simple animation and other events that happen at set intervals. The timer control is invisible at run time. Use an **OLE container** to link and embed objects from other applications in your Visual Basic application.

Data Access Controls

Use the *data control* to create applications to display, edit, and update information from many types of existing databases. You can also use various ActiveX controls to display information about the current records in a database. Visual Basic implements data access by incorporating the same database engine that powers Microsoft Access. For more information on data-access controls, see the many references in the *Data Access Guide* book in Visual Basic 6.0. See the *Guide to Data Access Objects* book in Visual Basic 5.0.

SET PROPERTIES WITH CODE

After you design and create your form, you set properties for the form(s) and each object (control) on the form. The advantage of setting properties is that Visual Basic does a lot of the coding for you. You can set properties using the Properties window at design time and using code at run time. You have written code to set properties several times while doing the hands-on exercises in this textbook. The syntax for general method is to write a line of code with the following syntax:

---

name.property = setting

where
   name is the name of the control or form
   . (period) is required between the name and property
   property is the name of the property you wish to set or modify
   = (equal) is required between the property and setting
   setting is the setting of the property exactly as you would set it using the Properties window

Examples:
   imgWorld.Visible = True
   txtName.Text = "Sarah"

THE ICON EXPLORER PROJECT

In the next hands-on exercise, we create an image-viewing application. Before we start, let's get a little background information. One of the enhancements to Visual Basic 5.0 was the ability to display GIF and JPEG files. These files are used extensively for graphics on the Web. You can now download graphics from the Web and use them in your Visual Basic projects. In previous versions of Visual Basic, you needed to use an image-converter program and convert the images to bitmaps (*bmp*) or Windows metafiles (*wmf*) first. Visual Basic also displays icon files, and many image-converter programs cannot. Visual Basic includes a large library of icon files, and the Icon Explorer project will allow you to see these icons.

Most commercial image-viewer programs allow you to see only a single image at a time. This can be very time consuming if you are looking through the hundreds of icons available. This project allows you to see all the icons available in the current folder simultaneously. Because icons are very small (usually either 16 by 16 pixels or 32 by 32 pixels), you can display a lot of them on a single form. The Icon Explorer project is designed to display 90 icons in order to accommodate the maximum number contained in a single folder in Visual Basic: the 89 icons in the *Misc* folder. The icons are displayed in an array of image controls. The name for all the image controls is *imgIcon,* so you can use a simple For loop to display all of the icons. The form was designed to fit in a 640-by-480-pixel display, so you should be able to view the icons on any personal computer.

Let's continue by creating the Icon Explorer application. This application uses the frame, image, drive list box, directory list box, file list box, and label controls.

HANDS-ON EXERCISE 2

Create the Icon Explorer Project Using File System Controls

Objective: Build the Icon Explorer application project; create controls using the file system tools from the toolbox; add existing forms; modify template forms. Use Figure 4.10 as a guide in the exercise.

STEP 1: Create a New Project

➤ Start Visual Basic. Click the New Project dialog box's **New tab**.

➤ Click the **Standard EXE icon**. Click the **Open button** to open a new project window. Set your Visual Basic options as shown in Chapter 2, Hands-on Exercise 1, Step 2 (page 47) if you want to ensure that the following steps look as much like the figures shown as possible.

➤ Pull down the Tools menu and select **Options**. Select the **Docking Tab** in the Options dialog box. Uncheck the **Properties Window** and **Project Explorer** boxes. Check the **OK button** to apply the new options.

STEP 2: Add the Existing Starter Form

➤ Click the toolbar's **Project Explorer button** to open the Project Explorer window. Double click the **Forms folder** to open it.

➤ Pull down the **Project menu** and select **Add Form** to display the Add Form dialog box. Click the **Existing tab**.

➤ Select the drive and folder where your data disk is located (*Exploring Visual Basic 6*).

➤ Click to select the **Icon Explorer Starter form**. Click the **Open button**. Click the dialog box's **Yes button** to upgrade the COMCTL32.OCX control.

➤ Double click the **Icon Explorer Starter form** in the Project Explorer window. The form will be displayed as shown in Figure 4.10a. Notice the form contains an array of image controls. The icons will be displayed in these controls.

Icon Explorer starter form

Control array containing images

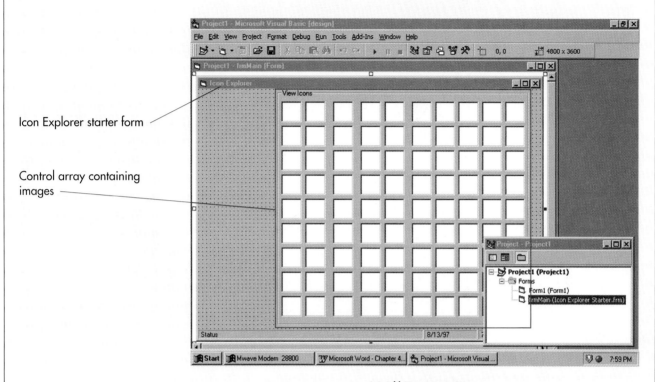

(a) Add Forms (step 2)

FIGURE 4.10   Hands-on Exercise 2

➤ Pull down the **File menu** and select **Save Icon Explorer Starter As** to display the Save File As dialog box. Select the drive and folder where you stored your data disk. Enter **Icon Explorer Main** in the File name text box. Click the **Save button** to save the form file and close the dialog box.

➤ You will be adding existing forms to this project and will not need Form1 (blank form), so remove it from the project. Click on **Form1** in the Project Explorer window.

➤ Pull down the **Project menu** and select **Remove Form1**. The Form1 form will be removed from the Project Explorer window.

➤ Close the Icon Explorer Main form window.

STEP 3: Add a Splash Form

➤ Pull down the **Project menu** and select **Add Form** to display the Add Form dialog box. Click the **New tab**.

➤ Click the **Splash Screen icon**. Click the **Open button**.

➤ Click the toolbar's **Properties Window button** to display the Properties window. Use Figure 4.10b as a guide in setting up your window so you can work with the form.

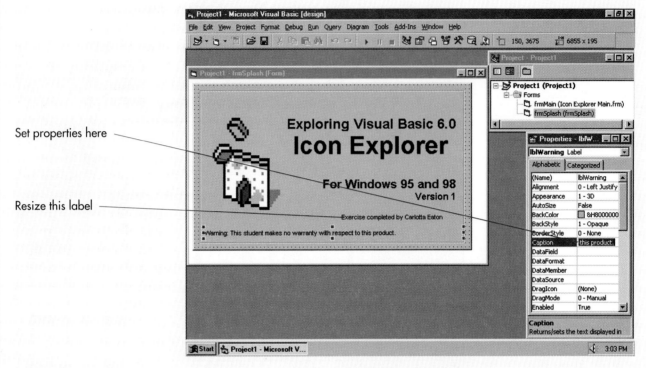

Set properties here

Resize this label

(b) Add a Splash Form (step 3)

FIGURE 4.10   Hands-on Exercise 2 (continued)

➤ Modify the form as shown in the figure. First, click the **License To label** to select it. Press the **Delete key** on your keyboard to delete the label.

➤ Select the **Company Product** label. Move to the Properties window and change the Caption property to **Exploring Visual Basic 6.0**.

➤ In the Form Designer window, click the **Product label** to select it. Move to the Properties window and change the caption property to **Icon Explorer**. Click the **Platform label** to select it. Move to the Properties window and change the Caption property to **For Windows 95 and 98**.

➤ Click the **Version label** to select it. Change the Caption property to **Version 1** in the Properties window.

➤ Click the **Copyright label** to select it. You are not the originator of this application, so press the **Delete key** on your keyboard to delete the label.

➤ Click the **Company label** to select it. Change the Caption property to **Exercise completed by** and add your name. The words may not fit on the form, so move the label to the left as needed.

➤ Click the **Warning label** to select it. Modify the label's Property setting to read **Warning: This student makes no warranty with respect to this product.**

➤ Your Splash form should look like the screen shown in Figure 4.10b.

➤ Pull down the **File menu** and select **Save frmSplash As** to display the Save File As dialog box. Select the drive and folder where you stored your data disk. Enter **Icon Explorer Splash** in the File name text box. Click the **Save button** to save the form file and close the dialog box.

➤ Close the Splash screen window.

➤ Pull down the **File menu** again and select **Save Project As** to display the dialog box. Notice that the Save in list box is set to the folder in which you saved the forms.

➤ Enter **Icon Explorer** in the File name text box. Click the **Save button** to save the project files and close the dialog box.

STEP 4: Add the Main Module

➤ Pull down the **Project menu** and select **Add Module** to display the Add Module dialog box. If necessary, click the **New tab**. Click the **Module icon** and then the **Open command button** to close the dialog box and add a new module in the Project Explorer window.

➤ Move to the Project Explorer window and double click **Module1**.

➤ The Code Editor window will be displayed with no code. Add the following code to the module:

```
Sub Main()
   'Purpose: Start the Icon Explorer project
   Dim frmMainForm As Form

  'Display the Splash form briefly
   frmSplash.Show
   frmSplash.Refresh

  'Create and load the main form
   Set frmMainForm = New frmMain
   Load frmMainForm

  'Unload the Splash form and display the Main form
   Unload frmSplash
   frmMainForm.Show
End Sub
```

➤ Click the Code Editor's **Procedure View button**. Select the **General object** and the **Declarations procedure**. There will not be any code displayed in the Code Editor window. Add the banner comments and the line of code as shown on page 182, changing to your name and the current date. The "Option Explicit" statement forces you to declare variables as an aid in debugging, as explained later in a tip box.

```
'****************************************************
' Programmer:    Carlotta Eaton
' Date:          June 30, 1998
' Source:        Icon Explorer Module.bas
' ID:            Chapter 4 Hands-on Exercise 2
' Purpose:       Practice creating forms for GUI
'                Display the icons included with VB
' Forms:         1) Icon Explorer Main
'                2) Icon Explorer Splash
'****************************************************
Option Explicit
```

➤ Click the **Full Module View button** to display the code as shown in Figure 4.10c.

Banner comments go here

Module declarations go here

Procedures start here

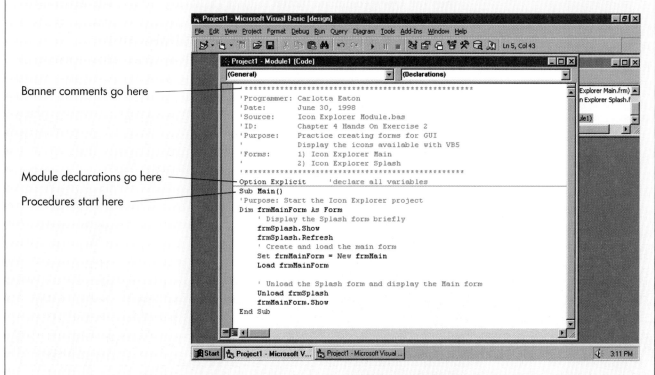

(c) Add the Main Module (step 4)

FIGURE 4.10   Hands-on Exercise 2 (continued)

➤ Pull down the **File menu** and select **Save Project** to display the Save File As dialog box, set to the folder where you saved your forms.

➤ Notice you are saving a module file, with the file extension *bas.* Enter **Icon Explorer Module** in the File name text box. Click the **Save button** to save the module file.

➤ Close the Code Editor window.

USE OPTION EXPLICIT

Add the Option Explicit statement to the Declarations section (immediately after the banner comments) of each form and module. This option checks your code to be sure all variables have been declared. This helps you in debugging and checks for typos for you.

STEP 5: Modify the Main Form

➤ Move to the Exploring Project window and double click the **Main form** to display it.

➤ Close the Project Explorer window. Maximize the Main form.

➤ Click the toolbar's **Toolbox button** to open the Toolbox.

➤ In the Toolbox, select the **Label tool**. Draw a label at the top left of the window as shown in Figure 4.10d. Click the toolbar's **Properties Window button** to open the Properties window.

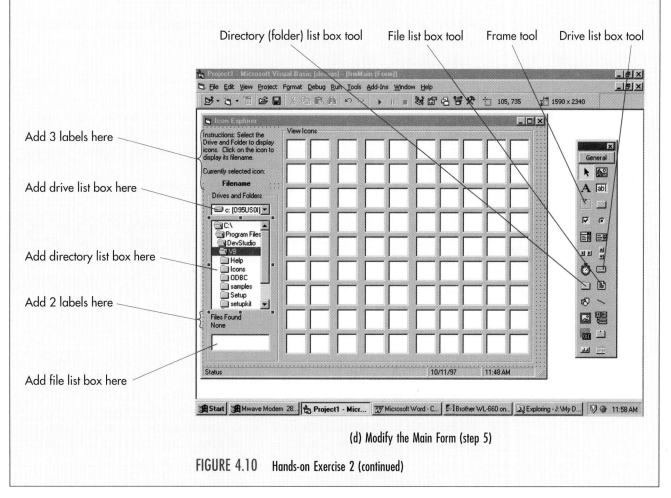

(d) Modify the Main Form (step 5)

FIGURE 4.10 Hands-on Exercise 2 (continued)

➤ Change the label's Name property to **lblInstructions** and its Caption property to **Instructions: Select the Drive and Folder to display icons. Click on the icon to display its file name.**

➤ In the Toolbox, select the **Label tool** again. Draw a label immediately below the previous label.

➤ Change the label's Name property to **lblCurrent** and its Caption property to **Currently selected icon**.

➤ In the Toolbox, select the **Label tool**. Draw a label immediately below the previous label.

➤ Change the label's Name property to **lblFilename**, its Alignment property to **2-Center**, its Caption property to **Filename**, and its Font to **Bold**.

➤ In the Toolbox, select the **Frame tool**. Draw a frame below the labels at the left side of the form as shown in Figure 4.10d.

➤ Open the Properties window and change the Name property to **fraFiles** and the Caption property to **Drives and Folders**.

➤ In the Toolbox, select the **Drive List Box tool**. Draw a drive box on the form within the top of the frame.

➤ Move to the Properties window and change the Name property to **drvDrive**.

➤ In the Toolbox, select the **Directory list box tool**. Draw a directory (folder) box on the form within the frame under the drive box.

➤ Move to the Properties window and change the Name property to **dirFolders**.

➤ In the Toolbox, select the **Label tool**. Draw a label within the frame under the directory box.

➤ Change the label's Name property to **lblFound** and its Caption property to **Files Found**.

➤ In the Toolbox, select the **Label tool**. Draw a label within the frame under the previous label.

➤ Change the label's Name property to **lblNumber** and its Caption property to **None**.

➤ In the Toolbox, select the **File list box tool**. Draw a file list box within the frame under the labels.

➤ Change the box's Name property to **filFiles** and its Pattern property to ***.ico**. The Pattern property selects which files to display. Change the Visible property to **False**.

➤ Your form should look like Figure 4.10d. Pull down the **File menu** and select **Save Icon Explorer Main. frm**.

ICON LIBRARY

An **_Icon Library_** is included with both Visual Basic 5.0 and 6.0. All **_icon files_** have the file extension _.ico_. You can find the icon files at Vb\Graphic\Icons, or alternatively at Microsoft Visual Studio\Common\Graphics\Icons. Also, check the Windows\Icons folder for more icons available on your computer.

STEP 6: Code the Main Form

➤ Close the Toolbox and the Properties windows.

➤ Double click on any control on the form to display the Code Editor window. Click the **Procedure View button**.

➤ Select the **General object** and the **Declarations procedure**.

➤ The initial code for the general section needs to be modified. Change the initial code to the code shown below and in Figure 4.10e. Also, change the **Programmer** name to your name and the **Date** to the current date.

```
'*****************************************************
'Programmer: Carlotta Eaton
'Date:       June 10, 1998
'Source:     Icon Explorer Main.frm
'ID:         Chapter 4 Hands On Exercise 2
'Purpose:    Practice creating forms for GUI
'            Display the icons available with VB5
'            Main form for the Icon Explorer project
'****************************************************
Option Explicit        'declare all variables
Const MaxArray As Integer = 89 'max icon boxes
'****************************************
```

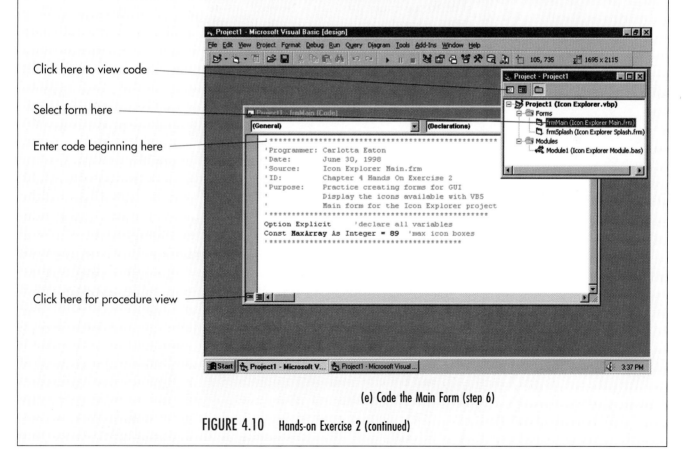

Click here to view code ——

Select form here ——

Enter code beginning here ——

Click here for procedure view ——

(e) Code the Main Form (step 6)

FIGURE 4.10   Hands-on Exercise 2 (continued)

➤ Select the **Form object** and the **Load procedure**. Add the following code to the event procedure:

```
Private Sub Form_Load()
Dim I As Integer 'loop counter
  'Hide all icon boxes
  For I = 0 To MaxArray
    imgIcon(I).Visible = False
  Next I
End Sub
```

➤ Select the **drvDrive object** and the **Change procedure**. Add the following code to the event procedure:

```
Private Sub drvDrive_Change()
'Purpose: Drive change event procedure
'        Link drive box to folders box
    dirFolders.Path = drvDrive.Drive
End Sub
```

➤ Select the **dirFolders object** and the **Change procedure**. Add the following code to the event procedure. Notice that the line DisplayIcon(I) is a comment. We will add this procedure to the project later.

```
Private Sub dirFolders_Change()
'Purpose: Folders change event procedure
'         Link folders box to file list box
'         Display icons in current folder

Dim I As Integer       'loop counter
Dim Max As Integer 'number of icons in current folder

  'Hide all icon boxes
  For I = 0 To MaxArray
    imgIcon(I).Visible = False
  Next I

  'Link the Folder list box to the Files list box
  filFiles.Path = dirFolders.Path

  'Count number of files in current folder
  Max = filFiles.ListCount
  lblNumber.Caption = Max

  'Display icons in current folder
  If Max > 0 Then
    For I = 0 To Max — 1
        'DisplayIcon (I)
    Next I
  End If

End Sub
```

➤ Select the **imgIcon object** and the **Click procedure**. Add the following code to the event procedure:

```
Private Sub imgIcon_Click(Index As Integer)
'Purpose: Display filename of current icon
Dim Filename as String

        'Get filename of current file
        Filename = filFiles.List(Index)

        'Display current filename
        lblFilename.Caption = Filename
End Sub
```

➤ Pull down the **File menu** and select **Save Icon Explorer Main.frm** to save your coding changes for this form.

STEP 7: Run and Debug the Project

➤ Pull down the **Project menu** and select **Project1 Properties**.

➤ Click the **General tab** as shown in Figure 4.10f. Click the **list box arrow** under **Startup Object** and select **Sub Main**. This option tells Visual Basic where to start when running the project.

➤ Click the **OK button** to save the option.

➤ Click the toolbar's **Start button** to run the project.

Pull down Project menu

Select Sub Main

Click here to continue

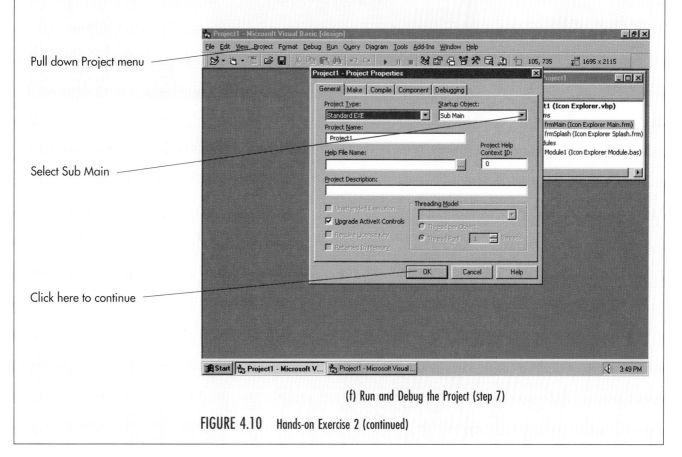

(f) Run and Debug the Project (step 7)

FIGURE 4.10   Hands-on Exercise 2 (continued)

➤ If the Save Changes message box is displayed, click **Yes** to continue and save changes to your forms and code.

➤ The Splash form will be displayed briefly, then the Main form will be displayed.

➤ Verify that the icon image boxes do not display.

➤ Click inside the **drive list box** and select the drive where Visual Basic is installed on your computer.

➤ Click inside the **folders list box** and select **Program Files**, then **Microsoft Visual Studio,** then **Common,** then **Graphics**, then the **Icons** folder, as shown in Figure 4.10g. This is the default location for installation of Visual Basic. You may have installed Visual Basic in a different location on your computer.

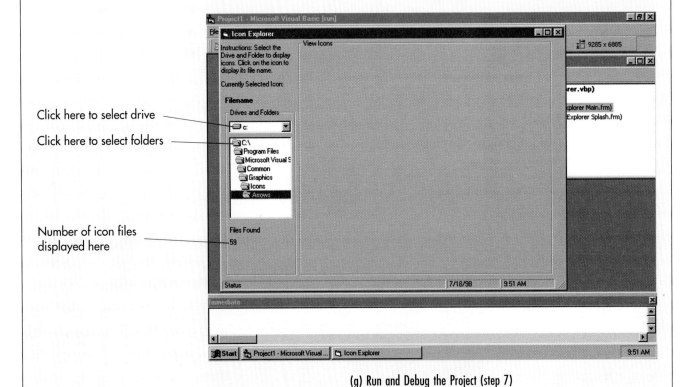

Click here to select drive

Click here to select folders

Number of icon files displayed here

(g) Run and Debug the Project (step 7)

FIGURE 4.10   Hands-on Exercise 2 (continued)

➤ Double click any folder below the Icons folder and notice the number label will update to show the number of icon files in the current folder.

➤ If you have made any errors, you may receive a warning message, or forms or file controls may not display correctly. Repeat any previous steps as needed to debug your project.

➤ Close the Icon Explorer project window.

START YOUR PROJECT

If your project has several forms or modules, you need to specify where to start the project. If you have more than one form, use code in a module to start up the project. This option is set under the Project Properties.

STEP 8: Add Code to Display Icons

➤ In the Project Explorer window, double click the **Main form** to open it.

➤ Click the toolbar's **Properties Window button** to open the Properties window.

➤ Double click the **directory list box** on the form to open the Code Editor window.

➤ Verify that the **dirFolders object** and the **Change procedure** are selected in the Code Editor window.

➤ Remove the apostrophe before the **DisplayIcon (I)** line of code to change it from a comment to active code.

➤ Immediately after the End Sub line of code add the code shown below:

```
Private Sub DisplayIcon(Index as Integer)
'Purpose: Display the icons in the current folder
Dim Path As String 'current path
Dim Filename As String 'next file in files list
Dim PathFilename As String 'path and file

'Look for error handling procedure
On Error GoTo PictureLoad_Error

        'Get current path and add \ if needed
        If Right$(dirFolders.Path, 1) = "\" Then
          Path = dirFolders.Path
        Else
          Path = dirFolders.Path & "\"
        End If

        'Get next filename in files list
        Filename = filFiles.list(Index)
        PathFilename = Path & Filename

        'Load icon into next image control
        imgIcon(Index).Picture = LoadPicture(PathFilename)
        imgIcon(Index).Visible = True

PictureLoad_Exit:
'If error when loading image, then exit procedure
        Exit Sub

PictureLoad_Error:
'Error handling code section
        Select Case Err
          Case 0 'no errors found
          Case Else
                MsgBox "Error loading icon file: " _
                    & vbCrLf & Err & " — " & Err.Description
        End Select
Resume PictureLoad_Exit
End Sub
```

STEP 9: Run and Debug the New Code

➤ Close any open windows.

➤ Click the toolbar's **Start button** to run the project.

➤ If the Save Changes message box is displayed, click **Yes** to continue and save changes to your forms and code.

➤ The Splash form will be displayed briefly, then the Main form will be displayed.

➤ Click inside the **drive list box** and select the drive where Visual Basic is installed on your computer.

➤ Click inside the **folders list box** and select **Program Files**, then **Microsoft Visual Basic**, then **Common**, then **Graphics**, then the **Icons** folder as shown in Figure 4.10h. This is the default location for installation of Visual Basic. Visual Basic may be installed in a different location on your computer.

This icon is selected —

File name for current icon displays here —

Select folder here —

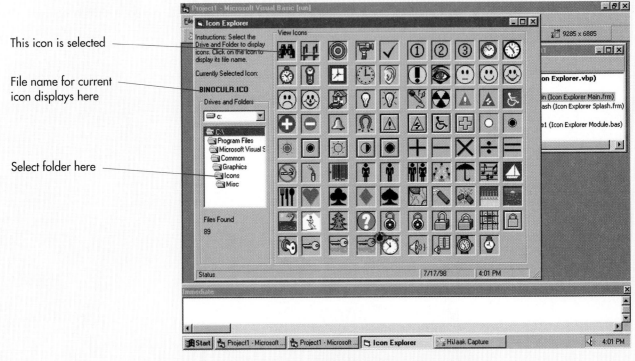

(h) Run and Debug the New Code (step 9)

FIGURE 4.10   Hands-on Exercise 2 (continued)

➤ Double click any folder below the Icons folder, The View Icons frame will display the images contained in that folder; the array of image controls will adjust automatically to the number of icons the folder contains.

➤ Click any icon to display its file name in bold letters.

➤ Test other folders to ensure that the icons are updated.

➤ The number label will update to show the number of icon files in the current folder.

➤ View the icons included with the Windows operating system. Click the **drive list box** and select the drive where Windows is installed on your computer.

➤ Click the **folders list box** and select **Windows**, and then **Icons**. The icons should display in the image controls. Click any icon to display its file name.

➤ If you have made any errors, you may receive a warning message, or forms or file controls may not display correctly. Repeat any previous steps as needed to debug your project.

➤ Close the Icon Explorer project window.

STEP 10: Print Your Project and Exit

➤ Pull down the **File menu** and select **Print** to display the Print dialog box.

➤ Select **Current Project** from the Range options as shown in Figure 4.10i.

Select form image here

Select project here

Select code here

Select form here

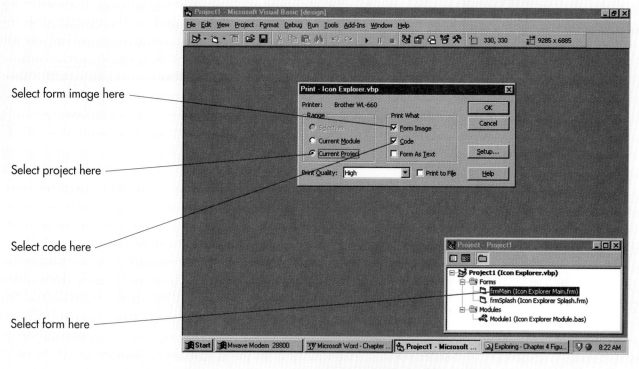

(i) Print Your Project and Exit (step 10)

FIGURE 4.10 Hands-on Exercise 2 (continued)

➤ Select **Form Image** and **Code** from the Print What options. Click the **OK button** to print the code and forms for the project.

➤ Several pages of code should print, and a page for each of the two forms. Examine the pages of code and verify that you understand what each of the procedures does.

➤ Close any open windows in the Visual Basic environment.

➤ Pull down the **File menu** and select **Exit**. The Save Changes message box will be displayed if you have not saved modifications made while debugging your project. Click **Yes** to save your changes and exit.

MENUS AND THE MENU EDITOR

Most people find it easier to point to and click items in a menu than to type commands. Therefore, most applications provide menus as a GUI component for giving commands to the computer. In this section, we will learn how to use menus in our applications.

One of our design principles was to follow the Microsoft guidelines for menu structure. When designing your menus, use the standard menu positions whenever possible. For example, the File command is always the first menu item on the menu bar, and Help is always the last. The menu bar is displayed immediately under the title bar in all Windows applications.

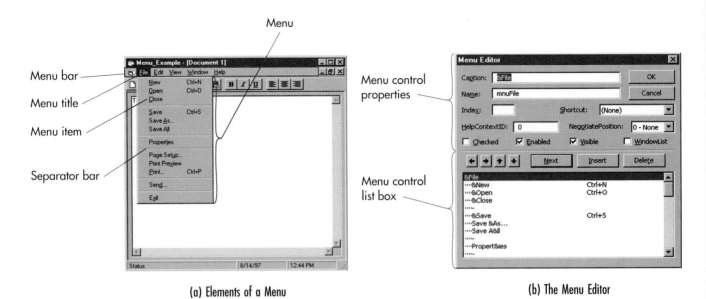

Menu

Menu bar

Menu title

Menu item

Separator bar

Menu control properties

Menu control list box

(a) Elements of a Menu

(b) The Menu Editor

FIGURE 4.11   Menus and the Menu Editor

Visual Basic includes the **Menu Editor** to make it easier to include menus in your applications. A simple menu example is shown in Figure 4.11a. The **menu bar** contains the menu titles that display across the top of the screen. The **menu titles** displayed in the figure are File, Edit, View, Window, and Help.

The Menu Editor window is shown in Figure 4.11b. Notice the top portion of the window allows you to set properties for the menu's controls. The bottom portion of the window is the menu control list box. As you add a menu, it is displayed here.

Setting Properties for Menu Commands

Most menu properties can be set using the Menu Editor. The three most important menu controls are the Name, Enabled, and Caption properties. These are the only properties you need to set most of the time. The **Name property** assigns the name you will use to refer to the menu control in your code. As a good programming practice, use the *mnu prefix* to designate a menu control. Notice that the File control is named mnuFile.

The **Enabled property** sets whether the menu control can respond to user actions. When the property is set to False, the menu item appears dimmed (grayed out) on the menu, and the user cannot select it. When the property is set to True, the menu item is displayed in black, and the user can select it. Setting the Enabled property to False for a menu title disables the entire menu because the user cannot click the title to get to any menu item. You can also disable or enable any menu control at run time by writing appropriate code.

The **Caption property** assigns the command that will be displayed on the menu bar or the submenus. You use the Caption property to assign keyboard access keys as well.

Access Keys

Notice that a letter is underlined for each menu command. The underlined letter defines the **access key** for the command. The user can use the keyboard instead of the mouse to select the menu commands by pressing the Alt key and the designated letter. For example, Alt+F is the keyboard access key for selecting

File from the menu bar. You assign an access key to a menu control in the Caption text box by typing an ampersand (&) immediately in front of the letter you want to be the access key. To assign X as the access key for the Exit command, enter E&xit as the caption.

Shortcut Keys

Frequently used menu items may be assigned a keyboard shortcut. A **keyboard shortcut** executes a menu item immediately. Keyboard shortcut keys are handy for commands that are available on submenus because the user only presses the Ctrl key and another character. This is quicker than the two-step process of selecting a menu title from the menu bar and then another command from a drop-down menu list. Commonly used shortcut keys are Ctrl+X for Cut, Ctrl+C for Copy, and Ctrl+V for Paste. You assign a shortcut key to a menu control by selecting a keyboard combination in the Shortcut combo box.

SHORTCUT KEYS

Shortcut keys appear automatically on the menu when you set the Shortcut property. You do not need to also enter the shortcut in the Caption property.

Separator Bar

Notice the separator bar displayed as a horizontal line below the Close commands on the menu. A **separator bar** is used to divide menu items into logical groups. To create a separator bar type a hyphen (-) in the Caption text box of a menu item.

Menu Design

Before using the Menu Editor, you must first design your menus. Decide the menu titles first and then the menu items. Menu design is important to the overall design of your Graphical User Interface. Let's add a few design rules for menus:

- Menu names should be short, usually a single word.
- Menu names should be unique for each menu. You can repeat a name in a different menu.
- Group menus commands logically. For example, you expect Cut, Copy, and Paste under the Edit command.
- Choose a logical access key for each menu item. Do not duplicate access keys. For example, Cut and Copy both start with a C, but assigning C to both commands could not possibly work. Use X (reminding you of scissors) for Cut and C for copy.
- Choose logical keyboard shortcuts for the most commonly used commands.

KEYBOARD SHORTCUTS: CUT, COPY, AND PASTE

Ctrl+X, Ctrl+C, and Ctrl+V are shortcuts to cut, copy, and paste, respectively. These shortcuts apply to Windows applications in general. They are logical if you realize the X reminds you of scissors or Xing out for cut, and the V for inserting or paste. The X, C, and V are also next to each other at the bottom-left side of the keyboard.

Let's continue the Learning Arithmetic project from Hands-on Exercise 1 and add a menu bar and menu items to the game. The menus were modeled after those of the Microsoft Solitaire game.

Add Menus to the Learning Arithmetic Project

Objective: Add a menu bar and more forms to the Learning Arithmetic game; use the Menu Editor to add menus; add code to display forms from the menu. Use Figure 4.12 as a guide for the exercise.

STEP 1: Open the Learning Arithmetic Project

➤ Start Visual Basic. Click the New Project dialog box's **Recent tab**.

➤ Click the **Learning Arithmetic file** to select it. Click the **Open button** to open the project. Set your Visual Basic options as shown in Chapter 2, Hands-on Exercise 1, Step 2 (page 47) if you want to ensure that the following steps look as much like the figures shown as possible.

➤ Pull down the **Tools** menu and select **Options**. Select the **Docking tab** in the Options dialog box. Uncheck the **Properties Window** and **Project Explorer** boxes. Click the **OK button** to apply the new options.

THE MOST RECENTLY OPENED FILES LIST

The easiest way to open a recently used project is to select it from the list of the most recently opened projects. This list is found at the end of the File menu.

STEP 2: Save the Project Files with a Different Name

➤ Open the **Project Explorer window** and double click the **Forms folder** to open it.

➤ Click the **About form** to select it.

➤ Pull down the **File menu** and select **Save Learning Arithmetic About As**. Select the drive and folder where you stored your data disk (*Exploring Visual Basic 6*) in the Save As dialog box. Enter **Learning Arithmetic with Menus About** in the File name text box.

➤ From the Project Explorer window, click the **Bears form** to select it. Pull down the **File menu** and select **Save Learning Arithmetic Bears As**.

➤ Enter **Learning Arithmetic with Menus Bears** in the File name text box. Click the **Save button** to save a copy of the file under a different file name.

➤ From the Project Explorer window, click the **Calculator form** to select it. Pull down the **File menu** and select **Save Learning Arithmetic Calculator As**.

➤ Enter **Learning Arithmetic with Menus Calculator** in the File name text box. Click the **Save button** to save a copy of the file under the new file name.

➤ From the Project Explorer window, click the **Splash form** to select it. Pull down the **File menu** and select **Save Learning Arithmetic Splash As**.

> Enter **Learning Arithmetic with Menus Splash** in the File name text box. Click the **Save button** to save a copy of the file under the new file name.

> From the Project Explorer window, double click the **Modules folder** to open it. Click the **Module1 file** to select it.

> Pull down the **File menu** and select **Save Learning Arithmetic Module As**. Enter **Learning Arithmetic with Menus Module** in the File name text box. Click the **Save button** to save a copy of the module under the new file name.

> Pull down the **File menu** and select **Save Project As** to display the Save Project As dialog box. Note that the Save in list box is set to the folder where you saved your forms and module. Enter **Learning Arithmetic with Menus** in the File name text box. Click the **Save button** to save the project file and close the dialog box.

STEP 3: Add Menu Titles

> Double click the **Calculator form** in the Project Explorer window to display the form.

> Pull down the **Tools menu** and select **Menu Editor** to open the Menu Editor window.

> In the top half of the Menu Editor window, click in the **Caption text box** and enter **&Game** as shown in Figure 4.12a. *&Game* will appear in the menu control list box at the bottom of the Menu Editor window.

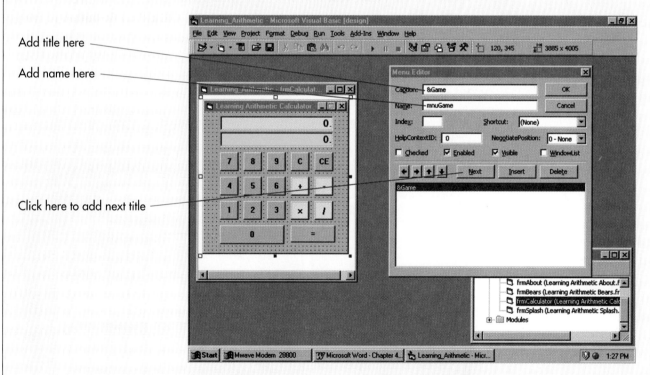

Add title here

Add name here

Click here to add next title

(a) Add Menu Titles (step 3)

FIGURE 4.12   Hands-on Exercise 3

> Click in the **Name text box** and enter **mnuGame**.

> Click the **Next command button** to add another menu title.

> Click in the **Caption text box** and enter **&Help**. *&Help* will appear in the menu control list box.

> Click in the **Name text box** and enter **mnuHelp**.

STEP 4: Add Menu Items

➤ Click the **Insert command button** to add a menu item under *Game*.

➤ Click in the **Caption text box** and enter **E&xit**.

➤ Click in the **Name text box** and enter **mnuExit**. E&xit should be selected in the menu control list box. Click the **right arrow button** to make the Exit command a submenu under *Game*.

➤ Click **&Help** in the menu control list box. Click the **Next command button** to add a submenu under Help.

➤ Move up and click in the **Caption text box** and enter **&How to Play Learning Arithmetic**.

➤ Click in the **Name text box** and enter **mnuHow**.

➤ Click the **right arrow button** to make this a submenu under *Help*.

➤ Click the **Next command button**.

➤ Move up and click in the **Caption text box** and enter a hyphen (-) to create a separator bar between menu items.

➤ Click in the **Name text box** and enter **mnuSeparator**.

➤ Click the **Next command button**.

➤ Click in the **Caption text box** and enter **&About Learning Arithmetic**.

➤ Click in the **Name text box** and enter **mnuAbout**.

➤ The Menu Editor should look like Figure 4.12b. Click the **OK button** to create the menus and exit the Menu Editor.

➤ You should now see your menu bar (Game Help) across the top of the Calculator window.

➤ Close the Calculator window.

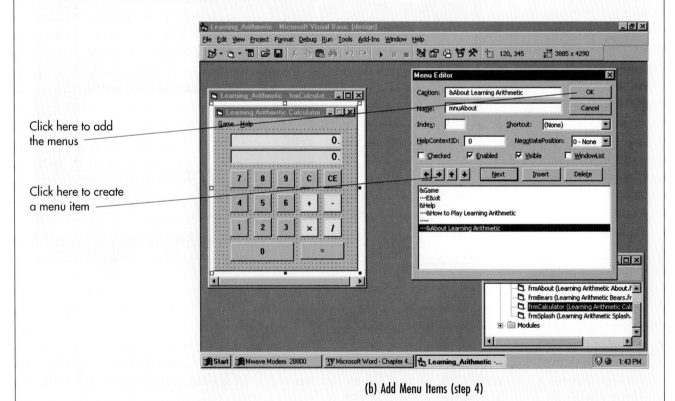

Click here to add the menus

Click here to create a menu item

(b) Add Menu Items (step 4)

FIGURE 4.12   Hands-on Exercise 3 (continued)

ARRANGING THE VISUAL BASIC DESKTOP

A *Visual Basic* project contains several objects that can be open at the same time. To size a window, point to any border or corner and drag in the desired direction. To move a window, point to the title bar and drag the window to its new location.

STEP 5: Modify the About Form

➤ In the Project Explorer window, double click the **About form** to display it.

➤ Open the Properties window. Verify that the Caption property for the form is **About Learning Arithmetic**. You may need to remove an underscore. Use Figure 4.12c as an aid to modify the form.

Add image here

Modify the labels

Modify properties here

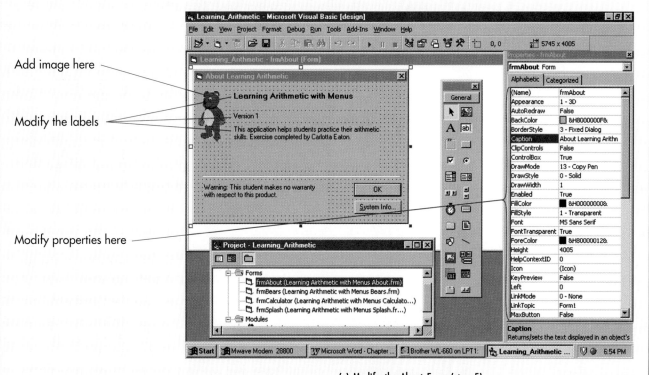

(c) Modify the About Form (step 5)

FIGURE 4.12   Hands-on Exercise 3 (continued)

➤ Click the **Application Title label** to select it. Change the Caption property to **Learning Arithmetic with Menus**. Change the Font property to **10 point, bold**.

➤ Click the **Version label** to select it. Change the Caption property to **Version 1**.

➤ Click the **App Description label** to select it. Modify the Caption property to **This application helps students practice their arithmetic skills. Exercise completed by Carlotta Eaton.** Change the name to your name.

➤ Click the Warning label to select it. Modify the Caption property to **Warning: This student makes no warranty with respect to this product.** You may need to resize the warning label smaller to avoid running over the command buttons.

➤ Click the **picture box control** to select it. Press the **Delete key** on your keyboard to delete the control. We will use the bear image here and will need to change its size. You cannot change the size of the image inside a picture box control. Therefore, you will replace the picture box with an image control on the form.

➤ Open the Toolbox and click the **Image tool**.

➤ Move to the Form Designer window and draw an image control to replace the picture box. Change the Name property to **imgLogo**. Change the Picture property to the drive and folder for your data disk (*Exploring Visual Basic 6*) and select the **bear.bmp** file.

➤ Change the Stretch property to **True** so that you can change the size of the bear.

➤ Click the **bear image** to display sizing handles. Grab a corner handle, drag the bear, and make it smaller as shown in the figure.

➤ Pull down the **File menu** and select **Save Learning Arithmetic with Menus About** to save your changes to the form.

➤ Close the About form.

THE ABOUT BOX

Most Windows applications have an *About* menu title. Clicking the menu title displays an About box identifying the application and the software vendor that created it. Visual Basic makes it easy to provide such About boxes. You can create an About box using a form or a dialog box.

STEP 6: Add the HowTo Form

➤ Close the Properties window and the Toolbox. Pull down the **Project menu** and select **Add Form**. Click the **New Tab** in the Add Form dialog box.

➤ Click the **Form icon** and click the **Open button** to open the new form.

➤ The new form will be displayed. Move the cursor to the bottom edge of the new form until the double-headed arrow appears. Click and drag the form until it is the approximate size shown in Figure 4.12d (page 200).

➤ Right click anywhere on the form and select **Properties** from the context menu. Set the following properties for the form:

Property	Setting
Name	frmHowTo
BorderStyle	1- Fixed Single
Caption	How To Play Learning Arithmetic
MaxButton	False

STEP 7: Add Controls to the HowTo Form

➤ Open the Toolbox and select the **Text Box tool**.

➤ Drag a text box almost as large as the form, as shown in the figure.

➤ Move to the Properties window and set the following properties:

Property	Setting
Name	txtHowTo
Appearance	0 – Flat
BackColor	Gray
BorderStyle	0 – None
Locked	True
MousePointer	1 – Arrow
MultiLine	True

➤ You will be adding long lines of text next, so drag the Properties window as wide as possible to allow enough room to enter the text.

➤ Click in the **Text property setting** and type in the first line as shown below and in Figure 4.12d. Press **enter**. Click the arrow in the setting box again and add the second line by pressing the **space bar** and then **enter**. Repeat until you have added all the lines.

```
Hello Parent, Teacher or Student,

1. The Learning Arithmetic game displays a math problem in the blue
   display area.
2. Click the number keys to display your answer in the yellow area.
3. Click the = key to check your answer.
     The problem and the correct answer appear in the blue area.
     If you were right, a bear appears on the second screen.
     If wrong, a bear disappears from the screen.

4. Click the CE key to clear your answer and try again. Or:
5. Click the C key to display another problem.
6. Click the +, -, x, or / key to change the type of problem.
7. To end the game, click the Close button in the upper right
   corner.

Have fun!
```

➤ Resize the Properties window so that you can see the HowTo window.

➤ Move to the Toolbox and click the **Command Button tool**. Drag a command button and place it on the form as shown in the figure.

➤ Move to the Properties window and set the following properties:

Property	Setting
Name	cmdOK
Caption	OK
Default	True

➤ Pull down the **File menu** and select **Save frmHowTo** to save your changes to the form.

➤ **Close** the Properties, Toolbox, and HowTo form windows.

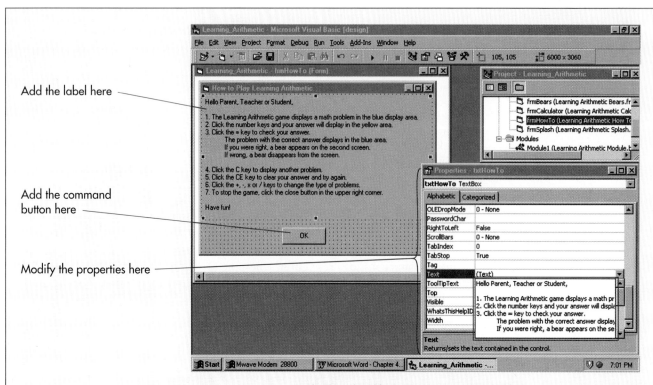

Add the label here

Add the command button here

Modify the properties here

(d) Add and Modify the HowTo Form (steps 6 and 7)

FIGURE 4.12 Hands-on Exercise 3 (continued)

STEP 8: Add Code to Activate the Menus

➤ Open the Project Explorer window and double click the **Calculator form** to display it.

➤ Click the **Game menu title** to display the drop-down menu.

➤ Click the **Exit menu item** to open the Code Editor window.

➤ Verify that the **mnuExit object** and **Click procedure** are selected.

➤ Add the code shown below and in Figure 4.12e for the event procedure.

```
Private Sub mnuExit_Click()
'Purpose: File...Exit menu event procedure
'         End game
  End
End Sub
```

➤ Select the **mnuAbout object** and the **Click procedure** in the Code Editor window.

➤ Add the code shown below and in the figure:

```
Private Sub mnuAbout_Click()
'Purpose: Help...About menu event procedure
'         Display About form
  frmAbout.Show
End Sub
```

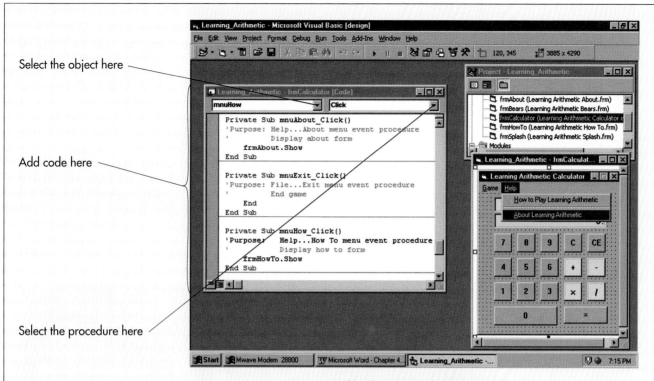

Select the object here

Add code here

Select the procedure here

(e) Add Code to Activate the Menus (step 8)

FIGURE 4.12 Hands-on Exercise 3 (continued)

➤ Select the **mnuHow** object and the **Click procedure**. Add the code shown below and in the figure:

```
Private Sub mnuHow_Click()
'Purpose: Help...How To menu event procedure
'          Display HowTo form
   frmHowTo.Show
End Sub
```

➤ Pull down the **File menu** and select **Save Learning Arithmetic with Menus Calculator**. Click the **Save button** to save your code changes.
➤ Close the Code Editor window and the Calculator form window.

USE RESTRAINT

More is not better, especially in the case of too many colors that detract from a form rather than enhance it. Visual Basic makes it very easy to switch foreground and background colors and change fonts and styles. Use restraint. A simple form is far more effective than one that uses too many fonts and colors simply because they are there.

STEP 9: Add Code for the HowTo Form

➤ Open the Project Explorer window and double click the **HowTo form** to open it.

➤ Double click the **OK button** to display the Code Editor window with the corresponding code.

➤ Add the code shown below and in Figure 4.12f:

```
Private Sub cmdOK_Click()
'Purpose: OK button click event procedure
'          Close the HowTo form
  Unload frmHowTo
End Sub
```

Double click here to display the form

Enter code here

Double click here to display code

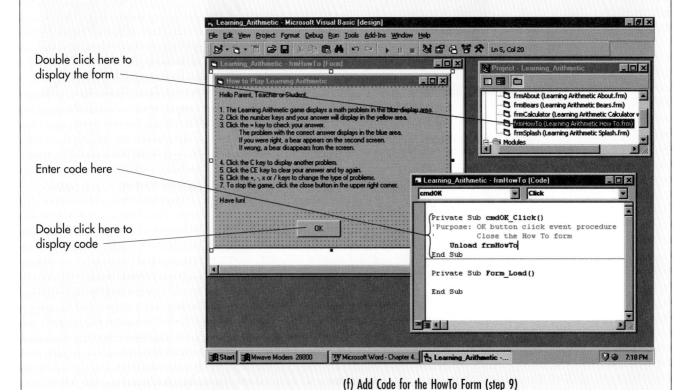

(f) Add Code for the HowTo Form (step 9)

FIGURE 4.12   Hands-on Exercise 3 (continued)

➤ Pull down the **File menu** and select **Save HowTo As**. Enter **Learning Arithmetic with Menus HowTo** in the File name text box. Click the **Save button** to save your form and code changes.

➤ Close the Code Editor window and the HowTo form window.

STEP 10: Add Code for the About Form

➤ In the Project Explorer window, double click the **About form** to open it.

➤ Double click the **OK button** to display the Code Editor window with the corresponding code.

➤ Modify the code to match that shown below:

```
Private Sub cmdOK_Click()
'Purpose: OK button click event procedure
'         Close the About form
  Unload frmAbout
End Sub
```

➤ Pull down the **File menu** and select **Save Learning Arithmetic with Menus About**. Click the **Save button** to save your code changes.

➤ Close the Code Editor window and the About form window.

STEP 11: Test the Menus and Forms

➤ Close any open windows.

➤ Click the toolbar's **Start** button. If the Save Changes message box is displayed, click **Yes** to save your file changes.

➤ The Splash form will be displayed briefly. The Calculator and Bear forms will be displayed.

➤ In the Calculator form, pull down the **Help menu** and select **How to Play Learning Arithmetic**.

➤ The HowTo form will be displayed, as shown in Figure 4.12g. Click the **OK button** to close the form.

➤ In the Calculator form, pull down the **Help menu**, and select **About Learning Arithmetic**.

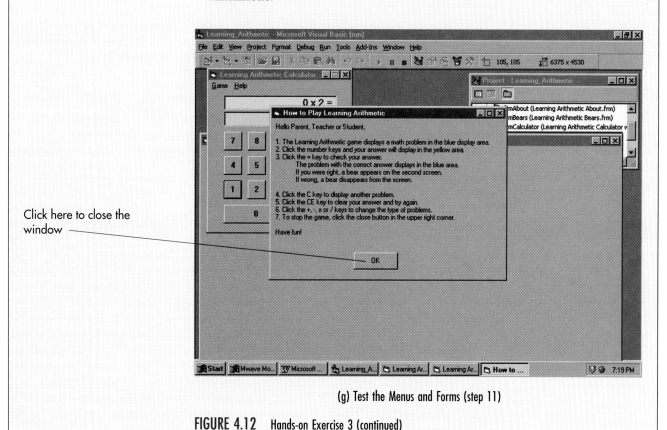

(g) Test the Menus and Forms (step 11)

FIGURE 4.12   Hands-on Exercise 3 (continued)

➤ The About form will be displayed, as shown in Figure 4.12h.

Click here to close the window

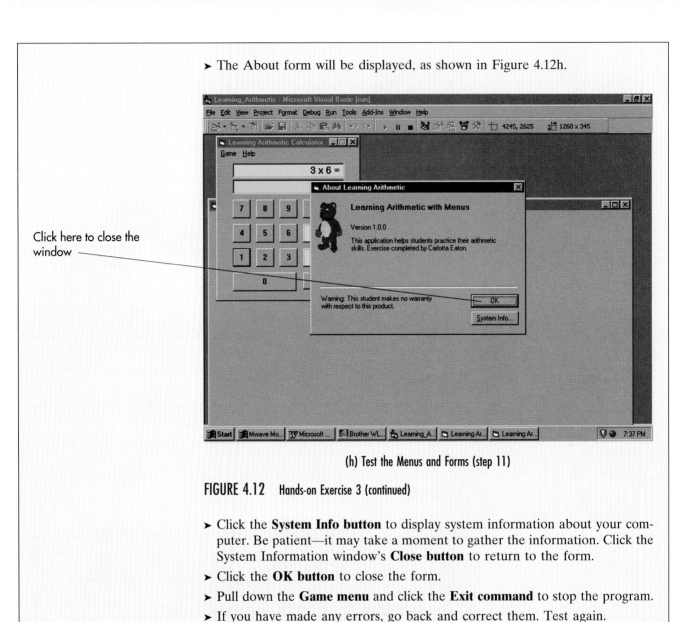

(h) Test the Menus and Forms (step 11)

FIGURE 4.12 Hands-on Exercise 3 (continued)

➤ Click the **System Info button** to display system information about your computer. Be patient—it may take a moment to gather the information. Click the System Information window's **Close button** to return to the form.

➤ Click the **OK button** to close the form.

➤ Pull down the **Game menu** and click the **Exit command** to stop the program.

➤ If you have made any errors, go back and correct them. Test again.

➤ When you finish, your menus and forms should display beautifully.

➤ Exit Visual Basic, saving any changes you have made.

SUMMARY

The chapter showed you how to design and create a Graphical User Interface for your applications. The design should take into consideration the five basic design principles of knowing your end user, being consistent, using informative graphics and messages, keeping it simple, and letting the user control the application. After designing the interface on paper, you can create forms for your screens and windows. Add controls to forms with tools from the Toolbox. The Toolbox always contains the pointer plus tools for creating 20 intrinsic controls. Intrinsic controls are available to add text, obtain input, add graphics, control the file system and data, and group objects. ActiveX controls and Insertable Objects can be added to the Toolbox at any time. Choose controls appropriate to the application. For example, use a File list box instead of an ordinary list box to display lists of files.

Set properties for the controls to determine how they look and behave. Properties can be set at design time or at run time. To change properties during run time, you need to add code to your project. Add menus to your project using the Menu Editor included with Visual Basic. You also add code to your project to activate the menus.

You created an application for children that used a calculator as a visual model. In the next hands-on exercise, you displayed the hundreds of icons that are included with Visual Basic and can be utilized in other projects. Finally, you created a simple menu that displayed different forms.

KEY WORDS AND CONCEPTS

Access key
ActiveX control
Check box control
Combo box control
Command button
 control
Control
Data control
Directory list box
 control
Drive list box control
Explorer-style interface
File list box control
Frame control
Graphical User Interface
 (GUI)

Horizontal scroll bar
 control
Image control
Insertable object
Intrinsic control
Keyboard shortcut
Label control
Line control
List box control
Menu
Menu bar
Menu Editor
Menu item
Menu title
Multiple Document
 Interface (MDI)

OLE container control
Option button control
Picture box control
Pointer
Property
Prototype
Single Document
 Interface (SDI)
Shape control
Text box control
Timer control
Toolbox
Usability test
Vertical scroll bar
 control

MULTIPLE CHOICE

1. When designing the Graphical User Interface for your end user, you should consider
   (a) the age of the end user
   (b) the reading ability of the end user
   (c) using graphics instead of words for preschoolers
   (d) all of the above

2. When designing a consistent Graphical User Interface, you should
   (a) be creative and use as many different fonts and colors as possible
   (b) follow the Windows conventions whenever possible
   (c) use a logical design for your menus and place them in different positions from most Windows applications
   (d) use as many different icons and graphics as possible

3. When designing the Graphical User Interface and using graphics,
   (a) use as many different icons and graphics as possible
   (b) use Windows graphics and icons as whenever possible
   (c) use graphics and icons to save time and money when translating to different languages for a worldwide market
   (d) items b and c

4. When designing the Graphical User Interface for user control,
   (a) direct the user as much as possible to follow a single predefined path
   (b) direct the user with the accompanying user manual at all times
   (c) let the user control the conversation with the mouse and keyboard
   (d) all of the above

5. A twip is
   (a) a screen-dependent unit of measurement for forms and controls
   (b) a screen-independent unit of measurement for forms and controls
   (c) an acronym for twenty picture elements
   (d) the dots on a monitor

6. The three broad categories for controls are
   (a) standard, default, and custom controls
   (b) basic, default, and custom controls
   (c) intrinsic, ActiveX, and insertable objects
   (d) standard, custom, and OLE controls

7. The control best suited to displaying text that the user cannot change and cannot click is called a
   (a) label
   (b) text box
   (c) command button
   (d) any of the above would be appropriate

8. The control used to logically group other controls is called a(n)
   (a) OLE container
   (b) frame control
   (c) data control
   (d) list control

9. The control that is capable of displaying an icon (using fewer resources) and being clicked to carry out a command is called a(n)
   (a) image
   (b) command button
   (c) picture box
   (d) shape

10. The control that is best suited to display a text button that could be clicked to carry out a command is a(n)
    (a) text box
    (b) label
    (c) command button
    (d) any of the above would be appropriate

11. The control that is best suited to display a list where only one choice is allowed is a(n)
   (a) check box
   (b) option button
   (c) combination box
   (d) list box

12. The control that is best suited to display a list where several choices are allowed is a(n)
   (a) check box
   (b) option button
   (c) combination list box
   (d) list box

13. The control that is best suited to display the location of a file that the user chooses is an
   (a) list box
   (b) drive list box, directory list box, and file list box utilized together
   (c) combination box
   (d) check box

14. You can set properties for forms and controls
   (a) at design time only
   (b) at run time only
   (c) at design time and run time
   (d) at run time only using code

15. The items displayed on the menu bar are called
   (a) menu items
   (b) menu titles
   (c) access keys
   (d) shortcut keys

ANSWERS

1. d	**6.** c	**11.** b
2. b	**7.** a	**12.** a
3. d	**8.** b	**13.** b
4. c	**9.** a	**14.** c
5. b	**10.** c	**15.** b

PRACTICE WITH VISUAL BASIC

LOCATE THE SAMPLES

You will be running several sample applications included with Visual Basic in these exercises. If you are using Visual Basic 6.0, look for them first in the default location by opening these folders: Microsoft Visual Studio, then Msdn98 (optionally 98vs, then 1033), then Samples, and finally Vb98. If you are using Visual Basic 5.0, open Microsoft Visual Studio, then Vb, then samples.

1. **Controls Demonstration Sample.** Run the *Control* sample project provided with Visual Basic to demonstrate the use of several controls in seven different forms. See the tip box "Locate the Samples" to help you find the sample applications. Open the Controls folder and run the project. Some of the forms are shown in Figure 4.13. As you execute the application, make a list of the controls contained on each of the forms. Submit your list to your instruction as evidence that you completed the exercise.

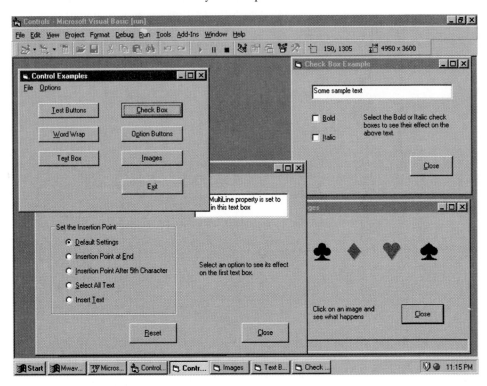

FIGURE 4.13   Screen for Practice Exercise 1: The Controls Sample Application

2. **MDI vs. SDI Interface Style.** Compare the sample Notepad applications coded in the two different interface styles: MDI (Multiple Document Interface) and SDI (Single Document Interface) as shown in Figure 4.14. The *MDInote* project is located in the MDI folder, and the *SDInote* project is located in the SDI folder. See the tip box "Locate the Samples" to help you find the sample projects.

(a) MDI Notepad   (b) SDI Notepad

FIGURE 4.14   Screens for Practice Exercise 2

Run both projects and keep a list of the differences between the two interface styles. List some advantages and disadvantages of each style. Which style do you prefer for this simple Notepad application? Why?

VIDEO CLIP

3. **A Successful Windows Application: Demonstration (Learning Edition Only).** This exercise requires that you be using the Learning Edition of Visual Basic 5.0 or 6.0, and that you have installed the *Learn Visual Basic Now* book on your hard drive or have access to it from the CD-ROM. This video clip, one of several included on the *Learn Visual Basic Now* CD, shows the components of a successful Windows application. Run and watch the animation clip to reinforce this material from the chapter. As you watch the video clip, keep a list of the components of a successful windows applications. Submit your list to your instructor as evidence that you completed this exercise. Watch and learn.

    a. Start Learn Visual Basic Now.

    b. Open the Chapter 1 book, then the Developing Visual Basic Programs book, and the Building the Program book.

    c. Open the Creating a User Interface topic. In the topic pane, click the animation icon.

    d. View the entire animation video clip.

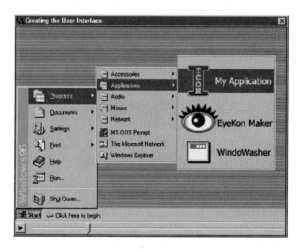

FIGURE 4.15   Screen for Practice Exercise 3: A Successful Windows Application

4. **Graphic Explorer Project.** Modify the Icon Explorer project you created in Hands-on Exercise 2 in this chapter. Change the interface to display several thumbnail images (small images) on a form. This application can be used to browse the images on your computer as well as images you download from the Internet. Save your project files as **Graphic Explorer** and your forms with appropriate names. Visual Basic 5.0 and 6.0 recognize the following graphic formats: bitmap (*.bmp*) files, icon (*.ico*) files, run-length encoded (*.rle*) files, metafile (*.wmf*) files, enhanced metafiles (*.emf*), GIF (*.gif*) files, and JPEG (*.jpg*) files. Use the LoadPicture function to load a graphic into a form's Picture property, a PictureBox control, or an Image control. This can be a very useful utility to browse the graphic files on your computer.

5. **My Calendar.** Use the ActiveX calendar control provided by Microsoft to create a calendar application. An example is shown in Figure 4.16. Pull down the Project menu and select Components. Click the Controls tab in the dialog box and select Microsoft Calendar Control 8.0 to add the control to your toolbox. Create forms using this ActiveX control and save your project as **My Calendar**. Set the properties to your birthdate. What day of the week were you born? Save your forms with appropriate file names.

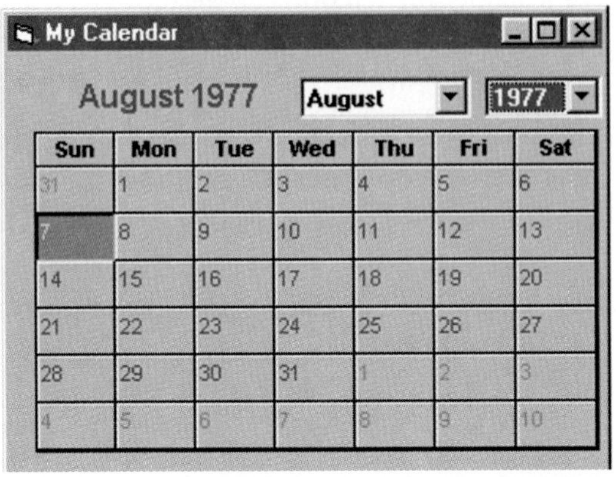

FIGURE 4.16   Screen for Practice Exercise 5: My Calendar

CASE STUDIES

Create a Prototype

Use the design guidelines to create a prototype Graphical User Interface for your favorite application. You can create an original application or redesign the interface for an application you have used in the past. Write down the specifications of the project first. Next, sketch the user interface on paper, remembering to keep your user in mind. Finally, create your interface using forms, controls, and the Menu Editor. Because this is a prototype, don't worry about the code to enable your interface as this point. Concentrate on the interface itself. If you are redesigning an existing interface, list the advantages of your new design. Make a printout of your forms and include them when submitting this case study to your instructor.

Insertable Objects

Use any Insertable Object provided in Visual Basic and create an application using the control. Choose a fun object such as the Midi Sequence that plays MIDI sound files or another object that looks interesting. If you are familiar with the Office applications, you may want to add a Word document, an Excel worksheet or chart, or maybe a PowerPoint slide. Add the Insertable Object to your Toolbox and then use the new tool to create the desired control on a form. Save your project as **Insertable Objects Case Study** and your forms with appropriate file names.

ActiveX Controls

Use any ActiveX control provided in Visual Basic and create an application using the control. Information on the ActiveX controls available can be found in Visual Basic Documentation. Open the **Reference** book, then the **Controls Reference** book, then the **ActiveX Controls** book for Visual Basic 6.0. You may want to add more fun to your projects and check out the animation, Multimedia MCI, or PictureClip controls. Save your project as **ActiveX Case Study** and your forms with appropriate file names.

ACTIVEX CONTROLS USING VISUAL BASIC 5.0

If you are using Visual Basic 5.0, open the *Visual Basic Help* book, and then the *Controls* book for more information on ActiveX controls.

Controls from the Web

There is a wealth of clip art and images available on the Web. There are also free demonstrations of Visual Basic controls available from third-party vendors available on the Web. Use a search engine and search for *"Visual Basic and ActiveX"* to start your search. You could start at one of the many Visual Basic Web addresses given in previous case studies and exercises in this book. There are ways to include animated GIF files, movie clips, sounds, and other multimedia objects in your projects. Create a project using the information you found on the Web. The information could be a new control, using existing controls in a creative way. Save your project as **Web Controls Case Study** and your forms with appropriate file names.

BASICS OF FILE INPUT AND OUTPUT: READING, WRITING, AND PRINTING TEXT FILES

OBJECTIVES

After this chapter you will be able to:

1. Explain the use of the common dialog control for Windows 95.
2. Use the common dialog control to display dialog boxes to open and save files, set printer options, and select colors and fonts.
3. Explain and implement common file input and output operations such as open, close, save, and print.
4. Write code to open an existing file and display text in a text box; save a modified text file from a text box to a selected file.
5. Distinguish between text files and binary files; explain the uses of special text file formats such as RTF and HTML.
6. Distinguish between sequential access, binary access, and random access to files.
7. Use the File System Object (FSO) model to process text files using sequential access.
8. Use string functions to modify text in a text box.
9. Print forms and text from your application.
10. Write code to handle errors by trapping problems and avoiding runtime error crashes.

OVERVIEW

This chapter demonstrates input/output techniques for working with text files. Input/Output, or simply I/O, refers to an operation, program, or device that enters data into a computer or extracts data from a computer.

We will utilize the Windows 95 operating system's most commonly used dialog boxes for working with files. These dialog boxes are displayed for opening, saving, and printing files, for selecting fonts and colors, and for displaying help.

The common dialog control in Visual Basic provides access to these Windows 95 dialog boxes. We choose the controls appropriate to display the corresponding dialog box. The control only displays a dialog box; additional code must be written to actually perform the box's function.

Access means to read data from or write data to a storage device such as a diskette or hard drive. There are three major types of file access for working with text files: sequential, random, and binary. (The Access application program is not to be confused with file access. Database files are not discussed in this chapter, but are detailed in Chapters 7 and 8.)

The File System Object (FSO) model is a new feature for Visual Basic 6.0. You will implement sequential access to text files using FSO (or alternatively the older file processing statements) in three hands-on exercises. The Sticky Pad project displays little yellow sticky notes on your screen. This is a fun project that can be useful as well.

WINDOWS DIALOG BOXES

The Windows operating system provides several dialog boxes. The Open dialog box displays when we open a file in applications such as Word, Excel, or PowerPoint. The Save As dialog box displays when we save a file with a new name. The Color dialog box displays when we change and select a color for fonts or borders. The Font dialog box displays when we change and select fonts. The Print dialog box displays when we select printer options. The Help dialog box can be used to run the Windows Help system and display help files.

The dialog boxes shown in Figure 5.1 are useful for working with files. The *Open* dialog box is displayed when opening files. The *Save As* dialog box is used when saving files. The *Print* dialog box is used to print files or select printer options.

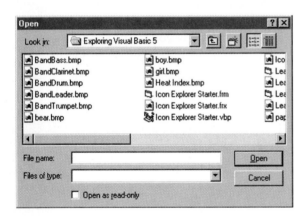

(a) Open Dialog Box

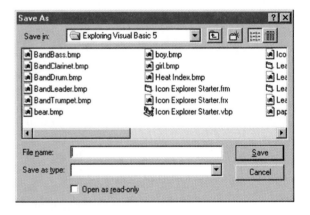

(b) Save As Dialog Box

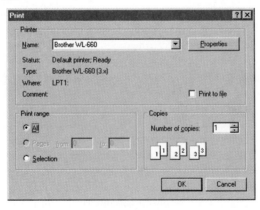

(c) Print Dialog Box

FIGURE 5.1 Dialog Boxes for Files

The dialog boxes shown in Figure 5.2 are useful when working with text. The **Font** dialog box is the standard technique for selecting fonts. The **Color** dialog box is used to select colors. The Help dialog box, not shown in the figure, is used to display Help files. Because the Microsoft Windows Help Compiler is required to build Help files, and is not a part of the Learning Edition of Visual Basic, we do not cover the Help dialog box in this chapter.

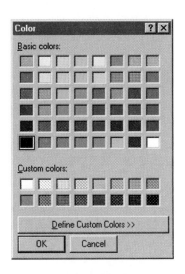

(a) Color Dialog Box

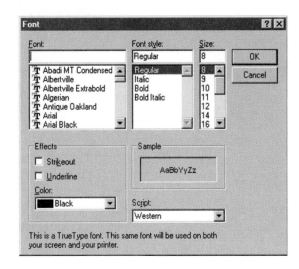

(b) Font Dialog Box

FIGURE 5.2   Common Dialog Boxes for Formatting Text

THE COMMON DIALOG CONTROL

FIGURE 5.3
The Common
Dialog Tool

The **common dialog control** provides access to the Windows operating system's most commonly used dialog boxes as shown in the previous figures. We choose the appropriate method for the common dialog control to display the corresponding dialog box. The control only displays a dialog box; additional code must be written to actually perform the box's function.

Recall that the dialog boxes invoked by the common dialog control are actually part of the Windows operating system. The control simply acts as an intermediary, or middleman, for the programmer. Microsoft included the code for the dialog boxes in the operating system to ensure that the boxes would have a standard look in Windows applications. The dialog boxes differ for Windows 3.x, Windows 95, and Windows 98. If you use the common dialog control, your dialog boxes should be consistent with the current version of the operating system.

To create a common dialog control, you simply select the **Common Dialog tool** (shown in Figure 5.3), from the Toolbox and place it on a form. It is an ActiveX control (not an intrinsic control), so it must be added to the Toolbox. Like the timer control, it is invisible at run time; and it controls the display of the various dialog boxes.

There are several properties associated with the common dialog control. The Filter property applies to the Open and Save As dialog boxes. The **Filter property** selects the files to display based on their file extensions. Most applications use this property to display only the files that can be modified with the application. For example, the Word application defaults to Word documents (*.*doc*) when opening files, and Excel defaults to (*.*xls*).

We will be working with text files in the exercises, so the Filter property will be set with code as shown below:

```
dlgCommon.Filter = "Text file (*.txt) | *.txt"
```

where the pipe symbol (|) separates a description of the filter which will appear in the dialog box's list box—*Text file (*.txt)*—from the filter itself—*.txt.*

The Windows 95 common dialog boxes are displayed by means of the common dialog control's methods. The syntax for the common dialog control's methods is shown in the following box:

CommonDialogName.Method
where
    CommonDialogName is the Name property assigned to the common
        dialog control
    Method is one of the following:
        ShowOpen displays the Open dialog box used for opening files
        ShowSave displays the Save As dialog box used for saving files
        ShowColor displays the Color dialog box used for setting or
            changing the color of text, background, etc.
        ShowFont displays the Font dialog box used for setting and changing
            the font, font size, and font styles
        ShowPrinter displays the Print dialog box used to select a printer and
            the number of printed copies
        ShowHelp starts the Windows Help engine

The Sticky Pad Project

Let's use the common dialog control in the Sticky Pad project. You probably use sticky notes for all sorts of things. Go into any office with a computer and you will probably see a sticky note attached to the monitor as a reminder. These are, of course, the Post-it™ Notes from 3M. They initially were yellow, but now they come in several colors and sizes, and can even be personalized. The Sticky Pad project is a simple computer version of the physical sticky pads. 3M markets an application called Post-it® Software Notes. Microsoft Outlook also contains a Notes feature, and lets you save sticky notes using the (*.msg*) extension.

The project can display a single sticky note or several, as shown in Figure 5.4. Each sticky note can be edited, resized, and moved anywhere on your screen. Each note is an instance of a form and is stored as a separate text file.

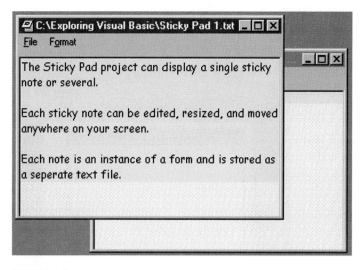

FIGURE 5.4   The Sticky Pad Project

Create the Sticky Pad Project Using the Common Dialog Control

Objective: Create a program to display sticky notes on the screen. Create a single form, and display several instances for the sticky notes. Use the common dialog control to display dialog boxes for working with text files. Use Figure 5.5 as a guide for the exercise.

STEP 1: Create a New Project and a New Form

➤ Start **Visual Basic**. Click the New Project dialog box's **New tab**.

➤ Click the **Standard EXE icon**. Click the **Open button** to open a new project window. Set your Visual Basic options as shown in Chapter 2, Hands-on Exercise 1, Step 2 (see page 47) if you want to ensure that the following steps look as much like the figures shown as possible.

➤ Pull down the **File menu** and select **Save Project** to name and save the project files. Enter **Sticky Pad** (was Form1) in the File name text box. Select the drive and folder where you stored your data disk (*Exploring Visual Basic 6*). Click the **Save button** to save the form file.

➤ In the Save Project As dialog box, enter **Sticky Pad** in the File name text box. Click the **Save button** to save the project file and close the dialog box.

➤ Click the **No button** in the Source Code Control dialog box.

➤ Open the Project Explorer and Properties windows. Use Figure 5.5a as a guide in setting up your screen display.

➤ Move to the Project Explorer window and click **Project1 (Sticky Pad.vbp)** to set the project's properties.

➤ Move to the Properties window and change the project's Name property to **StickyPad**.

➤ In the Project Explorer window, open the **Forms folder** and double click **Form1 (Sticky Pad.frm)** to display the Form Designer window. Move, undock, and resize the windows as appropriate so you can work with the form.

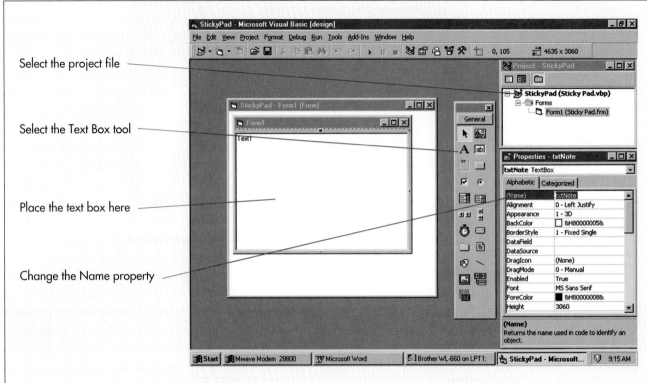

Select the project file

Select the Text Box tool

Place the text box here

Change the Name property

(a) Create a New Project and a New Form (step 1)

FIGURE 5.5   Hands-on Exercise 1

➤ Click the toolbar's **Toolbox button** to display the Toolbox. Select the **Text Box tool** and draw a text box on the form as shown in the figure.

➤ Move to the Properties window and change the following properties:

Property	Setting
Name	txtNote
MultiLine	True

STEP 2: Set the Form's Properties Using Code

➤ From the Properties window, change the following form properties:

Property	Setting
Name	frmStickyPad
Icon	Icons\Writing\Note02.ico

FIND THE ICON LIBRARY FILES

An Icon Library is included with both Visual Basic 5.0 and 6.0. You can find the icon files at \Vb\Graphics\Icons using Visual Basic 5.0, or alternatively at Microsoft Visual Studio\Common\Graphics\Icons using Visual Basic 6.0.

➤ Pull down the **View menu** and select **Code**. Click the **Object list box arrow** and select **Form**. Position the cursor below the Sub statement line and enter the following block of code, which loads the form and sets properties. The initial form will be centered on the screen. (We will see the meaning of the Me keyword later in the chapter.)

```
Private Sub Form_Load()
' Purpose: Loads a form
  Dim Inch As Integer
  Inch = 1440    '1440 twips = 1 logical inch

  With Me   'current note form
        'Application Title is Sticky Pad
        'Forms Count = number of forms loaded
        .Caption = App.Title & " " & Forms.Count
        'Set background to light yellow
        txtNote.BackColor = RGB(255, 255, 100)
        .Height = 2.5 * Inch
        .Width = 2.5 * Inch
  End With
  'Center initial form
  If Forms.Count = 1 Then
        Me.Move (Screen.Width - Me.Width) / 2, _
            (Screen.Height - Me.Height) /2
  End If
End Sub
```

➤ In the Procedures list box, select **Resize**. Enter the following code to resize the text box when the form is resized.

```
Private Sub Form_Resize()
' Purpose: Resize the text box when the form is resized
  Me.txtNote.Height = ScaleHeight
  Me.txtNote.Width = ScaleWidth
End Sub
```

STEP 3: Test the Form Code

➤ Close the Code Editor and Toolbox windows. Click the toolbar's **Start button**.

➤ If the Save Changes message box is displayed, click **Yes** to continue and save your coding changes.

CHOOSING COLORS WITH THE RGB FUNCTION

You can specify colors such as the background using the RGB function. The color is specified by giving its red, green, and blue components in the form of numbers between 0 and 255. For example:

White = RGB (255, 255, 255)   Black = RGB (0, 0, 0)
Yellow = RGB (255, 255, 0)   Gray = RGB (128, 128, 128)
Red = RGB(255, 0, 0)   Green = RGB(0, 255, 0)
Blue = RGB(0, 0, 255)   Light Yellow = RGB(255, 255, 100)

➤ Correct any typing errors.

➤ Your form should display as shown in Figure 5.5b. Enter text in the text box. The background should remain yellow.

➤ Minimize the form, and notice the yellow pad icon on the taskbar. Restore the form from the taskbar.

➤ Resize the form. The text box should resize with the form.

➤ Close the form.

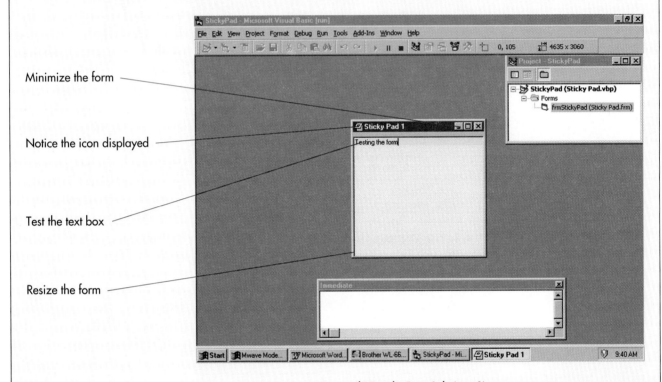

Minimize the form

Notice the icon displayed

Test the text box

Resize the form

(b) Test the Form Code (step 3)

FIGURE 5.5   Hands-on Exercise 1

STEP 4: Add the Common Dialog Control

➤ Click the toolbar's **Toolbox button** to display the Toolbox.

➤ If the Common Dialog tool is not displayed in the Toolbox, pull down the **Project menu** and select **Components**. Select the **Controls tab**. Check **Microsoft Common Dialog Control 5.0** or **6.0** component. Click the **OK button** to add the tool to the Toolbox.

➤ Select the **Common Dialog tool** as shown in Figure 5.5c.

➤ Move to the form and draw the control. You cannot resize the control, and it will not display at run time, so position is not important.

➤ Move to the Properties window and change the control's Name property to **dlgDialogs**.

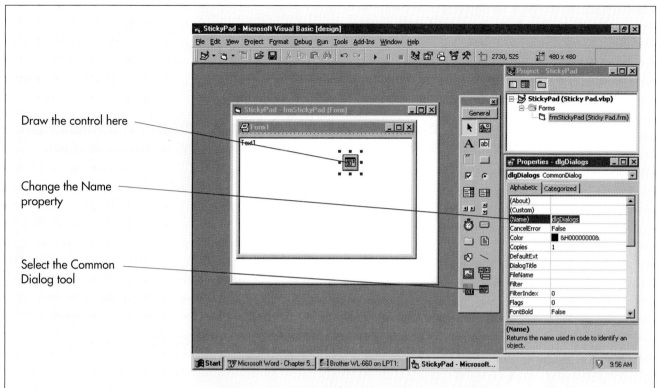

Draw the control here

Change the Name property

Select the Common Dialog tool

(c) Add the Common Dialog Control (step 4)

FIGURE 5.5   Hands-on Exercise 1

ACTIVEX CONTROLS

The Learning Edition automatically displays only the intrinsic controls in the Toolbox. The common dialog control is an ActiveX control, so it is not automatically displayed. The Professional and Enterprise editions have a larger selection of ActiveX controls than the Learning Edition.

STEP 5: Create the Menus

➤ Click the form to select it.

➤ Pull down the **Tools menu** and select **Menu Editor**. Enter the following menu items:

Level	Caption	Name
Title	&File	mnuFile
Menu Item	&New Note	mnuNew
Menu Item	&Open Note...	mnuOpen
Menu Item	&Save Note / Save Note As...	mnuSave
Menu Item	&Close Note without Saving	mnuClose
Menu Item	-	mnuDash1
Menu Item	Print Set&up...	mnuSetup
Menu Item	&Print Note...	mnuPrint
Menu Item	-	mnuDash2
Menu Item	E&xit	mnuExit
Title	F&ormat	mnuFormat
Menu Item	&Font...	mnuFont
Menu Item	&Background...	mnuColor

➤ Click the **OK button** to create the menu. Remember that an ellipsis (...) indicates that choosing the menu item will display a dialog box. You will use the common dialog control to display the appropriate dialog box.

➤ Go to the form and pull down the **File menu**. The menu will look like Figure 5.5d.

➤ Pull down the form's **Format menu**. The menu will look like Figure 5.5e.

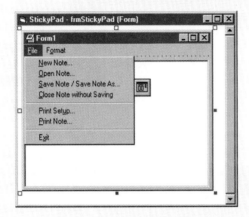

(d) Create the File Menu (step 5)

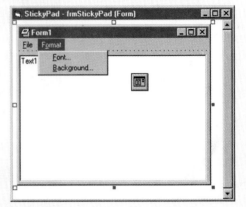

(e) Create the Format Menu (step 5)

FIGURE 5.5   Hands-on Exercise 1

STICKY PAD MENUS

The menus for this project are a little different from the Windows 95 standards. Since we can use the Save As dialog box to save the sticky note with the current name or a new name, we'll use a single menu item instead of two. We are also including a *Close Note without Saving* menu item to close a note without saving changes. Alternatively, we could have used the Exit menu item, and displayed a Save Changes message box.

STEP 6: Add Code for the New Note and Exit Menus

➤ Close the Toolbox.

➤ Move to the Form Designer window and pull down the form's **File menu**.

➤ Select the menu item **New Note** to display the Code window.

➤ Add the following block of code for the New Note menu event procedure.

```
Private Sub mnuNew_Click()
' Purpose: Menu - display a new note
   Dim frmNote As Form      'new note form
   Dim Top As Integer       'top position of form
   Dim Left As Integer      'left position of form
   Dim Inch As Integer      '1440 twips = logical inch

Inch = 1440

   'Get current note's screen position
   Top = Me.Top
   Left = Me.Left

   'Open new form in a new window
   'Load and display down and right 1/4 inch
   Set frmNote = New frmStickyPad
```

```
frmNote.Move Left + (0.25 * Inch), _
    Top + (0.25 * Inch)
  frmNote.Show
End Sub
```

➤ In the Code Editor window's Object list box, select **mnuExit**.
➤ Add the following block of code for the Exit menu event procedure.

```
Private Sub mnuExit_Click()
' Purpose: Menu - Exit the application
  End
End Sub
```

STEP 7: Test the New Note and Exit Menus

➤ Close the Code Editor window, and any other open windows.
➤ Click the toolbar's **Start button** to test your code. Click the **Yes button** to save your code changes.
➤ Correct any typing errors.
➤ The startup StickyPad form will display in the center of the screen.
➤ Pull down the form's **File menu** and select **New Note**. Another note will display down and to the right of the first note. Notice the title bar displays "Sticky Pad 2."
➤ Pull down this form's **File menu** and select **New Note** to display a third note.
➤ Pull down the third form's **File menu** and select **New Note** to display a fourth note. Your screen will appear as shown in Figure 5.5f.

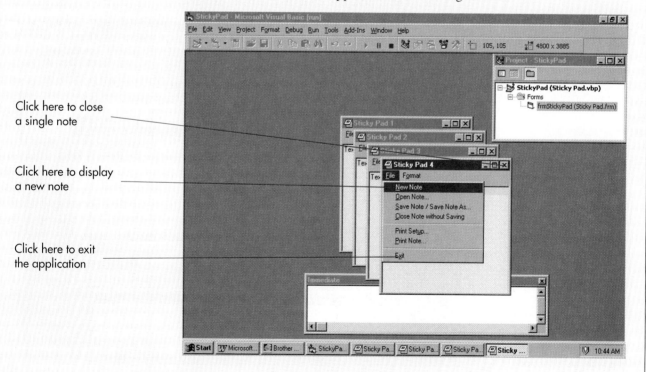

(f) Test the New Note and Exit Menus (step 7)

FIGURE 5.5   Hands-on Exercise 1

➤ Click the note's **Close button** to close a single note.

➤ Pull down a note's **File menu** and select **Exit** to end the application.

STEP 8: Display the Open Dialog Box

➤ Pull down the **View menu** and select **Code**.

➤ In the Code Editor window's Object list box, select **mnuOpen**.

➤ Add the following block of code for the Open menu event procedure:

```
Private Sub mnuOpen_Click()
'Purpose: Menu - Open a sticky pad (text) file
  Dim Pathname As String    'path of selected file
  'Display only text files
  DlgDialogs.Filter = "Text files (*.txt)|*.txt"
  dlgDialogs.ShowOpen    'display the Open dialog box
  Pathname = dlgDialogs.filename    'store selected filename
  Me.Caption = UCase(Pathname)    'reset title bar
End Sub
```

➤ Close the Code Editor window.

➤ Click the toolbar's **Start button** to test your code. Click the **Yes button** to save your code changes.

➤ Correct any typing errors.

➤ The startup Sticky Pad form will display in the center of the screen. Pull down the form's **File menu** and select **Open Note**.

➤ The Open dialog box will display as shown in Figure 5.5g. The Filter property filters the files, so that only files with the *.txt* extension are listed. Notice that the dialog box works, but no code has been implemented yet to actually open a file. You'll add this code in the next exercise.

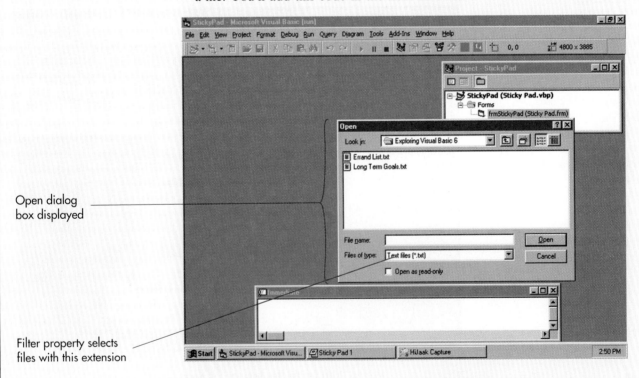

Open dialog box displayed

Filter property selects files with this extension

(g) Display the Open Dialog Box (step 8)

FIGURE 5.5 Hands-on Exercise 1

➤ Close the Open dialog box.

➤ Pull down the form's **File menu** and select **Exit** to exit the application.

STEP 9: Display the Save As Dialog Box

➤ Pull down the **View menu** and select **Code**.

➤ In the Code Editor window's Object list box, select **mnuSave**.

➤ Add the following block of code for the Save menu event procedure:

```
Private Sub mnuSave_Click()
' Purpose: Menu - Save the current sticky pad (text) file
  Dim Pathname As String    'current filename
  dlgDialogs.filename = Me.Caption    'get current filename
  dlgDialogs.Filter = "Text files (*.txt)|*.txt"
  dlgDialogs.ShowSave    'display the Save As dialog box
End Sub
```

➤ Close the Code Editor window.

➤ Click the toolbar's **Start button** to test your code. Click the **Yes button** to save your code changes.

➤ The startup Sticky Pad form will display in the center of the screen. Pull down the form's **File menu** and select **Save Note/ Save Note As**.

➤ The Save As dialog box will display as shown in Figure 5.5h. Notice that the dialog box works, but no code has been implemented yet to actually save a file. You'll add this code in the next exercise.

Save As dialog
box displayed

Current file name
displayed here

Filter property selects
files with .txt file extension

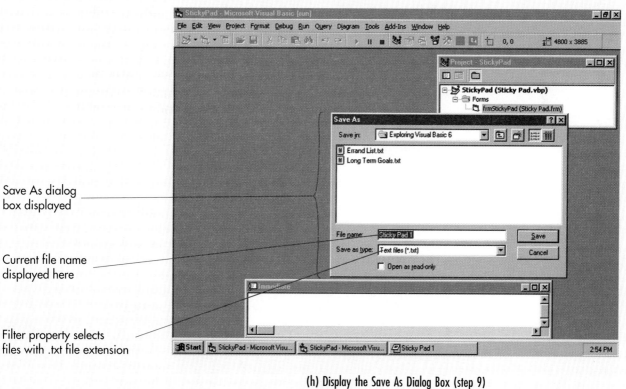

(h) Display the Save As Dialog Box (step 9)

FIGURE 5.5   Hands-on Exercise 1

➤ Close the Save As dialog box.

➤ Pull down the form's **File menu** and select **Exit** to exit the application.

STEP 10: Add and Test Code for the Close Note Menu

➤ Pull down the **View menu** and select **Code**.

➤ In the Code Editor window's Object list box, select **mnuClose**.

➤ Add the following block of code for the Close Note menu event procedure:

```
Private Sub mnuClose_Click()
' Purpose: Menu - Close Note event
'        Close current note without saving
'        Remove the note from screen and memory
  Unload Me
End Sub
```

➤ Close the Code Editor window.

➤ Click the toolbar's **Start button** to test your code. Click the **Yes button** to save your code changes. Correct any typing errors.

➤ The startup Sticky Pad form will display in the center of the screen. Pull down the form's **File menu** and select **New Note**. Another note will display in a cascade fashion.

➤ On the top note, pull down **File menu** and select **Close Note without Saving**. The top note will close, and the initial note will remain displayed on the screen.

➤ Pull down the **File menu** and select **Exit** to exit the application.

STEP 11: Add Banner Comments

➤ Pull down the **View menu** and select **Code**.

➤ In the Code Editor window's Object list box, select **General**.

➤ Add the following block of banner comments to document the project. Change the comments to include your name and the current date:

```
****************************************************************
Programmer:    Carlotta Eaton
Date:          June 30, 1998
Source:        Sticky Pad.vbp
ID:            Chapter 5 Hands-On Exercises 1, 2, and 3
Purpose:       Display little sticky notes on the screen
               that can open, print, and save text files
Events:        New Note, Open Note, Save Note,
               Close Note (don't save), Print Setup,
               Print Note, Fonts, Color, and Exit
Forms:         frmStickyPad
****************************************************************
Option Explicit
```

> ► Close the Code Editor window.

> ► Click the toolbar's **Start button** to test your code. Click the **Yes button** to save your code changes.

> ► The startup Sticky Pad form will display in the center of the screen.

> ► Pull down the form's **File menu** and select **Exit** to end the application.

> ► Click the toolbar's **Save button** to save your project changes.

> ► Pull down Visual Basic's **File menu** and select **Exit** if you are not continuing to the next exercise at this time.

INSTANCES AND CLASSES

Let's review what you have done so far in the Sticky Pad project. First, you created a form. Next, in the Sticky Pad project you used the Menu Editor and added several commands under the File menu. Next, you added the common dialog control to your form. The common dialog control gives a professional look to your Sticky Pad project. Finally you added code for the File menus and displayed the Open and Save common dialogs.

The Sticky Pad project displays several copies, called instances, of the same form. Let's define some more object-oriented programming terms. A *class* is the formal definition of an object. (Objects were discussed earlier on page 10 of this book.) At run time, a class acts as a template to create objects. The class defines the properties and methods of an object. You are actually creating a class every time you create a new form. Forms are actually classes. You use the Form Designer window along with the Properties window to define the class. When you run the project, the form is displayed. The form displayed at run time is called an instance of the class. An *instance* is one of the set of objects that belong to the same class.

CLASS MODULE STEP BY STEP

If you are using Visual Basic 6.0, you can find this Help topic by pulling down the Help menu and selecting Contents. Now open the *Using Visual Basic* book, then the *Programmer's Guide*, then the *Part 2* book, then *Programming with Objects*, and finally the *Creating Your Own Classes* book. If you are using Visual Basic 5.0, you can find this topic by pulling down the Help menu and selecting Books Online. Now open the *Programmer's Guide* and continue as directed above.

One analogy to help you distinguish a class from an instance is to think of a class as a gingerbread man cookie cutter. The cookie cutter defines the basic cookie (object). Each cookie would be an instance. Each cookie can be decorated entirely differently (different properties), but each is still a gingerbread man. You can actually write an entire module of code to define a class, and this module is called a class module. For more information, see the Help topic "Class Module Step by Step." Creating your own classes is beyond the scope of this book.

The project looks great so far, but it still doesn't do anything with files. Let's look at the commands that allow your project to work with text files.

TYPES OF FILES

First, a little about files. A **file** is a block of information stored on disk or another media. A file may contain a program, a document, or a collection of data. Here we will look at text files, binary files, and RTF format files. Databases are another matter altogether, and we will discuss them in Chapter 7 and 8.

Text Files

A **text file** is a file that contains lines of written information that can be sent directly to the screen or printer using ordinary operating system commands. The Window's Notepad accessory creates text files using the **.txt file extension**. In the days of DOS, most editors were called text editors, and created simple text files. Most DOS computers use the ASCII character set; therefore text files are often called **ASCII files**. The **text box control** you have been using throughout the exercises has the capability to display text files.

Binary Files

Today we have word processing applications, such as Word, WordPerfect, and WordPro. These applications create documents (*.doc*) that are saved in a binary file format. A **binary file** contains bits that do not necessarily represent printable text. Application software is required to print or view a binary file. You can create and save a Word document that contains only text, and then open it using Notepad. The binary file will probably look like gibberish, and you may be able to recognize only a few characters. You can open the same file with Word, and everything will be readable. The term binary file is also used to denote executable **machine language files**, as discussed in Chapter 1 (see pages 38–39). Most word processing applications can save files as text files (*.txt*), but the fonts, font sizes, and other formatting information will not be saved.

RTF and HTML File Formats

Visual Basic provides another control for text files called **rich text box control**. This control displays Rich Text Format files that are saved using the .RTF file extension. The **Rich Text Format (RTF)** is a standard developed by Microsoft Corporation to format documents. RTF files are actually text files with special commands to indicate formatting information, such as fonts and margins. **Hypertext Markup Language (HTML)** is another special format for text files.

HTML is used to define documents on the World Wide Web. You can design HTML Web pages in Visual Basic 6.0 using the DHTML Page Designer.

These formats are a happy medium between the word processing document (binary files) and plain text files. An RTF file can contain basic formatting commands for different fonts, font sizes, and even font colors. The Window's WordPad accessory can save files in RTF, TXT, or DOC file formats. Some formatting information is lost when converting from a binary (*.doc*) format to the RTF format. Most of today's word processing applications can also save files in the RTF format. The **rich text box control** uses the RTF format. This control and the DHTML Page Designer are available in the Professional and Enterprise editions of Visual Basic.

DESIGN HTML WEB PAGES

For more information on designing Web pages with DHTML technology, pull down the Help menu and select Contents, then open the *Using Visual Basic* book. Next, open the *Component Tools Guide* book, then *Building Internet Applications*, and finally *Developing DHTML Applications*. The DHTML Page Designer is not available in Visual Basic 5.0.

FILE-ACCESS METHODS

Input/Output, or simply I/O, refers to an operation, program, or device that enters data into a computer or extracts data from a computer. Note that the process is viewed from the point of the view of the computer, not the human end user. We read a file as input to the computer, and write a file as output from the computer. The text box control will be used to display text read from a file.

Access means to read data from or write data to a storage device such as a diskette or hard drive. Visual Basic can access files in three different ways: sequential, random, and binary. Sequential access is used to read and write text files in continuous blocks. Random access is used to read and write text or binary files structured as fixed-length records. Binary access is used to read and write files that are structured according to an application's specifications, and varies from application to application.

Sequential Access

Sequential access was designed to be used with plain text files. Each letter entered is stored as an alphanumeric character, or a special formatting character such as a tab or line break. Access to the file is sequential, which means that to get to the middle of the file, you must first read from the beginning. A cassette tape is an example of a sequential access device. To play song number 3, you must either play songs 1 and 2 first or wind the tape from the beginning until you reach song 3. You will be using sequential access in the next hands-on exercise.

Random Access

Random access was designed to be used with files that are composed of records of identical length. Since each record is exactly the same length, you can randomly move from record to record. To continue the music analogy, a CD player is an example of a random access device. You can play song number 3 by simply selecting song 3, and the CD will instantly access the correct song. You can randomly access each song easily in any order. (The analogy isn't exact, because the songs on a CD don't have to be of the same length.) You will practice random access in Chapter 7.

USING RANDOM FILE ACCESS

For more information, see the topic "Using Random File Access." If you're using Visual Basic 6.0, pull down the Help menu and select Contents, then open the *Using Visual Basic* book, then the *Programmer's Guide* book, then the *Part 2* book, and finally the *Processing Files with Older I/O Statements and Functions* book to locate this topic. If you're using Visual Basic 5.0, pull down the Help menu and select Books Online. Open the *Programmer's Guide*, then the *Part 2* book, then the *Accessing Data* book, and finally the *Processing Files* book.

Binary Access

Binary access is similar to random access except that the files can have records of various lengths, or not contain any records at all. An application creates and reads the file, and must know exactly how the file was written to read it correctly. This gives you a lot of flexibility, but it is also more complicated than sequential or random access.

USING BINARY FILE ACCESS

For more information, see the topic "Using Binary File Access." You can find the topic by following the instructions for the topic "Using Random File Access" in the previous tip box.

READING AND WRITING FILES

Now we know a little more about text files. Visual Basic provides many functions that are used to read and write text files. We will only be using the commands for sequential access. Before we can read a file, we need to open it. This is accomplished using the **Open statement**. We read the file using the **Input ( ) function** or the **Input # statement**. After we finish reading the file, we need to close it using the **Close statement**.

To save a file, we open it again and then save it using the **Print # statement**. Visual Basic contains several other functions and statements for file I/O that are beyond the scope of this book. For more information, see the Help topic "Processing Files", as instructed in the first tip box on this page.

The Open Statement

The *Open statement* provides access to a file for reading or writing. The simple syntax for the Open statement is shown in the box below:

Open *pathname* **For** *mode* **As** *#filenumber*
where
> *Pathname* is a string that specifies a filename, and may include the folder and drive.
> *Mode* specifies the access mode and must be one of the following: **Append, Binary, Input, Output,** or **Random**. Random is the default if not specified.
> *Filenumber* is a valid file number in the range 1 to 511, inclusive. The **FreeFile** function is used to obtain the next available file number.

Example: `Open Filename For Input As #1`

The Close Statement

Immediately after a file is read or written to, it is closed using the Close statement. This concludes the input/output (I/O) to the file. When a file is closed, it is no longer associated with a file number. The simple syntax for the Close statement is shown in the box below:

Close *#filenumber*
where
> *Filenumber* is any valid file number. If the file number is omitted, all active files are closed.

Example: `Close #1`

The LOF (Length of File) Function

The *LOF (Length of File) function* finds the length of an opened file. The length is returned as a Long data type. The simple syntax for the LOF function is shown in the box below:

LOF(*filenumber*)
where
> *filenumber* is an **Integer** containing a valid file number.

Example: `FileLength = LOF(1)`

The Input Function

The *Input function* reads a file opened for input into a string or a data type containing text such as a text box. This function is used only with files opened in input or binary mode. The input function is usually used for reading files written using the Print # or Put functions. The simple syntax for the Input function is shown in the box below:

> **Input**(*charnumber, filenumber*)
> where
>   *Charnumber* is the number of characters to read
>   *Filenumber* is any valid file number
> *Example*: `String = Input(Number, 1)`

The Print # Statement

The ***Print # statement*** writes text to a file sequentially. The simple syntax for the Print # statement is shown in the box below:

> **Print #***filenumber, outputname*
> where
>   *filenumber* is any valid file number
>   *outputname* is the object to be printed
> *Example:* `Print #1, txtNote`

Now that we have looked at the details of the file input/output functions and statements, let's put them all together. The following simple program segment opens, reads, and writes to a text file using sequential access.

```
Sub FileIO()
  Dim Pathname As String
  Dim FileLength As Long
  'txtNote is a text box control on the current form

  'Read the file
  Open Pathname For Input As #1
  FileLength = LOF(1)
  txtFile = Input(FileLength, 1)
  Close #1

  'Do some other stuff here

  'Now ready to save the file
  Open Pathname for Output As #1
  Print #1, txtNote
  Close #1
End Sub
```

THE FILE SYSTEM OBJECT

The ***File System Object (FSO)*** model is a new feature for Visual Basic 6.0. It provides an object-based tool for working with drives, folders, and files. The model also makes processing files easier. The File System Object model has five objects: Drive, Folder, Files, FileSystemObject, and TextStream. The ***Drive object*** allows you to get information about a drive such as available space. The ***Folder object*** gives you the ability to create, change, move, and delete folders, and gain information about folders such as their name. The ***Files object*** allows you to create, delete, and move files, and gain information about files such as their names and paths. The *FileSystemObject object* is the primary object of the model, and contains methods that allow you to manipulate drives, folders, and files. The *TextStream object* enables you to read and write text files. A drawback to the FSO model is that is does not as yet support random or binary files. You can continue to use the statements discussed in the previous section to create and manipulate random and binary files.

We are interested in reading and writing text files at this point. The TextStream object and its methods are used for file input and output. If we were deleting or moving files to different folders, the Files object would be appropriate. Before we can use any of the FSO objects, we must first create an object using the *CreateObject function*. This function has been enhanced in Visual Basic 6.0, to support FSO objects.

The CreateObject Function

The CreateObject function creates and returns a reference to a File System Object and other ActiveX objects. The simple syntax is shown in the following box:

CreateObject*(ClassName)*
where
     ClassName uses the syntax of AppName.ObjectType
Example: `Set fso = CreateObject("Scripting.FileSystemObject")`

The OpenTextFile Method

After we create a file system object, we use it to open a specified text file using the OpenTextFile method. The *OpenTextFile method* opens a text stream object that is used for sequential access to a file. The syntax is shown in the following box:

---

*Object.***OpenTextFile***(filename, iomode, create, format)*
where
    Object is the name of a file system object
    Filename is the name of the file to open
    Iomode can be one of two constants, either **ForReading** or
        ForAppending
    Create is a boolean value; the value is **True** if a new file is created;
        False if it isn't created. The default is False.
    Format can be one of three constants. If omitted, the file is opened
    as ASCII.
        TristateUseDefault (or –2) opens the file using the system default.
        TristateTrue (or –1) opens the file as Unicode used for Windows NT
        TristateFalse (or 0) opens the file as ASCII.
Examples:
```
  Set ts  =  fso.OpenTextFile("c:\testfile.txt", _
             ForReading, False, TristateFalse)
  Set ts  =  fso.OpenTextFile("c:\testfile.txt", _
             ForAppending, True, TristateUseDefault)
```

The TextStream Object

After we have opened the file, we are ready to read, write, or close the file. The TextStream object is used for sequential processing of a file. The syntax for the TextStream object's methods is shown below. Note that this is only a partial listing.

TextStreamName.Method or *TextStreamName.Property*
where
    TextStreamName is the name assigned to the textstream using the File Sytem Object
    Method is one of the following:
        Close closes an open textstream file
        Read reads a specified number of characters from a textstream file
        ReadAll reads the entire textstream file
        ReadLine reads the next line from the textstream file
        Skipline skips the next line in a textstream file
        Write writes a specified string to a textsteam file
        WriteLine writes a specified string and the newline character
    Property is one of the following:
        AtEndofLine returns True if at the end of a line marker, and False otherwise
        AtEndofStream returns True if at the end of a textstream file, and False otherwise

Examples:
```
txtNote = ts.ReadAll
ts.Write "This is a test."
ts.Close
```

Now that we have looked at the details of the File System Object model, let's put the statements together. The following simple procedure opens a file, writes, and closes a text file using sequential access.

```
Sub OpenTextFile( )
Const ForReading = 1
Const ForWriting = 2
Const ForAppending = 3
  Dim fso    'File System Object
  Dim textfile    'Textstream file

  Set fso = CreateObject("Scripting.FileSystemObject")
  Set textfile = fso.OpenTextFile("c:\testfile.txt", _
        ForWriting, True, TristateFalse)
  textfile.Write "This is a test."
  textfile.Close
End Sub
```

HANDLING INPUT/OUTPUT ERRORS

When you work with files and printers, many unexpected events can cause problems. A diskette can be removed from the drive, a file may be deleted, or a printer may be turned off. Recall from Chapter 2 (page 63) that a ***bug*** is a mistake in a computer program. Bugs fall into at least three different categories. ***Compiler errors*** occur when the rules of the Visual Basic programming language were not followed. These errors are displayed in red when using the Code Editor, and are usually the easiest to correct. **Runtime errors** occur when executing a project. **Logic errors** happen when the programmer makes a mistake in understanding the problem, or implements the problem incorrectly. Logic errors are usually the hardest for programmers to find and correct.

To avoid many runtime errors, we need to add error handling code to our procedures. In the following example, we added a special code segment labeled *Error Handler*.

```
Sub FileIO()
 ' Purpose: Error handling example
   Dim Pathname As String 'path of selected file
   On Error GoTo ErrorHandler  'set up the error handler
   'Insert code to open, save, or print file here
   'No errors encountered here
   Exit Sub
ErrorHandler:
   'Display a message box, and exit procedure
   MsgBox "Cannot complete file operation"
   Exit Sub
End Sub
```

The **On Error statement** must be the first executable statement in the procedure. If an error is encountered, the program will execute the code immediately after the *ErrorHandler* statement as specified in the On Error statement. We need to place an *Exit Sub* statement immediately in front of this statement to avoid executing the error handling code when no error exists.

DEBUGGING YOUR CODE AND HANDLING ERRORS

For more information, see the Help topic "Debugging Your Code and Handling Errors." If you're using Visual Basic 6, pull down the Help menu and select Contents, then open the *Using Visual Basic* book. If you're using Visual Basic 5, pull down the Help menu and select Books Online. Open the *Programmer's Guide* book and then the *Part 2* book.

Now we have the file I/O and error handling information we need to work with text files. We'll add code for the Format menu, and display the Color and Font dialog boxes. We will use the Font dialog box to change the fonts displayed in the form, and the Color dialog box to change the background color of the displayed sticky note. Color and font changes can be saved using the rich text box control, but not with the intrinsic text box control. The rich text box control is available in the Professional and Enterprise editions of Visual Basic, and this control can be substituted for the text box control in the next hands-on exercise. Let's continue the Sticky Pad project and use a text box on the form to display a text file. Then we'll add the file input/output code to read and write to the text files.

Add File I/O to the Sticky Pad Project

Objective: Continue building the Sticky Pad project. Add code to open, read, close, and write to a text file using the text box control. Add code for the Format menu to display the Color and Font dialog boxes using the common dialog control. Use Figure 5.6 as a guide for the exercise.

STEP 1: Open the Sticky Pad Project

➤ Start **Visual Basic**. Click the **Recent tab** in the New Project dialog box. Select the **Sticky Pad project** from the previous hands-on exercise. Click the **Open command button** to open the project.

➤ If the Project Explorer window is not open, click the toolbar's **Project Explorer button** to open it. If necessary, double click the **Forms folder** in the Project Explorer window to expand it and show its contents. Double click the **Sticky Pad form**. The Form Designer window will display the form as you left off from the previous exercise.

STEP 2: Add Code to Open a Text File

➤ Pull down the **View menu**, and select **Code** to open the Code Editor window.

➤ In the Object list box, select **mnuOpen**.

➤ Add the boldfaced lines of code to the Open event procedure:

```
Private Sub mnuOpen_Click()
' Purpose: Menu - Open a sticky pad (text) file
  Dim Pathname As String    'path of selected file
  On Error GoTo OpenError 'set up the error handler
  'set up filter for text files with txt file extension
  dlgDialogs.Filter = "Text files (*.txt)|*.txt"
  dlgDialogs.ShowOpen   'display the Open dialog box
  'User did not select a filename
  If Len(dlgDialogs.filename) = 0 Then
       Exit Sub   'user did not select a filename
  End If
  'Store selected filename
  Pathname = dlgDialogs.filename
  Open Pathname For Input As #1    'open file
  Me.Caption = UCase(Pathname)   'reset title bar
  txtNote = Input(LOF(1), 1) 'read file into text box
  Close #1   'close file
  Exit Sub
OpenError:
  MsgBox "Can't open sticky note file " & Pathname
  Exit Sub
End Sub
```

➤ Close the Code Editor window.

➤ Click the toolbar's **Start button** to test your new code. Click the **Yes button** to save your code changes. Correct any typing errors.

➤ Pull down the form's **File menu** and select **Open Note**. The Open dialog box will display.

➤ Select the drive and folder where you stored your data disk (*Exploring Visual Basic 6*). Select the file named **Errand List** and click the **Open button**.

ALTERNATIVE CODE USING FSO WITH VISUAL BASIC 6.0

The code shown in the previous code box will work properly for both Visual Basic 5.0 and 6.0. If you are using Visual Basic 6.0, you can substitute the following code in the mnuOpen procedure:

```
Dim Pathname As String
Const ForReading = 1
Dim fso      'File System Object
Dim textfile 'Textstream file
...
Pathname = dlgDialogs.FileName
Set fso = CreateObject("Scripting.FileSystemObject")
Set textfile = fso.OpenTextFile(Pathname, ForReading)
TxtNote = textfile.ReadAll
Me.Caption = Ucase(Pathname)
Textfile.Close
```

➤ The file will display in the text box. Grab the right border of the form and stretch the form until you can read the entire filename in the title bar.

➤ Pull down the form's **File menu** and select **New Note**. A new note will display cascaded.

➤ Pull down the new form's **File menu** and select **Open Note**. The Open dialog box will display.

➤ The Open dialog box will still be set to the disk and folder you last used. Select the file named **Long Term Goals** and click the **Open button**.

➤ The file will display in the text box. Grab the right border of the form and stretch the form until you can read the entire filename in the title bar.

➤ Grab each form by its title bar and move it until your screen matches Figure 5.6a.

Displays the *Errand List* file

Displays the *Long Term Goals* file

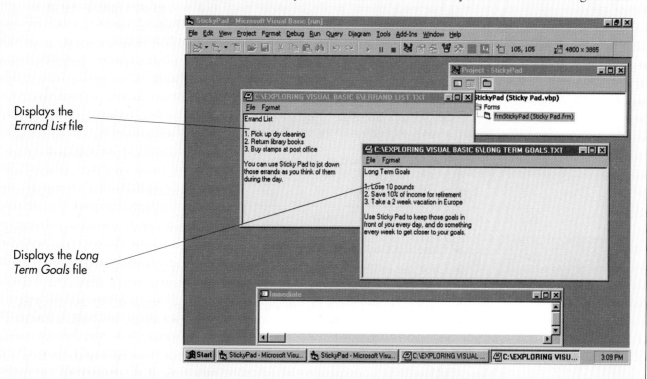

(a) Add Code to Open Text File (step 2)

FIGURE 5.6   Hands-on Exercise 2

➤ Pull down either form's **File menu** and select **Exit** to end the application.

STEP 3: Add Code to Save a Text File

➤ Pull down the **View menu**, and select **Code** to open the Code Editor window.

➤ Click the Object text box's **drop down arrow** and select **mnuSave**.

➤ Add the boldfaced lines of code shown below to the Save event procedure:

```
Private Sub mnuSave_Click()
'Purpose: Menu - Save the current sticky pad (text file)
  Dim Pathname As String    'current filename
  On Error GoTo SaveError    'set up error handler
  dlgDialogs.filename = Me.Caption    'get current filename
  'set up filter for text files with txt file extension
  dlgDialogs.Filter = "Text files (*.txt)|*.txt"
  dlgDialogs.ShowSave    'display the Save As dialog box
  Pathname = dlgDialogs.filename    'get user selection
  Me.Caption = Pathname    'change title bar
  Open Pathname For Output As #1    'open file to write
  Print #1, txtNote.Text    'write text box to file
  Close #1    'close file
  Exit Sub
SaveError:
  MsgBox "Can't save sticky note file " & Pathname
  Exit Sub
End Sub
```

ALTERNATIVE CODE USING FSO WITH VISUAL BASIC 6.0

The code shown in the previous code box will work properly for both Visual Basic 5.0 and 6.0. If you are using Visual Basic 6.0, you can substitute the following code in the mnuSave procedure:

```
Dim Pathname As String
Const ForWriting = 2
Dim fso    'File System Object
Dim textfile    'Textstream file
...
Me.Caption = Pathname
Set fso = CreateObject("Scripting.FileSystemObject")
Set textfile = fso.OpenTextFile(Pathname, ForWriting, True)
textfile.Write(txtNote.Text)
Me.Caption = Ucase(Pathname)
Textfile.Close
```

➤ Close the Code Editor window.

➤ Click the toolbar's **Start button** to test your new code. Click the **Yes button** to save your code changes. Correct any typing errors.

➤ Pull down the form's **File menu** and select **Open Note**. Select the drive and folder where you stored your data disk (*Exploring Visual Basic 6*). Select the file named **Errand List** and click the **Open button**.

➤ The file will display in the text box. Select the last three lines of the note and delete them. Then enter the following new task at the bottom of the list: **4. Pick up milk and bread.**

➤ Pull down the form's **File menu** and select **Save Note / Save Note As**. The Save As dialog box will display.

➤ The filename *Errand List* will display in the Filename text box. Change the filename to **Errand List Changed**.

➤ Click the **Save button** to save the file changes. Notice that the title bar updates to reflect the new filename.

➤ Verify that the file was saved. Pull down the form's **File menu** and select **New Note**. Close the previous sticky pad window.

➤ Pull down the form's **File menu** and select **Open Note**. Select the **Errand List Changed** file. The file with your changes will display.

➤ Double check that the original file was not changed. Pull down the form's **File menu** and select **New Note**.

➤ Pull down the form's **File menu** and select **Open Note**. Select the **Errand List** file. This file should display as shown in Figure 5.6b.

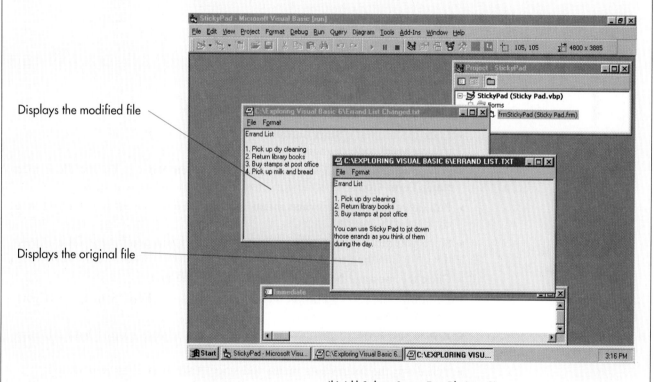

Displays the modified file

Displays the original file

(b) Add Code to Save a Text File (step 2)

FIGURE 5.6   Hands-on Exercise 2

➤ Pull down the form's **File menu** and select **Exit** to end the application.

STEP 4: Add Code to Display the Font Dialog Box

➤ Pull down the **View menu** and select **Code** to open the Code Editor window.

➤ In the Code Editor window's Object list box, select **mnuFont**.

➤ Add the lines of code shown below to the Font event procedure:

```
Private Sub mnuFont_Click()
'Purpose: Menu - User can change font
  Dim Pathname As String
  On Error GoTo FontError   'set up error handler
  'Display screen & printer fonts
  dlgDialogs.Flags = cdlCFBoth
  dlgDialogs.ShowFont
  'Apply user selections to text box
  With Me.txtNote
       .FontName   =   dlgDialogs.FontName
       .FontSize   =   dlgDialogs.FontSize
       .FontBold   =   dlgDialogs.FontBold
       .FontItalic =   dlgDialogs.FontItalic
  End With
  Exit Sub
FontError:
  Pathname = Me.Caption
  MsgBox "Can't set fonts for sticky pad file " & Pathname
  Exit Sub
End Sub
```

STEP 5: Test the Font Dialog Box

➤ Close the Code Editor window.

➤ Click the toolbar's **Start button** to test your new code. Click the **Yes button** to save your code changes.

➤ Pull down the form's **File menu** and select **Open Note**. Select the file named **Long Term Goals**. The file contents will display in the text box.

➤ Pull down the form's **Format menu** and select **Font**. Do not select a font, and click the **OK button**.

➤ Since you did not select a font, a runtime error was generated and executed the error handling code. The message box will display as shown in Figure 5.6c.

➤ Click the message box's **OK button** to close the box.

➤ Pull down the form's **Format menu** again and select **Font**. Select one of your favorite fonts in a 16pt size.

➤ Resize the form to display the entire text. The font Comic Sans MS was selected in Figure 5.6d.

➤ Pull down the form's **File menu** and select **Exit** to end the application.

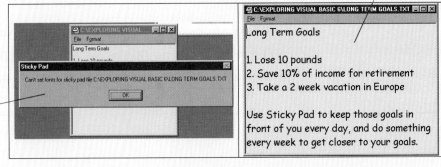

Displays with selected font

Displays message box

(c) Test the Message Box (step 5)   (d) Test the Font Dialog Box (step 5)

FIGURE 5.6   Hands-on Exercise 2

STEP 6: Add Code to Display the Color Dialog Box

➤ Pull down the **View menu** and select **Code** to open the Code Editor window.

➤ In the Code Editor window's Object list box, select **mnuColor**.

➤ Add the lines of code shown below to the Color event procedure:

```
Private Sub mnuColor_Click()
' Purpose: Menu - Change sticky note background color
  dlgDialogs.ShowColor
  Me.txtNote.BackColor = dlgDialogs.Color
End Sub
```

➤ Close the Code Editor window.

➤ Click the toolbar's **Start button** to test your new code. Click the **Yes button** to save your code changes.

➤ Pull down the form's **File menu** and select **Open Note**. Select the **Long Term Goals** file. The file contents will display in the text box.

➤ Pull down the form's **Format menu** and select **Background**.

➤ The Color dialog box will display. Click the **Define Custom Colors** button to display the screen shown in Figure 5.6e.

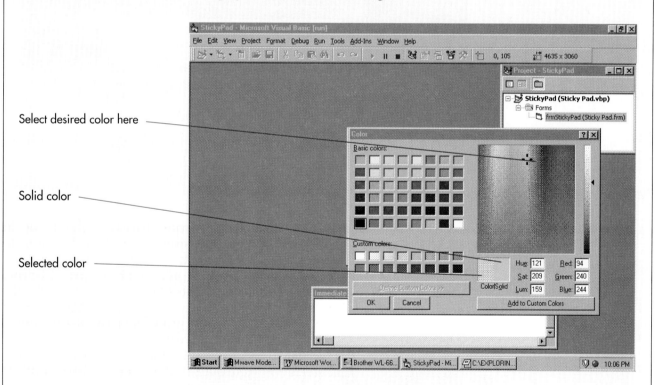

Select desired color here

Solid color

Selected color

(e) Specify a Background Color (step 6)

FIGURE 5.6   Hands-on Exercise 2

➤ Experiment with different colors and click the **OK button** to check the background color. Notice the **Selected color**, and **Solid color boxes** as shown in the figure. If the two colors are different, then the background color will be two-toned for the text box. If the background color under text displays gray, go back and select another color.

> ➤ The result of choosing a light blue color is shown in Figure 5.6f.
> ➤ Pull down the form's **File menu** and select **Exit** to end the application.
> ➤ Click the toolbar's **Save button** to save your project changes.
> ➤ Pull down the **File menu** and select **Exit** if you are not continuing to the next exercise at this time.

Background color changed to light blue

(f) Test the Selected Color (step 6)

FIGURE 5.6   Hands-on Exercise 2

WORKING WITH STRINGS

Let's review what you accomplished in the previous hands-on exercise for the Sticky Pad project. First, you added code to open a text file and display the contents in the text box. Next, you added code to write the text box contents to a file. Along the way, you opened and closed files as appropriate. You added code to display the Font dialog box, and change the text box font. Finally, you added code to display the Color dialog box, and change the text box background color. You also included error-handling code with each procedure. You also performed a simple string process within the Open menu procedure in Step 2.

You used the ***Len function*** to find the length of the pathname that was stored as a string. The filename stored was "*C:\Exploring Visual Basic 6\Errand List.txt.*" You found the length of the string using the following block of code:

```
If Len(dlgDialogs.filename) = 0 Then
   Exit Sub
End If
```

In this case, the string was the filename selected by the user in the Save As dialog box. If the length of the string is equal to 0, then the user did not select a file, and the event procedure is exited immediately and a file is not saved. Visual Basic provides many functions to help us work with strings.

The **InStr function** searches a string for a substring. The **Left function** finds the leftmost characters of a string, and the **Right function** finds the rightmost characters of a string. The **Mid function** finds characters in the middle of a string. Let's look at these functions in detail.

The Len (Length of String) Function

The Len function finds the length of a string. The length is returned as a Long data type. The simple syntax for the Len function is shown in the box below:

> **Len** *(string | varname)*
> where
> > Either a *string* or a *varname* is given, but not both.
> > *String* is any valid string expression.
> > *Varname* is any valid variable name.
> *Example:* `If Len(Filename) = 0 Then Exit Sub`

The InStr (In String) Function

The InStr function searches for the first occurrence of a substring in a string. The position is returned as a Long data type. The InStr function returns 0 if the string does not contain the substring, The simple syntax for the InStr function is shown in the box below:

> **InStr***(startposition, string, substring)*
> where
> > *startposition* sets the starting position for each search. If omitted, search
> > > begins at the first character position.
> > *string* is the string you are searching
> > *substring* is the substring you are looking for
> *Example:* `Position = InStr(pathname, "\")`

The Left Function

The Left function returns a string containing the specified number of characters from the leftmost characters of a string. The simple syntax for the Left function is shown in the box below:

> **Left** *(string, length)*
> where
> > *string* is any valid string expression
> > *length* is a Long data type indicating the number of characters to return.
> *Example:* `FirstEight = Left(string, 8)`

The Right Function

The Right function returns a string containing the specified number of characters from the rightmost characters of a string. The simple syntax for the Right function is shown in the box below:

> **Right** *(string, length)*
> where
> > *string* is any valid string expression
> > *length* is a Long data type indicating the number of characters to return.
>
> *Example:* `LastEight = Right(string, 8)`

The Mid Function

The Mid function returns a string containing the specified number of characters from the middle of a string. The simple syntax for the Mid function is shown in the box below:

> **Mid***(string, startposition, length)*
> where
> > *string* is any valid string expression
> > *startposition* sets the starting position for extracting the substring
> > *length* is a Long data type indicating the number of characters to return
>
> *Example:* `MiddleWord = Mid(string, start, 6)`

> ### MORE ON SYNTAX
>
> This textbook gives the simple syntax for the Visual Basic string functions. The online documentation gives more details for each function or statement. If you're using Visual Basic 6.0, pull down the Help menu and select Contents, then open the *Language Reference book*. If you're using Visual Basic 5.0, pull down the Help menu and select Books Online; open the *Visual Basic Help* book and then the *Language Reference* book. The information is organized by functions, statements, keywords, etc. Open the appropriate book, and then select the desired function or statement.

All the string functions are very useful when working with text and strings or extracting substrings from strings. The following code block separates the complete path name of a file into two parts, the path, and the filename.

```
Private Sub ExtractFilename()
'Position in string to start search
  Dim StartPosition As Integer
  Dim NextPosition As Integer   'position found in string
  Dim Pathname   'complete pathname of current file
  Dim Path As String   'path including drive and folders
  Dim Filename As String   'filename from pathname

StartPosition = 1
NextPosition = 1
Length = Len(Pathname)
'Search for "\" as separator between folders
Do Until NextPosition = 0
      NextPosition = InStr(StartPosition, Pathname, "\")
      If NextPosition > 0 Then   'found \
          Path = Left(Pathname, NextPosition)
          Filename = Right(Pathname, (Length - NextPosition))
      End If
      Text1.Text = Path   'display path in text box
      Text2.Text = Filename   'display filename in text box
      StartPosition = NextPosition + 1
Loop
End Sub
```

WORKING WITH PRINTERS

Next let's concentrate on printing. We added a menu item called Print Note in the Sticky Pad project, and we need to know how to implement the code. First, let's learn a little about printing and printers. We can print three different ways using Visual Basic. (1) We can create a form, and then print the form. (2) We can send text and graphics to the default printer using the system defaults. (3) We can display the Print dialog boxes to offer the user printing options, set the printer options, and send the text and graphics to the user's choice of printers and print. Let's examine these three methods in more detail.

Print a Form

By now, we have a lot of practice creating forms. We can print them from Visual Basic menus, but we want to print forms from within our own applications. This can be accomplished using the PrintForm method. The ***PrintForm method*** prints out a bitmap image of the form. This is the easiest method for printing using Visual Basic. The simple syntax for the PrintForm method is shown in the box below:

*FormName.***Printform**
where
    FormName is a form object. If this object is omitted, the selected form
        (with the current focus) is printed.
Example: `frmMain.PrintForm`

This is a quick and easy method for printing text and graphics, but it produces disappointing results as shown in Figure 5.7a. The resolution is printed at the screen resolution (generally about 72 to 96 dots per inch). Ink jet and laser printers are capable of 300, 600, and 1200 dots per inch, and this method does not take advantage of the printer capabilities. An example printout using the default printer and fonts is shown in Figure 5.7b. You can see the difference in the quality of the printing.

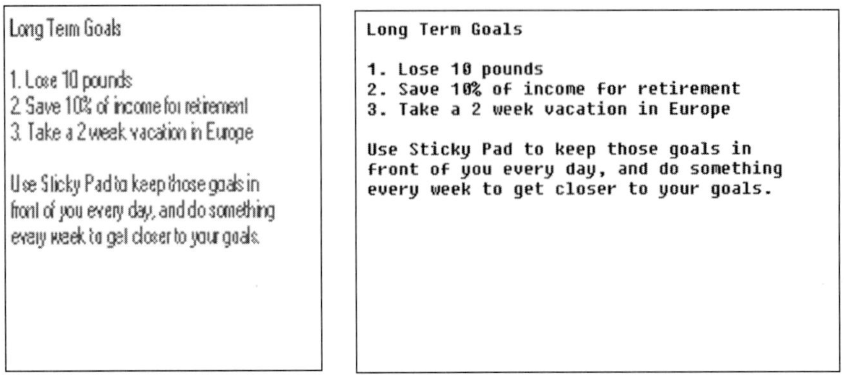

(a) Print Form Method   (b) Print Using Default Method

FIGURE 5.7   Printing Methods

To print using this method, we could print the Sticky Pad form with the following code for the Print event procedure:

```
Private Sub mnuPrint_Click()
'Purpose: Menu Print Form event
  On Error GoTo PrintError   'set up error handler
  Me.PrintForm
  Exit Sub
PrintError:
  MsgBox "Can't print sticky note file " & Pathname
End Sub
```

The Printers Collection

The second procedure for printing is to send the text and graphics to the default printer using the system defaults. The default printer is set in the Printers collection. The ***Printers collection*** is simply the set of printers available for your computer. We can view the Printers collection in Windows 95 by clicking the Start button and selecting Settings, then Printers. Alternatively, we can also go through the Control Panel and select Printers. An example Windows 95 Printers window is shown in Figure 5.8. Network printers as well as local printers are included. Notice that the Printers collection can include objects that are not really printers, but that can produce output, such as the fax modem and the file objects. To send text to the default printer, we need to work with the Printer object.

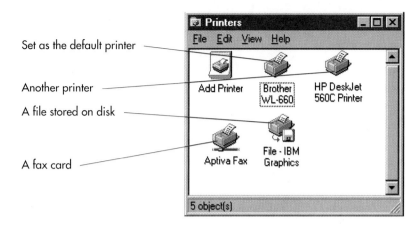

Set as the default printer

Another printer

A file stored on disk

A fax card

FIGURE 5.8   The Printers Collection

WORKING WITH THE PRINTER OBJECT

The **_Printer object_** is a device-independent drawing space that supports text and graphics in Visual Basic. The Printer object provides the highest print quality with a variety of printers. Instead of writing all the code for printing, we use the Printer object that is controlled by the Windows operating system, which has the capability to translate the text and graphics to the printer for us. Of course, the obvious drawback to this method is the printing speed.

The Printer object probably works differently than you would expect. The Printer object can be thought of as a logical drawing area divided into pages. You send the signal to start the print job, then place text or graphic objects anywhere and in any order on the page. When you have finished drawing the page, send the signal to start printing the page. Then you can start a new page if needed and continue the process. The Printer object is programmed using several methods, with the syntax as shown below:

Printer._Method_
where
    Printer is the default printer
    Method is one of the following:

METHOD	DESCRIPTION
Print _Objectname_	Places the named object on the current page
New Page	Starts a new page in the current print job
End Doc	Signals the end of a print job
KillDoc	Terminates the current print job

Example:
```
'Print current textbox contents
Printer.Print ;
Printer.Print txtNote.Text
Printer.EndDoc
```

In the above example, the first line of code initializes the print job and prepares it for accepting font changes and other printer settings if needed. The next line of code sends the text box object to the printer. The last line of code actually prints the text and finishes the print job.

As another example, the following event procedure prints the text box in the Sticky Pad project using the operating system printer defaults:

```
Private Sub mnuPrint_Click()
' Purpose: Menu Print Note using System Defaults
  On Error GoTo PrintError      'set up error handler
  Printer.Print ;              'initialize printer
  Printer.Print Me.Caption      'send filename to printer
  Printer.Print vbCrLf;        'send Line Feed character
  Printer.Print Me.txtNote      'send note to printer
  Printer.EndDoc               'print note and end job
  Exit Sub
PrintError:
  MsgBox "Can't print sticky note file " & Pathname
End Sub
```

Setting Printer Object Properties

Sending text to the default printer is an easy method for printing, and it produces better quality text than the PrintForm method. However, it uses the default printer, the default font, and the default margins as set by the operating system (Windows 95). We can use the Printer object properties to give us more control over the printed results. We cannot set the Printer object properties at design time (as we can for controls and forms). We must set the properties for the Printer object at run time. Luckily, this is not difficult. Here is the syntax of the most useful properties for printing text.

Printer._Property_
where
  Printer is the default printer
  Property is one of the following:

PROPERTY	DESCRIPTION
FontName	Sets the font name for the text
FontSize	Sets the font size for the text
FontBold	"True" setting sets to the bold font style
FontItalic	"True" setting sets to the italic font style
ScaleLeft	Measured in twips, placement for the object to start from the left edge of the paper
ScaleTop	Measured in twips, placement for the object to start from the top edge of the paper
Page	Contains the page number that is being printed

Example:
```
'Print text box in Bold, Times New Roman font
Printer.FontName = "Times New Roman"
PrinterFontBold = True
Printer.Print ;
Printer.Print txtNote.Text
Printer.EndDoc
```

The third printing procedure is to use the Windows 95 Print dialog box to give the user more control over the printing process. The common dialog control provides two dialog boxes that can be displayed for the user: the Print Setup and the Print dialog box, as shown in Figure 5.9.

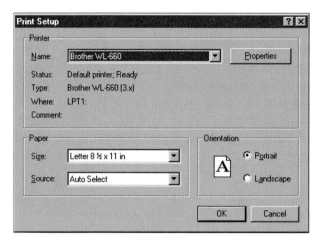

(a) Print Setup Dialog Box

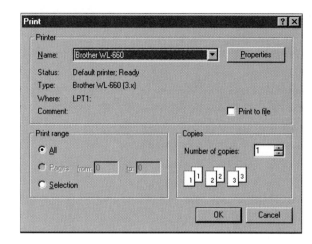

(b) Print Dialog Box

FIGURE 5.9   Print Display Boxes

Set the Flags Property

Another property available for the common dialog control is the *Flags property*. This property sets flags (on and off switches) prior to displaying the Print or Print Setup dialog box using the common dialog control. The syntax for this property is shown below:

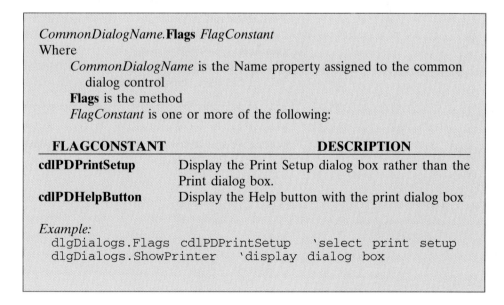

CommonDialogName.**Flags** *FlagConstant*
Where
    CommonDialogName is the Name property assigned to the common
        dialog control
    Flags is the method
    FlagConstant is one or more of the following:

FLAGCONSTANT	DESCRIPTION
cdlPDPrintSetup	Display the Print Setup dialog box rather than the Print dialog box.
cdlPDHelpButton	Display the Help button with the print dialog box

Example:
```
dlgDialogs.Flags cdlPDPrintSetup   'select print setup
dlgDialogs.ShowPrinter   'display dialog box
```

MORE ON THE FLAGS PROPERTY

Fifteen different constants can be set with the Flags property for the Print dialog boxes. See the topic "Flags Property (Print Dialog)" for more information on the Flag constants. If you're using Visual Basic 6.0, pull down the Help menu and select Contents, then open the Reference book, then the *Language Reference* book, then the *Properties* book, and finally the *F* books. If you're using Visual Basic 5.0, pull down the Help menu, select Online Books, then open the *Visual Basic Help, Language Reference, Properties* and finally the *F* books.

Set More Properties for Printing

There are more properties for the common dialog control that are useful for printing. The following properties contain information about the user's selections from the Print dialog box. The syntax for these properties is shown below:

CommonDialogName.Method
where
    CommonDialogName is the Name property assigned to the common
        dialog control
    Method is one of the following:

METHOD	DESCRIPTION
Copies	The number of copies to print
FromPage	The page to start printing
ToPage	The page to stop printing
hDC	This is the selected printer managed by the Windows 95 operating system (handle Device Context)
PrinterDefault = Setting	If True prints with the current printer

Example:
```
dlgDialogs.PrinterDefault = True
dlgDialogs.ShowPrinter
```

Now that we know how to print from an application, let's add printing capability to the Sticky Pad project.

Add Printing Capability to the Sticky Pad Project

Objective: Display the Print Setup and Print dialog boxes using the common dialog control. Print a text box using the options selected by the user. Use Figure 5.10 as a guide for the exercise.

STEP 1: Open the Sticky Pad project

➤ Start **Visual Basic**. Click the **Recent tab** in the New Project dialog box. Select the **Sticky Pad project** from the previous hands-on exercise. Click the **Open command button** to open the project.

➤ If the Project Explorer window is not open, click the toolbar's **Project Explorer button** to open it. If necessary, double click the **Forms folder** in the Project Explorer window to expand it and show its contents. Double click the **Sticky Pad form**. The Form Designer window will display the form as you left off from the previous exercise.

➤ Pull down the **View menu** and select **Code** to display the Code Editor window.

STEP 2: Display the Print Setup Dialog Box

➤ In the Code Editor window's Object list box, select **mnuSetup**.

➤ Add the following block of code for the Setup menu event procedure:

```
Sub mnuSetup_Click()
'Purpose: Menu - display the Print Setup dialog box
  'Choose the Print Setup dialog box instead of Print
  dlgDialogs.Flags = cdlPDPrintSetup
  dlgDialogs.PrinterDefault = True   'default printer
  dlgDialogs.ShowPrinter   'show printer setup dialog box
End Sub
```

➤ Close the Code Editor window.

➤ Click the toolbar's **Start button** to test your code. Click the **Yes button** to save your code changes.

➤ Correct any typing errors.

➤ The startup Sticky Pad form will display in the center of the screen. Pull down the form's **File menu** and select **Print Setup**.

➤ The Print Setup dialog box will display as shown in Figure 5.10a (on the next page). Notice that the dialog box works, and the code to change the default printer has already been added. Click the **Cancel button** to close the Print Setup dialog box.

➤ Pull down the **File menu** and select **Exit** to exit the application.

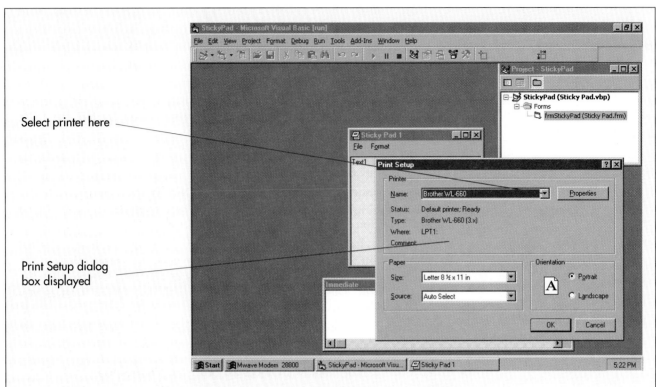

Select printer here

Print Setup dialog box displayed

(a) Display the Print Setup Dialog Box (step 2)

FIGURE 5.10   Hands-on Exercise 3

STEP 3: Display the Print Dialog Box

➤ Pull down the **View menu** and select **Code** to open the Code Editor window.

➤ In the Code Editor window's Object list box, select **mnuPrint**.

➤ Add the following block of code for the Print (Print Note) menu event procedure:

```
Private Sub mnuPrint_Click()
'Purpose: Menu - display the Print dialog box
  dlgDialogs.ShowPrinter  'Display the Print dialog box
End Sub
```

➤ Close the Code Editor window.

➤ Click the toolbar's **Start button** to test your code. Click the **Yes button** to save your code changes.

➤ Correct any typing errors.

➤ The startup Sticky Pad form will display in the center of the screen. Pull down the form's **File menu** and select **Print Note**.

➤ The Print dialog box will display as shown in Figure 5.10b. Notice that the dialog box works, but no code has been implemented yet to actually print a file. You'll add this code in the next steps. Click the **Cancel button** to close the Print dialog box.

➤ Pull down the **File menu** and select **Exit** to exit the application.

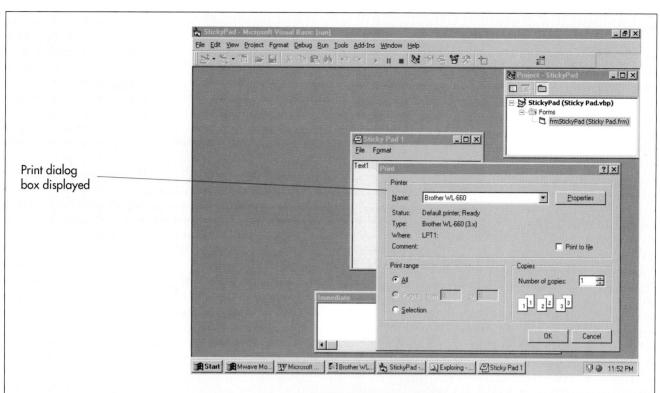

Print dialog box displayed

(b) Display the Print Dialog Box (step 3)

FIGURE 5.10   Hands-on Exercise 3

STEP 4: Add Code to Print the Header

➤ Pull down the **View menu**, and select **Code** to display the Code Editor window.

➤ In the Code Editor window's Object list box, select **mnuPrint**. Add the boldfaced lines of code to the Print event procedure as shown below:

```
Private Sub mnuPrint_Click()
'Purpose: Menu - Print the file using User selections
  Dim Cancel As Boolean          'user clicked Cancel
  Dim Inch As Integer            '1440 twips = logical inch
  Dim Position As Integer        'position in string
  Dim Textbuffer As String       'copy of text box
  Dim PrintLine As String        'current line of text to print
  'CR is carriage return character (paragraph mark)
  Dim CR As String
  Dim Pathname As String         'current filename
  Dim Footer As String           'footer to print
  Dim Length As String           'length of current string

  On Error GoTo PrintError
  Cancel = False                 'reset Cancel button
  Inch = 1440                    '1440 twips = logical inch
  'Set Flags options for the Print Dialog box
  'Disable the Selection option button
  'Disable the pages option button
  dlgDialogs.Flags = cdlPDHidePrintToFile _
     Or cdlPDNoSelection _
     Or cdlPDNoPageNums
  dlgDialogs.CancelError = True  'Cancel signals an error
  'set default printer to selection
  dlgDialogs.PrinterDefault = True
```

```
        dlgDialogs.Copies = 1
        dlgDialogs.ShowPrinter   'display the Print dialog box

        If Cancel = True then Exit Sub   'user clicked cancel
            'Otherwise continue and print
            Printer.Print ; 'initialize printer
            'Set up font selections
            Printer.FontName = Me.txtNote.FontName
            Printer.FontSize = Me.txtNote.FontSize
            Printer.FontBold = Me.txtNote.FontBold
            Printer.FontItalic = Me.txtNote.FontItalic
            '************************************************
            ' Print Header centered 3/4" from top of page
            '************************************************
            Pathname = Me.Caption   'get filename from title bar
            Printer.CurrentX = (Printer.ScaleWidth - _
                Printer.TextWidth(Pathname)) / 2
            Printer.CurrentY = 0.75 * Inch   'top margin
            'Send pathname to printer object
            Printer.Print Pathname
            '***********************************
            'Add more code here later in step 6
            '***********************************
    Printer.EndDoc   'print text and end job
    Exit Sub
PrintError:
    If Err.Number = cdlCancel Then   'user clicked Cancel
        Cancel = True
        Resume Next
    End If
    MsgBox "Can't print sticky pad file " & Pathname
    Exit Sub
End Sub
```

STEP 5: Test the Print Header Code

➤ Close the Code Editor window.

➤ Click the toolbar's **Start button** to test your code. Click the **Yes button** to save your code changes.

➤ Correct any typing errors.

➤ The startup Sticky Pad form will display in the center of the screen. Pull down the **File menu** and select **Open Note**.

➤ Select the appropriate disk and folder for your data disk (*Exploring Visual Basic 6*), and select the **Long Term Goals** file. Click the **Open button** to continue.

➤ Pull down the **Format menu** and select **Font**. Change the font to **Comic Sans MS** or another font, with a point size of **18**. Click the **OK button** to continue.

➤ Pull down the form's **File menu** and select **Print Note**.

➤ The Print dialog box will be displayed. Select a printer and click **OK**.

➤ The header of *Long Term Goals* (showing the file's name and path) will print in the center of the page about an inch from the top of the page, as shown in Figure 5.10c. The actual top margin will vary depending on the printable area of your printer.

➤ Pull down the **File menu** and select **Exit** to end the application.

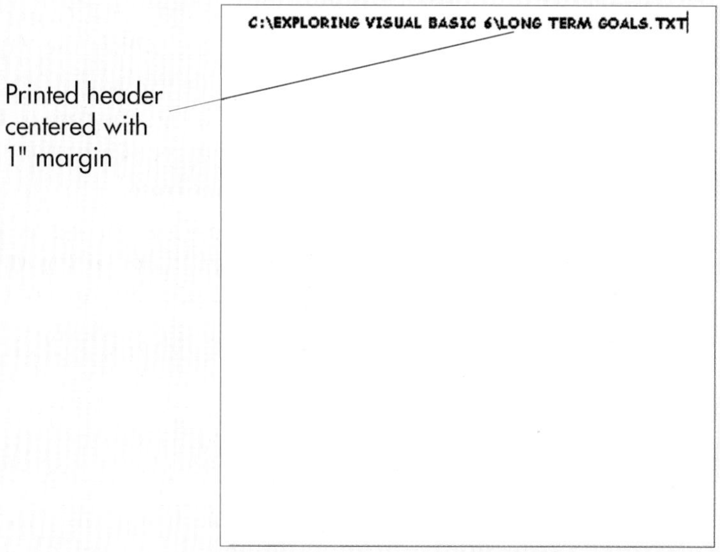

Printed header
centered with
1" margin

```
C:\EXPLORING VISUAL BASIC 6\LONG TERM GOALS.TXT|
```

(c) Add Code to Print the Header (step 5)

FIGURE 5.10   Hands-on Exercise 3

Step 6: Add and Test the Print Footer Code
➤ Pull down the **View menu** and select **Code** to open the Code Editor window.
➤ In the Code Editor window's Object list box, select **mnuPrint**.
➤ Add the boldfaced block of code immediately after the comment block as shown below:

```
'*************************************
'Add more code here later in step 6
'*************************************


'**********************************************
'Print Footer centered 3/4" from bottom of page
'**********************************************
Footer = Date$   'get system date
Printer.CurrentX = (Printer.ScaleWidth - _
   Printer.TextWidth(Footer)) / 2
Printer.CurrentY = Printer.ScaleHeight - _
   (0.75 * Inch)
Printer.Print Footer   'send footer to printer


'*************************************
'Add more code here later in step 7
'*************************************
```

➤ Close the Code Editor window.
➤ Click the toolbar's **Start button** to test your code. Click the **Yes button** to save your code changes.
➤ Correct any typing errors.
➤ The startup Sticky Pad form will display in the center of the screen. Pull down the form's **File menu** and select **Open Note**.

➤ Select the appropriate disk and folder for your data disk (*Exploring Visual Basic 6*), and select the **Long Term Goals** file. Click the **Open button** to continue.

➤ Pull down the **Format menu** and select **Font**. Change the font to **Comic Sans MS** or another font, with a point size of **18**. Click the **OK button** to continue.

➤ Pull down the form's **File menu** and select **Print Note**.

➤ The footer consisting of the current date will print in the center of the page about an inch from the bottom of the page, as shown in Figure 5.10d. The actual bottom margin will vary depending on the printable area of your printer.

➤ Pull down the **File menu** and select **Exit** to end the application.

SAVE PAPER WITH DEBUG PRINTING

While testing statements that print, you can change the **Printer.Print** statements to **Debug.Print** to print to the Immediate window instead of the printer. After your program prints the correct information, you can change the statements back to Printer.Print.

STEP 7: Add and Test the Print Text Box Code

➤ Pull down the **View menu** and select **Code** to open the Code Editor window.

➤ Add the boldfaced block of code to replace the comment line, "Add more code here later."

```
'****************************************
'Add more code here later in step 7
'****************************************


'*********************************************
' Send text box to printer 1 line at a time
'*********************************************

Printer.CurrentY = Inch * 1.5   'top margin
Printer.CurrentX = Inch   'left margin
Textbuffer = Me.txtNote.Text
'CR is carriage return and line feed chars
'also called paragraph marks
CR = Chr(13) & Chr(10)
Length = Len(Textbuffer)
    Do Until Length < 3   'CR + LF = 2 char
        'search for CR characters
        Position = InStr(1, Textbuffer, CR)
        If Position > 0 Then
            PrintLine = Left(Textbuffer, Position - 1)
            Textbuffer = Right(Textbuffer, _
                Length - Position - 1)
            Length = Len(Textbuffer)
        Else:
            PrintLine = Textbuffer 'last line of text
            Length = 0
        End If
        Printer.CurrentX = Inch
        Printer.Print PrintLine   'print current line
    Loop
```

➤ Close the Code Editor window.

➤ Click the toolbar's **Start button** to test your code. Click the **Yes button** to save your code changes.

➤ Correct any typing errors.

➤ The startup Sticky Pad form will display in the center of the screen. Pull down the form's **File menu** and select **Open Note**.

➤ Select the appropriate disk and folder for your data disk (*Exploring Visual Basic 6*), and select the **Long Term Goals** file. Click the **Open button** to continue.

➤ Pull down the **Format menu** and select **Font**. Change the font to **Comic Sans MS** or another font, with a point size of **18**. Click the **OK button** to continue.

➤ Pull down the form's **File menu** and select **Print Note**.

➤ The Print dialog box will be displayed. Select a printer and click the **OK button**.

➤ The entire text box contents will print with about 1 1/2" inch left margin as shown in Figure 5.10e. The actual margin will vary depending on the printable area of your printer.

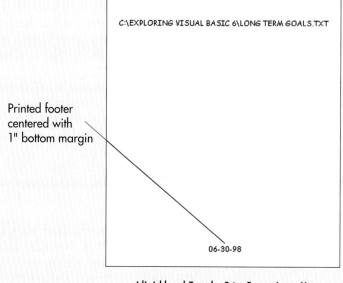

Printed footer centered with 1" bottom margin

(d) Add and Test the Print Footer (step 6)

(e) Add and Test the Print Text Box Code (step 7)

FIGURE 5.10   Hands-on Exercise 3 (continued)

➤ Pull down the **File menu** and select **Exit** to end the application.

➤ Pull down the **File menu** and select **Exit** to exit Visual Basic.

➤ Congratulations! You have now finished the Sticky Pad project.

The common dialog control gives access to the Windows 95 common dialog boxes. The ShowOpen, and ShowSave methods, used with files, display the Open dialog and the Save As dialog boxes. The Print Setup and Print dialog boxes are displayed with the ShowPrinter method. The ShowColor method sets or changes colors, and the ShowFont method sets or changes font characteristics.

A class is the formal definition of an object and includes the methods and properties of the class. A form is a class. An instance is one of the set of objects that belong to the same class. The Me keyword is a special purpose variable that helps refer to a particular instance of a class.

A file is a block of information stored on disk or another media. A text file contains lines of written information that can be sent directly to the screen or printer using ordinary operating system commands. The text box control is used to display text files. Application software is required to view or print a binary file. Executable machine language files are saved in the binary format as well. The RTF format is a special text format that can be displayed with the rich text box control. The rich text box control is not available in the Learning Edition of Visual Basic. The HTML format is another special text format that is used to format Web documents

Sequential file access was designed to be used with plain text files and is read sequentially much like a cassette tape. Random access was designed to be used with files that are composed of records of identical length, and is read much like an audio CD. Binary access is similar to random access except the files can have varying record lengths, or no records at all.

The Open statement is used to open a file. The Input( ) function and Input # statement are used to read the file into a text box. After reading or writing a file, we close it using the Close statement. The Print # statement writes the contents of a text box to a file. The examples in this chapter use sequential access for text files.

The File System Object (FSO) model, a new feature in Visual Basic 6, provides an object-based tool for working with drives, folders, and files. The model also makes processing sequential access to text files easier. The FSO model does not currently support random or binary file access.

A bug is a mistake in a computer program. Compiler errors occur when the rules of the Visual Basic programming language are not followed. Runtime errors occur when executing a project. Logic errors happen when the programmer makes a mistake in understanding or implementing the problem. Error handling code is used to avoid many runtime errors when working with files.

The Printers collection is the set of printers available for your computer. The PrintForm method prints out a bitmap image of a form at low resolution. A text box can be sent to the Printer object and printed using the default printer with the default margins and fonts. The Printer object is a device-independent drawing space that supports text and graphics. The Print Setup and Print dialog boxes give the user more control over the printing process.

Binary access
Binary file
Bug
Class
Close statement
CommonDialog control
Compiler errors
CreateObject function
Debug.Print statement
Default printer
File
FileSystem object
File System Object
   (FSO) model
Filter property
Flag property
FormsCount method
HTML format

Input function
Instance
InStr (In String)
   function
Left function
Len (Length of String)
   function
LOF (Length of File)
   function
Logic errors
Me keyword
Mid function
Open statement
OpenTextFile method
Print # statement
Printers collection
Printer object
PrintForm method

Random access
RGB (Red, Green,
   Blue) function
Rich text box control
Right function
RTF format
Runtime errors
Sequential access
ShowColor method
ShowFont method
ShowHelp method
ShowOpen method
ShowPrinter method
ShowSave method
Text box control
Text file
TextStream object

MULTIPLE CHOICE

1. The common dialog control
   (a) Contains the code to display the Windows 95 dialog boxes
   (b) Displays dialog boxes and opens and saves files
   (c) Acts as a "middleman" to the Windows 95 operating system dialog boxes
   (d) Gives a professional look to your code, so your interface will be different
      from the operating system

2. In the analogy of a cookie cutter and cookies to a class and an instance
   (a) The cookie cutter is the class, and a cookie is an instance
   (b) The cookie cutter is an instance
   (c) The cookie is the class
   (d) None of the above

3. If you clicked on a command button on the second form currently displayed
   at run time, the Me keyword refers to
   (a) All of the forms currently displayed
   (b) The second form
   (c) The second form or any control contained on the second form
   (d) Only the initial form

4. A file is defined as:
   (a) A block of information stored on disk or another media
   (b) Lines of written information that can be sent directly to the printer
   (c) Containing bits that do not necessarily represent printable text
   (d) A happy medium between binary and text file formats

5. The Rich Text Format (RTF) is a standard developed by Microsoft that is used to
   - (a) Save files using the WordPad accessory available with Windows 95
   - (b) Save files using the Notepad accessory available with Windows 95
   - (c) Save files in the primary format used by Word
   - (d) Save files in the primary format used by WordPerfect

6. The HTML format used to format and display web documents is actually a special case of a
   - (a) Text file
   - (b) RTF file format
   - (c) Binary file format
   - (d) None of the above

7. Which access method was designed to be used with plain text files, and accesses data much like a cassette tape?
   - (a) Random access
   - (b) Sequential access
   - (c) Binary access
   - (d) None of the above

8. Before we read a file into a text box, we must first
   - (a) Use the Open statement to open it
   - (b) Use the Close statement to close it
   - (c) Use the Input statement
   - (d) Use the Input # statement

9. Immediately after a file is read or written to, the following statement must be used
   - (a) Open statement
   - (b) Print # statement
   - (c) Close statement
   - (d) Input statement

10. Visual Basic 6's File System Object (FSO) model currently supports the following type of file access:
    - (a) Binary
    - (b) Sequential
    - (c) Binary
    - (d) All of the above

11. This type of error is generally the hardest for programmers to find and correct
    - (a) Compiler error
    - (b) Runtime error
    - (c) Logic error
    - (d) All are equally difficult to debug

12. We include error handlers in our code to handle a
    - (a) Compiler error
    - (b) Runtime error
    - (c) Logic error
    - (d) Any of the above

13. The On Error statement is included in a procedure to trap errors. Where should this statement be located?

(a) As the last statement in the procedure

(b) Immediately after the procedure's declaration statement

(c) As the first statement in the error handling code section

(d) The position of the statement in the procedure is not important

14. The following function searches a string for a substring:

(a) The Left function

(b) The Right function

(c) The InStr function

(d) The Mid function

15. The Printer object is used to print text and graphics. You should send text and graphics to the printer objects in the following order:

(a) top to bottom, left to right

(b) bottom to top, left to right

(c) top to bottom, right to left

(d) the order is not important

ANSWERS

1. c	**6.** a	**11.** c
2. a	**7.** b	**12.** b
3. c	**8.** a	**13.** b
4. a	**9.** c	**14.** c
5. a	**10.** b	**15.** d

PRACTICE WITH VISUAL BASIC

1. Common Dialog Demo. Create a project that demonstrates the common dialog control. Your code only needs to display the common dialogs. You don't need to include code to actually open, save, or print files. Save your project as *Common Dialog Demo.vbp* and your form as *Common Dialog Demo.frm*. Add the command buttons shown in Figure 5-11, and the corresponding events to display the common dialogs.

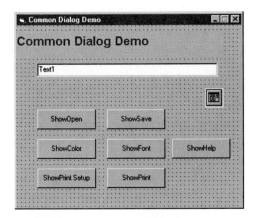

FIGURE 5.11 Screen for Practice Exercise 1: Common Dialog Demo

Remember the common dialog control has to be added to the Toolbox, and the ShowPrinter method is used to display both the Print Setup and Print dialog boxes. You will also need to set the Flags property to display the Print Setup dialog box.

The following code can be used to display the help files for Visual Basic for the ShowHelp command button event procedure:

```
Private Sub cmdHelp_Click()
'Purpose:  Display the Help common dialog box
'Modified from the VB Help Code Example
'the textbox is named txtNote
'the common dialog control is named dlgDialogs

On Error GoTo HelpError
  txtNote.Text = "Help dialog box"
      ' SetdlgDialogs.HelpFile = "VB5.HLP"
    'Set up to display VB general help
    dlgDialogs.HelpCommand = cdlHelpContentsHelponHelp
    ' Display Visual Basic general Help topic.
    dlgDialogs.ShowHelp
    Exit Sub
HelpError:
    MsgBox ("Help error")
    Exit Sub
End Sub
```

Make a printout of your form and code, to submit to your instructor.

2. **Print Demonstration.** Create a project that demonstrates the print and the print setup dialog boxes using the common dialog control. Save your project as *Print Demonstration.vbp* and your form as *Print Demonstration.frm*. The form for the project is shown in Figure 5-12.

Click here to exit

Click here to print to the Immediate window

Debug. Print results display here

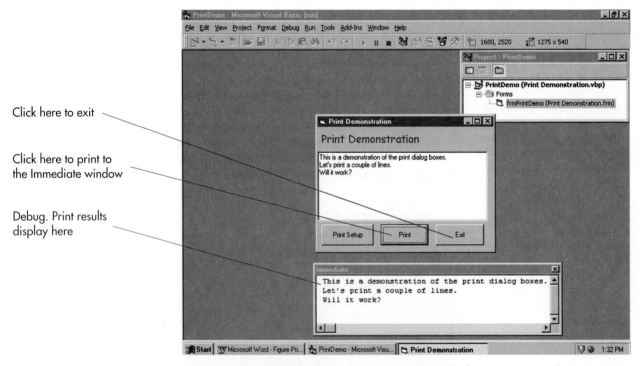

FIGURE 5.12   Screen for Practice Exercise 2: Print Demonstration

a. The Print Setup command button displays the Print Setup dialog box and changes the default printer to the user selection. The Print command button sends the text box contents to the selected printer object, and then prints using the default printer settings.

b. Code and test your project.

c. Change the project by using the *Debug.Print* command in place of the *Printer.Print txtNote.Text* command. Test the project again. You should see the printout displayed in the Immediate window, as shown in the figure.

d. Make a printout of your form and code to submit to your instructor.

3. **ANSI Values Demo.** You used string functions in the Print event for Hands-on Exercise 3 of this chapter. In this exercise, you will create a project using these string functions. ANSI (American National Standards Institute) is a standards organization that creates standards for many industries, and many of them are for computers. The ANSI character set is used in the Windows interface.

a. Read more about the ANSI character set in the topic "ANSI, DBCS, and Unicode (Definitions)" before beginning this project. Pull down the Help menu and select Index. Enter ANSI in the text box. Double click *ANSI character standard* from the list to display the topic.

b. Double click *ANSI* and then *Character Set (0–127)* to display the character code set. After viewing, close the Help window.

c. Create the form as shown in Figure 5-13a.

d. Use the ExtractFilename procedure code example for the Mid function as a guide, and create a project to extract the contents of a text box one character at a time.

e. Click the *Extract Next Character* button. This command button:

   ■ Removes a character from the top text box. Use the Right and Left string functions to extract the characters.

   ■ Displays the extracted character in the character text box.

   ■ Displays the ANSI code for the individual character in the ANSI value text box, as shown in Figure 5-13b. Use the ASC function to find the ANSI code for a character.

Click here ⟶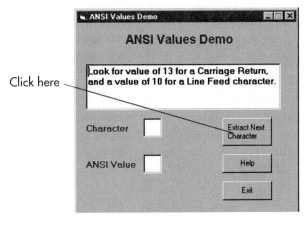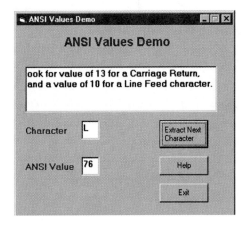

(a) Initial Screen   (b) Screen Results

FIGURE 5.13   Screen For Practice Exercise 3: ANSI Values Demo

f. Creating help files is outside the capabilities provided by the Learning Edition of Visual Basic. However, we can display the Online Help about ANSI codes provided by Visual Basic 5.0. If you are using Visual Basic 6.0, use the code given in the Common Dialog Demo practice exercise and display the basic help. If you are using Visual Basic 5.0, the Help command button should display the ANSI help file, using the following code:

```
Private Sub cmdHelp_Click()
'Purpose: Display a Help screen for ANSI character set
  'dlgHelp is the name of the common dialog control
  dlgHelp.HelpContext = "ANSI"
  dlgHelp.HelpFile = "VB5.HLP"
  dlgHelp.HelpKey = "ANSI"
  dlgHelp.HelpCommand = cdlHelpKey
  dlgHelp.ShowHelp
End Sub
```

   g. Save your project as *ANSI Values Demo.vbp* and your form as *ANSI Values Demo.frm.*

   h. Make a printout of your form and code to submit to your instructor.

4. **Clipboard Demo.** We have used several operating system objects that are provided with Visual Basic: App (Application), Printer, Debug (Immediate window), Err (error handling numbers), and Screen. Visual Basic also provides the operating system Clipboard object. The Clipboard object provides access to the system clipboard, which is commonly used to cut and paste.

There are several methods available for working with text on the clipboard, and others for working with graphics. For example, the Clear method clears the clipboard.

   a. Create a form as shown in Figure 5.14a and save it as *Clipboard Demo.frm.* Save your project as *Clipboard Demo.vbp.*

   b. Use the Menu Editor to create the Edit menu shown in Figure 5.14b. The File menu will contain the Exit item.

- The Cut menu item will place the selected text on the clipboard and remove it from the text box, as shown in Figure 5.14c.
- The Copy menu item will place the selected text on the clipboard and leave it in the text box.
- The Paste menu item will place the current contents of the clipboard into the text box.
- The Select All menu item will select the entire text box contents in preparation for cutting, copying, or pasting.

   c. See the Help topic "Cutting, Copying, and Pasting Text with the Clipboard" for excellent code examples and more about the Clipboard object. Open the Visual Basic Documentation (or Books Online), and select the Index button. Enter *clipboard* in the text box. Double click *transferring text and graphics* in the list. In the topic pane, select the topic. Use the SetText method to put text on the Clipboard and the GetText method to get text from the Clipboard to a text box.

   d. See the Help topic "Working with Selected Text" for code examples for selecting text. This topic is also in the *Working with Text and Graphics* book as described in the previous step. Click the Locate button if using Visual Basic 6.0, or the Contents tab if using Visual Basic 5.0. Use the SelStart and SelLength methods of the text box to select all or a portion of the text box.

   e. Make a printout of your form and code to submit to your instructor.

5. **Using Extra Forms: Video Clip (Learning Edition Only).** This exercise requires that you be using the Learning Edition of Visual Basic and that you have installed the *Learn Visual Basic Now* book on your hard drive or have access to it from the CD-ROM. This video clip shows how extra forms are used in applications. It also demonstrates the difference between a modal and a nonmodal form. Watch and learn. To start the video clip:

   a. Start *Learn Visual Basic Now.*

   b. Open the Chapter 7 book as shown in Figure 5.15.

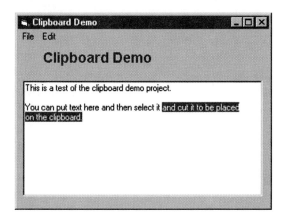

(a) Select Text

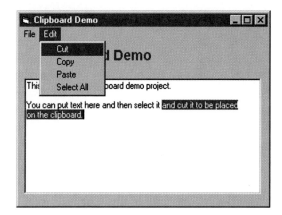

(b) Select Cut Menu Item

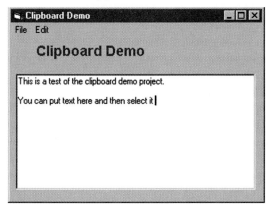

(c) Screen Results

FIGURE 5.14   Screen for Practice Exercise 4: Clipboard Demo

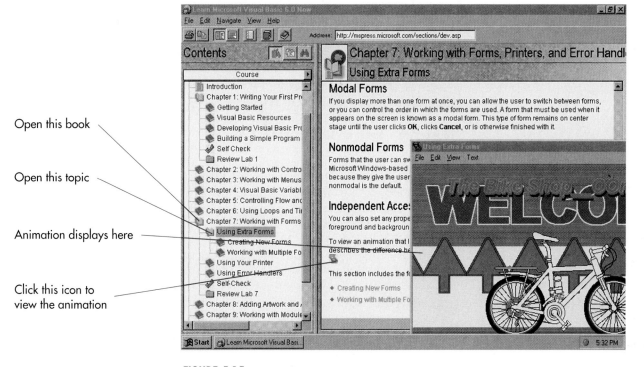

Open this book

Open this topic

Animation displays here

Click this icon to
view the animation

FIGURE 5.15   Screen for Practice Exercise 5: Using Extra Forms

c. Open the "Using Extra Forms" book. In the Topic pane, scroll down to the bottom, and click the Video animation clip icon.

d. View the entire video clip.

6. Printing Text: Audio Clip (Learning Edition Only). This exercise requires that you be using the Learning Edition of Visual Basic and that you have installed the *Learn Visual Basic Now* book on your hard drive or have access to it from the CD-ROM. This audio clip explains the different methods and statements using with the Printer object. This online chapter gives more information about the Printer object, printing text, and printing graphics. Listen and learn. To start the audio clip:

a. Start *Learn Visual Basic Now*.

b. Open the *Chapter 7* book as shown in Figure 5.16.

c. Open the "Using Your Printer" book.

d. Open the "Printing Text" topic.

e. In the Topic pane, click the Audio clip icon to listen to the narration.

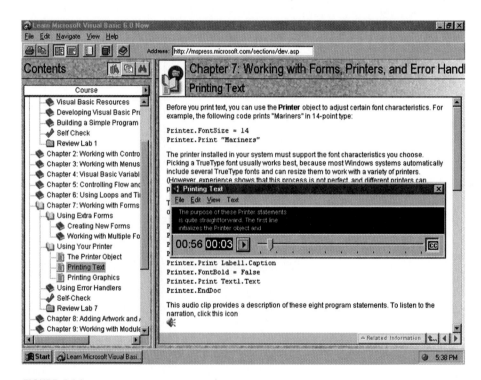

FIGURE 5.16   Screen for Practice Exercise 6: Printing Text

7. Processing Text Demonstrations: Video Clip (Learning Edition Only). This exercise requires that you be using the Learning Edition of Visual Basic and that you have installed the *Learn Visual Basic Now* book on your hard drive or have access to it from the CD-ROM. There are two demonstrations about working with text files. The first video clip demonstrates a very simple text browser that opens a text file and displays it in a text box. It reviews the methods used in the hands-on exercises for this chapter. The second clip demonstrates creating new text files. To start the video clips:

a. Start *Learn Visual Basic Now*.

b. Open the *Chapter 10* book as shown in Figure 5.17.

c. Open the "Displaying Text Files" book.

d. Open the "Text Browser Demonstration" topic. In the Topic pane, click the video clip icon to start the video clip.

e. For the second demonstration, open the "Creating New Text Files" book.

f. Open the "Demonstration: Quick Note Utility" topic. In the Topic pane, click the video clip to start the second video clip.

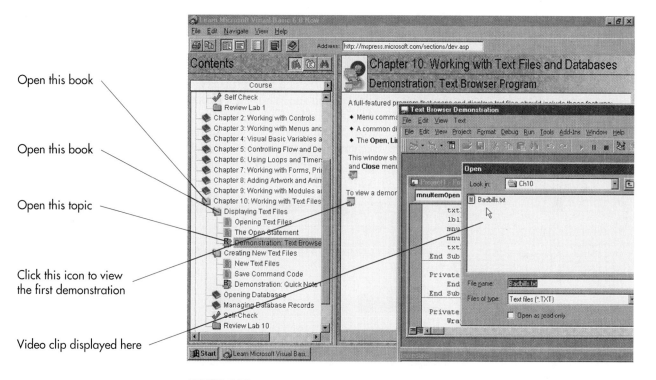

Open this book

Open this book

Open this topic

Click this icon to view the first demonstration

Video clip displayed here

FIGURE 5.17   Screen for Practice Exercise 7: Processing Text

Case Studies

Personal Text Editor

Create your own personal text editor using the text input/output processing, printing, and dialog box information gained from this chapter. Decide on the form size, color, and text properties before you start. Look at the Windows Notepad and WordPad Accessory menus for functions and menu positioning. Would you like to include a Find function in your text editor? Check out the MDI Notepad sample project included with Visual Basic for code examples for the Find menu function. When you have finished, create an executable version of your project. Name the project and the primary form *Personal Text Editor*. Make a printout of all your forms, menus, and code to submit to your instructor.

The Rich Text Box Control

This case study requires that you be using the Professional or Enterprise Editions of Visual Basic. Create a project called *Rich Sticky Pad*. Start with the Sticky Pad project you created in the hands-on exercises for this chapter. Replace the text box with a rich text box control. This is not as drastic as it seems. Name the new control txtNote, and very little code will need to be modified. Most of the text box code will still work with the new control. What makes this control a richer text box? Add or modify the menus to provide these enhancements. Make a printout of your form, menus, and code to submit to your instructor.

Ask the Pros

Sometimes you just cannot find what you are looking for using Visual Basic Books Online. There are hundreds of code examples available, so be sure to check for an example when you are learning a new property, method, function, or object. There is more help available from the Web. Check out *www.inquiry.com*. A sample page from the site is shown in Figure 5.18. (Fawcette Technical Publications provides this site.) This site provides an answer to your programming inquiries from the pros: Development Exchange editors and professional programmers. First select your programming language and then enter your question. You will get technical tips and sample code in response. Write a one-page summary of the results of an inquiry.

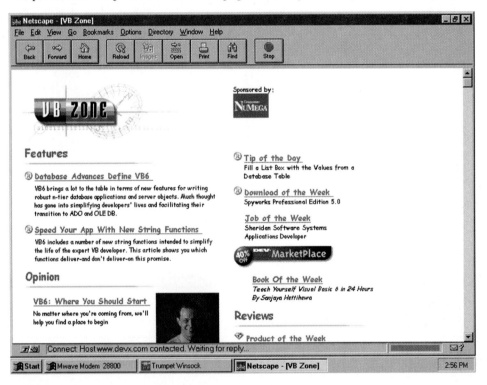

FIGURE 5.18   Screen for Case Study 1: Ask the Pros

Enhance with Extra Forms

Enhance the Sticky Pad project and include more forms. Add a Splash screen and an About form . Name your project *Extra Sticky Pad.vbp*, and your forms *Extra Sticky Pad.frm*, *Extra Sticky Pad Splash.frm*, and *Extra Sticky Pad About.frm*. Set the project properties and use these settings in the Splash screen. Use the yellow notebook icon from the Form Icon property on both new forms. Add a Main procedure to the project to briefly display the splash screen. Make a printout of all your forms, menus, and code to submit to your instructor.

PROGRAMMING WITH OFFICE 97: THE OLE CONTAINER CONTROL AND AUTOMATION

6

OBJECTIVES

After reading this chapter, you will be able to:

1. Explain the progression of data-sharing technologies in the Windows operating-system environment from the clipboard to DDE to OLE and ActiveX.
2. Explain Object Linking and Embedding; differentiate between an embedded object and a linked one.
3. Understand and use the old and new terms for data-sharing technologies.
4. Use the OLE container control to embed an object within a form and link an object to a form.
5. Explain the technology known as automation; use automation to create an application with components and functions available in Office 97 applications.

OVERVIEW

One of the major benefits when programming with Visual Basic is the ability to utilize code contained in other applications. The primary applications we'll be working with are contained in Microsoft Office 97: Word for word processing, Excel for spreadsheets, PowerPoint for slide presentations, and Access for databases. Remember that the Visual Basic Applications Edition 5.0 (VBA) is built into all of the Office 97 applications and is used to customize any of them—for instance by creating a macro or code module to be used within the application environment. Visual Basic can be thought of as the glue that binds all these applications' objects together.

In this chapter, we are working from outside the Office applications, in the Visual Basic interactive development environment (IDE). We will create Visual Basic applications that utilize the spell-checking and grammar-checking code contained in Word. We will also use the mathematical capabilities of Excel in the Mortgage Minder application.

This chapter will introduce you to Object Linking and Embedding (OLE). This technology allows you to employ data and components from one application in another application. One way to take advantage of the OLE technology is by using the OLE container control. The OLE container control can be placed on a form, and then any object such as a Word document, an Excel spreadsheet or chart, or a PowerPoint slide can be embedded in or linked to the Visual Basic form.

We will also introduce automation, a powerful tool that allows us to work with programmable data objects. With automation, (formerly called OLE Automation in Version 4), a programmable data object can be displayed on a form, or we can work with it in the background without displaying the interface at all. The power of automation and OLE will be demonstrated in the hands-on exercises.

Over the years, Microsoft has introduced several ways to share data between Windows applications. We will briefly describe the different technologies: the clipboard, DDE, ActiveX, and of course OLE. Some of the terminology has also changed over time, so we will list the old and new terms used with OLE.

SHARING DATA BETWEEN APPLICATIONS

When Windows was first introduced, the only way that application developers could share data between applications was by using the Windows clipboard. The clipboard was also available in operating systems such as Macintosh (by Apple Computer) and OS/2 (by IBM and Microsoft).

The Clipboard

The *clipboard* is a holding area where information can be copied and transferred to another application. The clipboard is usually used to copy, cut, and paste objects between applications. You probably have experience with the clipboard from using the Office applications, Word, Excel, PowerPoint, or Access.

However, the clipboard has its limitations. First, it is limited to a single object. A new object replaces any object currently contained on the clipboard. The clipboard is a storage area in memory. This means any object on the clipboard is erased when you turn off the computer. There is also no way to automatically update data placed on the clipboard.

Dynamic Data Exchange (DDE)

Dynamic Date Exchange was introduced in later versions of Windows and in OS/2 to overcome the limitations of the clipboard. *Dynamic Data Exchange (DDE)* is a mechanism where applications can exchange data and commands with each other while they are running. A connection (or link) is made between the two applications called the source and destination. The destination application can initiate a DDE conversation and request data in the form of text, numbers, or graphical images from the source application The data will be automatically updated and transferred.

Object Linking and Embedding (OLE)

Introduced with Windows 3.1, Object Linking and Embedding is a more sophisticated technique for achieving the same results as DDE, and is not limited to data and commands. *Object Linking and Embedding (OLE)* is a method of combining data created and processed by different applications. The resulting documents, containing elements from more than one application, are called to create **compound documents**. OLE is really Object Linking or Embedding (it doesn't both link and embed at the same time). An **embedded object** is copied and stored in the **container document** and becomes part of the document. A linked object is stored as a separate file, and a link to that file is placed in the **container document**. When the **linked object** is updated, the container document is automatically updated as well.

For example, if you create a compound document by *linking* an Excel worksheet to a Word document, Word is the container application and Excel is the server application. If you modify the worksheet, the modifications will automatically be displayed in the Word document. If you *embed* the worksheet in the Word document and then modify the worksheet, the modifications will not be displayed in the Word document. Obviously, you choose to link or embed an object depending on the situation.

New and Old OLE Terminology

The application that receives the object is called the **container application**. Prior to Office 97 and Visual Basic 5.0, the container was called the **client** or **destination**. Previously the OLE container control was called the **OLE client control**.

The application that created the object is called the **server application**. Prior to Office 97 and Visual Basic 5.0, the server was called the **source**. In earlier versions of Visual Basic, applications that created and exposed objects were called **OLE servers** or **OLE automation servers**. Today, these applications are called **ActiveX servers** or simply **ActiveX components**.

ActiveX Technology

The term "ActiveX" originally referred to software components that were created using OLE technology and designed specifically for the World Wide Web. With Visual Basic 5, Microsoft changed the definition of the term to encompass a broader range of components. **ActiveX** now refers to a wide range of communication techniques where an application makes its capabilities available to another application. The two applications can reside on the same computer, or be connected by a local area network, or the Internet. You can create an ActiveX code component, an ActiveX control, an ActiveX document, an ActiveX library, and more. You need the Professional or Enterprise Editions of Visual Basic to create ActiveX controls or ActiveX documents. This textbook makes use of the Learning Edition, so creating ActiveX components is beyond its scope. To see the benefits of OLE technology, therefore, we will use the OLE container. We utilized the common dialog control, also an ActiveX control, previously in Chapter 5.

THE OLE CONTAINER CONTROL

The OLE container control in Visual Basic makes it easy for programmers to take advantage of OLE. The **OLE container control** permits an OLE object to be inserted during design or while the application is running. Of course, you need to add code to insert an object at run time.

Insert an OLE Object at Design Time

To insert an OLE object at design time, simply place an OLE container control on the form. When you do this, the Insert Object dialog box is automatically displayed

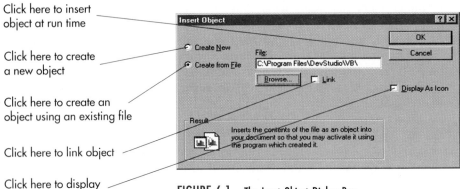

Click here to insert
object at run time

Click here to create
a new object

Click here to create an
object using an existing file

Click here to link object

Click here to display
an icon only

FIGURE 6.1 The Inset Object Dialog Box

as shown in Figure 6.1, allowing you to insert or paste the desired object into the control. You have three major options at this point:

1. You can create a new object or use an existing object by selecting the appropriate option button.
2. You can choose whether to link or to embed the object. To link the object, select the Link check box; otherwise the object will be embedded.
3. You can choose to display the object as an icon. To display only an icon, select the Display As Icon check box; otherwise the object will be displayed.

Insert an OLE Object at Run Time

To insert an OLE object at run time, simply place an OLE container control on the form. When the Insert Object dialog box is displayed, click the Cancel command button to leave the container empty. You will add code to insert the OLE object when the application is running.

To create an OLE object at run time, use either the **CreateEmbed** or **CreateLink** method. The syntax follows:

> *OLEcontainer.***CreateEmbed** *sourcefile*
>   or
> *OLEcontainer.***CreateLink** *sourcefile*
> where
>   *OLEcontainer* is the name of the OLE container control
>   **CreateEmbed** or **CreateLink** is required as the method used
>   *sourcefile* is the location of the source file for the object
>
> ***Examples:***
> ```
> OleWorksheet.CreateEmbed  "c:\data\report.xls"
> OleWorksheet.CreateLink   "c:\data\report.xls"
> ```

In-place Activation

The OLE container control also supports in-place activation. ***In-place activation*** allows direct editing of the OLE object placed in the OLE container control. When editing OLE objects in previous versions of Visual Basic, the server application started in its own window, where the object could be edited. When you finished, you closed the server application window. This newer version of OLE allows the object to be displayed and edited within the Visual Basic form.

In-place activation is set by using the ***Auto-Activate property*** for the OLE container control. Depending on the intended use of the OLE container object, the control may be activated manually, when it receives focus, when it is double clicked, or automatically.

LEARN BY DOING

The following exercise demonstrates in-place activation and use of the OLE container control. You will place an OLE container control on several forms. You will place the same existing Excel worksheet onto four different forms. Each form demonstrates a different ways to use OLE: linking, embedding, displaying an icon, and pasting. The difference between linking and embedding will be demonstrated. You will start with an existing project that has the form templates created for you. The code to display the various forms has already been written as well. You will add the OLE container controls to the form, and run the project to test the forms.

HANDS-ON EXERCISE 1

OLE Container Demonstration

Objective: Use the OLE container control to embed and link an Excel spreadsheet. Use Figure 6.2 as a guide for the exercise.

STEP 1: Open and Save the OLE Starter Project

➤ Start Visual Basic. Click the New Project dialog box's **Existing tab**.

➤ Select the disk and folder where your data disk is stored (*Exploring Visual Basic 6*). Select the **OLE Starter project**. Click the **Open button** to open the project.

➤ Open the Project Explorer window. Select the project.

➤ Pull down the **File menu** and select **Save Project As**.

➤ Select the disk and folder where your data disk is stored (*Exploring Visual Basic 6*). Enter **OLE Container Demo** in the File name text box. Click the **Save command button** to save the project.

➤ In the Project Explorer window, click the **plus sign** beside the Forms folder to display the list of forms. Next you will save each form with a new name (*OLE Container Demo*) in the same folder.

➤ First, select the first form, **frmEmbed**.

➤ Next, pull down the **File menu** and select **Save OLE Starter Embed.frm As**.

➤ The Save in list box will be set to the folder where you saved the project. Enter **OLE Container Demo Embed** in the File name text box. Click the **Save command button** to save the form.

➤ Repeat this procedure for the other four forms. The forms should be named:
  • *OLE Container Demo Icon*
  • *OLE Container Demo Link*
  • *OLE Container Demo Main*
  • *OLE Container Demo Paste*

➤ Select the Main form and click the **View Code button** to display the Code Editor window.

➤ Change the programmer name and date to your name and the current date.

➤ Scroll and read the program code. Immediately after the banner comments is the Declarations section. All the forms are declared here. Notice that each command button (and click event) displays a different form.

➤ **Close** the Code Editor window. Click the toolbar's **Start button** to run the project.

➤ Click the **Yes button** to save your project changes if needed.

➤ The Main form will display as shown in Figure 6.2a.

Display the Embed form

Display the Paste form

Display the Link form

Display the Icon form

Exit the Application

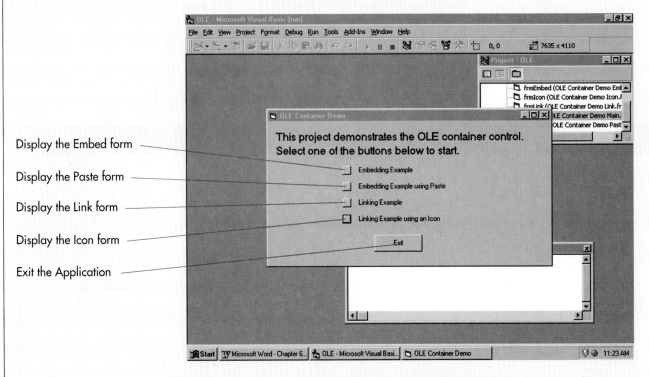

(a) Open and Save the OLE Starter Project (step 1)

FIGURE 6.2   Hands-on Exercise 1

➤ Click the **Embedding Example button** to display the Embed form. Click the **Close button** to close the form.

➤ Click the **Embedding Example using Paste button** to display the Paste form. Click the **Close button** to close the form.

➤ Click the **Linking Example button** to display the Link form. Click the **Close button** to close the form.

➤ Click the **Linking Example using Icon button** to display the Icon form. Click the **Close button** to close the form.

➤ Click the **Exit button** to stop execution.

STEP 2: Add the OLE Container Control to the Embed Form

➤ Double click the **Embed form** in the Project Explorer window to display the form.

➤ Click the toolbar's **Toolbox button**.

➤ Select the **OLE Container tool** and draw the container on the form. Click the **Create from File option button** to display the Insert Object dialog box as shown in Figure 6.2b.

➤ Select the dialog box's **Create from File option button**. Click the **Browse button** and select the **OLE Container Demo.xls file** in the *Exploring Visual Basic 6* folder. Click the **Insert button** to return to the dialog box.

➤ Click the **OK button** to display the worksheet in the OLE Container area. This may take a moment, so be patient.

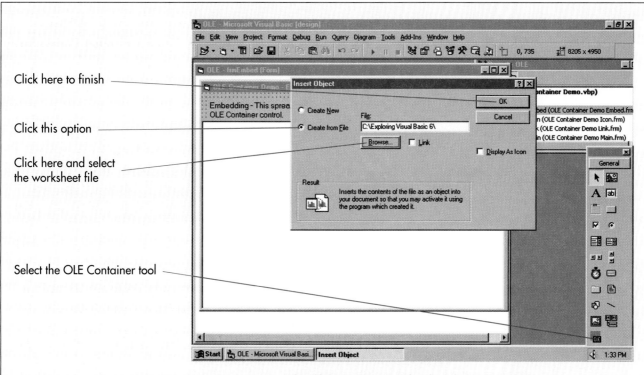

Click here to finish

Click this option

Click here and select
the worksheet file

Select the OLE Container tool

(b) Add the Container Control to the Embed Form (step 2)

FIGURE 6.2 Hands-on Exercise 1 (continued)

➤ The form will look like Figure 6.2c at this point. You may need to resize the OLE container or form to display the worksheet contents as shown in the figure.

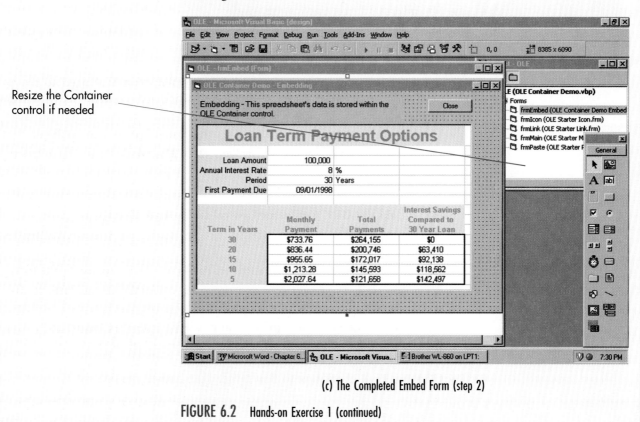

Resize the Container
control if needed

(c) The Completed Embed Form (step 2)

FIGURE 6.2 Hands-on Exercise 1 (continued)

➤ Move to the Properties window and set the Name property to **oleSheet**.

➤ Pull down the **File menu** and select **Save OLE Container Demo Embed.frm** to save your changes.

➤ Close the form window

EXCEL 97 REQUIRED

Microsoft Excel 97 is required to complete this exercise. If you do not have Excel installed on your computer the Excel spreadsheets will not display in the forms.

STEP 3: Add the OLE Container Control to the Paste Form

➤ Double click the **Paste form** in the Project Explorer window to display the form.

➤ Select the **OLE Container tool** and draw the container on the form to display the Insert Object dialog box.

➤ Click the **Cancel button** to exit the dialog box. This time you will paste the worksheet into the OLE container control.

➤ Click the taskbar's **Start button** and start the Excel 97 application.

➤ In Excel, click the Standard toolbar's **Open button**.

➤ Select the disk and folder where your data disk is stored (*Exploring Visual Basic 6*). Select the **OLE Container Demo.xls file** and click the **Open button** to open the workbook.

➤ Select cells **A1 through D15**. Click the toolbar's **Copy button**.

➤ Minimize the Excel application window.

➤ The OLE container will still be selected in the Visual Basic window. Click the toolbar's **Paste button** to paste the worksheet into the OLE container control area.

➤ The form will look like Figure 6.2d at this point. You may need to resize the OLE container or form to display the worksheet contents as shown in the figure.

➤ Move to the Properties window and set the Name property to **oleSheet**.

➤ Pull down the **File menu** and select **Save OLE Container Demo Paste.frm** to save your changes.

➤ Close the form window.

STEP 4: Add the OLE Container Control to the Link Form

➤ Exit the Excel application to avoid a binding error when you link the worksheet to this form.

➤ Double click the **Link form** in the Project Explorer window to display the form.

➤ Select the **OLE Container tool** and draw the container on the form to display the Insert Object dialog box.

➤ Select the **Create from File option button**. Click the **Browse button** and select the **OLE Container Demo.xls** file in the *Exploring Visual Basic 6* folder. Click the **Insert button** to return to the dialog box.

➤ Click the **Link check box** to link rather than embed the file.

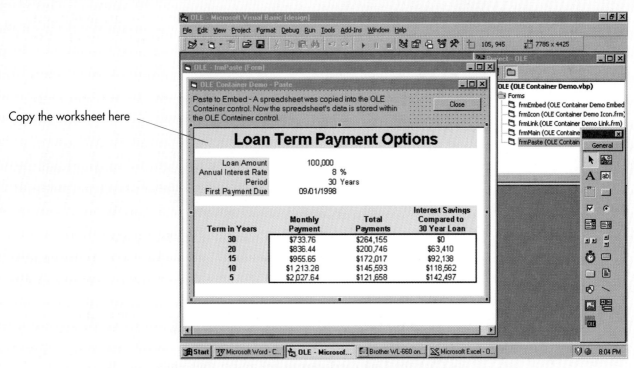

Copy the worksheet here

(d) Add the Container Control to the Paste Form (step 3)

FIGURE 6.2 Hands-on Exercise 1 (continued)

➤ Click the **OK button** to display the worksheet in the OLE container area. This may take a moment, so be patient.

➤ The form will look like Figure 6.2e at this point. You may need to resize the OLE container or form to display the worksheet contents as shown in the figure.

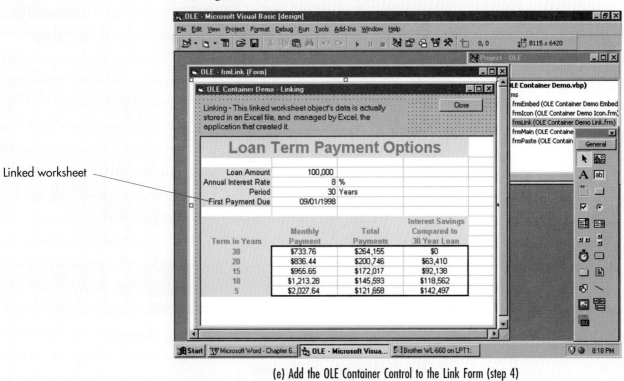

Linked worksheet

(e) Add the OLE Container Control to the Link Form (step 4)

FIGURE 6.2 Hands-on Exercise 1 (continued)

➤ Move to the Properties window and set the Name property to **oleSheet**.

➤ Pull down the **File menu** and select **Save OLE Container Demo Link.frm** to save your changes.

➤ Close the form window.

BINDING AND BINDING ERRORS

Binding is the process of starting the appropriate applications (such as Excel in this exercise) when running your project. If the application is already running and you try to start it, then a Binding Error is generated.

STEP 5: Add the OLE Container Control to the Icon Form

➤ Double click the **Icon form** in the Project Explorer window to display the form.

➤ Select the **OLE Container tool** and draw the container on the form to display the Insert Object dialog box.

➤ Select the **Create from File option button**. Click the **Browse button** and select the **OLE Container Demo.xls file** in the *Exploring Visual Basic 6* folder. Click the **Insert button** to return to the dialog box.

➤ Click the **Link check box** to link rather than embed the file.

➤ Click the **Display as Icon check box** to display an icon instead of the worksheet.

➤ Click the **OK button** to display the icon in the OLE container area.

➤ You may need to resize the OLE Container or form to display the icon as shown in the figure.

Worksheet linked and
displayed as an icon

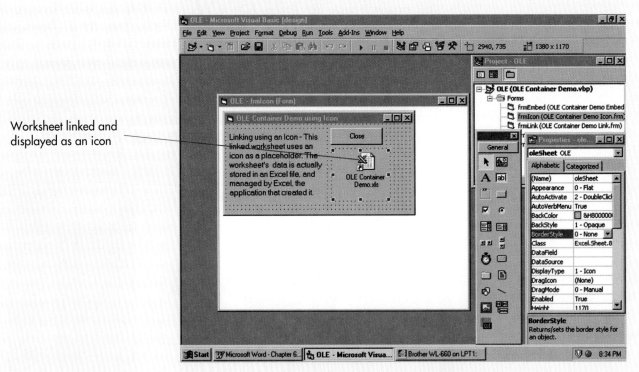

(f) Add the OLE Container Control to the Icon Form (step 5)

FIGURE 6.2   Hands-on Exercise 1 (continued)

➤ Move to the Properties window and set the following properties:

Property	Setting
Name	oleSheet
Appearance	0 - Flat
BackColor	Scroll Bars (gray)
BorderStyle	0 - None

➤ The form will look like Figure 6.2f at this point.

➤ Pull down the **File menu** and select **Save OLE Container Demo Icon.frm** to save your changes.

➤ Close the form window.

STEP 6: Modify the Source Worksheet

➤ Start Excel again and open the **OLE Container Demo.xls workbook** in the *Exploring Visual Basic 6* folder.

➤ Select **cell B3** and change the Loan Amount value to **75000**.

➤ Select **cell B4** and change the Interest Rate value to **7.5** as shown in Figure 6.2g.

➤ Click the toolbar's **Save button** to save your changes.

➤ Exit Excel.

STEP 7: Test the Embedded Objects

➤ Close the Properties window, the Toolbox, and the Form Designer window.

➤ Click the toolbar's **Start button** to execute the project.

➤ Click the **Yes button** to save the changes to your project if needed.

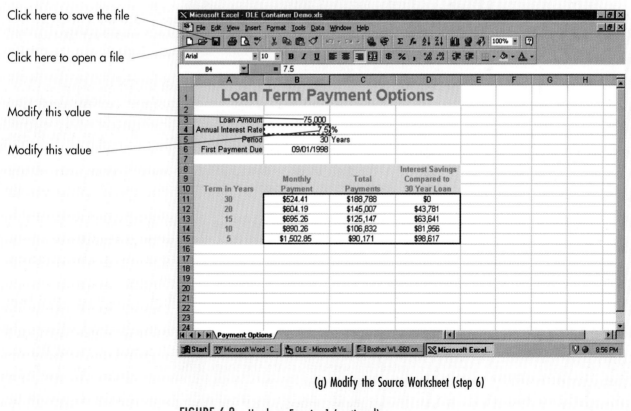

(g) Modify the Source Worksheet (step 6)

FIGURE 6.2 Hands-on Exercise 1 (continued)

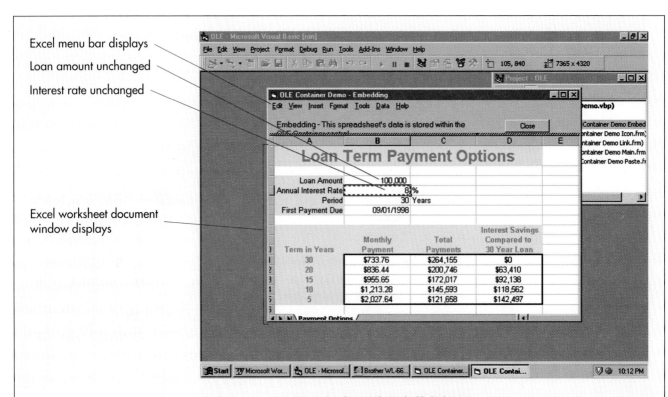

Excel menu bar displays

Loan amount unchanged

Interest rate unchanged

Excel worksheet document window displays

(h) Test the Embedded Objects (step 7)

FIGURE 6.2 Hands-on Exercise 1 (continued)

➤ The Main form will display. Click the **Embedding Example button**.

➤ The Embed form will display. Notice that the Loan Amount is $100,000 and the Interest Rate is 8%, as it was when you embedded the worksheet. The values did not change when you modified the source worksheet. Because you embedded this worksheet in the form, it did not change when the original worksheet was modified.

➤ Double click the worksheet to activate the Excel worksheet object as shown in Figure 6.2h. The worksheet remains unchanged, and the Excel application menu bar is displayed across the top of the form. Notice that the File menu is missing from the menu bar. You need to add code if you want to save changes to an embedded object.

➤ Pull down the **Edit menu** and examine it. It contains menu items such as Delete Sheet that are commonly displayed with Excel. Do not select any menu items.

➤ Examine the Excel worksheet document window and note that it displays the row headings on the left side and the column headings along the top.

➤ Click the **Close button**. The Excel menu bar and document windows disappear.

➤ Click the **Close button** again to close the Embed form.

➤ The Main form is now displayed. Click the **Embedding Example using Paste button** to display the Paste form.

➤ Notice that the Loan Amount is $100,000 and the Interest Rate is 8%, as it was when you pasted the worksheet into the OLE container control. Because you pasted this worksheet into the form, it did not change when the original worksheet was modified.

➤ Double click the worksheet to activate the Excel worksheet object.

➤ Examine the menu bar and the worksheet window. They appear as they did in the Embed form.

➤ Click the **Close button** to close the Excel windows.

➤ Click the **Close button** again to close the Paste form.

STEP 8: Test the Linked Objects

➤ Click the **Linking Example button** to display the Link form.

➤ Examine the spreadsheet. The Loan Amount is $100,000 and the Interest Rate is 8%. The container image has not changed yet. Double click the worksheet to activate the Excel worksheet object as shown in Figure 6.2i.

➤ Notice that the worksheet displays the updated loan amount of $75,000 and the updated interest rate of 7.5%. These values are displayed from the linked worksheet, not from the image in the OLE container control.

➤ The Link form has disappeared, and the entire Excel application window and document windows are displayed. The menu bar contains the File menu, and several toolbars are displayed. You can change cell values and save them as well.

➤ Do not make any changes to the worksheet, and close the Excel application window.

➤ The worksheet may resize and look different, and the values will be updated to the modified values. The worksheet may resize so that it is difficult to read.

➤ Click the **Close button** to close the Link form.

➤ The Main form is displayed again. Click the **Linking Example using Icon button** to display the Icon form.

➤ Double click the **Excel icon** to activate the linked worksheet.

➤ The entire Excel application window and document windows will display. The menu bar contains the File menu just as it did with the Link form.

➤ The worksheet displays the updated loan amount of $75,000 and the updated interest rate of 7.5%. These values are displayed from the linked worksheet.

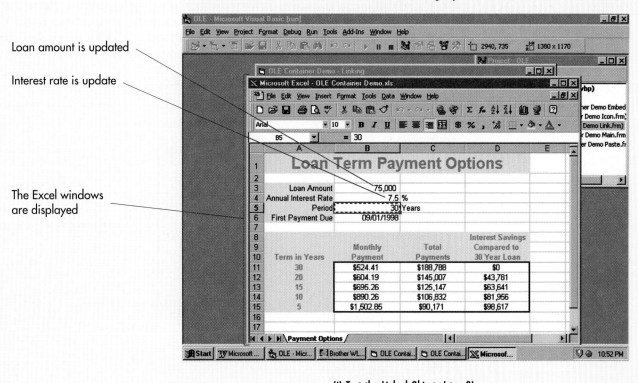

(i) Test the Linked Objects (step 8)

FIGURE 6.2   Hands-on Exercise 1 (continued)

> ➤ Close the Excel application window.
>
> ➤ Click the **Close button** to close the Icon form.
>
> ➤ Click the **Exit button** to exit the OLE Container Demo application.
>
> ➤ Exit the Visual Basic environment, and save changes to your project if you are not continuing on to another exercise at this time.

AUTOMATION

Automation is a Visual Basic technology that allows us to use code and objects from other Windows applications in our Visual Basic applications. (This technology was called *OLE automation* in versions of Visual Basic previous to Version 5.) For example, if we want to provide spell check and grammar check capabilities in our application, we can use the functions that are available in Word 97 instead of coding it from scratch. Automation provides powerful capabilities with a minimum of code. We can, for instance, perform calculations in a spreadsheet and display the results in a form. You will perform both of these tasks in the next two exercises. Remember that the referenced application must be available to the local computer for it to be able to use automation. That is, an application using automation with Excel cannot be run on a computer that does not have Excel installed.

Available References

To use automation, we first need to determine what automation objects are available on our computer. Next, we need to figure out which functions or methods to use to provide the desired capability in our application. We can use the *References dialog box* to determine which application objects are available to our computer. To display the References dialog box (shown in Figure 6.3a), pull down Visual Basic's Project menu and select References. In this example, notice we have Excel objects, Outlook, PowerPoint, Word, and many more objects available to us. We decide that we need the spell-check capabilities available in Word, so we select the Microsoft Word 8.0 Object Library (for Word 97).

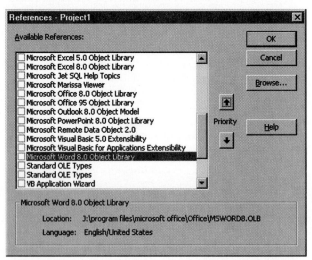

(a) The References Dialog Box

FIGURE 6.3   Using Automation

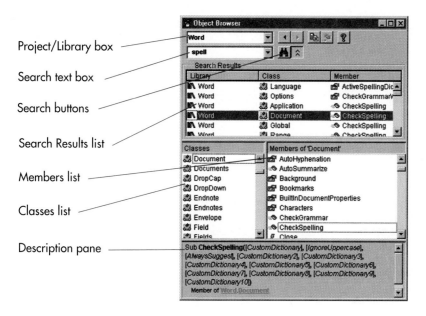

Project/Library box

Search text box

Search buttons

Search Results list

Members list

Classes list

Description pane

(b) The Object Browser

FIGURE 6.3   Using Automation (continued)

The Object Browser

Now we need to find the function or method to use for spell-check capability. We use the **Object Browser** to explore the object library for the selected application. We used the References dialog box to add the Word 8.0 library to our project. Now we can use the Object Browser to search for a likely method or function. To display the Object Browser window (shown in Figure 6.3b), click the toolbar's Object Browser button. Alternatively, pull down the Project menu and select Object Browser.

We have several libraries available, so first we select the Word library in the Project/Library box. Next, we enter *spell* in the Search text box. The matching methods, properties, and functions are displayed in the Search Results list. We next select *CheckSpelling* to display more information. The middle pane of the window displays the classes, functions, and methods available in the Word library. The syntax for the selected function is displayed in the Description pane of the window.

Viewing Object Hierarchies

The Object Browser allows you to browse an application and all its objects, methods, properties, and functions. Sometimes it is hard to see the full picture because you are only seeing bits and pieces. You can view all the objects available within an application by using the online Help available with the application. For example, start the Word application. Then pull down the Help menu and select Contents and Index. Scroll down and open the *Microsoft Word Visual Basic Reference* book. Now open the *Visual Basic Reference* topic and the *Getting Started with Visual Basic* book. Finally, open the *Microsoft Word Objects* topic to display the screen shown in Figure 6.3c (on the next page). This help screen gives you an overview of the objects available with the desired application. For more information, see other topics within the Word Online Help.

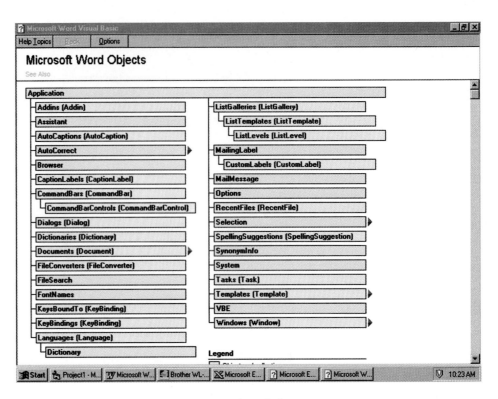

(c) Microsoft Word Objects

FIGURE 6.3   Using Automation (continued)

Create an Automation Object

Before we can use the power of automation, we need to declare and create the automation object in our code. First, we need to declare the object. The following are examples:

```
Dim oleObject As Object
Dim wrdApp As Word.Application
Dim wrdDoc As Word.Document
Dim xlsApp As Excel.Application
Dim xlsWorkbook As Excel.Workbook
Dim xlsWorksheet As Excel.Worksheet
```

Notice that we can either declare a variable as an Object type or be more specific. When we declare the Object type, Visual Basic must use *late binding*. When we declare the specific object type, such as Word.Document, Visual Basic can use early binding. Visual Basic knows exactly the type of object desired so the time required to set properties or use methods is faster. *Early binding* generally executes faster, so we will use this technique in the following exercises.

The CreateObject Function

To create a new, empty automation object, we use the Set statement with the **CreateObject function**. We used this function earlier in Chapter 5 to create TextStream objects using the File System Object (FSO) model. The simple syntax to help us work with Office applications is shown below:

```
Set objectname = CreateObject (Application.Object)
where
        Set is the required command
        objectname is the name of the automation object
        CreateObject is the required function
        Application is the class name of the application
        Object is the type of object

Examples:
        Set xlsSheet = CreateObject("Excel.Sheet")
        Set xlsChart = CreateObject("Excel.Chart")
        Set xlApp = CreateObject("Excel.Application")
        Set wdDoc = CreateObject("Word.Document")
```

The GetObject Function

To create a new automation object from an existing file, we use the Set statement with the **GetObject function**. The syntax is shown below:

```
Set objectname = GetObject (filename)
where
        Set is the required command
        objectname is the name of the automation object
        GetObject is the required function
        filename is the location of the existing file
```

(continued)

Release an Automation Object

When we are finished with an automation object, we need to remove the object from memory with the Set statement and the Nothing keyword. The ***Nothing keyword*** is used to disassociate a variable name from an actual object. Use the ***Set statement*** to assign Nothing to an object variable. The syntax is shown below:

Set *objectname* = **Nothing**
    where
        Set is the required command
        objectname is the variable name used to refer to an object
        Nothing is the required keyword

Examples:

```
        Set xlsChart = Nothing
        Set wdDoc = Nothing
```

In the next exercise, you will create an application that spell-checks and grammar-checks the contents of a text box. You will use the power of automation with Word to add this capability to your application. You will not be using an OLE container in this example because the text will be displayed in a text box.

The Spell Pad Project Using Automation

Objective: Create a simple notepad application that can spell check and grammar check. Use Figure 6.4 as a guide for the exercise.

STEP 1: Create the Spell Pad Form

➤ Start Visual Basic. Click the New Project dialog box's **New tab**.

➤ Click the **Standard EXE icon**. Click the **Open button** to open a new project window. Set your Visual Basic options as shown in Chapter 2, Hands-on Exercise 1, Step 2 (see page 48) if you want to ensure that the following steps look as much like the figures shown as possible.

➤ Pull down the **File menu** and select **Save Form1 As** to display the Save File As dialog box. Select the drive and folder where you stored your data disk (*Exploring Visual Basic 6*). Enter **Spell Pad** in the File name text box. Click the **Save button** to save the form file and close the dialog box.

➤ Pull down the **File menu** again and select **Save Project As** to display the Save Project As dialog box. Notice that the Save in list box is set to the folder in which you saved the form. Enter **Spell Pad** in the File name text box. Click the **Save button** to save the project files and close the dialog box.

➤ Open the Project Explorer, Form Designer, Properties, and Toolbox windows. Use Figure 6.4a as a guide in setting up your screen display. Move and resize the windows as appropriate so you can work with the form.

Change project name to Spell Pad

Writing icon displays here

Use a handle to resize the form

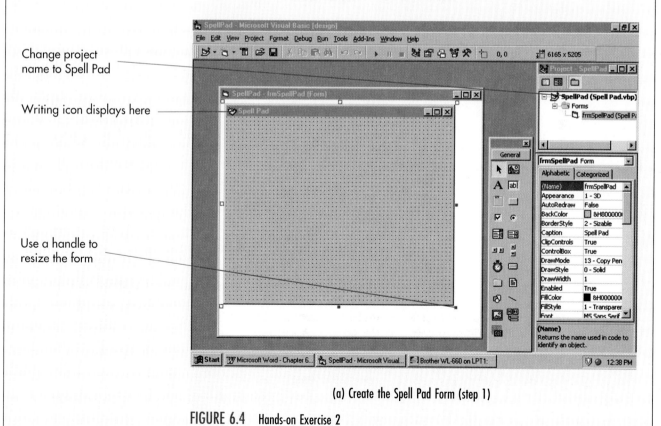

(a) Create the Spell Pad Form (step 1)

FIGURE 6.4 Hands-on Exercise 2

➤ Select **Project1** from the Project Explorer window.

➤ Move to the Properties window and change the project's Name property to **SpellPad**.

➤ Move to the Form Designer window and select the form. Move and resize it to the size shown in the figure.

➤ With the form still selected, move to the Properties window and set the following properties for the form:

Property	Setting
Name	frmSpellPad
Caption	Spell Pad
Icon	Icons\Writing\Note16.ico Note: This Icon is located in the Icon Library.

STEP 2: Add Menus and Set the Form Properties

➤ Pull down the **Tools menu** and select **Menu Editor** to open the Menu Editor window.

➤ Enter the following menu items:

Level	Caption	Name
Title	&File	mnuFile
Menu Item	E&xit	mnuExit
Title	&Tools	mnuTools
Menu Item	&Spell Check...	mnuSpell
Menu Item	Spell and &Grammar Check...	mnuGrammar

➤ Click the **OK button** to create the menu. The items with the ellipses (...) indicate that a dialog box will be displayed. You will add code to display the Word dialog boxes later.

➤ Select the **TextBox tool** from the Toolbox. Move to the form, then drag and drop to place the control immediately below the menu bar as shown in Figure 6.4b. Move to the Properties window and set the following properties for the text box:

Property	Setting
Name	txtNote
MultiLine	True

➤ From the Form Design window, pull down the **File menu** to test and display the Exit menu item.

➤ Pull down the **Tools menu** to test and display the menu as shown in the figure.

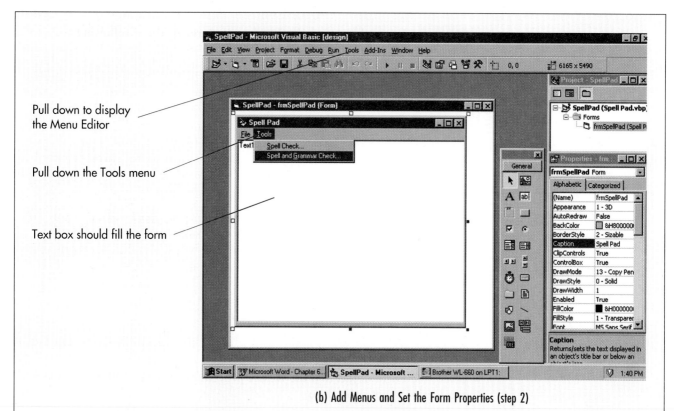

Pull down to display the Menu Editor

Pull down the Tools menu

Text box should fill the form

(b) Add Menus and Set the Form Properties (step 2)

FIGURE 6.4   Hands-on Exercise 2 (continued)

STEP 3: Add Code to Display the Form

➤ Close the Toolbox and Properties windows.

➤ Pull down the form's **File menu** and select **Exit** to display the Code Editor window.

➤ Add the following code to the Exit menu event procedure:

```
Private Sub mnuExit_Click()
' Purpose: Exit the application
        End
End Sub
```

➤ Select the **General object** and the **Declarations procedure**. Add the banner comment code to the Declarations section:

```
'*****************************************************
' Programmer:   Carlotta Eaton
' Date:         June 30, 1998
' Source:       Spell Pad.vbp
' ID:           Chapter 6 Hands-on Exercise 2
' Purpose:      Demonstrate Automation using Word
'               Add Spell checking and grammar checking
'               'capabilities to a text box
' Events:       Exit, Spell Check, Grammar Check
' Forms:        Spell Pad.frm
' References:   None
'*****************************************************
Option Explicit
```

➤ Select the **Form object** and the **Load procedure**. Add the following code to the Load event procedure:

```
Private Sub Form_Load()
' Purpose: Set form properties and load form
        Dim Inch As Integer
        Inch = 1440    '1440 twips = 1 logical inch

        With Me 'current form
                Height = 3 * Inch
                Width = 5 * Inch
                txtNote.BackColor = RGB(255, 255, 255) 'white
                txtNote.Text = "Enter text here."
        End With

        'Center form
        Me.Move (Screen.Width - Me.Width) / 2, _
         (Screen.Height - Me.Height) / 2
End Sub
```

➤ Select the **Form object** and the **Resize procedure**. Add the following code to the Resize event procedure:

```
Private Sub Form_Resize()
' Purpose: Resize the textbox when the form is resized
   Me.txtNote.Height = ScaleHeight
   Me.txtNote.Width = ScaleWidth
End Sub
```

➤ Close the Code Editor window.

STEP 4: Test the Form Code

➤ Click the toolbar's **Start button**. Click the **Yes button** to save your code and form changes if needed.

➤ The screen will display as shown in Figure 6.4c. Examine the size of the form. It should be approximately 3 by 5 inches, which is the size of a standard index card.

➤ The words "Enter text here" will display in the text box.

➤ Select an edge of the form and drag it to resize it. The text box should resize with the form.

➤ Type a few lines of text in the text box. You should be able to type several lines of text because the Multiline property is set to True.

➤ If a compilation error is displayed, correct any typos in the code.

➤ Pull down the form's **File menu** and select **Exit** to stop running the application.

STEP 5: Add the Word Library Reference to Your Project

➤ Pull down **Project menu** and select **References** to display the dialog box shown in Figure 6.4d.

➤ Select the check box beside **Microsoft Word 8.0 Object Library** to add a reference to this object library to your project. You may need to scroll to display the Word reference.

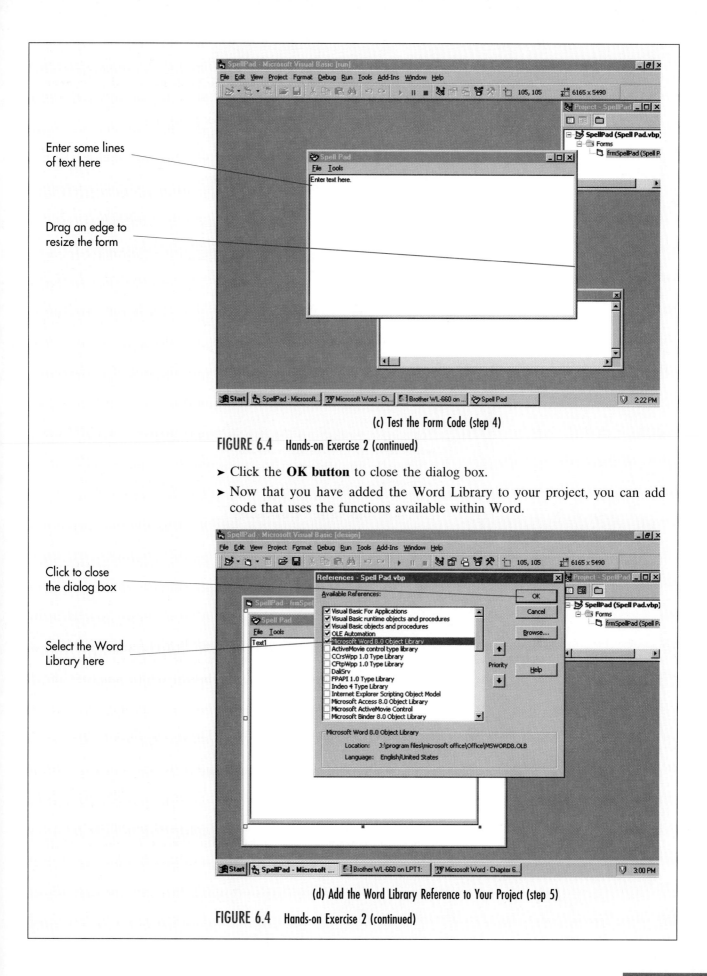

Enter some lines
of text here

Drag an edge to
resize the form

(c) Test the Form Code (step 4)

FIGURE 6.4   Hands-on Exercise 2 (continued)

➤ Click the **OK button** to close the dialog box.

➤ Now that you have added the Word Library to your project, you can add code that uses the functions available within Word.

Click to close
the dialog box

Select the Word
Library here

(d) Add the Word Library Reference to Your Project (step 5)

FIGURE 6.4   Hands-on Exercise 2 (continued)

STEP 6: Add Code to the Spell-Check Menu

➤ From the Form Designer window, pull down the **Tools menu** and select **Spell Check** to display the Code Editor window.

➤ Add the following code to the Spell menu event procedure:

```
Private Sub mnuSpell_Click()
' Purpose: Use Automation and Word to add spell check
        'Declare a variable for the Word application object
        Dim wdDocument As Word.Application

        'Create a Word object and a new Word document
        Set wdDocument = CreateObject("Word.Application")
        wdDocument.Documents.Add

        'Set the Word selection as the text box contents
        wdDocument.Selection.Text = txtNote.Text
        'Call the check spelling function
        wdDocument.ActiveDocument.CheckSpelling

        'Put the spell-checked text into the text box
        txtNote.Text = wdDocument.Selection.Text

        'Quit Word without saving changes within Word
        wdDocument.ActiveDocument.Close _
            SaveChanges:=wdDoNotSaveChanges
        wdDocument.Quit

        'Release Word object from memory
        Set wdDocument = Nothing
End Sub
```

➤ Close the Code Editor window.

STEP 7: Test the Spell-Check Menu

➤ If you have the Word application open, save changes to your document and exit Word to avoid Component Busy errors while you are running your VB project.

➤ Click the toolbar's **Start button**. Click the **Yes button** to save your code and project changes.

➤ Delete **Enter text here** from the text box.

➤ Enter **I am using VB automtion and the Word Libray**. into the text box. The misspellings are intentional.

➤ Pull down the **Tools menu** and select **Spell Check**.

➤ The Spelling dialog box will display as shown in Figure 6.4e. Notice the Word task may be added to the taskbar.

➤ The misspelled word will be highlighted, and suggested respellings will be offered. Select the correct spelling and click the **Change button** to change the spelling.

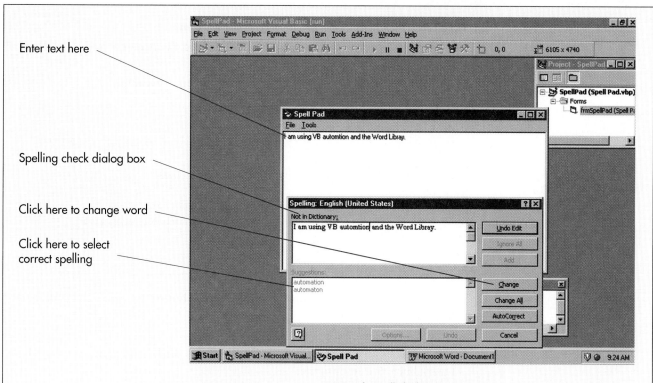

Enter text here

Spelling check dialog box

Click here to change word

Click here to select
correct spelling

(e) Test the Spell Checking Menu (step 7)

FIGURE 6.4   Hands-on Exercise 2 (continued)

➤ Continue until all the words are correctly spelled. When you click the **Change button** to correct the last misspelling, the dialog box closes. (Alternatively, you can click the box's Close button.)

➤ As the dialog box closes, the Word window flashes briefly on the screen before the Word application quits. You will add code in the next step to fix this.

➤ The sentence with the corrected spellings now appears in the text box.

➤ Pull down the **File menu** and select **Exit** to stop your application.

COMPONENT BUSY ERRORS

The Component Busy message box is displayed if the application (such as Word in this exercise) is busy doing something else when you call it. To fix the problem, you can click the Switch To button to go to the application (Word) and finish the current process, or click Retry to give the application more time to finish, or click Cancel to cancel the Visual Basic use of the application

STEP 8: Add More Code to the Spell-Check Menu

➤ From the Form Designer window, pull down the **Tools menu**, and select **Spell Check** to display the Code Editor window.

➤ Add the boldfaced code to the Spell menu event procedure.

```
wdDocument.Documents.Add

'Set the Word selection as the text box contents
wdDocument.Selection.Text = txtNote.Text

'Minimize Word window to avoid window flash
Word.Application.WindowState = wdWindowStateMinimize

'Call the check spelling function
```

➤ Click the toolbar's **Start button**. Click the **Yes button** to save your code and project changes if needed.

➤ Delete **Enter text here** from the text box.

➤ Enter **I am using VB automtion and the Word lbary.** into the text box. The misspellings are intentional.

➤ Pull down the **Tools menu** and select **Spell Check**. The Spelling dialog box will display. Correct the misspelled words, and click the **Change button**.

➤ Wait a moment for the dialog box to close. The Word document window should not display this time.

STEP 9: Add Code for Multiple Lines of Text

➤ Go back to the text box, and press **Enter** and add **Watch the reslts of multiple lines**.

➤ Press **Enter** twice and add **Programmed by name**. Substitute your name here.

➤ Pull down the **Tools menu** and select **Spell Check**. Correct the misspelled word (results), and click the **Change button**.

➤ Wait a moment for the dialog box to close. Examine the text box, and notice that a special carriage return symbol, "|", has been inserted at the beginning of the second line as shown in Figure 6.4f.

➤ The inserted symbol occurs because Word and the Visual Basic text box control handle the carriage return and line feed characters a bit differently. Next, let's add some code to handle multiple lines of text correctly.

➤ Pull down the form's **File menu** and select **Exit** to stop your application.

➤ From the Form Designer window, pull down the form's **Tools menu** and select **Spell Check** to display the Code Editor window.

➤ Change the line of code as shown below as indicated by the bold font:

```
'Put the spell checked text into the text box
txtNote.Text = AddLF (wdDocument.Selection.Text)
```

➤ Now add the AddLF function to your code. Select the **General object** and the **Declarations procedure**. Immediately after the Option Explicit line add the following:

```
Private Function AddLF(txtBuffer As String) As String
' Purpose: Add LF character to the end of each line
        Dim txtClean As String          'clean string w/o chars
        Dim CR As String                'carriage return character
        Dim LF As String                'line feed character
        Dim Length As Integer           'length of text string
        Dim Position As Integer         'position of char in string

        'Initialize variables
        CR = Chr(13)    'carriage return
        LF = Chr(10)    'line feed
        txtClean = ""   'empty string
        Length = Len(txtBuffer)
        Do Until Length < 2 'CF + LF = 2 chars
            Position = InStr(1, txtBuffer, CR)
            If Position > 0 Then
                'Remove CR char, replace with LF
                txtClean = txtClean & Left _
                    (txtBuffer, Position) & LF
                txtBuffer = Right(txtBuffer, _
                    Length - Position)
                Length = Len(txtBuffer)
            Else:
                txtClean = txtClean & txtBuffer
                Length = 0
            End If
        Loop
        AddLF = txtClean   'return clean string
End Function
```

➤ Close the Code Editor window.

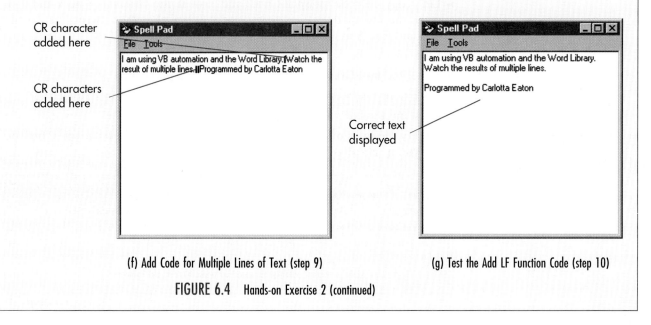

(f) Add Code for Multiple Lines of Text (step 9)   (g) Test the Add LF Function Code (step 10)

FIGURE 6.4   Hands-on Exercise 2 (continued)

STEP 10: Test the AddLF Function Code

➤ Click the toolbar's **Start button**. Click the **Yes button** to save your code changes if needed.

➤ Delete **Enter text here** from the text box.

➤ Enter **I am using VB automation and the Word Library**. into the textbox.

➤ Press **Enter** and add **Watch the reslts of multiple lines**.

➤ Press the **Enter key** twice and add **Programmed by name**. Substitute your name here.

➤ Pull down the **Tools menu** and select **Spell Check**. Correct the misspelled word (*results*), and click the **Change button**.

➤ Wait a moment for the dialog box to close.

➤ Examine the text box. There will be multiple lines of text as shown in Figure 6.4g (see previous page).

➤ Pull down the **File Menu** and select **Exit** to stop your application.

NONPRINTABLE SPECIAL CHARACTERS

There are several special characters used to format text. Two of these are the Linefeed and Carriage Return characters. The *Linefeed character* moves down to the next line, and is represented by 10 in the ANSI code set. The *Carriage Return character* moves to the leftmost margin on the same line, and is represented by 13 in the ANSI code set. The *Chr function* returns character strings and is especially useful when working with nonprintable characters. Another term used by programmers is the *NewLine character* that combines the Carriage Return and Linefeed characters Chr(13) and Chr(10) together.

STEP 11: Add Code to the Grammar Check Menu

➤ From the Form Designer window, pull down the **Tools menu** and select **Spell Check** to display the Code Editor window.

➤ Let's copy the code for Spell Check and paste it into Grammar Check and then make the few modifications to the code. Select all code between the Private Sub and End Sub lines of code.

➤ Click the toolbar's **Copy button**.

➤ Select the **mnuGrammar object** and the **Click procedure**.

➤ Place your insertion bar immediately after the Private Sub statement.

➤ Click the toolbar's **Paste button** to insert the lines of code.

➤ Modify the lines of code as shown below. The changes are shown in bold to aid you in making the necessary changes:

```
Private Sub mnuGrammar_Click()
' Purpose: Use Automation and Word to add grammar check
'Declare a variable for the Word application object
Dim wdDocument As Word.Application


        'Create a Word object and a new Word document
```

(continued)

```
                Set wdDocument = CreateObject("Word.Application")
                wdDocument.Documents.Add

                'Set the Word selection as the text box contents
                wdDocument.Selection.Text = txtNote.Text

                'Minimize Word window to avoid window flash
                Word.Application.WindowState = wdWindowStateMinimize

                'Call the check grammar function
                wdDocument.ActiveDocument.CheckGrammar

                'Put the grammar-checked text into the text box
                txtNote.Text = AddLF(wdDocument.Selection.Text)

                'Quit Word without saving changes within Word
                wdDocument.ActiveDocument.Close _
                        SaveChanges:=wdDoNotSaveChanges
                wdDocument.Quit
                'Release Word object from memory
                Set wdDocument = Nothing
        End Sub
```

➤ Close the Code Editor window.

STEP 12: Test the Grammar Check Menu

➤ Click the toolbar's **Start button**. Click the **Yes button** to save your code and project changes.

➤ Delete **Enter text here** from the text box.

➤ Enter **i am using VB automation and the Word Library**. The misspellings are intentional.

➤ Press **Enter**.

➤ Enter **this tiem I am checking grammar as well as spelling**.

➤ Pull down the **Tools menu** and select **Spell and Grammar Check**.

➤ The Spelling and Grammar dialog box will display as shown in Figure 6.4h (on the next page).

➤ Grammar errors will be displayed in green, and spelling errors will be displayed in red. Select the corrections, and click the **Change button** to apply the changes.

➤ Continue until all the words are corrected in the sentences. When you click the **Change button** to correct the last mistake, the dialog box closes. (Alternatively, you can click the box's Close button.)

➤ When the dialog box closes, the corrected sentences appear in the text box.

➤ Pull down the **File menu** and select **Exit** to stop your application.

➤ **Exit** Visual Basic, and save your project changes if needed.

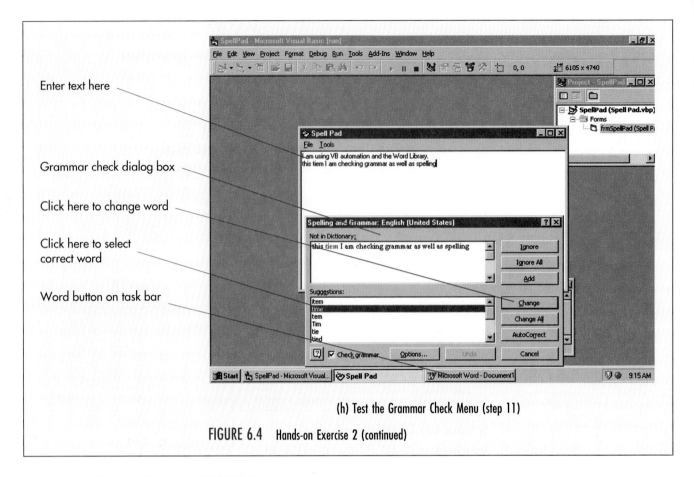

Enter text here

Grammar check dialog box

Click here to change word

Click here to select correct word

Word button on task bar

(h) Test the Grammar Check Menu (step 11)

FIGURE 6.4 Hands-on Exercise 2 (continued)

SAVING OLE OBJECTS

In the previous exercises, we did not save any changes made to the objects embedded or linked to the form using the OLE container control. We can save changes using the OLE container control's SaveToFile method. We can read a file into the OLE container control using the ReadFromFile method.

SaveToFile Method

We can use the *SaveToFile method* to save an OLE object to a data file. The file will be saved in binary format. The syntax is shown below:

> *Objectname*.**SaveToFile** *filenumber*
> where
>   *Objectname* is the name of the OLE object
>   **SaveToFile** is the required method
>   *filenumber* is the number of the file, and must correspond to an open
>   binary file

ReadFromFile Method

We can use the ***ReadFromFile method*** to retrieve an OLE object from a data file. The file will be retrieved in binary format. The syntax is shown below:

*Objectname.***ReadFromFile** *filenumber*
where
     Objectname is the name of the OLE object
     ReadFromFile is the required method
     filenumber is the number of the file, and must correspond to an open
         binary file

For example, we could use the following code to open, read, and save a file to and from an OLE container control.

```
' oleObject is the name of the OLE container control

'Open File
FileNumber = FreeFile
Open "MyFile.dat" For Binary As #FileNumber

' Read File
oleObject.ReadFromFile FileNumber

' Save File
oleObject.SaveToFile FileNumber

' Close File
Close #FileNumber
```

THE MORTGAGE MINDER PROJECT

Now let's apply the use of the OLE container control and automation by creating a more sophisticated project. We have created an Excel workbook called Mortgage Minder. It consists of four worksheets. The first worksheet is called Setup and is shown in Figure 6.5a (on the next page). It contains the setup values and assumptions needed to calculate the other three worksheets.

Notice that many of the values have been named. This makes it easier to refer to the values in the other worksheets and our Visual Basic program. For example, cell B2 is named *Amount for the Loan Amount*. The other named references are shown in the figure. All the changes to the values are made on this worksheet. We do not edit the other worksheets; instead they are updated via references to this first worksheet.

Take a look at the Term Options worksheet shown in Figure 6.5b. This worksheet calculates monthly payments for several term options ranging from 5 years to 30 years. The monthly payment calculations are made using Excel's PMT function. The assumptions listed at the top of the worksheet are taken from the Setup

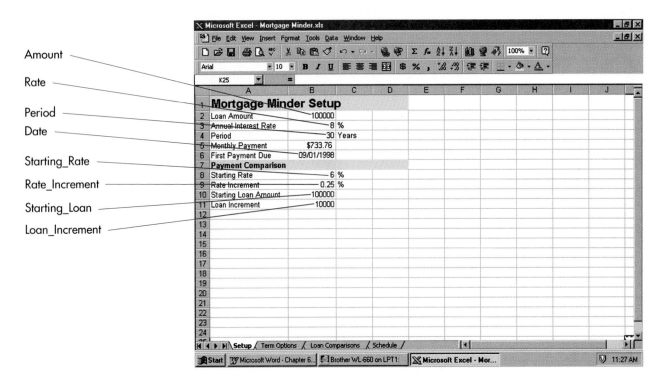

Amount

Rate

Period

Date

Starting_Rate

Rate_Increment

Starting_Loan

Loan_Increment

(a) The Setup Worksheet

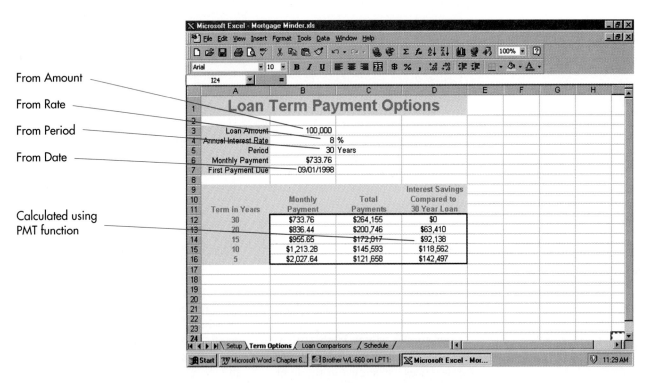

From Amount

From Rate

From Period

From Date

Calculated using
PMT function

(b) The Term Options Worksheet

FIGURE 6.5   The Mortgage Minder Project

worksheet. For example, the Loan Amount is set in the Setup worksheet with the named reference called Amount. The other references are shown in the figure.

Next, examine the Loan Comparisons worksheet shown in Figure 6.5c. This worksheet calculates difference loan amounts with varying interest rates. Again

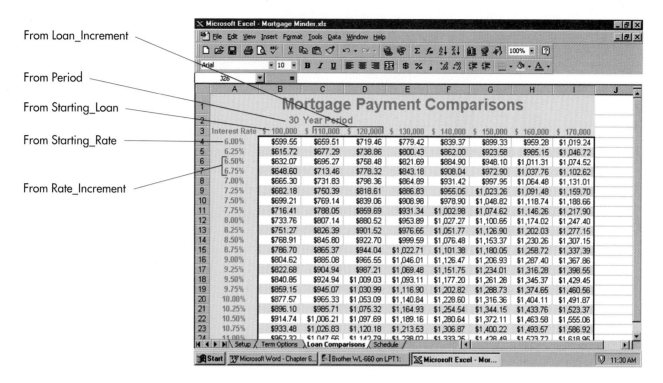

From Loan_Increment

From Period

From Starting_Loan

From Starting_Rate

From Rate_Increment

(c) The Loan Comparisons Worksheet

FIGURE 6.5 The Mortgage Minder Project (continued)

the assumptions listed at the top and left side of the worksheet are not edited on this worksheet. Instead the values are taken from the Setup worksheet. For example, the Starting_Loan amount of $100,000 is referenced from the first worksheet. The other references are shown in the figure.

Finally, examine the Schedule worksheet shown in Figure 6.5d (on the next page). This worksheet calculates the amortization schedule for the life of the loan. The worksheet is very long because it lists the amounts for 30 years. Again, the assumptions listed at the top of the worksheet are not edited on this worksheet. Instead, the values are taken from the Setup worksheet. For example, the Amount of $100,000 is referenced from the first worksheet. The other references are shown in the figure. The values in the body of the worksheet are calculated using the PMT function and other formulas. The workbook is available in the data disk, and is called *Mortgage Minder.xls*.

For this application, we do not want the end user to modify the worksheets directly. We have put a lot of work into setting up the first worksheet (called Setup) and referencing the appropriate values for the other three worksheets. We have also included several functions and formulas in the body of the worksheets, and we do not want the user to corrupt these cells.

We decide to use Visual Basic to create a user interface for this Excel workbook. We create a different form for each worksheet. We want the user to be able to edit only the values shown in the Setup worksheet, so we will create a form to display these values. The initial form, called Main, is displayed in Figure 6.5e (on the next page). Examine the figure, and notice the values are labeled to correspond to the Setup worksheet. The second form is displayed in Figure 6.5f (on the next page), and is used in the Loan Comparisons worksheet. The values are also labeled here to correspond with the Setup worksheet.

We will also create forms to display the other three worksheets. Since we do not want the user to be able to edit or save the actual worksheets, we will embed the worksheets in the OLE container control. We do want the latest updates from the Setup worksheet to be displayed in the other worksheets, so we will embed the worksheets at run time.

From Rate

From Date

From Period

From Amount

Calculated using PMT
function and formulas

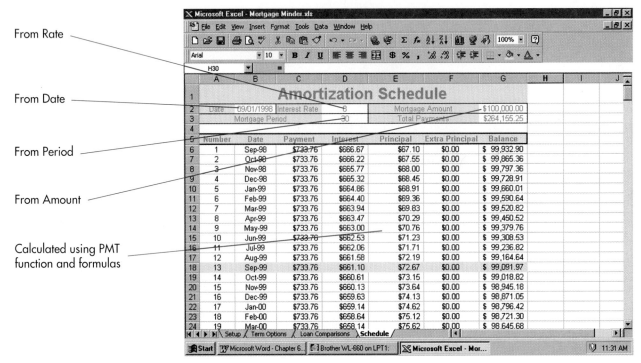

(d) The Schedule Worksheet

Amount

Rate

Date

Period

Starting_Rate

Rate_Increment

Starting_Loan

Loan_Increment

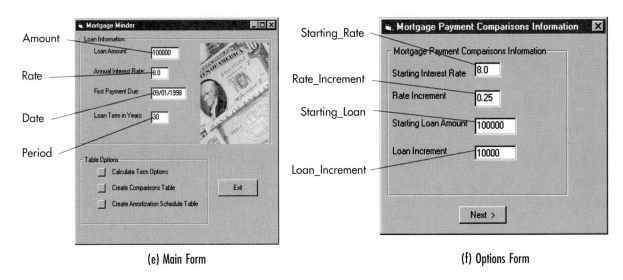

(e) Main Form

(f) Options Form

FIGURE 6.5   The Mortgage Minder Project (continued)

Learn by Doing

Now that you understand the purpose of the Mortgage Minder application, let's actually work with it. There are six different forms in the project. All of the forms have been started for you. A Splash form introduces the project. The Main form is shown in Figure 6.5e. When the user selects the Calculate Term Options button, the Options form is displayed with the embedded Term Options worksheet. When the user selects the Create Comparisons Table button, the form as shown in Figure 6.5f is displayed. After the user modifies the values and clicks the Next command button, the Compare form is displayed with the embedded Loan Comparisons worksheet. Finally, when the user selects Create Amortization Schedule Table, the Schedule form is displayed with the embedded Schedule worksheet.

The Mortgage Minder Project

Objective: To use automation with Excel and the OLE container to display several Excel worksheets. Create a project to compute mortgage payments, compare interest rates, and create an amortization table. Use Figure 6.3 as a guide for the exercise.

STEP 1: Open and Save the Project and Module Files

➤ Start Visual Basic. Click the New Project dialog box's **Existing tab**.

➤ Select the disk and folder where your data disk is stored (*Exploring Visual Basic 6*). Select the **Mortgage Starter project**. Click the **Open button** to open the project.

➤ Open the Project Explorer and Properties windows.

➤ Move to the Project Explorer window and click the **plus sign** beside the Modules folder to display the list of modules.

➤ Move to the Project Explorer window and click the **plus sign** beside the Forms folder to display the list of forms.

➤ Select the **Module1 module**. Move to the Properties window and change the Name property to **Module**.

➤ Click the **View Code button** to display the Code Editor window as shown in Figure 6.6a.

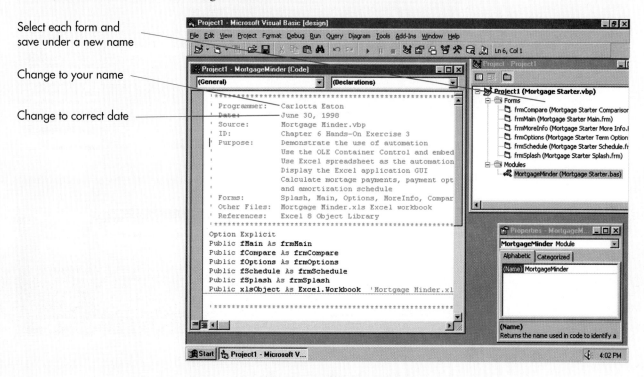

Select each form and save under a new name

Change to your name

Change to correct date

(a) Open and Save the Mortgage Starter Project (step 1)

FIGURE 6.6   Hands-on Exercise 3

➤ Change the programmer name and the date to your name and the current date.

➤ Scroll and read the program code. The Declarations section immediately follows the banner comment section. The Excel object and all the forms are declared here. The code in this module displays the Splash form.

➤ Pull down the **File menu** and select **Save Mortgage Starter.bas As**.

➤ Select the disk and folder where your data disk is stored (*Exploring Visual Basic 6*).

➤ Enter **Mortgage Minder** in the File name text box. Click the **Save button** to save the module file.

➤ Select **Project1** in the Project Explorer window. Move to the Properties window and change the Name property to **MortgageMinder** (no spaces).

➤ Pull down the **File menu** and select **Save Project As**. The Save in list box will be set to the folder where you saved the module.

➤ Enter **Mortgage Minder** in the File name text box. Click the **Save button** to save the project file.

STEP 2: Save the Form Files

➤ Close the Code Editor window.

➤ Double click the **Splash form** to display it. Click the **View Code button** to display the Code Editor window.

➤ Select the **Form object** and the **Load procedure**.

➤ Change the programmer name to your name as shown in Figure 6.6b.

Select the Splash form

Change to your name

Change to your school

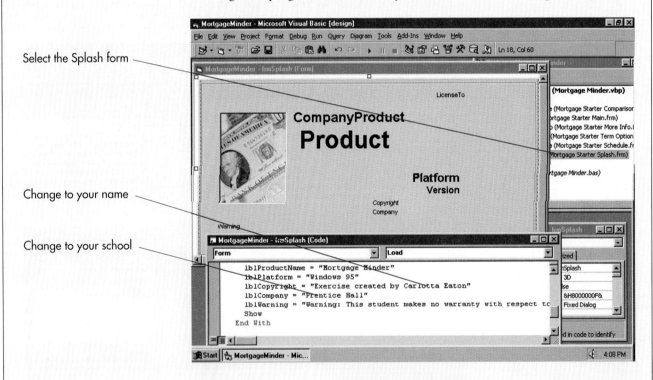

(b) Save the Form Files (step 2)

FIGURE 6.6   Hands-on Exercise 3 (continued)

➤ Change *Prentice Hall* to the name of your school.

➤ Next, pull down the File menu, and select **Save Mortgage Starter Splash As**.

➤ Enter **Mortgage Minder Splash** in the File name text box. The Save in list box will be set to the folder where you saved the project.

➤ Repeat this procedure for the other 5 forms. Select the form from the Project Explorer window. Then pull down the **File menu** and select **Save form As**. When you finish, the form files should be saved as:

- *Mortgage Minder Comparisons*
- *Mortgage Minder Main*
- *Mortgage Minder More Info*
- *Mortgage Minder Term Options*
- *Mortgage Minder Schedule*
- *Mortgage Minder Splash*

➤ Close the Code Editor window if it is still displayed.

STEP 3: Test the Existing Forms

➤ Click the toolbar's **Start button** to run the project. Click the **Yes button** to save your project changes if needed.

➤ The Splash form will display as shown in Figure 6.6c. Click the **OK button** to display the next form.

➤ Next, the Main form will display as shown in Figure 6.6d. The form is titled *Mortgage Minder*.

➤ Click the command button beside **Create Comparisons Table** to display the next form.

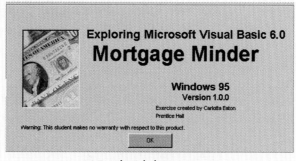

(c) Test the Splash Form (step 3)

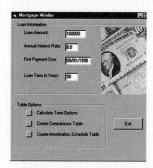

(d) Test the Main Form (step 3)

FIGURE 6.6   Hands-on Exercise 3 (continued)

➤ The More Info form will display (on top of the main form). The form is titled *Mortgage Payment Comparisons Information* as shown in Figure 6.6e (on the next page). Click the **Next command button** to display the Compare form.

➤ The Compare form will display as shown in Figure 6.6f (on the next page). The form is titled *Mortgage Payment Comparisons*. Click the **Close button** to redisplay the Main form.

➤ Click the command button beside **Calculate Term Options**. The Options form will display. The form looks like Figure 6.6f except the form is titled *Calculate Term Options*. Click the **Close button** to redisplay the Main form.

➤ Click the command button beside **Create Amortization Schedule Table**. The Schedule form will display. The form looks like Figure 6.6f except the form is titled *Amortization Schedule*. Click the **Close button** to redisplay the Main form.

➤ Click the **Exit button** to exit the application.

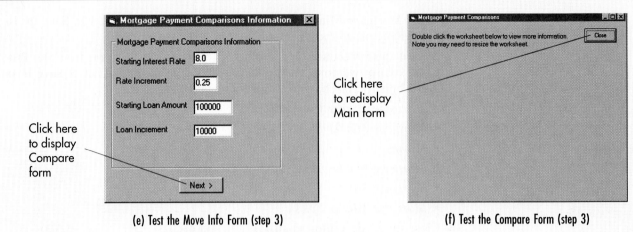

Click here
to display
Compare
form

Click here
to redisplay
Main form

(e) Test the Move Info Form (step 3)

(f) Test the Compare Form (step 3)

FIGURE 6.6   Hands-on Exercise 3 (continued)

STEP 4: Modify the Options Form

➤ In the Project Explorer window, double click the **Options form** to display it.

➤ Click the toolbar's **Toolbox button**.

➤ Select the **OLE Container tool** and draw the container on the form as large as possible within the current form size.

➤ The Insert Object dialog box will display. Click the **Cancel button**. You will be selecting the object with code later.

➤ Move to the Properties window and change the Name property to **oleWorksheet**.

➤ Pull down the **View menu** and select **Code** to display the Code Editor window.

➤ Select the **Form object** and the **Load procedure**.

➤ Insert the following lines of code immediately after the comment line:

```
' Add code here to display Excel
      xlsObject.Worksheets("Term Options").Activate
      'display worksheet in OLE container
      With oleWorksheet
            .CreateEmbed App.Path & "\Mortgage Minder.xls"
            .Visible = True
      End With
```

➤ This code embeds the Mortgage Minder workbook in the OLE container control. It also activates the Term Options worksheet in the Mortgage Minder workbook.

➤ Scroll to read the rest of the code for this form. Notice that the Close button unloads the current form and then redisplays the Main form.

➤ Close the Code Editor window.

STEP 5: Test the Options Form

➤ Click the toolbar's **Start button** to test your changes. Click the **Yes button** to save your project changes if needed.

➤ The Splash form will display. Click the **OK button** to display the Main form.

➤ Click the command button beside **Calculate Term Options** to display the Options form.

- ➤ The Options form will display with the worksheet titled *Loan Term Payment Options*.
- ➤ Double click the **worksheet** to invoke active editing. You may need to grab a handle and drag the worksheet to enlarge it as shown in the figure.
- ➤ Click the **Close button**. The form will appear as shown in Figure 6.6g.

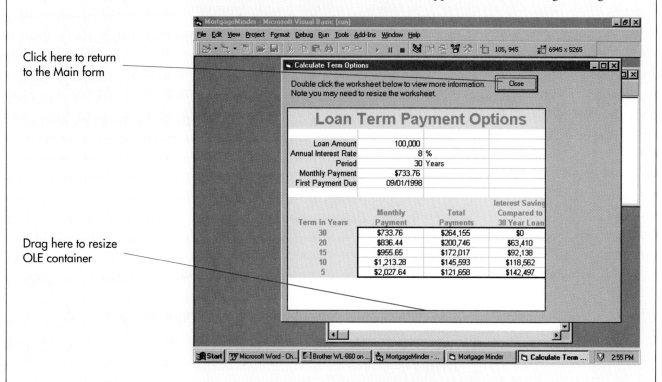

Click here to return to the Main form

Drag here to resize OLE container

(g) Test the Options Form (step 5)

FIGURE 6.6 Hands-on Exercise 3 (continued)

- ➤ Click the **Close button** again to redisplay the Main form.
- ➤ Change the Loan Amount to **150000**, and enter **15** for the Loan Term in Years.
- ➤ Click the command button beside **Calculate Term Options** to display the Options form.
- ➤ The Options form will display with the new data. Examine the worksheet. The new monthly payment is **$1,433.48**.
- ➤ Click the **Close button** to return to the Main form.
- ➤ Click the **Exit button** to exit the application.

STEP 6: Modify the Compare Form

- ➤ In the Project Explorer window, double click the **Compare form** to display it.
- ➤ Select the **OLE Container tool** from the Toolbox and draw the container on the form as large as possible within the current form size.
- ➤ The Insert Object dialog box will display. Click the **Cancel button**. You will be selecting the object with code later.
- ➤ Move to the Properties window and change the Name property to **oleWorksheet**.
- ➤ Pull down the **View menu** and select **Code** to display the Code Editor window.
- ➤ Select the **Form object** and the **Load procedure**.

➤ Insert the following lines of code immediately after the comment line:

```
' Add code here to display Excel worksheet
      xlsObject.Worksheets("Loan Comparisons").Activate
      'display worksheet in OLE container
      With oleWorksheet
            .CreateEmbed App.Path & "\Mortgage Minder.xls"
            .Visible = True
      End With
```

➤ This code embeds the Mortgage Minder workbook in the OLE container control. It also activates the Loan Comparisons worksheet in the workbook.

➤ Scroll to read the rest of the code for this form. Notice that the Close button unloads the current form and then redisplays the Main form.

➤ Close the Code Editor window.

STEP 7: Test the Compare Form

➤ Click the toolbar's **Start button** to test your changes. Click the **Yes button** to save your changes if needed

➤ The Splash form will display. Click the **OK button** to display the Main form.

➤ Change the Loan amount to **80000**.

➤ Click the command button beside **Create Comparisons Table** to display the Compare form.

➤ The More Info form will display. Notice the loan amount automatically updates to 80000.

➤ Change the Loan Increment to **5000**.

➤ Click the **Next command button**.

➤ The Compare form will display with the worksheet titled *Mortgage Payment Comparisons*.

➤ The first cell will display $587.01 for $80,000 at an 8% interest rate. The next column will be labeled 85,000 then 90,000 since you specified a $5000 increment.

➤ Double click the **worksheet** to invoke active editing. You may need to grab a handle and drag the worksheet to enlarge it as shown in the figure.

➤ Click the **Close button**. The form will appear as shown in Figure 6.6h.

➤ Click the **Close button** again to redisplay the Main form.

➤ Click the **Exit button** to exit the application.

STEP 8: Modify the Schedule Form

➤ In the Project Explorer window, double click the **Schedule form** to display it.

➤ Select the **OLE Container tool** and draw the container on the form as large as possible within the current form size.

➤ The Insert Object dialog box will display. Click the **Cancel button**. You will be selecting the object with code later.

➤ Move to the Properties window and change the Name property to **oleWorksheet**.

➤ Pull down the **View menu** and select **Code** to display the Code Editor window.

➤ Select the **Form object** and the **Load procedure**.

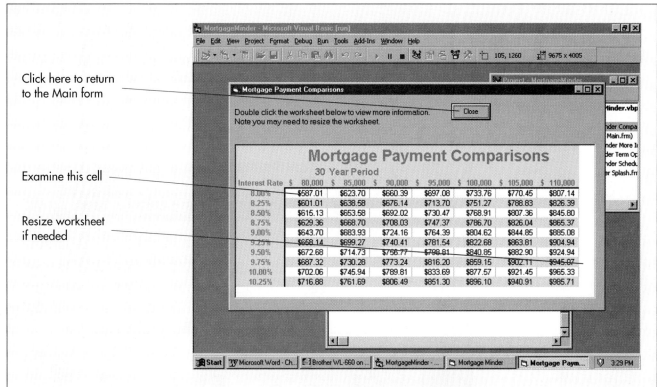

Click here to return to the Main form

Examine this cell

Resize worksheet if needed

(h) Test the Compare Form (step 7)

FIGURE 6.6   Hands-on Exercise 3 (continued)

➤ Insert the following lines of code immediately after the comment line:

```
' Add code here to display Excel worksheet
      xlsObject.Worksheets("Schedule").Activate
      'display worksheet in OLE container
      With oleWorksheet
            .Visible = True
            .CreateEmbed App.Path & "\Mortgage Minder.xls"
      End With
```

➤ This code embeds the Mortgage Minder workbook in the OLE container control. It also activates the Schedule worksheet of the workbook.

➤ Scroll to read the rest of the code for this form. Notice that the Close button unloads the current form and then redisplays the Main form.

➤ Close the Code Editor window.

STEP 9: Test the Schedule Form

➤ Click the toolbar's **Start button** to test your changes. Click the **Yes button** to save your changes if needed.

➤ The Splash form will display. Click the **OK button** to display the Main form.

➤ Change the Loan Amount to **115000**, the First Payment Due date to **01/01/1998**, and enter **15** for the Loan Term.

➤ Click the command button beside **Create Amortization Schedule Table** to display the Schedule form.

➤ The Schedule form will display. Notice the parameters are automatically updated in the worksheet.

➤ Double click the **worksheet** to invoke active editing. You may need to grab a handle and drag the worksheet to enlarge it as shown in the figure.

➤ The payment is computed at $1,099.00 for $115,000, at an 8% interest rate for 15 years. Each row calculates the mortgage balance at the end of the month.

➤ Click the **Close button**. The form will appear as shown in Figure 6.6i.

➤ Click the **Close button** again to redisplay the Main form.

➤ Click the **Exit button** to exit the application.

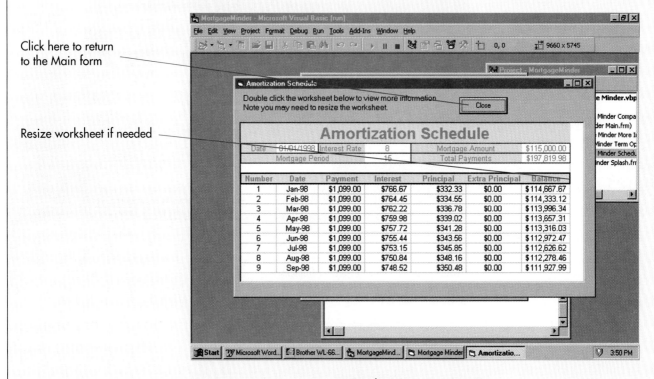

(i) Test the Compare Form (step 9)

FIGURE 6.6 Hands-on Exercise 3 (continued)

TROUBLE DISPLAYING DATES?

If your Schedule form does not display the payment dates correctly, you may not have the Excel 97 Analysis ToolPak loaded on your computer. To correct this problem, bring up Excel 97, and pull down the Tools menu. Select the Add-ins menu item, and check to select the Analysis TookPak add-in. If the Add-in is not listed, then you need to install this option using the Windows Control Panel.

This chapter showed you how to utilize code contained in other applications using the OLE container control and automation. All the Office 97 applications are ActiveX servers, so we can reference and use their libraries, and use their objects, methods, and functions. You can customize any Office application and use the same programming language—Visual Basic. Visual Basic can be thought of as the glue that binds all these applications' objects together. You can customize Office applications from within the application using VBA (Visual Basic for Applications). In this chapter, we worked with Visual Basic from outside the Office applications.

Microsoft has introduced various ways to share data between Windows applications. At first there was only the clipboard. Next came DDE, then OLE, and finally the newest ActiveX technologies. The terminology for what are now called servers and containers has changed over time.

This chapter introduced you to Object Linking and Embedding. OLE allows you to combine data and components from multiple applications to create compound documents. We used the OLE container control to take advantage of the OLE technology. We placed an OLE container control on a form, and learned how to paste, embed, and link an Excel worksheet to the Visual Basic form.

We introduced automation. Automation is a powerful tool that allows us to work with programmable data objects. A programmable data object can be displayed on a form, or we can work with it in the background without displaying the interface at all. We created the Spell Pad application that utilized the spell-checking and grammar-checking code contained in Word.

Finally, we utilized the OLE container control together with an Excel workbook with several worksheets to create the Mortgage Minder application. We combined the mathematical capabilities of Excel with the forms and code in Visual Basic to create a sophisticated application.

KEY WORDS AND CONCEPTS

ActiveX servers	Dynamic Data Exchange (DDE)	Nothing keyword
Auto-activate property		Object browser
Automation	Early binding	Object Linking and Embedding (OLE)
Clipboard	Embedded object	
Container application	GetObject function	OLE container control
CreateEmbed method	In-place activation	ReadFromFile method
CreateLink method	Late binding	References dialog
CreateObject function	Linked object	SaveToFile method
		Server application

MULTIPLE CHOICE

1. Which of the following methods of data sharing between Windows applications was available first?
   (a) ActiveX
   (b) Dynamic Date Exchange (DDE)
   (c) Object Linking and Embedding (OLE)
   (d) Clipboard

2. Which of the following is not a limitation of the Windows clipboard?
    (a) Only one object can be placed on the clipboard at any time
    (b) The objects cannot be automatically updated
    (c) The only way to access the clipboard is through cut, copy, and paste operations
    (d) All of the above are limitations of the clipboard

3. Which of the following terms was used in previous versions of Visual Basic to mean the OLE container control?
    (a) OLE server control
    (b) OLE client
    (c) OLE client control
    (d) OLE automation

4. Which of the following terms was **not** used in previous versions of Visual Basic to denote an ActiveX server?
    (a) OLE source
    (b) OLE destination
    (c) OLE server
    (d) OLE automation server

5. What happens when you double click an OLE container control at run time?
    (a) In-place activation
    (b) Activation of the server application outside of Visual Basic
    (c) Out-of-place activation
    (d) In-place editing

6. Under which circumstances would you choose linking over embedding?
    a) When the server object is constantly changing and you need the latest version
    b) When the same object is referenced from many different documents
    c) Both (a) and (b)
    d) Neither (a) nor (b)

7. Under which circumstances would you choose embedding over linking?
    (a) When you need to run the Visual Basic program on a different machine from where the original server object is located
    (b) When the server object is constantly changing and you want the embedded object to remain static
    (c) Both (a) and (b)
    (d) Neither (a) nor (b)

8. Which of the following can be created as an embedded object using the OLE container control?
    (a) A chart created by Microsoft Excel
    (b) A worksheet created by Microsoft Excel
    (c) A document created by Microsoft Word
    (d) All of the above

9. What happens if you draw an OLE container control on a form but click the Cancel button on the Insert Object dialog box?
    (a) The OLE container control is deleted
    (b) The OLE container control is empty, and needs code to insert the object at run time
    (c) The Insert Object dialog box reports an error, and waits for you to select an object
    (d) There is no Cancel button on the Insert Object dialog box

10. An embedded object can be added to a form in an OLE container control
    (a) At design time
    (b) At run time
    (c) Both (a) and (b)
    (d) Neither (a) nor (b)

11. Which type of object can be displayed as an icon on a form in an OLE container control
    (a) An embedded object
    (b) A pasted object
    (c) A linked object
    (d) All of the above

12. How do we add a library of available objects to our Visual Basic project?
    a) Pull down the Project menu and select References
    b) Pull down the Project menu and select Object Browser
    c) Click the toolbar's Object Browser button
    d) Press the F2 key

13. The Object Browser allows us to view which of the following?
    a) Classes
    b) Methods
    c) Functions
    d) All of the above

14. If we declare a variable of type Object, which of the following binding methods will Visual Basic use?
    (a) Late binding
    (b) Early binding
    (c) Either of the above depending on the rest of the code
    (d) None of the above

15. When we are finished with an automation object, we should
    (a) Release the object using the Set statement with the Nothing keyword
    (b) Quit the server application
    (c) Close any open files
    (d) Open any closed files

ANSWERS

1. d	**6.** c	**11.** d
2. d	**7.** c	**12.** a
3. c	**8.** d	**13.** d
4. b	**9.** b	**14.** a
5. a	**10.** c	**15.** a

Practice with Visual Basic

VIDEO
CLIP

1. **Using the OLE Container Control (Learning Edition Only)** This exercise requires that you be using the Learning Edition of Visual Basic, and that you have installed the *Learn Visual Basic Now* book on your hard drive or have access to it from the CD-ROM. This demonstration illustrates using the OLE container control to display a Paint object. Run and watch the demonstration to reinforce this material from the chapter.

   a. Start *Learn Visual Basic Now*.

   b. Open the *Chapter 2* book and the *Working with Other Applications* book as shown in Figure 6.7.

   c. Open the "OLE" or "OLE Control" topic.

   d. Read the information about OLE.

   e. Scroll to the bottom of the topic pane and click the Demonstration icon.

   f. View the entire Visual Basic demonstration.

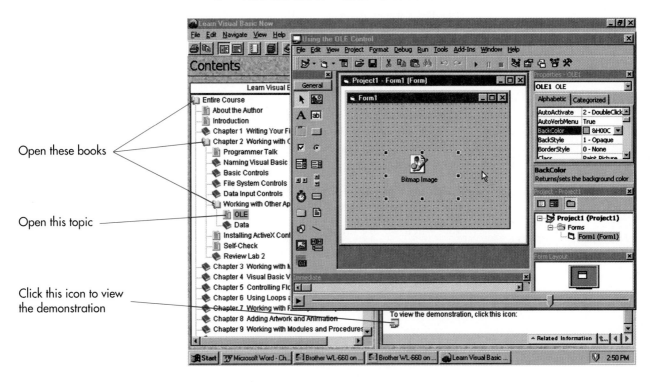

FIGURE 6.7 Screen for Exercise 1: Using the OLE Container Control

VIDEO
CLIP

2. **In the Kitchen with Automation (Learning Edition Only)** This exercise requires that you be using the Learning Edition of Visual Basic and that you have installed the *Learn Visual Basic Now* book on your hard drive or have access to it from the CD-ROM. This video clip draws an analogy between cooking in the kitchen and automation. Run and watch the video clip to reinforce this material from the chapter.

   a. Start *Learn Visual Basic Now*.

   b. Open the *Chapter 11* book. If you are using Visual Basic 5, also open the *Using Application Objects* book.

   c. Open the "Understanding Automation" topic.

   d. Read the information shown in the topic pane.

e. Click the Expert Point of View icon in the topic pane.

f. View the entire video clip.

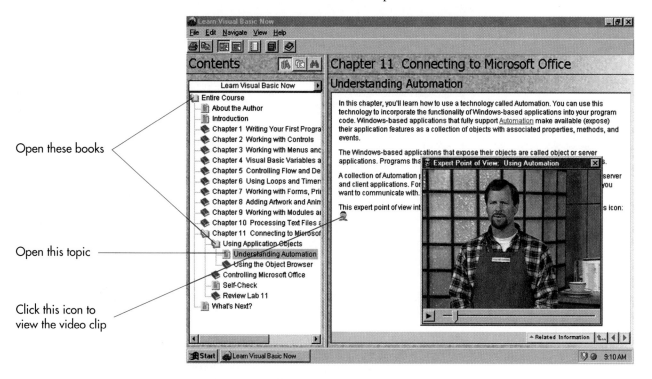

Open these books

Open this topic

Click this icon to
view the video clip

FIGURE 6.8   Screen for Exercise 2: In the Kitchen with Automation

3. **Sample Word Automation (Learning Edition Only)** This exercise requires that you be using the Learning Edition of Visual Basic and that you have installed the *Learn Visual Basic Now* book on your hard drive or have access to it from the CD-ROM. This demonstration shows you have to use Word spell-check function as you did in Hands-on Exercise 2 of this chapter. You will be amazed at how quickly you can recreate the starting portion of this exercise. Run and watch the demonstration to reinforce this material from the chapter.

a. Start *Learn Visual Basic Now*.

b. Open the *Chapter 11* book. Open the *Controlling Microsoft Office* book, and then the *Microsoft Word* book or topic.

c. If you are using Visual Basic 5, also open the "Sample Word Automation" topic.

d. Click the Video Clip icon in the topic pane.

e. View the entire demonstration.

LOCATE THE SAMPLES

You will be running several sample applications included with Visual Basic in these exercises. If you are using Visual Basic 6.0, look for them first in the default location by opening these folders: Microsoft Visual Studio, then Msdn98 (optionally 98vs, then 1033), then Samples, and finally Vb98. If you are using Visual Basic 5.0, open Microsoft Visual Studio, then Vb, then samples.

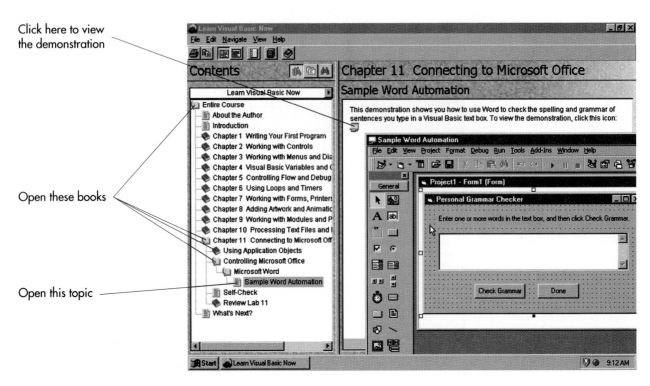

Click here to view the demonstration

Open these books

Open this topic

FIGURE 6.9   Screen for Exercise 3: Sample Word Automation

4. OLE Container Sample Application There are several interesting sample projects included with Visual Basic. Run the *Olecont* sample project (located in the *Olecont* folder) as shown in Figure 6.10. Open the *olecont.vbp* project file and run the project.

  a. Click the toolbar's **Start button** to run the sample application.

  b. Pull down the **File menu** and select **About** to read the project instructions.

  c. Pull down the **File menu** again and select **New**.

  d. The Insert Object dialog box will display.

  e. Select the **Create New** option button.

  f. Select **Bitmap image** as the Object type.

  g. Click the **OK button** to insert the object.

  h. The Paint application will display within the OLE container control area on the form.

  i. Create a simple Paint drawing.

  j. When you have finished the drawing, pull down the **Close OLE object menu** to return to Visual Basic.

  k. Pull down the **File menu** and select **Save As**.

  l. Select the folder for your data disk (*Exploring Visual Basic 6*), and save the file as **OLE and Paint**. The file extension of OLE will automatically be added.

  m. Close the Paint.Picture Object (child) window.

  n. Pull down the **File menu** again and select **Open**.

  o. Select the same folder, and select the **OLE and Paint file**.

  p. Click the **Open button** to redisplay your Paint creation.

  q. Close the windows and exit the project.

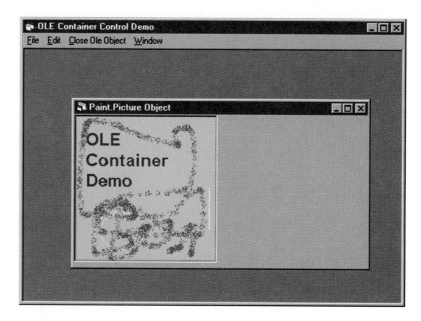

FIGURE 6.10 Screen for Exercise 4: OLE Container Sample Application

5. **More Spell Check** Enhance the Sticky Pad project you created in Chapter 5 with spell-check and grammar-check capabilities. Open the *Sticky Pad* project that you completed in Chapter 5 Hands-on Exercise 3. Follow the instructions from Hands-on Exercise 2 in this chapter to add the spell check and grammar check capabilities. Save your completed project as ***Sticky Pad Spell***. Remember to save your forms with the new project name. Print out your form and code, or turn in your project and form files on disk to your instructor.

6. **OLE and PowerPoint** Create a graphic user interface (GUI) for the PowerPoint presentations included on your data disk. There are three PowerPoint presentations named OLE History, OLE Works, and OLE Container. Create a Splash form as shown in Figure 6.11a. The graphic for this form is named *VB-Book.jpg* and is available on the data disk. Change the name on the form to your name. The Main form should look similar to Figure 6.11b. Create the labels to describe the three presentations, and place an OLE container beneath each. Embed the PowerPoint files in the appropriate OLE container using the Display as Icon option. The names of the presentations are shown in the figure.

(a) Splash Form

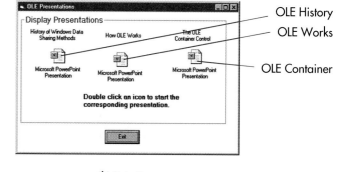

(b) Main Form

FIGURE 6.11 Screen for Exercise 6: OLE and PowerPoint

Programming with PowerPoint

Create at least three different short PowerPoint presentations on related topics. Create a Visual Basic program that displays each of the presentations when selected. You may design your forms to look similar to Figure 6.11 if you wish. Save the forms and project with the name ***Programming with PowerPoint***. Create an appropriate Splash form to initialize your project. Make a printout of your forms and code, or submit a disk containing the project to your instructor.

Careers in Visual Basic

There are many career opportunities available for employees with Visual Basic skills. Go to the CareerLink site at *www.careerlink.windx.com* or your favorite jobs Web site. From the home page, look under the Job Seekers category for appropriate links. On the next page, you can select a programming language as shown in Figure 6.12. You can also select the area you would like to live. Read at least three different job descriptions that spark your interest, and use Microsoft Word or another word processor to create a professional-looking summary document. Submit your summary and a hard copy of the three jobs you reviewed to your instructor.

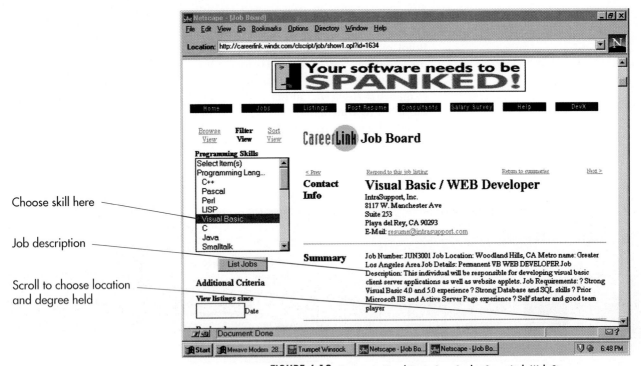

FIGURE 6.12 Careers in Visual Basic Case Study: CareerLink Web Site

Programming a Handheld PC

Microsoft has added the Windows CE Version 2.0 operating systems for Handheld PCs to its operating system list. *The Windows CE Toolkit for Visual Basic* is also available. Information about this toolkit is available at:

www.microsoft.com/windowscs/hpc/developer/products/vbce.htm

as of this writing. If the URL listed here doesn't work, start at *www.microsoft.com* and search for Visual Basic and Windows CE. Read about creating applications for these small devices. Use Microsoft Word or another word processor to create a professional-looking one-page summary of information about this toolkit. Submit your summary to your instructor.

Programming with Excel

Create an Excel workbook with at least two related worksheets. Create a Visual Basic program that gets input or updates the worksheet. Use the Mortgage Minder project created in Hands-on Exercise 3 as a guide for this project. Create an appropriate Splash form to initialize your project. Save the forms and project with the name *Programming with Excel*. Make a printout of your forms and code, or submit a disk containing the project to your instructor.

7

DATABASE BASICS: TABLES, RECORDS, AND FIELDS

OBJECTIVES

After reading this chapter, you will be able to:

1. Explain the differences between a flat-file database and a relational database.
2. Explain the basic terminology for databases such as *table*, *record*, and *field*.
3. Implement a flat-file database using random access.
4. Explain the use of the Microsoft FlexGrid control.

OVERVIEW

In this chapter, we will be working with a simple database created using Visual Basic. The database project we'll develop is very simple and stores celebrity birthdays. It demonstrates the basics of do-it-yourself database programming, and other Visual Basic techniques. It's not a database we would actually use to keep track of celebrity birthdays because it lacks a number of features that most end users would consider essential.

First, we will define some basic database concepts such as tables, records, and fields. Then we will create a flat-file database that consists of a single table.

We will also utilize the Microsoft FlexGrid control to display this table. The FlexGrid control is an ActiveX control. As its name indicates, it is very flexible, and can be used to display many types of information in a grid or tabular format.

The project is completed in the three hands-on exercises for the chapter. After you complete this project, you'll have a simple, functional program that demonstrates database fundamental concepts. We'll build on this knowledge in Chapter 8 where we use the controls designed especially for databases.

A **database** is a collection of data for a particular purpose that is stored and later retrieved. Databases are used to store data about clients, products, inventory, students, courses, and much more. The data in a database is stored in one or more tables. If a database has only one table, it is often called a **flat-file database**. A **relational database** usually consists of more than one table, and also joins and cross-references the information between them. A database **table** has rows and columns just like tables that we create with a word processor, but it has special requirements.

Each row in a database table represents a record, as shown in Figure 7.1. The figure displays the database table design for the Birthday Database that we'll be creating in the hands-on exercises. A **record** stores data about a single client, product, inventory item, student, course, or other entity. In this case, there are four records, and each record stores information about a single person. Each record consists of several fields. A **field** is the smallest unit of data (or fact) that we store in a database. Each column in the table represents a field. In our example each person record consists of seven fields—last name, first name, birthdate, occupation, birthplace, state, and country.

Field names

Last Name	First Name	Birthdate	Occupation	Birthplace	State	Country
Bergen	Candice	5/9/46	Actor / Actress	Beverly Hills	CA	USA
Dion	Celine	3/30/68	Musician / Singer	Charlemagne	Quebec	Canada
Nicholson	Jack	4/22/37	Actor / Actress	Neptune	NJ	USA
Seymour	Jane	2/15/51	Actor / Actress	Hilling	Middlesex	England

A record

FIGURE 7.1   Birthday Database Table

The Type Statement

Records for a flat-file database have to be defined using code. We define a record by creating a new data type. The **Type statement** allows us to create our own data types called **user-defined data types**. (Some programming languages use the term **programmer-defined data type**, which is more logical since it is the programmer, not the end user, who creates the new type.) Creating a new type is a two-step process. First, we declare the type, and then we declare a variable of the new type.

Let's return to the example shown in Figure 7.1, where we want to store birthday data about celebrities. Each of the seven fields would be appropriately stored as strings except for the birthdate field, which would be stored as a date.

We could name this new data type **Person**. Then we would need a variable using the new defined type, such as **CurrentRecord**. The simple syntax for the Type statement is shown below:

```
Type variablename
    elementname1 As datatype
    elementname2 As datatype...
End Type
where
    variablename is a programmer-named variable
    elementname is a programmer-named element (or field) contained
        within the new type
    datatype is a Visual Basic data type such as Integer, Currency, or
        String etc.

Example:
    Type Person
        FirstName As String * 25
        LastName As String * 50
        Birthdate As Date
        Occupation As String * 35
        City As String * 25
        State As String * 25
        Country As String * 2
    End Type
```

Next we need to declare a new variable with the new data type. For example:

```
Public CurrentRecord As Person
```

LEARN BY DOING

First, we will create a flat-file database, with records of equal length. Many databases were originally created this way. The term *flat-file* is used for a simple, single-table database. We already know all about reading and writing to files from Chapter 5. We'll store the records in binary file format, and use random access rather than sequential access, because that's faster with such records. We will define our records using the Type statement.

RANDOM ACCESS

Visual Basic 6 provides a new feature called the File System Object (FSO) model. This feature was discussed in Chapter 5. FSO does not currently support random access. Therefore, we are using the older Open, Close, Get, and Put statements for file I/O in this exercise.

Today there are more sophisticated application and programming tools specially designed for creating database projects, and these will be used in the next chapter. Figure 7.2 shows the form used to add, display, and edit records stored in the Birthday Database.

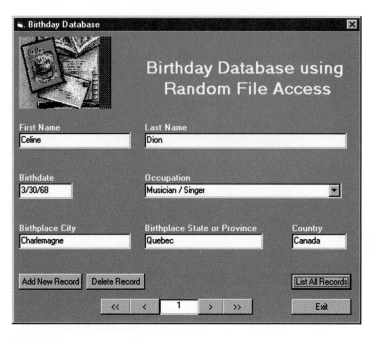

FIGURE 7.2   Birthday Database Main Form

HANDS-ON EXERCISE 1

Birthday Database

Objective: To define and create a new flat-file database using random access. Store the records in binary format. Create the forms and module for the database. Define the record structure using the Type statement. Use Figure 7.3 as a guide for the exercise.

STEP 1: Create a New Project

➤ Start **Visual Basic**. Click the New Project dialog box's **New tab**. Click the **Standard EXE icon**. Click the **Open button** to open the new project.

➤ Pull down the **File menu** and select **Save Project As**.

➤ Select the disk and folder where your data disk is stored (*Exploring Visual Basic 6*). Enter **Birthday Database Main** in the File Name text box, and click the **Save button** to save the form.

➤ The Save Project As dialog box will display next. Enter **Birthday Database** in the File Name text box. Click the **Save button** to save the project.

➤ Click the toolbar's **Properties Window button**. Ensure the form is selected, and move to the Properties window. Change the Name Property to **frmMain** and the Caption property to **Birthday Database**.

➤ Pull down the **Project menu** and select **Add Form**. Select the Add Form dialog box's **Splash Screen icon**. Click the **Open button** to add the form.

➤ Pull down the **File menu** and select **Save frmSplash As**. Enter **Birthday Data-base Splash** in the File Name text box. Click the **Save button** to save the form.

➤ Pull down the **Project menu** and select **Add Module**. Click the Add Module dialog box's **New tab**. Click the **Module icon**. Click the **Open button** to add the module to your project.

➤ Pull down the **File menu** and select **Save Module1 As**. Enter **Birthday Data-base** in the File Name text box. Click the **Save button** to save the module.

STEP 2: Set Properties for the Splash Form

➤ Click the toolbar's **Project Explorer button**. Move to the window and open the Forms folder.

➤ Double click the **Splash form** to display it. Select the form.

➤ In the Properties window, change the BackColor property to **teal** (6th column, 5th row of the palette).

➤ Select the **frame**, and change the BackColor property to **teal**.

➤ Select the **first label**, hold down the **Ctrl** key and select **all of the labels** on the form. Change the BackColor property to **teal**, and the ForeColor property to **white**.

➤ Select the **Image**. Select the **Picture property setting**, and then select the folder where your data disk is stored (*Exploring Visual Basic 6*). Select the **Birthday.bmp file**.

➤ Change the Stretch property to **False**. Drag and move the picture down a bit, and stretch the CompanyProduct label across the top of the image as shown in Figure 7.3a.

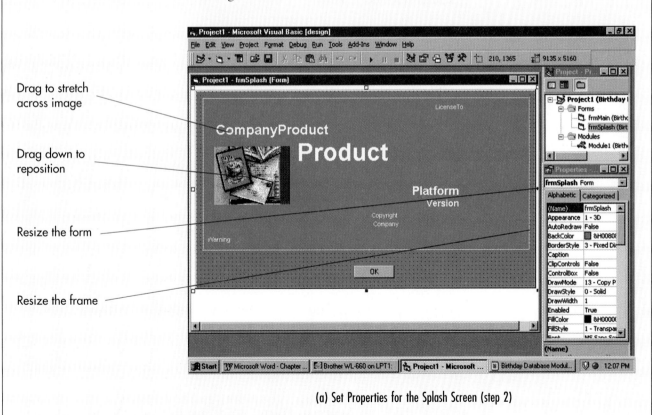

(a) Set Properties for the Splash Screen (step 2)

FIGURE 7.3   Hands-on Exercise 1

➤ Resize the form to include room for the OK command button. Click the toolbar's **Toolbox button**.

➤ Select the **Command Button tool** and draw the OK button as shown in the figure. Change the Name property to **cmdOK** and the Caption property to **OK**.

STEP 3: Add Code to the Splash Form

➤ Click the **View Code button** in the Project Explorer window.

➤ Select the **cmdOK object** and the **Click procedure**. Add the following code to the Splash form:

```
'*********************************************************************
Private Sub cmdOK_Click()
'Purpose: Unload Splash form, start database
    Call Start
    Unload Me
End Sub
```

➤ Select the **Form object** and the **Load procedure**. The two lines that begin with lblVersion and lblProductName are already included in the procedure. Add the following code to the load Splash form procedure. Remember to change the Copyright label to your name and the Company label to your college or university name.

```
'*********************************************************************
Private Sub Form_Load()
'Purpose: Display the Splash form
    With Me
        Move (Screen.Width - .Width) / 2, _
                (Screen.Height - .Height) / 2
        Show
        lblVersion.Caption = "Version " & App.Major & "." & _
                App.Minor & "." & App.Revision
        lblProductName.Caption = App.Title
        lblLicenseTo = " "
        lblCompanyProduct = "Exploring Visual Basic 6.0"
        lblPlatform = "Windows 95 and 98"
        lblCopyright = "Exercise created by Carlotta Eaton"
        lblCompany = "Prentice Hall"
        lblWarning = " Warning: This student makes no warranty"
        lblWarning = lblWarning & " with respect to this product."
        Refresh
    End With
End Sub
```

➤ Delete the **Form_KeyPress, Frame1_Click**, and **lblProductName_Click event procedures** from the form code.

➤ Close the Code Editor window and any other open windows.

SET FORM'S PROPERTIES AT RUN TIME

Step 3 demonstrates how to set the properties for the form's labels at run time. You must set the form name during design, but most other properties can be set or changed at run time or design time. Having completed Step 3, what would you say are the advantages of each technique?

STEP 4: Add Code and Test the Module

➤ In the Project Explorer window double click the **module** to display its code window.

➤ The line that includes "Option Explicit" may already be included in the procedure.

➤ Add the following code to the module, changing to your name and the current date:

```
'****************************************************************
'  Programmer:      Carlotta Eaton
'  Date:            June 30, 1998
'  Source:          Birthday Database.vbp
'  ID:              Chapter 7 Hands On Exercises 1, 2, and 3
'  Purpose:         Create a flat-file database
'                   Open, read, write, binary file with random access
'                   Use Microsoft FlexGrid and combo box controls
'  Functions:       Main, Start, AddRecord, SaveRecord, DeleteRecord
'                   and DisplayRecord
'  Forms:           Splash, Main, and List
'  References:      None
'****************************************************************
Option Explicit
Public Sub Main()
'Purpose: Open database file, display Splash form
    frmSplash.Show 'Display Splash form
End Sub
'****************************************************************
Public Sub Start()
'Purpose: Display Main form and start database
    frmMain.Show
End Sub
```

➤ Close the Code Editor window.

➤ In the Project Explorer window, right click the **Project**, and select **Project1 properties**. Change the Startup Object to **Sub Main**. Click the **OK button**.

➤ Pull down the **Tools menu** and select **Options**. Click the **Environment tab**. In the "When a program starts" frame, click the **Prompt to Save Changes option button**. Click the **OK button**. This ensures that you will be prompted to save your code changes.

➤ Click the toolbar's **Start button**. Click the **Yes button** to save your code and form changes.

➤ The Splash screen will display. Examine the size of the form to ensure that all of the words are displayed.

➤ Click the **OK button**. The blank Main form will display.

➤ Click the **Close button** in the top corner of the form to exit the application.

➤ If the form or frame was not large enough to display all labels as shown in Figure 7.3b, enlarge any objects necessary in the Form Designer window. Retest for size before continuing.

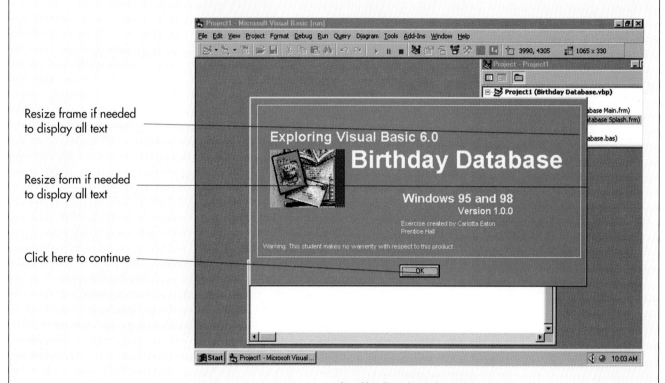

Resize frame if needed to display all text

Resize form if needed to display all text

Click here to continue

(b) Add Code and Test the Module (step 4)

FIGURE 7.3   Hands-on Exercise 1 (continued)

STEP 5: Create the Main Form

➤ In the Project Explorer window, double click **the Main form** to display it.

➤ Select the form and change the BackColor property to **teal**.

➤ Add the image control, label controls, text boxes, and command buttons to the form as shown in Figure 7.3c. Resize your form if needed.

➤ Change the Picture property to **birthday.bmp** for the image in the upper left corner of the form.

➤ Select the **title label**, and name the label **lblTitle**. Change the font size to 18, and the alignment to Center.

➤ The 7 fields for the database have two controls for each field. Corresponding controls have matching suffixes. For example, the label for the FirstName field is named **lblFirstName**, and the text box is named **txtFirstName**. Change the Caption and Name properties for all the label controls as shown in the figure.

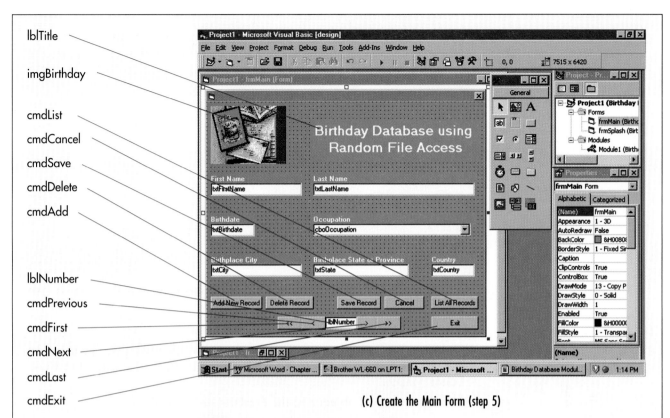

lblTitle

imgBirthday

cmdList
cmdCancel
cmdSave
cmdDelete
cmdAdd

lblNumber
cmdPrevious
cmdFirst
cmdNext
cmdLast
cmdExit

(c) Create the Main Form (step 5)

FIGURE 7.3   Hands-on Exercise 1 (continued)

➤ After placing the controls on the form, select all the label boxes by clicking the first one, holding down the Ctrl button, and selecting all other labels except the one in the middle of the navigation buttons. Change the Back-Color property to **teal** and the ForeColor property to **white**.

➤ The name for each text box is displayed in the figure to aid you in naming the controls. The other control names are labeled in the figure. Change the Name property for all the text box controls and command buttons. Change the Text property to a **blank** for all the text boxes.

➤ The Occupation field uses a combo box instead of a text box. Name the combo box **cboOccupation** as shown.

➤ Change the Name property for the first line of command buttons as shown. The buttons are named **cmdAdd**, **cmdDelete**, **cmdSave**, **cmdCancel**, and **cmdList** respectively.

➤ Change the Name property and the Caption property for the bottom line of command buttons to navigate the database and the label. The buttons are named **cmdFirst, cmdPrevious, cmdNext**, and **cmdLast** respectively.

➤ The label control in the middle is named **lblNumber**. Change the Alignment property to **2-Center**, the BackColor property to **white**, the ForeColor property to **black**. (This control may look like a text box, but it is a label here.)

➤ Change the Tab order as shown below to make entering information into the database much easier and more logical for the end user. Change the TabIndex property for any control as needed:

Control Name	TabIndex Property
txtFirstName	1
txtLastName	2
txtBirthdate	3
cboOccupation	4
txtCity	5
txtState	6
txtCountry	7

➤ Pull down the **File menu** and select **Save Birthday Database Main.frm** to save your changes.

STEP 6: Add Record Declarations to the Module

➤ Close the Form Design window, Properties window and the Toolbox. In the Project Explorer window, double click **Module1** to display the Code Editor window.

➤ Select the **General object** and the **Declarations procedure**.

➤ The banner comment will be displayed at the top of the window (as added in Step 4).

➤ In the top of the code shown below, you are defining the record called Person, which has 7 fields that match the fields in the Main form you just created.

➤ Several variables are created to temporarily store the data record number and the contents of a record while you are processing the database.

➤ The database filename is stored as a constant, *Birthday Database.dat*, and will be created in the current folder (*Exploring Visual Basic 6*).

➤ Append the following code immediately after the banner comments (after the line "Option Explicit"):

```
Option Explicit
'************* Declarations ***************************************
Public Type Person 'Define fields for a record
    FirstName As String * 25
    LastName As String * 50
    Birthdate As Date
    Occupation As String * 35
    City As String * 25
    State As String * 25
    Country As String * 25
End Type


'Stores data for current record
Public CurrentRecord As Person 'Record to hold current birthday
Public NewRecord As Boolean 'True means record not saved yet


'Record counters
Public RecordNumber As Integer 'Record key in file
```

(continued)

```
Public MaxNumber As Integer 'Maximum number of records in file
Public OldRecordNumber As Integer 'Previous record key

'File where database is stored
Public PathFilename As String 'Current path and filename
Public FileNumber As Integer 'Operating System assigned file number
Public Const FILENAME = "Birthday Database.dat" 'file for database
```

GOOD PROGRAMMING PRACTICE: PUBLIC VARIABLES

A good rule of thumb is to define variables with the smallest scope possible. *Public variables* (also called *global variables*) are a convenient way to share data among forms. Recall that public variables declared in a module are available everywhere in the application. It is a good programming practice to declare all public variables in the same module for an application (as demonstrated in step 6).

STEP 7: Add More Code to the Main Procedure

➤ Select the **Main Procedure**. This procedure opens the file for random access processing, calculates the number of files, and displays the Splash form.

➤ Append the existing code (entered in Step 4) as follows:

```
'*************************************************************************
Public Sub Main()
'Purpose: Open database file, display Splash form
Dim RecordSize As Integer

    PathFilename = App.Path & "\" & FILENAME
    FileNumber = FreeFile   'VB function to get next free file number

    RecordSize = Len(CurrentRecord) 'get length of a record
    Open PathFilename For Random As #FileNumber Len = RecordSize

    'Find number of records in file
    MaxNumber = (LOF(FileNumber) / RecordSize)

    frmSplash.Show 'Display Splash form
End Sub
```

STEP 8: Add More Code to the Start Procedure

➤ Select the **Start procedure**, and modify the existing code (entered in Step 4) as follows:

```
'************************************************************************
Public Sub Start()
'Purpose: Display Main form and start database
Dim Reply As Integer
Const NewMsg = "New database, want to start entering birthdays?"
    If MaxNumber = 0 Then    'brand new database
        Reply = MsgBox(NewMsg, vbYesNo, "New database")
    If Reply = vbYes Then
            NewRecord = True
            frmMain.Show
            'Call AddRecord
        Else
            Close(FileNumber)
            End
        End If
    Else   'records exist, display first record
        RecordNumber = 1
        NewRecord = False
        frmMain.Show
        'Call DisplayRecord(RecordNumber)
    End If
End Sub
```

ADD PROCEDURES LATER

In Step 8, notice that two lines that call procedures are comments. The procedures will be added in the next hands-on exercise. If you remove the comment indicator (') now, you will get a runtime error when testing.

STEP 9: Test the Start Procedure

➤ Close the Code Editor window (and any other windows that may still be open.) Click the toolbar's **Start button** to test your code.

➤ If displayed, click the **Yes button** to save the changes to your project.

➤ When the Splash form is displayed, click the **OK button** to continue. The New Database message box will display as shown in Figure 7.3d.

➤ Click the **No button** to test your exit code. The application will end.

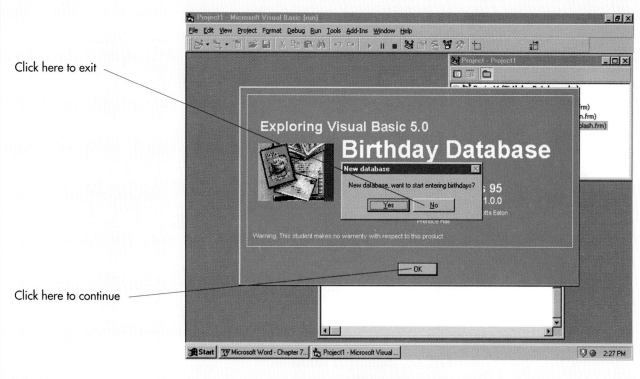

Click here to exit

Click here to continue

(d) Test the Start Procedure (step 9)

FIGURE 7.3 Hands-on Exercise 1 (continued)

➤ If you received any compiler errors, correct your code and retest until all errors have been corrected in your code.

➤ If you are not continuing to the next hands-on exercise at this time, exit Visual Basic.

MESSAGE BOX DISPLAY

When you test your Start procedure in Step 9, the Splash form may unload completely before the message box displays. Other times, the message box will overlay the Splash screen as shown in the figure. Examine the code and notice that the Splash screen's OK button executes the Unload code, and then the message box code executes. Depending on your computer, the timing will vary and either may occur.

NAVIGATING THE DATABASE

Navigating refers to finding your way around the database, and locating the item needed. We added five controls to navigate the database in the previous hands-on exercise. Together as a set, these controls imitate the data control. These five controls and the data control are shown in Figure 7.4 (on the next page). The first control (cmdFirst) moves to the first record in the database, and the second (cmdPrevious) moves to the previous record. The label control (lblNumber) displays the record number of the current record. The fourth control (cmdNext) moves to the next record, and the fifth control (cmdLast) moves to the last record in the database. We need to add code to navigate the records using these five controls.

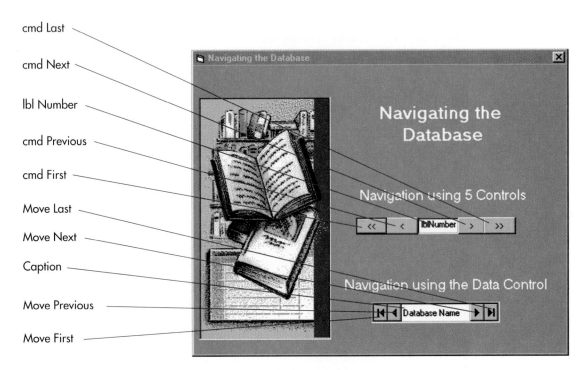

cmd Last
cmd Next
lbl Number
cmd Previous
cmd First
Move Last
Move Next
Caption
Move Previous
Move First

FIGURE 7.4 Navigating the Database

We'll look at the data control in much more detail in the next chapter. You'll see the benefits of the data control that automatically navigates the database for you without writing code. We'll code event procedures in the Main form to navigate the Birthday Database in the next hands-on exercise.

Recall that we declared several variables and the record type in the code module. Why bother with a separate module? A code module is the best place to declare variables and define types that will be used by several forms. Another important reason is that a code module can be reused as a software component. We may want to write another database application in the future, and the major procedures will be contained in a single module, instead of scattered throughout several forms. The following variables were declared in the code module to store record numbers, data, and flags so that we can keep track of the records in the database.

- *CurrentRecord* stores all the data from the current record.
- *NewRecord* is a flag that is set to True if the record still needs to be written to the database file.
- *RecordNumber* is the record number currently displayed on the Main form.
- *MaxNumber* is the number of records currently stored in the database.
- *OldRecordNumber* is the number of the previous record displayed on the Main form.

In the next hands-on exercises you will add more procedures to the code module that are called from the remaining command buttons. These procedures are listed below:

- *Main* opens the database file, and displays the Splash form.
- *Start* displays the Main form.
- *AddRecord* adds a new record to the database (called from the cmdNew Click event procedure).
- *DeleteRecord* deletes the current record from the database (called from the cmdDelete Click event procedure).

- *SaveRecord* writes the contents of the Main form to the current record in the database file (called from several event procedures).
- *DisplayRecord* reads the appropriate record from the database file and displays the contents in the Main form (called from several event procedures).
- *ExitApplication* closes the database file, unloads the Main form and ends the application (called from cmdExit Click event procedure).

Additional Improvements

After you have completed all the hands-on exercises in this chapter, you will have a good overview of the process of reading and storing records in a flat-file database. However, the Birthday Database does have some drawbacks that could be improved with additional code. The most obvious disadvantage is that you cannot search for a record based on a name or a birth date. It would also be nice to be able to print labels or a report from the database.

Another shortcoming is the way deleted records are handled. The application does not actually delete any records; instead, the contents are simply erased from the file, and the string "Record Deleted" is stored in the First Name field. The blank records take up space in the file, and they are displayed when we navigate through the records. There are several approaches to overcome this shortcoming. You could add code to skip over any records that contain the string "Record Deleted." You could add code to find the first deleted record, and overwrite it when you add a new record. If there are no deleted records, then you could add the new record at the end of the database. These improvements are left as practice exercises for the reader.

The purpose of the Birthday Database is to demonstrate how to create a simple database application without the overhead of Visual Basic's specialized database tools. As discussed in Chapter 1, remember to use the right tool for the job. You can make up your own mind depending on the job at hand.

HANDS-ON EXERCISE 2

Continue the Birthday Database

Objective: Add code to enable the Main form. Add code to add records to the database. Add code to navigate the records and display a record. Use Figure 7.5 as a guide for the exercise.

STEP 1: Add Code for the AddRecord Procedure

➤ If you did not continue from the previous exercise, start **Visual Basic**. Click the New Project dialog box's **Existing tab**. Select the disk and folder where your data disk is stored (*Exploring Visual Basic 6*). Select the **Birthday Database file**. Click the **Open button** to open the project from the previous exercise.

➤ Click the toolbar's **Project Explorer button** to display the window.

➤ Open the Forms folder and select the **Main form**. Click the **View Code button** to open the Code Editor window.

➤ Select the **General object** and the **Start procedure**.

➤ Delete the apostrophe in front of the line "Call AddRecord." This changes the line from a comment to a line that is executed.

➤ Delete the apostrophe in front of the line "Call DisplayRecord (Record-Number)". This line will also be executed.

➤ Scroll to the bottom of the Code Editor window, and append the following code for the AddRecord procedure. This procedure clears the contents of the Main form and adds a new record to the existing database.

```
'*********************************************************************
Public Sub AddRecord()
' Purpose:    Add a new record to the database
'             New Record command button was clicked
        NewRecord = True
        OldRecordNumber = RecordNumber 'save current record number
        'Toggle command button display
        With frmMain
            .cmdAdd.Visible = False
            .cmdDelete.Visible = False
            .cmdSave.Visible = True
            .cmdCancel.Visible = True

            .lblNumber = "New" 'current record number

            'Initialize data contents
            .txtFirstName = ""
            .txtLastName = ""
            .txtBirthdate = ""
            .cboOccupation.Text = ""
            .txtCity = ""
            .txtState = ""
            .txtCountry = ""

            'Set the focus to the first text box
            .txtFirstName.SetFocus
        End With
End Sub
```

STEP 2: Add Code for the DisplayRecord Procedure

➤ Scroll to the bottom of the Code Editor window, and append the following code for the DisplayRecord procedure. This procedure displays the current record in the Main form.

```
'*********************************************************************
Public Sub DisplayRecord(Record As Integer)
' Purpose: Read the specified record from the database and
'          display it in the form
    Get #FileNumber, RecordNumber, CurrentRecord

    With frmMain
        .txtFirstName = CurrentRecord.FirstName
        .txtLastName = CurrentRecord.LastName
        .txtBirthdate = CurrentRecord.Birthdate
        .cboOccupation.Text = CurrentRecord.Occupation
        .txtCity = CurrentRecord.City
        .txtState = CurrentRecord.State
        .txtCountry = CurrentRecord.Country
```

(continued)

```
            .lblNumber = RecordNumber
        End With
        OldRecordNumber = RecordNumber 'store in case of cancels
    End Sub
```

STEP 3: Add Code for the Save Record Procedure

➤ Scroll to the bottom of the Code Editor window, append the following code for the SaveRecord procedure. This procedure saves the data displayed in the Main form as a record in the database.

```
'*******************************************************************
Public Sub SaveRecord()
' Purpose: Save the contents of the form to the database file
    If NewRecord = True Then
        OldRecordNumber = RecordNumber    'remember previous record
        MaxNumber = MaxNumber + 1         'increment record counter
        RecordNumber = MaxNumber          'current record position
    End If

    With frmMain 'copy current form contents to record
        .lblNumber = RecordNumber
        CurrentRecord.FirstName = .txtFirstName
        CurrentRecord.LastName = .txtLastName
        CurrentRecord.Birthdate = DateValue(.txtBirthdate)
        CurrentRecord.Occupation = .cboOccupation.Text
        CurrentRecord.City = .txtCity
        CurrentRecord.State = .txtState
        CurrentRecord.Country = .txtCountry
     End With
     'Save record to database file
     Put #FileNumber, RecordNumber, CurrentRecord
     NewRecord = False
End Sub
```

STEP 4: Add Code for the Exit Application Procedure

➤ At the bottom of the Code Editor window, **add the following code** for the ExitApplication procedure. This procedure closes the database file before exiting the application.

```
'*******************************************************************
Public Sub ExitApplication()
' Purpose: Close files needed to exit application
    'Close the database file
    Close #FileNumber

    'Unload the Main form
    Unload frmMain
End Sub
```

STEP 5: Add Code to Load the Main Form

➤ Close the Code Editor window. In the Project Explorer window, select the **Main form**. Click the **View Code button** to edit the code.

➤ Select the **Form object** and the **Load procedure**. This procedure loads the Main form that displays the current record. It also creates the list for the combo box. Add the following code to the procedure:

```
'***************************************************************
Private Sub Form_Load()
' Purpose: Display the Main database form

    'Initialize Combo box
    With cboOccupation
            .AddItem "Actor / Actress"
            .AddItem "Artist / Painter / Sculptor"
            .AddItem "Author / Columnist / Writer"
            .AddItem "Comedian / Comedianne"
            .AddItem "Model / Supermodel"
            .AddItem "Politician / Ruler"
            .AddItem "Musician / Singer"
            .AddItem "Composer / Songwriter"
            .AddItem "Talk show host"
            .AddItem "Athlete"
            .AddItem "Movie Director / Producer"
    End With

    'Center form
    With Me
        Move (Screen.Width - .Width) / 2, _
            (Screen.Height - .Height) / 2
        .Caption = App.Title
        .Refresh
    End With

End Sub
```

CENTER FORM WITH CODE

You can specify the position of a form on the screen at design time using the Form Layout window. An alternative to this is to use code to specify the position at run time. In Step 5, you added code that is classically used to center a form on the screen.

STEP 6: Add Code to Unload the Main Form

➤ Select the **QueryUnload procedure** and add the following code. This procedure verifies that the user intended to exit the application.

```
'**********************************************************************
Private Sub Form_QueryUnload(Cancel As Integer, UnloadMode As Integer)
'Purpose: Confirm user wants to end application
Dim Reply As Integer
Const ExitMsg = "Are you sure you want to exit?"

    Reply = MsgBox(ExitMsg, vbYesNo + vbQuestion)
        If Reply = vbYes Then
            Call ExitApplication
        Else
            Cancel = True
        End If
End Sub
```

GOOD PROGRAMMING PRACTICE: USE CONSTANTS FOR MESSAGES

Use a constant for the string displayed in a message box. This keeps all the messages in the top of the procedure, making them easy to find and change in the future. Many large projects have a single module that contains only the constant declarations for messages.

STEP 7: Add Code for the Add and Save Record Command Buttons

➤ Select the **cmdAdd object** and the **Click procedure**. This procedure displays the appropriate command buttons and calls the AddRecord procedure (located in the module code). Add the following code to the procedure:

```
'**********************************************************************
Private Sub cmdAdd_Click()
'Purpose: Add a new record to the database
        NewRecord = True
        Call AddRecord

        'Toggle command button display
        cmdAdd.Visible = False
        cmdDelete.Visible = False
        cmdSave.Visible = True
        cmdCancel.Visible = True
End Sub
```

➤ Select the **cmdSave object** and the **Click procedure**. This procedure displays the appropriate command buttons and calls the SaveRecord procedure to store the current new record to the database. Add the following code to the procedure:

```
'***********************************************************************
Private Sub cmdSave_Click()
'Purpose: Save contents of current record to database
Dim Reply As Integer

    Call SaveRecord
    NewRecord = False
    'Toggle command button display
    cmdAdd.Visible = True
    cmdDelete.Visible = True
    cmdSave.Visible = False
    cmdCancel.Visible = False
End Sub'
```

➤ Select the **cmdExit object** and the **Click procedure**. This procedure displays the appropriate command buttons and calls the SaveRecord procedure to store the current new record to the database. This calls the ExitApplication procedure added in step 4. Add the following code to the procedure:

```
Private Sub cmdExit_Click()
'Purpose: End the application
    Call ExitApplication
End Sub
```

NEW VISUAL BASIC 6 FEATURE: RESOURCE EDITOR

One of the many new features of Visual Basic 6 is the Resource Editor. A *resource file* (file extension *.res*) allows you to collect all of the text and bitmaps for an application in one place. To add the Resource Editor, pull down the Add-Ins menu and select Add-In Manager. Select VB 6 Resource Editor from the list, and select the Loaded/Unloaded option. The Resource Editor is available from either the Standard toolbar or the Tools menu.

STEP 8: Test the Start Procedure
➤ Close the Code Editor window (and any other windows that may still be open). Click the toolbar's **Start button** to test your code.
➤ Click the **Yes button** to save the changes to your project.
➤ The Splash form will display. Click the **OK button** to continue.
➤ The New Database message box will display as shown in Figure 7.5a.
➤ Click the **No button** to test your exit code. The application will end.

STEP 9: Test the Code for a New Database
➤ Click the toolbar's **Start button** to test more of your code.
➤ When the Splash form is displayed, click the **OK button** to continue.

Click here to exit

Click here to display
Main form

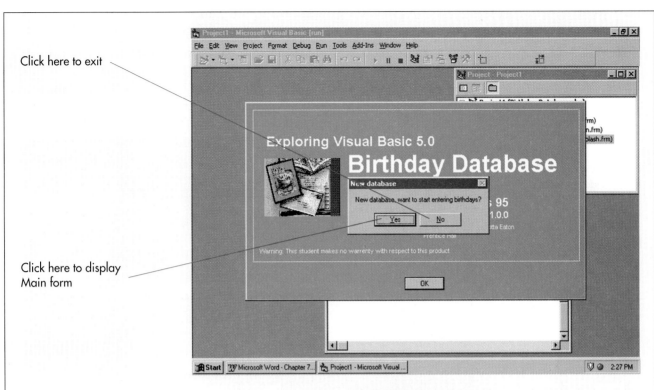

(a) Test the Start Procedure (step 8)

FIGURE 7.5   Hands-on Exercise 2

➤ The New Database dialog box will display. This time click the **Yes button** to continue.

➤ The Main form will display with blank text boxes as shown in Figure 7.5b.

Enter data here

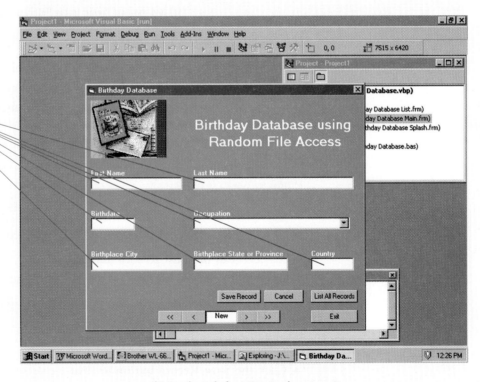

(b) Test the Code for a New Database (step 9)

FIGURE 7.5   Hands-on Exercise 2

STEP 10: Add the First Record to the Database

➤ Add some celebrity birthdays to your database. Add the following data for the first record: **Celine Dion, 03/30/1968**.

➤ Click the **combo box's arrow** to display the drop-down list as shown in Figure 7.5c. Scroll and select **Musician/Singer** from the list.

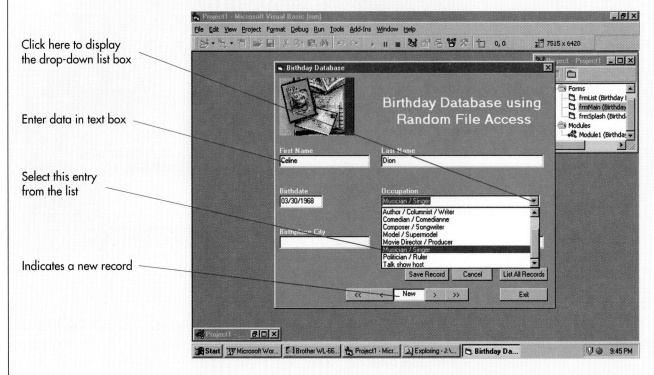

Click here to display the drop-down list box

Enter data in text box

Select this entry from the list

Indicates a new record

(c) Add the First Record to the Database (step 10)

FIGURE 7.5   Hands-on Exercise 2 (continued)

➤ Enter **Charlemagne, Quebec, Canada** for her birthplace.

➤ Click the **Save Record button** to save your entry.

➤ Notice the Save Record and Cancel buttons disappear, and the Add New Record and Delete buttons are now visible.

➤ Click the **Add New Record button**, and add the following entry:

```
Mel Gibson, 01/03/1956, Actor/Actress, Peekskill, NY, USA
```

➤ Click the **Save Record button** to save the record.

STEP 11: Add the Last Record and Exit

➤ Click the Add New Record button, and add the following entry:

```
Jane Seymour, 02/15/1951, Actor/Actress, Hilling, Middlesex, England
```

➤ Click the **Save Record button** to save the record.

➤ Click the **Exit button** to end the application. The Birthday Database message box will display, as shown in Figure 7.5d.

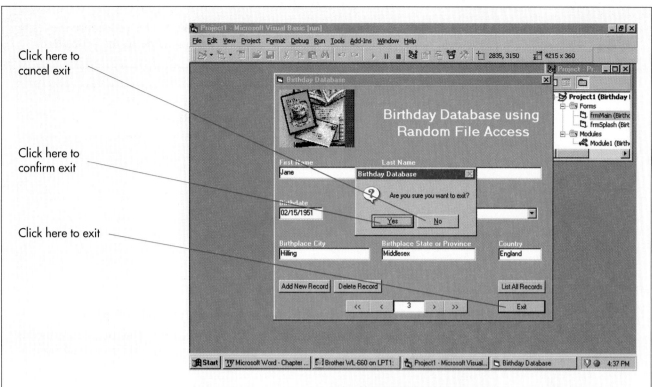

Click here to cancel exit

Click here to confirm exit

Click here to exit

(d) Add Last Record and Exit (step 11)

FIGURE 7.5   Hands-on Exercise 2 (continued)

➤ Click the **No button** to test this portion of your code. The message box will close and the Main form will remain on the screen.

➤ Click the **Exit button** to end the application. The Birthday Database message box will display.

➤ This time, click the **Yes button** to test this portion of your code. The message box and Main forms will close, and end the application.

STEP 12: Add Code for the First and Last Navigation Buttons

➤ Open the Forms folder and select the **Main form**. Click the **View Code button** to open the Code Editor window.

➤ Select the **cmdFirst object** and the **Click procedure**. This procedure moves to the first record and displays it. Add the following code to the procedure.

```
'*****************************************************************
Private Sub cmdFirst_Click()
' Purpose: Move to the first record in the database
    If NewRecord Then Exit Sub 'button should not work here
    Call SaveRecord 'save any changes
    If RecordNumber = 1 Then
        MsgBox ("Already at first record!")
        Exit Sub 'cannot move any further
    End If
    RecordNumber = 1
    Call DisplayRecord(RecordNumber)
End Sub
```

➤ Select the **cmdLast object** and the **Click procedure**. This procedure moves to the last record and displays it. Add the following code to the procedure:

```
'*********************************************************************
Private Sub cmdLast_Click()
' Purpose: Move to the last record in the database
    If NewRecord Then Exit Sub 'button should not work
    Call SaveRecord 'save any changes
    If RecordNumber = MaxNumber Then
        MsgBox ("Already at last record!")
        Exit Sub 'cannot move any further
    End If
    RecordNumber = MaxNumber
    Call DisplayRecord(RecordNumber)
End Sub
```

STEP 13: Add Code for the Next and Previous Navigation Buttons

➤ Select the **cmdNext object** and the **Click procedure**. This procedure moves to the next record in the database and displays it. Add the following code to the procedure:

```
'*********************************************************************
Private Sub cmdNext_Click()
' Purpose: Move to the next record in the database
    If NewRecord Then Exit Sub 'cannot move forward any more
    Call SaveRecord 'save any changes
    If RecordNumber = MaxNumber Then
        MsgBox ("Already at last record!")
        Exit Sub 'cannot move any further
    End If
    RecordNumber = RecordNumber + 1
    Call DisplayRecord(RecordNumber)
End Sub
```

➤ Select the **cmdPrevious object** and the **Click procedure**. This procedure moves to the previous record and displays it. Add the following code to the procedure:

```
'*********************************************************************
Private Sub cmdPrevious_Click()
' Purpose: Move to the previous record in the database
    If NewRecord Then Exit Sub 'button should not work now
    Call SaveRecord 'save any changes
    If RecordNumber = 1 Then
        MsgBox ("Already at first record!")
        Exit Sub 'cannot move any further
    End If
    RecordNumber = RecordNumber - 1
    Call DisplayRecord(RecordNumber)
End Sub
```

STEP 14: Test the Navigation Buttons

➤ Run the application again to test the navigation buttons, and verify that the records were saved.

➤ Close the Code Editor window and any other open windows. Click the toolbar's **Start button**.

➤ If prompted, click the **Yes button** to save the changes to your project.

➤ Click the Splash window's **OK button** to continue.

➤ The Main form will open, with Celine Dion's data displayed as the first record as shown in Figure 7.5e.

Last

Next

Current Record
Number

Previous

First

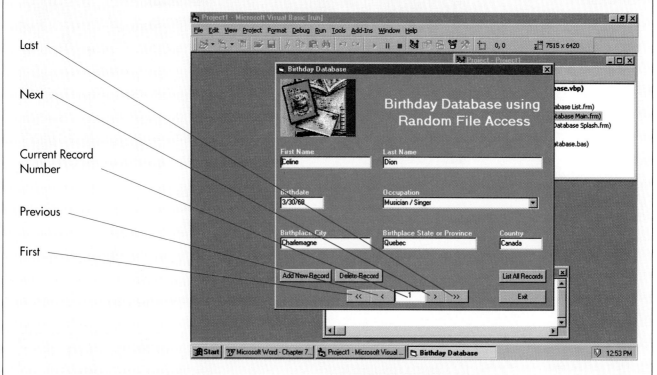

(e) Test the Navigation Buttons (step 14)

FIGURE 7.5   Hands-on Exercise 2 (continued)

➤ Click the **Next button** (looks like >) to display the second record, the data for Mel Gibson.

➤ Click the **Next button** again to display the last record, the data for Jane Seymour.

➤ Notice that the label for the record number in the middle of the navigation buttons changes as you move among the records.

STEP 15: Test and Add More Records

➤ Click the **Next button** again. A message box like that in Figure 7.5f (on the next page) will indicate that you are already at the last record. Click the **OK button** to continue.

➤ Click the **First button** (looks like <<) to return to Celine Dion's data. Click the **Previous button** (looks like <). A message box will indicate that you are already at the first record.

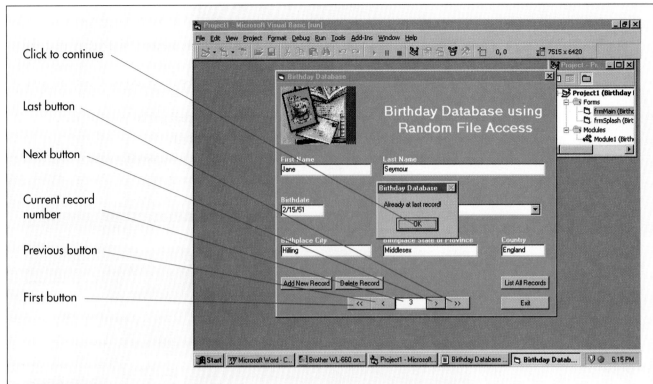

Click to continue

Last button

Next button

Current record number

Previous button

First button

(f) Test the Navigation Buttons (step 14)

FIGURE 7.5   Hands-on Exercise 2 (continued)

➤ Click the **Last button** (looks like >>) to return to Jane Seymour's data.
➤ Click the **Previous button** to return to Mel Gibson's data.
➤ Click the **Add New Record button**. Enter the following data:

```
Jack Nicholson, 04/22/1937, Actor / Actress, Neptune, NJ, USA
```

➤ Click the **Save Record button** to save the record.
➤ Click the **Add New Record button** again, and enter the following data:

```
Candice Bergen, 05/09/1946, Actor / Actress, Los Angeles, CA, USA
```

➤ Click the **Save Record button** to save the record.

STEP 16: Exit the Application

➤ Click the **Exit button** and then the message box's **Yes button** to exit the application.
➤ If you are not continuing to the next hands-on exercise at this time, exit Visual Basic.
➤ You will add the code for the "Delete Record" and "List all Records" command buttons in the next hands-on exercise.

Visual Basic contains the **Microsoft FlexGrid control** that is specially designed to display tables or grids of data arranged in rows and columns. Using this control, you can sort, merge, and format tables containing strings and pictures. Figure 7.6a shows the MSFlexGrid tool in the Toolbox. The Microsoft FlexGrid control shown in Figure 7.6b displays 7 columns and 5 rows of data. The control can be used with or without a database, so it is a versatile control for displaying tables of information.

The Flex
Grid tool

(a) The Toolbox

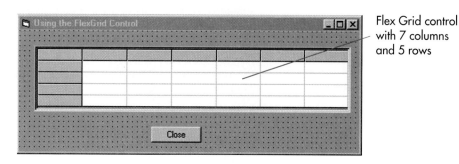

Flex Grid control
with 7 columns
and 5 rows

(b) A Form with a FlexGrid Control

FIGURE 7.6   The Microsoft FlexGrid control

The FlexGrid control is not an intrinsic control, so it needs to be added to the Toolbox before it can be used. (Pull down the Project menu, select Components, click the Controls tab, click the check box beside Microsoft FlexGrid Control, and then click the OK button.)

FlexGrid Properties

The Microsoft FlexGrid control has over 100 properties that can be set at design time or run time. We will list only the most commonly used properties here:

Property	Description
Name	Name used to refer to the control in the code
Cols	Number of columns displayed
Rows	Number of rows displayed
Col	Current column in grid
Row	Current row in the grid
ColWidth	Width of the current column
RowHeight	Height of the current row
Text	Contents of current cell

There are many methods available as well, such as Sort and Refresh. The Sort method sorts on the current column. For more information, see the topic "Using the Microsoft (Hierarchical) FlexGrid Control." If you are using Visual Basic 6, you can find this topic by pulling down the Help menu and selecting Contents. Now open the *Using Visual Basic* book, then the *Programmer's Guide*, then the

Part 2 book, and finally the *Using Visual Basic's Standard Controls* book. If you are using Visual Basic 5, you can find this topic by pulling down the Help menu and selecting Books Online. Now open the *Programmer's Guide* and continue as directed above.

NEW AND IMPROVED FLEXGRID

An updated version of the Microsoft FlexGrid control is available with Visual Basic 6, numbered 6.0. The previous version, available in Visual Basic 5, was numbered 5.0. A new control, called the **Hierarchical FlexGrid**, is also available. The MSHFlexGrid control provides advanced features for displaying data in a grid format. For more information, use the Visual Basic Documentation. Open the *What's New in Visual Basic* book and select the topic "What's New in Controls."

Now we can finish the Birthday Database project by adding code for the List All Records command button. We'll use the Microsoft FlexGrid control with a new form to display the records.

HANDS-ON EXERCISE 3

Finish the Birthday Database

Objective: Add the code for the Cancel and Delete buttons. Add a new form and the code to display all the records in the database. Use the Microsoft FlexGrid control to display the records in a table format. Use Figure 7.7 as a guide for the exercise.

STEP 1: Add Code for the Cancel Button

➤ If you did not continue from the previous exercise, start **Visual Basic**. Click the New Project dialog box's **Existing tab**. Select the disk and folder where your data disk is stored (*Exploring Visual Basic 6*). Select the **Birthday Database file**. Click the **Open button** to open the project from the previous exercise.

➤ Click the toolbar's **Project Explorer button** to display the window.

➤ Open the Forms folder and select the **Main form**. Click the **View Code button** to open the Code Editor window.

➤ Select the **cmdCancel object** and the **Click procedure**. This procedure cancels a new record before you add it to the database. Add the following code to the procedure:

```
'****************************************************************
Private Sub cmdCancel_Click()
' Purpose: Do not save new record just entered
    RecordNumber = OldRecordNumber
    NewRecord = False

    'Toggle command button display
    cmdAdd.Visible = True
    cmdDelete.Visible = True
```

(continued)

```
        cmdSave.Visible = False
        cmdCancel.Visible = False
        Call DisplayRecord(RecordNumber)
End Sub
```

STEP 2: Add Code for the Delete Button

➤ Select the **cmdDelete object** and the **Click procedure**. This procedure displays a message box, and then calls the DeleteRecord procedure from the code module. Add the following code to the procedure:

```
'*******************************************************************
Private Sub cmdDelete_Click()
'Purpose: Delete the current record from the database
Dim Reply As Integer
Const ConfirmMsg = "Delete this person?"
    Reply = MsgBox(ConfirmMsg, vbYesNo + vbQuestion)
    If Reply = vbYes Then Call DeleteRecord 'delete record
End Sub
```

➤ Move to the Project Explorer window and select the **Module**. Click the **View Code button** to edit the code.

➤ This procedure doesn't actually delete a record; instead, it erases the data from the record and replaces the first name with "Record Deleted" and the birth date with the current date. Add the following code to the bottom of the module:

```
'*******************************************************************
Public Sub DeleteRecord()
'Purpose: Delete current record
Const DeletedMsg = "Record Deleted"
    With frmMain
        .txtFirstName = DeletedMsg
        .txtLastName = ""
        .txtBirthdate = Date 'get current system date
        .cboOccupation.Text = ""
        .txtCity = ""
        .txtState = ""
        .txtCountry = ""
    End With
    Call SaveRecord 'save deleted msg to file
End Sub
```

STEP 3: Test the Delete Button

➤ Close the Code Editor windows. Click the toolbar's **Start button**. Click the **Yes button** to save your project changes.

➤ Click the Splash window's **OK button** to continue.

➤ The Main form will display with Celine Dion's data.

➤ Click the **Next button** to display Mel Gibson's data. Click the **Delete button**.
➤ The message box in Figure 7.7a will ask you to confirm the deletion.

Click here to cancel deletion

Click here to confirm deletion

Click here to delete record

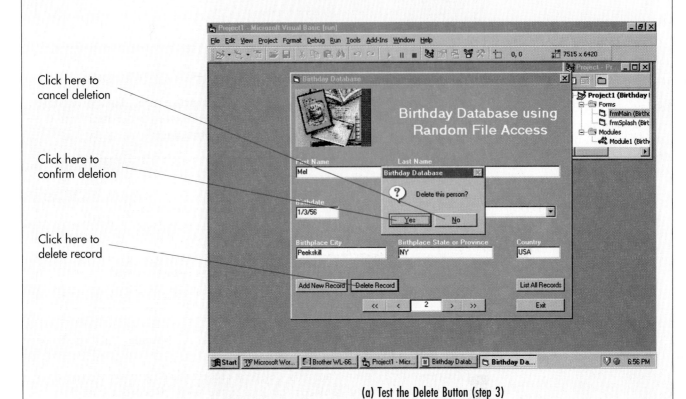

(a) Test the Delete Button (step 3)

FIGURE 7.7   Hands-on Exercise 3

➤ Click the **No button** to cancel the deletion.
➤ Click the **Delete button** again, and this time delete the record.
➤ The words "Record Deleted" will display and be stored in the FirstName field for this record as shown in Figure 7.7b. The current system date will be stored in the Birthdate field.

STEP 4: Test the Cancel Button

➤ Click the **Add New Record button**. Enter the following data:

```
Tim Allen, 06/13/1953, Actor / Actress, Denver, CO, USA
```

➤ Click the **Cancel button** to change your mind as shown in Figure 7.7c.
➤ The data will be cleared from the fields on the form, and return to the original record.

STEP 5: Create the List Form

➤ Pull down the **Project menu** and select **Add Form**.
➤ Click the **New tab** and select the **Form icon**. Click the **Open button** to add the form to your project.
➤ Pull down the **File menu** and select **Save Form1 As**.

Name replaced here

Current system date displays here

Data deleted here

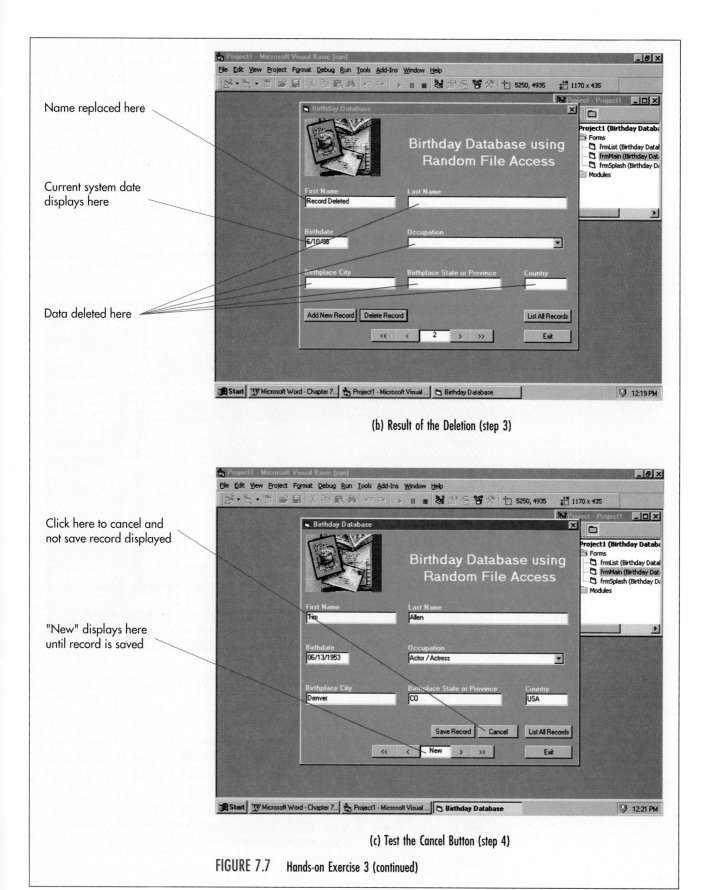

(b) Result of the Deletion (step 3)

Click here to cancel and not save record displayed

"New" displays here until record is saved

(c) Test the Cancel Button (step 4)

FIGURE 7.7   Hands-on Exercise 3 (continued)

➤ Select the disk and folder where your data disk is stored (*Exploring Visual Basic 6*). Enter **Birthday Database List** in the File name text box. Click the **Save button**.

➤ Click the toolbar's **Properties Window button**. Open the Form Designer window if it is not currently displayed.

➤ Select the **form**, and change the Name property to **frmList**. Change the Caption property to **List All Records**. Change the BackColor property to **teal**.

➤ Click the toolbar's **Toolbox button**.

➤ Add two command buttons to the top of the form as shown in Figure 7.7d. Set the first command button's Name property to **cmdSort** and its Caption property to **Sort by Last Name**.

➤ Set the second command button's Name property to **cmdClose** and its Caption property to **Close**.

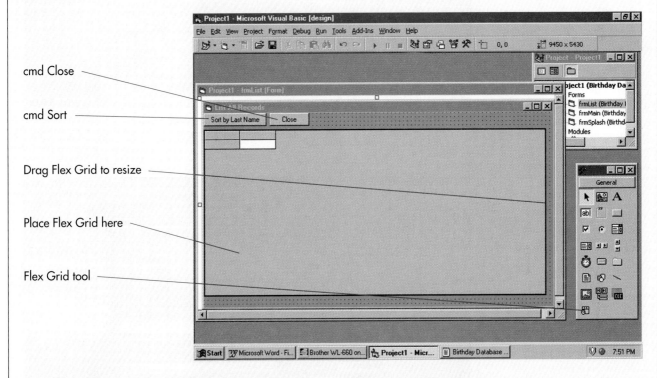

(d) Create the List Form (step 5)

FIGURE 7.7   Hands-on Exercise 3 (continued)

➤ Pull down the **Project menu** and select **Components**. Click the **Controls tab**. You may need to scroll to see the **Microsoft FlexGrid Control 6.0** (or **5.0**). Click the check box beside the control name. Click the **OK button** to add the control to the Toolbox.

➤ Select the **FlexGrid tool** from the Toolbox. Draw the control on the form as shown in the figure. Set the Name property to **msgTable**. Set the AllowUserResizing property to **1 -flexResizeColumns**. Resize the form and FlexGrid control to the approximate size shown.

STEP 6: Add Code for the List Form

➤ Double click the **Close button** to open the Code Editor window. Add the following code to the event procedure:

```
'***********************************************************************
Private Sub cmdClose_Click()
'Purpose: Close List form
    Unload Me
End Sub
```

➤ Select the **cmdSort object** and the **Click procedure**. This procedure sorts the database by the LastName field. Add the following code to the procedure:

```
'***********************************************************************
Private Sub cmdSort_Click()
'Purpose: Sort the grid using the Last Name column
    msgTable.ColSel = 1 'Select Last Name column
    msgTable.Sort = 1 'Generic ascending
        msgTable.Refresh
End Sub
```

➤ Select the **Form object** and the **Load procedure**. Add the following code to the procedure:

```
'***********************************************************************
Private Sub Form_Load()
'Purpose: Display a list of all the database records
'         in the FlexGrid
'Center Form
    Me.Move (Screen.Width - Me.Width) / 2, _
        (Screen.Height - Me.Height) / 2
End Sub
```

➤ In the Project Explorer window, select the **Main form** and click the **View Code button**.

➤ Select the **cmdList object** and the **Click procedure**. This procedure displays the List form. Add the following code to the procedure:

```
'***********************************************************************
Private Sub cmdList_Click()
'Purpose: Show all records in database
    frmList.Show
End Sub
```

STEP 7: Test the List Form

➤ **Close** the Code Editor window and any other open windows. Click the toolbar's **Start button**. Click the **Yes button** to save your project changes.

➤ Click the Splash screen's **OK button**. The Main form will display. Click the **List All Records button**.

➤ The List form will display. The form has not changed from the design shown in the previous Figure 7.7d (on page 352).

➤ The FlexGrid is currently empty. You need to add code to display the database in the grid. Click the **Close button** to close the form.

➤ Click the **Exit** button and then the click **Yes** to exit the application.

STEP 8: Add Code for the FlexGrid

➤ In the Project Explorer window, select the **List form** and click the **View Code button**.

➤ Select the **Form object** and the **Load procedure**. Add the boldfaced lines of code to the procedure immediately after the comment line:

```
'****************************************************************
Private Sub Form_Load()
'Purpose: Display a list of all the database records
'          in the Flexgrid

    Call GridHeadings 'fill headings of FlexGrid
    Call GridCells 'fill cells of FlexGrid

    'Center Form
    Me.Move (Screen.Width - Me.Width) / 2, _
        (Screen.Height - Me.Height) / 2
End Sub
```

STEP 9: Add Code for the GridHeadings Procedure

➤ Add the following new procedure to the bottom of the Code Editor window. This procedure fills the headings of the FlexGrid control with the field names of the database.

```
'****************************************************************
Private Sub GridHeadings()
'Purpose: Fill FlexGrid Column Headings
Const MAXCOLS = 8 'number of columns in FlexGrid
    msgTable.Cols = MAXCOLS 'initialize number of columns
    msgTable.Row = 0
    With msgTable
        .Col = 0
        .Text = "Number"
        .Col = 1
        .Text = "Last Name"
        .Col = 2
        .Text = "First Name"
```

(continued)

```
                .Col = 3
                .Text = "Birthdate"
                .Col = 4
                .Text = "Occupation"
                .Col = 5
                .Text = "Birthplace"
                .Col = 6
                .Text = "State"
                .Col = 7
                .Text = "Country"
        End With
End Sub
```

NAMING CONSTANTS

Many programmers use the naming convention of using all uppercase letters when naming constants. This reminds the programmer that the value remains constant during run time. This convention is used for the MAXCOLS constant in the GridCells procedure.

STEP 10: Add Code for the GridCells Procedure

➤ Add the following new procedure to the bottom of the Code Editor window. This procedure displays the records of the database in the FlexGrid control.

```
'**********************************************************************
Private Sub GridCells()
Dim R, C As Integer      'row and column counters
Dim Buffer As String     'text buffer
Dim MaxRows As Integer   'maximum number of rows in grid
Const MAXCOLS = 8        'number of columns in FlexGrid

   msgTable.Cols = MAXCOLS 'initialize number of columns

    'FlexGrid initial settings
    MaxRows = MaxNumber
    msgTable.Rows = MaxRows + 1 'add 1 for table heading

    'Fill FlexGrid rows with records
    For R = 1 To MaxRows
        msgTable.Row = R
        msgTable.Col = 0
        Get #FileNumber, R, CurrentRecord
        msgTable.Col = 0
        msgTable.Text = R

        With msgTable
            .Col = 1
            .Text = RTrim$(CurrentRecord.LastName)
```

(continued)

```
                    .Col = 2
                    .Text = RTrim$(CurrentRecord.FirstName)
                    .Col = 3
                    .Text = RTrim$(CurrentRecord.Birthdate)
                    .Col = 4
                    .Text = RTrim$(CurrentRecord.Occupation)
                    .Col = 5
                    .Text = RTrim$(CurrentRecord.City)
                    .Col = 6
                    .Text = RTrim$(CurrentRecord.State)
                    .Col = 7
                    .Text = RTrim$(CurrentRecord.Country)
            End With
        Next R
End Sub
```

STEP 11: Test the FlexGrid Control

➤ Close the Code Editor window and any other open windows. Click the toolbar's **Start button**. Click the **Yes button** to save your project changes.

➤ Click the Splash screen's **OK button**. The Main form will display.

➤ Click the **List All Records button**. The List form will display as shown in Figure 7.7e. Notice that the deleted records are displayed because they are still saved in the database file.

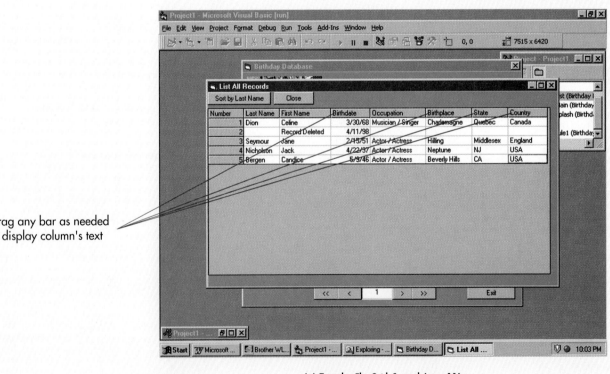

Drag any bar as needed to display column's text

(e) Test the FlexGrid Control (step 11)

FIGURE 7.7   Hands-on Exercise 3 (continued)

> Click any vertical line in the heading in the grid, and drag it to display the complete words in each column. Continue across all the columns as shown in the figure.

> Click the **Sort by Last Name button**. The rows will be sorted as shown in Figure 7.7f.

Click here to close the form

Click here to sort the list

List is sorted by Last Name

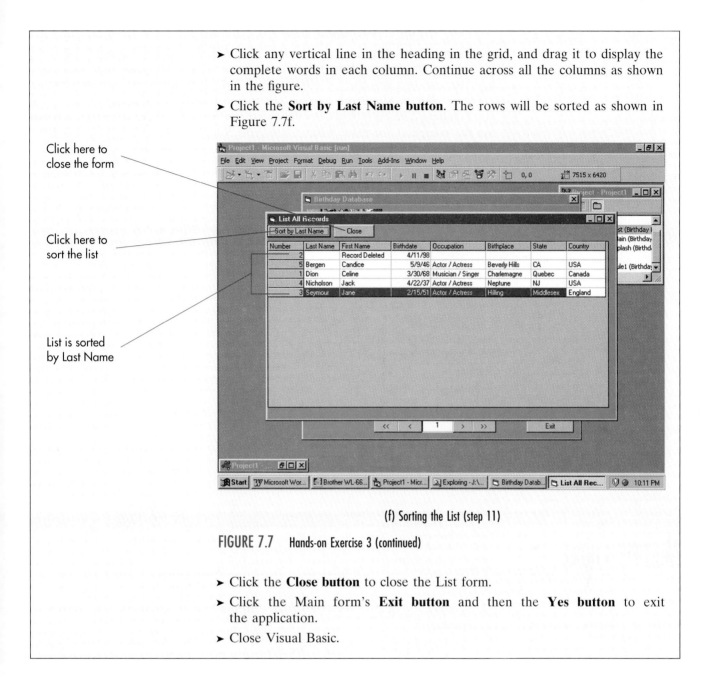

(f) Sorting the List (step 11)

FIGURE 7.7   Hands-on Exercise 3 (continued)

> Click the **Close button** to close the List form.
> Click the Main form's **Exit button** and then the **Yes button** to exit the application.
> Close Visual Basic.

SUMMARY

A database is a collection of data for a particular purpose that is stored and later retrieved. A table consists of rows and columns where each column is a field and each row is a record. A record stores data about a single entity, such as a client, product, inventory item, student, or course. Each record in the table consists of several fields. A field is the smallest unit of data that we store in a database.

A database may consist of a single table, in which case it is sometimes referred to as a flat-file database. The Type statement allows us to create our own data types, and can be used to define records in a flat-file database. The Microsoft FlexGrid control is specially designed to display tables or grids of data arranged in rows and columns. It can be bound to a database or used without a database.

The Birthday Database project demonstrates how to create a simple database application without the overhead of Visual Basic's specialized database tools. It read and stored records in a flat-file database. The project has some shortcomings that can be overcome by adding more code, or using a specialized database program such as Microsoft Access. The most obvious disadvantage is searching and handling deleted records. As discussed in Chapter 1, there are many ways to use the computer for many tasks. After you complete Chapter 8, you can make up your own mind on the tools depending on the job at hand.

KEY WORDS AND CONCEPTS

Data control
Database
Field
Flat-file database
Microsoft FlexGrid control
Microsoft Hierarchical FlexGrid control
Record
Relational database
Table
Type statement

MULTIPLE CHOICE

1. A collection of data for a particular purpose that is stored and later retrieved is called a
   (a) Record
   (b) Database
   (c) Field
   (d) Table

2. Which sequence represents the hierarchy of terms, from smallest to largest?
   (a) Database, table, record, field
   (b) Record, database, field, table
   (c) Field, record, table, database
   (d) Record, table, database, field

3. An advantage to flat-file databases is
   (a) They can contain many tables just like a relational database
   (b) They can be used without installing a database application such as Access
   (c) They are limited to a single table
   (d) The programmer has to include code for every database operation needed

4. An advantage to using an Access database over flat-flat databases is
    (a) The database can contain many tables
    (b) Tools are available to help you create forms and reports
    (c) The code for accessing the data is written for you
    (d) All of the above

5. Which of the following is represented by a row in a table?
    (a) Field
    (b) Record
    (c) Database
    (d) None of the above

6. The Type statement is used to
    (a) Define user-defined data types such to create database records
    (b) Define programmer-defined data types
    (c) Define new data types such as customized records for a database
    (d) All of the above

7. Which of the following controls did not act as a navigation button in the database you created in the hands-on exercises?
    (a) CmdFirst
    (b) CmdPrevious
    (c) lblNumber
    (d) CmdNext
    (e) CmdLast

8. Most real-life databases contain many capabilities. Which of the following capabilities was not coded in the hands-on exercises for this chapter?
    (a) Deleting records
    (b) Adding new records
    (c) Modifying records
    (d) Searching for records

9. Which of the following statements is false about the Microsoft FlexGrid control?
    (a) It is specially designed to display information arranged in rows and columns
    (b) It can sort, merge, and format tables
    (c) It must be used with a database
    (d) It is not an intrinsic control, so it needs to be added to the toolbox

10. Which of the following methods is the least appropriate for deleting records in a database?
    (a) Blank out the fields in a record, and use a field as a record deleted indicator
    (b) Display a message box informing the user that the record was deleted, but do not modify the record
    (c) Modify a single field to indicate a deleted record, and skip over the record when navigating the database
    (d) Actually delete the record from the database, and reuse the spot for new records

11. Which of the following is not a characteristic of the database you created in the chapter's hands-on exercises?
    (a) It is very simple
    (b) It demonstrates several key features of flat-file databases
    (c) It would be appropriate for a real-life database
    (d) It demonstrates the basics of do-it-yourself database programming

12. Which of the following fields would be most appropriate if you were searching for a celebrity whose birthday is the same as yours?
    (a) Country
    (b) Firstname
    (c) Birthdate
    (d) Lastname

13. What is the purpose of the Main form in this chapter's hands-on exercises?
    (a) It is used as a splash screen to introduce the application
    (b) It is used to display, add, and delete a record from the database
    (c) It is used to display all the records in the database
    (d) It is used to display a single record in the database, but cannot be used to add or delete records

14. What is the purpose of the List form in this chapter's hands-on exercises?
    (a) It is used as a splash screen to introduce the application
    (b) It is used to display, add, and delete a record from the database
    (c) It is used to display all the records in the database in a FlexGrid control
    (d) It is used to display a list of the only the names of all the records in the database

15. Which of the following descriptions does not match the purpose of the procedure created in this chapter's hands-on exercises?
    (a) Start—opens the database file, and displays the splash form
    (b) ExitApplication—closes the database file, unloads the main form and ends the application
    (c) SaveRecord—saves the contents of the main form to the current record in the database file
    (d) DisplayRecord—reads the appropriate record from the database and displays the contents in the main form

ANSWERS

1. b	6. d	11. c
2. c	7. c	12. c
3. b	8. d	13. b
4. d	9. c	14. c
5. b	10. b	15. a

PRACTICE WITH VISUAL BASIC

1. **WindChill Table.** Create a project that demonstrates the MS FlexGrid control. Create an application that displays the wind chill temperatures in a FlexGrid control. The formula to calculate Wind Chill factors is given in Hands-on Exercise 1 in Chapter 3 on page 104. The temperature values should range from -35 to +35 degrees Fahrenheit in the grid columns. The wind speeds should range from 5 to 45 miles per hour, down the rows of the grid. Add the graphic *WindChill.bmp* available on the data disk, to the right of the grid as shown in Figure 7.8. Loop through the values and call the WindChill function to calculate the needed values, and display the value in the appropriate grid cell. Name the project and form file **Wind Chill Grid**. Make a printout of your form and code, or save the projects files on disk, and submit to your instructor.

Column heading label here

MS Flex Grid control here

Wind Chill image here

Row heading label here

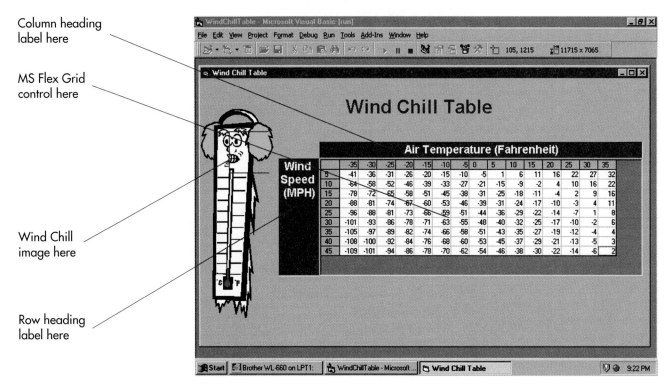

FIGURE 7.8   Screen for Practice Exercise 1: Wind Chill Table

2. **Personal Address Book.** Create a new database to store addresses, telephone numbers, and e-mail addresses using a flat-file database. Use the Birthday Database created in the hands-on exercises as a model for this exercise. The table should contain fields such as LastName, FirstName, Address, City, State, Country, ZipCode, HomePhone, BusinessPhone, Email, and Birthday. You may also include other fields as appropriate for your needs. Name the database, project, and form file **Personal Address Book**. Make a printout of your form and code, or save the project files on disk, and submit to your instructor.

3. **Practice with Access.** If you have previous experience with Access, create a new database using the Database Wizard included with Access. Choose from such pre-designed databases as Address Book, Book Collection, Contact Management, Music Collection, Video Collection, and many more. The switchboard and an example form are shown for the Workout database in Figure 7.9. Name your database *Practice with Access*. Select the option to include sample data on the Wizard screen. Add at least six more records to the new database with appropriate valid data. Print out a report from the database with the added records, or save the database file on disk, and submit to your instructor.

Wizard with
Workout Database

Workout history
form displayed

Save database
as Access Demo

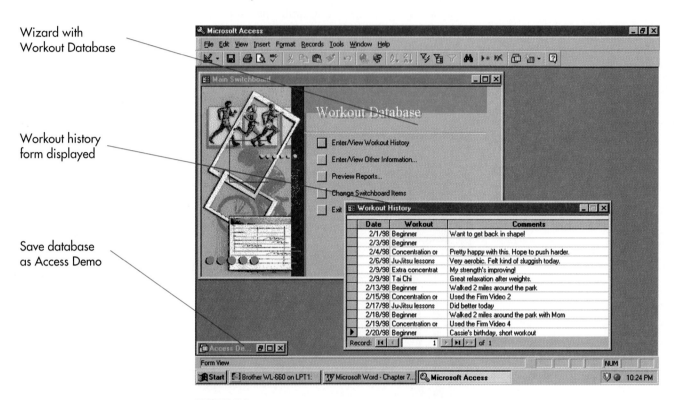

FIGURE 7.9   Screen for Practice Exercise 6: Access Demo

4. **Birthday Deletion Improvement.** The Birthday Database created in the hands-on exercises leaves room for improvement. Start with the database as completed in Hands-on Exercise 3 and change the procedures for deleting a record. Change the navigation event procedures so that any deleted record is skipped and not displayed using the Main form. Rename the project and form files *Birthday Deletion Improvement*. Make a printout of your form and code, or save the project files on disk, and submit to your instructor.

CASE STUDIES

Database Mystery

The Microsoft Web site has a short animation with a more light-hearted view of databases. To view the animation, go to the Microsoft Web site at **www.microsoft.com**. Use the product search engine and go to Access 97. From the Access 97 home page select the link called ***Are Databases a Mystery to You?*** The first page of the animation is shown in Figure 7.10. Relax and enjoy the show.

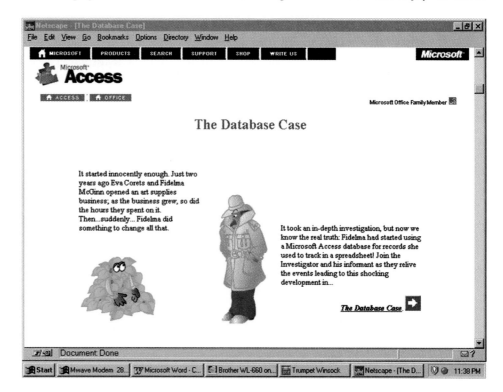

FIGURE 7.10   Screen for the Database Mystery Case Study

Beginning Database Design

Design a database that would be useful to you. Select something other than names, addresses, or contacts. Sketch on paper the table(s) that would be appropriate for your database along with the fields for each table. Decide on a name, data type, and size for each field. Draw the input form on paper for your database. Also, design at least two other forms such as a Splash screen, List screen, Help screen, or About screen. Submit your design sketches to your instructor.

Flat-file Database

Design and implement a database that would be useful to you. Select something other than names, addresses, or contacts. You can start with the *Beginning Database Design* case study, or design an entirely new database. Decide and create fields with appropriate names, data types, and sizes and code using Visual Basic's Type statement. Create at least two forms in your project such as a Splash screen, List screen, Help screen, or About screen. Save your database and project files as *Flat-file Database*. Print out the forms and code from your application, or save the project files on disk, and submit to your instructor.

FlexGrid Case Study

Design and create a project that demonstrates the MS FlexGrid control. This project does not need to include a database. Instead, choose a project that displays calculated information in tabular format. The calculated values could be a simple as a multiplication table to monthly payments to a complicated formula. Code a function to do the calculations. Remember to include appropriate column and row headings so the grid will be easy to read. Add an appropriate graphic to the grid form or a Splash screen for your project. Name the project and form file *FlexGrid Case Study*. Make a printout of your form(s) and code, or save the project files on disk, and submit to your instructor.

RELATIONAL DATABASES: ACTIVEX DATABASE CONTROLS

OVERVIEW

In this chapter, we will be working with the Access database application contained in Microsoft Office. We'll create a database application using an existing Access database. Access is a relational database program, the most popular type of database in use today. Relational databases are easy to create, build, and maintain, allowing us to add new fields and tables at any time. Relational databases consist of tables made up of rows and columns, and can be composed of a single table or several tables to describe our data.

To minimize the amount of code we must write, we will use the data-bound controls designed for databases. These include the data control, the data-bound list box, the data-bound combo box, and the data-bound grid. These controls are different from Visual Basic's intrinsic list box and combo box controls. The Learning Edition of Visual Basic refers to these database-specialized controls as standard ActiveX controls. They have to be added to the Toolbox manually. Together with the Microsoft FlexGrid and common dialog controls, they complete our list of standard ActiveX controls.

We will also use several intrinsic controls that are data-aware in our database applications. These controls include the label, text box, check box, list box, combo box, image, picture, and OLE container controls. The Professional and Enterprise editions of Visual Basic 6 also include data-aware controls such as the masked edit and rich text box controls, but we do not use them in the chapter.

All three editions of Visual Basic include the Visual Data Manager, which can be used to define and create new databases. This is a benefit if we do not have Access installed on our computer.

Visual Basic's Application Wizard helps us create applications for existing databases. The new Data Form Wizard helps us to create forms for our database tables. We will use the forms generated by the wizard in the final hands-on exercise in the chapter.

APPLICATION WIZARD IN VISUAL BASIC 5

The Application Wizard in Visual Basic 5 generates applications as well as forms for databases. The Data Form Wizard in Visual Basic 6 generates only database forms, and the Application Wizard continues to help you build applications and general forms such as Splash and About forms.

RELATIONAL DATABASES

Relational databases are composed of tables and relationships. A *table* consists of rows and columns where each column is a field and each row is a record. A *relationship* is an association established between fields in two tables. A relationship can be one-to-one, many-to-many, or one-to-many. Relational databases are the most popular database model today because they are easier to modify when needs change than other models such as hierarchical, network, and object. Oracle is a very popular relational database for mainframe computers.

Access is a relational database application included with Microsoft Office Professional. A database created by an application such as *Microsoft Access* is a collection of forms, reports, tables, queries, macros, and modules. We have been creating forms throughout our study of Visual Basic. Forms for Access databases are created the same way, and we have some special tools to help in creating these forms.

Let's examine an Access database called Birthday Access. This database, like the Birthday Database in Chapter 7, will store celebrities' birthdays. This time we are not limited to a single table. In the previous chapter, we used a combo box to select and display the occupation in the flat-file implementation. This time we will use a more sophisticated approach, with two tables. The first table, called Birthdays, will store the same 7 fields, but will store only a code, called OccCode, for the occupation. A second table, called Occupations, will store the lookup codes for the list of occupations. The tables and relationship are shown in Figure 8.1a.

A *primary key* is a field or combination of fields that uniquely determines a record in the database. The field named Key serves as the primary key for the Birthdays table. We use the AutoNumber data type for this field, to automatically generate a new record number when we add a new record.

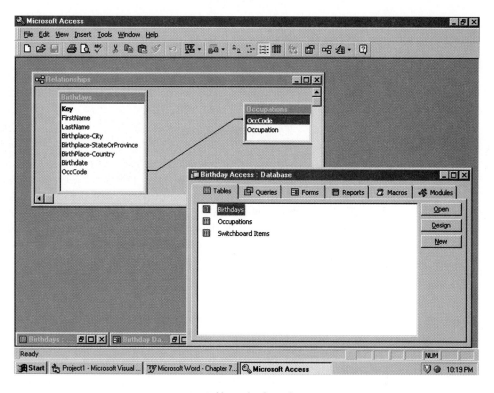

(a) Tables and Relationships

FIGURE 8.1   The Birthday Access Database

The OccCode field is the primary key field for the Occupations table. This field is also used in the Birthdays table, but there it is a foreign key. A *foreign key* is a non-primary-key field in a table that also serves as a primary key in another table. Including the primary key of one table as a field in another table is the method used to define the relationships in relational databases.

Several records are stored in the database, as shown in Figure 8.1b. This figure displays the Birthdays table in Access's Datasheet view, where one can add and edit records in the database. The Occupations table is shown in Datasheet view in Figure 8.1c.

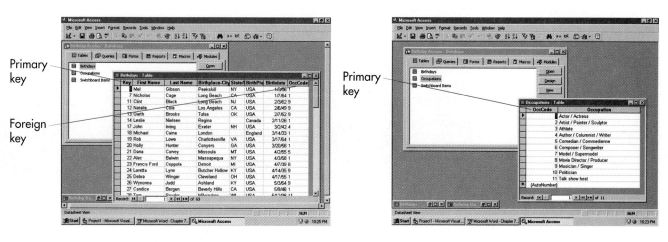

(b) The Birthdays Table

(c) The Occupations Table

FIGURE 8.1   The Birthday Access Database (continued)

Visual Basic provides four controls specially designed to work with databases: the data control, the data-bound list, the data-bound combo, and the data-bound grid. These four controls are available in all three editions of Visual Basic.

The Data Control

We use the intrinsic *data control* for each table that we want to work with in a database. For the Birthday Database project, we would need a data control for the Birthdays table and another one for the Occupations table, as shown in Figure 8.1d. The data control uses the *Microsoft Jet database engine*, which is the same database engine that powers Microsoft Access. As you will see in the next two exercises, the data control allows access to a database without writing much code. The data control navigates the database for us automatically. It has buttons to move to the first, previous, next, and last records, as shown in the figure.

Data Control Properties

As usual, we need to set properties for the data control before we can utilize its capabilities. First, we set the *DatabaseName property* to the path and filename of the database. Next, we select the appropriate table from the list displayed for the *RecordSource property*. We need a data control for every table used in the database, so we will set the RecordSource to Birthdays for the first control and to Occupations for the second.

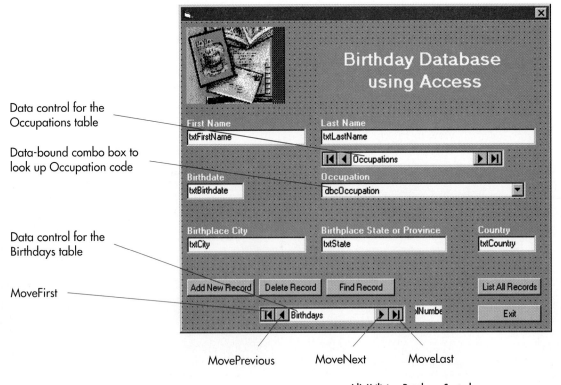

(d) Utilizing Database Controls

FIGURE 8.1   The Birthday Access Database (continued)

After we set the two properties for a data control, we can add the data-bound list, combo, or grid controls to display the table's fields on a form. The **data-bound list control** displays a list box using a field in a database. The **data-bound combo control** displays a combo box using a database field. The **data-bound grid control** is similar to the MS FlexGrid control except that it must be used with a database. The data-bound grid control also enables editing of the database, whereas the MS FlexGrid control does not.

The **ActiveX database controls** are not intrinsic, so they must be added to the Toolbox before they can be used. (Pull down the Project menu, select Components, click the Controls tab, and click the check boxes beside Microsoft Data Bound List Controls 5.0 (DBlist and DBcombo) and beside Microsoft Data Bound Grid Control. Then click the OK button to add the controls to the Toolbox.) These tools are displayed in Figure 8.2.

Data-bound List and Combo Control Properties

Usually, when working with the DBList and DBCombo controls, we utilize two Data controls. The first one is used to fill the list, in our example the data control for the Occupations table (named datOccupations). The second one is used to manage the records to update. In our example the data control for the Birthdays table (named datBirthdays). We need to set properties for the controls before we can utilize them. To automatically fill the list or combo-box with data, set the **Row Source**, **List Field**, and **Text** properties. Use the **Data Source**, **Data Field**, and **Bound Column** properties to manage the records for updating.

The properties are dependent upon each other, so they must be set in the proper order. First, to fill the data-bound list, or combo, we set the *Row Source property* to the name of the corresponding data control (datOccupations). Next, select the appropriate field from the list displayed in the *List Field property* (Occupation) to set the property . Finally, set the *Text property* to the name of the control to display the data (usually the control itself).

Next, to manage and update records, set the *Data Source property* to the name of the corresponding data control (datBirthdays) to manage the Birthdays table. Next, select the appropriate field from the list displayed in the *Data Field property* (OccCode) to set the property. Finally, we select and set the *Bound property* to the name of field to update (usually the same as the Data Field property).

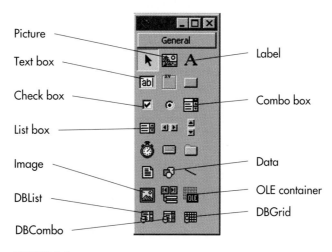

FIGURE 8.2 Database Tools

Data-bound Grid Control Properties

The data-bound grid control displays a selection of records and fields from a database table. Each cell of the DBGrid can hold either text or pictures. Cells can be edited and the changes can be stored in the database. Set the *Data Source property* to the name of the corresponding data control (datBirthdays) to display. The DBGrid is automatically filled and its column headers are set from the database table. At design time, you can set the DBGrid's column width and row height.

INTRINSIC DATA-AWARE CONTROLS

Other data-aware controls that can be used to display data fields in a database are the picture, label, text box, check box, image, OLE container, list box, and combo box, as shown in previous Figure 8.2. With these controls, we use properties to indicate which database table and field we want to display.

Data-aware Control Properties

Once the data control is placed and the properties are set, we have access to all the tables and fields in the database. Next, we need to associate the controls to display the data from the appropriate field. This is accomplished with the control's Data Source and Data Field properties. The **Data Source property** is set to the name of the corresponding data control to select the appropriate table. The **Data Field property** is set to the name of the desired field in the table.

For example, the FirstName field should be displayed in a text box, so we draw a text box on the form. First, we set the text box's **DataSource property** to the name of the appropriate data control, such as *datBirthdays*. Next, we use the **DataField property** to select the field we want to display in the text box, such as *FirstName*. Once you understand how to use these two basic properties, the database is relatively easy to program.

Database Front-end Applications

A database front-end is an application that can be used to display and modify the data in a database. The "back end" is the set of related database tables—in this example the Access database. Our front-end application shields the end user from the complexities of Access. Access can be very intimidating with all its tables, queries, forms, reports, macros, and modules. Access also makes it very easy to change the design of a table or relationship. You probably do not want the end users modifying the design, and the application prevents this problem. We'll create a front-end application to the existing Birthday Access database in the next two hands-on exercises.

HANDS-ON EXERCISE 1

Birthday Database Using Access

Objective: Create a front end application to an existing Access database. Use the data control and data-bound combo control specially designed to work with databases. Use other data-aware controls such as text boxes. Use Figure 8.3 as a guide for the exercise.

STEP 1: Create the Project and Add Forms

➤ Start **Visual Basic**. Click the New Project dialog box's **New tab**. Click the **Standard EXE icon**. Click the **Open button** to open the new project.

➤ The Form Designer window should be displayed. Right click anywhere within the new Form1 form and select **Properties** from the shortcut menu. Set the Name property to **frmList**.

➤ Pull down the **File menu** and select **Save frmList As**. Select the disk and folder where your data disk is stored (*Exploring Visual Basic 6*). Enter *Birthday Access List* in the File name text box to save the form.

➤ You created a Splash form and Main form in the hands-on exercises in the previous chapter that you can use to start this project. Pull down the **Project menu** and select **Add Form**.

➤ Click the **Existing tab** and select the disk and folder where your data disk is stored (*Exploring Visual Basic 6*). (Alternatively, if you did not complete the project, it is also available on the data disk as Birthday Access Starter.)

➤ Select **Birthday Database Splash** (or Birthday Access Starter Splash). Click the **Open button**. In the Project Explorer window, select the **Splash form**. Pull down the **File menu** and save the form as **Birthday Access Splash**.

➤ Pull down the **Project menu** and select **Add Form**. Click the **Existing tab** and select **Birthday Database Main** (or Birthday Access Starter Main). Click the **Open button**.

➤ In the Project Explorer window, select the **Main form**. Pull down the **File menu** and save the form as **Birthday Access Main**. Change the Caption property to **Birthday Access**.

➤ Pull down the **Project menu** and select **Add Module**. Click the **Existing Tab** and select **Birthday Database** (or Birthday Access Starter). Click the **Open button**. In the Project Explorer window, select the **Module**. Pull down the **File menu** and save the module as **Birthday Access**.

➤ In the Project Explorer window right click **Project1** and select **Project1 Properties**. Change the Startup Object to **Sub Main**. Click the **OK button**.

➤ Finally, save the project. Pull down the **File menu** and select **Save Project As**.

➤ The disk and folder where your data disk is stored (*Exploring Visual Basic 6*) should be displayed. Enter **Birthday Access** in the File name text box to save the project.

➤ Your forms and module should now be named as shown in Figure 8.3a.

STEP 2: Edit the Main Form

➤ Close the List form window. Double click the **Main form** in the Project Explorer window.

➤ Select the **title label**. Change the Caption property to **Birthday Database Using Access**. You may need to resize the label.

➤ Delete the four **navigation buttons** at the bottom of the form and the **label** in the middle. You will place the data control in this location later.

➤ Delete the **Save Record** and **Cancel** command buttons. The data control automatically saves new records as you add them, so you will not need these buttons.

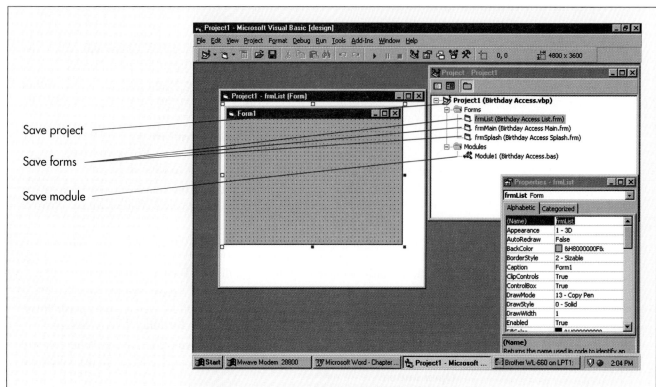

Save project
Save forms
Save module

(a) Create the Project and Add Forms (step 1)

FIGURE 8.3 Hands-on Exercise 3

SETTING PROPERTIES: ORDER IS IMPORTANT

When setting properties for the specialized data controls and the data aware controls, you need to set the controls in a certain order. Notice the properties are not listed alphabetically in this exercise, but by setting order. Set the properties in the correct order, and simply select a property from a list instead of typing it in.

STEP 3: Add the Data Control

➤ Click the toolbar's **Toolbox button**. Select the **Data tool**, and draw the control at the bottom of the form as shown in Figure 8.3b.

➤ Set the following properties for the data control:

Property	Setting
Name	datBirthdays
Caption	Birthdays
Connect	Access
DatabaseName	Select the disk and folder for your data disk (*Exploring Visual Basic 6*) and the *Birthday Access.mdb* file
RecordSource	Select **Birthdays** from the list

➤ Select the **text box** for the First Name field. Select and set the DataSource property to **datBirthdays**.

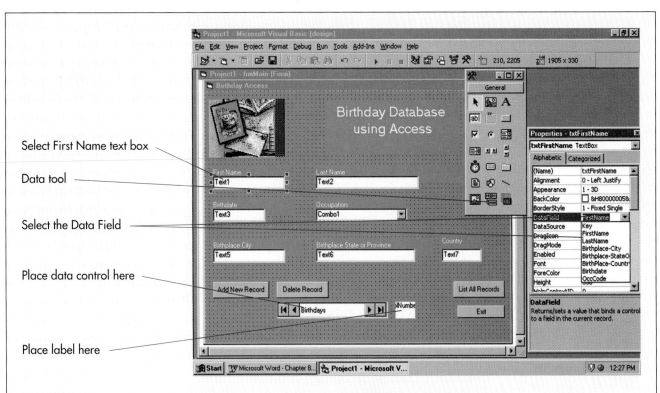

Select First Name text box

Data tool

Select the Data Field

Place data control here

Place label here

(b) Add the Data Control (step 3)

FIGURE 8.3   Hands-on Exercise 1 (continued)

➤ Select and set the DataField property to **FirstName** as shown in the figure.

➤ Repeat the process for the other text boxes on the form. Set the DataSource property to **datBirthdays**. Set the DataField property as shown below:

Control	DataField Property Setting
txtLastName	LastName
txtBirthdate	Birthdate
txtCity	Birthplace-City
txtState	Birthplace-StateOrProvince
txtCountry	Birthplace-Country

➤ Move to the Toolbox and select the **Label tool**. Draw the label to the right of the data control as shown in the figure. Set the following properties for the label:

Property	Setting
Name	lblNumber
Alignment	2 - Center
BackColor	White
Caption	lblNumber
DataSource	Select **datBirthdays**
DataField	Select **Key**

STEP 4: Edit the Module Code

➤ Close the Toolbox and Form Designer windows.

➤ In the Project Explorer window, select **Module1** and click the **View Code button**.

➤ Scroll to the top of the code. Modify the banner comment as shown below. Change the date to the current date.

```
'*********************************************************************
' Programmer:    Carlotta Eaton
' Date:          April 6, 1998
' Source:        Birthday Access.vbp
' ID:            Chapter 8 Hands On Exercises 1 and 2
' Purpose:       Create a front end to an existing Access database
'                Open, read, write, save to an Access database
'                Use the Data, DBCombo, and DBList controls
' Functions:     Main, Start, AddRecord, DeleteRecord,
'                ExitApplication, and FindRecord
' Forms:         Splash, Main and List
' References:    None
'*********************************************************************
Option Explicit
```

➤ Delete the **Declarations section** of code.

➤ Delete the **SaveRecord** and **DisplayRecord procedures**.

➤ Delete the code between the purpose comment and the End Sub statements in the **AddRecord** and **DeleteRecord procedures**. We'll add code to these procedures in the next exercise.

➤ Edit the **Main** and **Start procedures** as shown below:

```
'**********************************************************
Public Sub Main()
'Purpose: Display Splash form
        frmSplash.Show
End Sub
'**********************************************************
Public Sub Start()
'Purpose: Display Main form and start database
        frmMain.Show
End Sub
```

➤ Edit the **ExitApplication procedure** as shown below:

```
'**********************************************************
Public Sub ExitApplication()
'Purpose: Exit the application
        Unload frmMain
        End
End Sub
```

STEP 5: Edit the Main Form Code

➤ In the Project Explorer window, select **frmMain** and click the **View Code button**.

➤ Delete the event procedure for the following objects: **cmdCancel** (if still available), **cmdFirst**, **cmdLast**, **cmdNext**, **cmdPrevious**, and **cmdSave**. Since you deleted the corresponding controls from the form, you will not be able to select the procedures from the Object list.

➤ Edit the cmdAdd object's Click event procedure as shown below:

```
Private Sub cmdAdd_Click()
'Purpose: Add a new record to the database
       Call AddRecord
End Sub
```

➤ Edit the cmdDelete Click event procedure as shown below:

```
'*************************************************************
Private Sub cmdDelete_Click()
'Purpose: Display msg box and call the delete record procedure
Dim Reply As Integer
       'Verify user wants to delete current record
       Reply = MsgBox("Delete this person?", vbYesNo + vbQuestion)
       If Reply = vbYes Then Call DeleteRecord
End Sub
```

➤ Edit the Form Load event procedure as shown below:

```
'*****************************************************************
Private Sub Form_Load()
'Purpose: Display the Main database form

       'Center form
       With Me
          Move (Screen.Width - .Width) / 2, _
               (Screen.Height - .Height) / 2
          .Caption = App.Title
          .Refresh
       End With
End Sub
```

STEP 6: Verify Unchanged Code for the Main Form

➤ Ensure that the code for the cmdList Click event procedure remains unchanged as shown below:

```
'*****************************************************************
Private Sub cmdList_Click()
'Purpose: Show all records in database
       frmList.Show
End Sub
```

➤ Ensure the code for the Form QueryUnload event procedure remains unchanged as shown below:

```
'*******************************************************************
Private Sub Form_QueryUnload(Cancel As Integer,_
       UnloadMode As Integer)
'Purpose: Confirm user wants to end application
Dim Reply As Integer
Const ExitMsg = "Are you sure you want to exit?"

       Reply = MsgBox(ExitMsg, vbYesNo + vbQuestion)
       If Reply = vbYes Then
              Call ExitApplication
       Else
              Cancel = True
       End If

End Sub
```

➤ Ensure the code for the cmdExit Click event procedure remains unchanged as shown below:

```
'*******************************************************************
Private Sub cmdExit_Click()
'Purpose: End the application
       Call ExitApplication
End Sub
```

STEP 7: Test the Splash and Main Forms

➤ Close the Code Editor windows. Click the toolbar's **Start button** to test your code.

➤ Click the **Yes button** to save your changes.

➤ The Splash form will display as shown in Figure 8.3c.

➤ Click the **OK button** to continue. The Main form will display as shown in Figure 8.3d.

➤ The data control will navigate through the records in the existing database. The first record stored is Mel Gibson.

➤ Click the **Last button** to display the record for Donald Fagen (record number 80).

➤ Click the **Previous button** to display the record for Glenn Close (record number 78).

➤ Click the **First button** to display Mel Gibson again.

➤ Click the **Next button** to display Nicholas Cage (record number 7).

➤ Click any of the navigation buttons to move to another record.

➤ Notice the Occupation combo box needs to be coded, and the List All Records button also needs code. You'll add this code next.

➤ Click the **Exit button**. Click the **Yes button** to confirm.

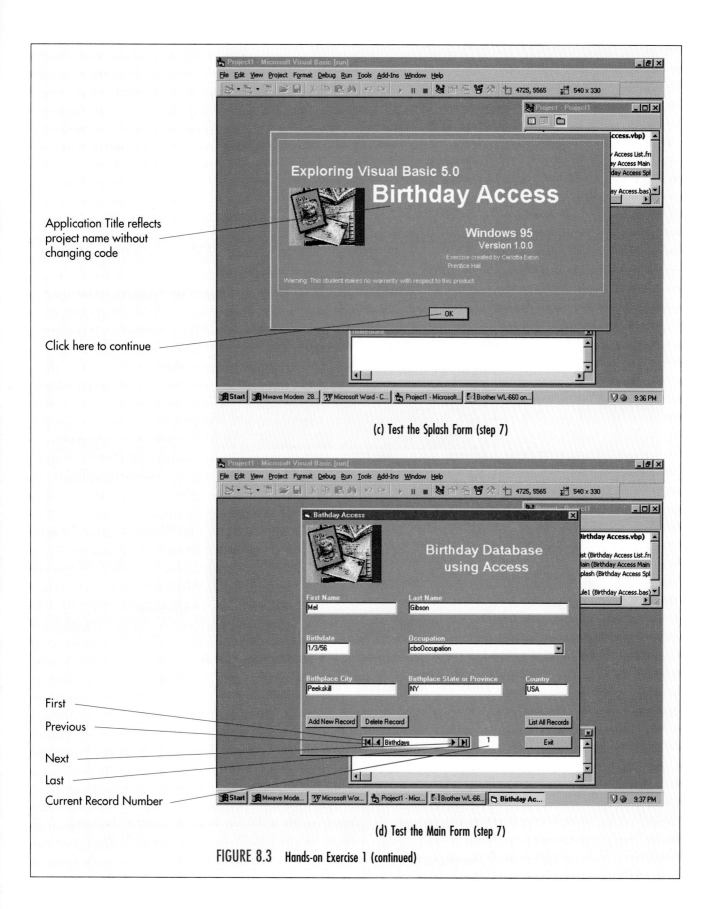

Application Title reflects project name without changing code

Click here to continue

(c) Test the Splash Form (step 7)

First
Previous
Next
Last
Current Record Number

(d) Test the Main Form (step 7)

FIGURE 8.3   Hands-on Exercise 1 (continued)

RECORD NUMBERS

Access automatically numbers the records and this number is used as the primary key. The record numbers will have gaps between them if records have been deleted. Access does not reuse the primary key, and the deleted records are not displayed.

STEP 8: Add Another Data Control

➤ In the Project Explorer window, double click the **Main form** to display it.

➤ Click the toolbar's **Toolbox button**. Select the **Data tool** from the Toolbox, and draw it immediately above the combo box as shown in Figure 8.3e.

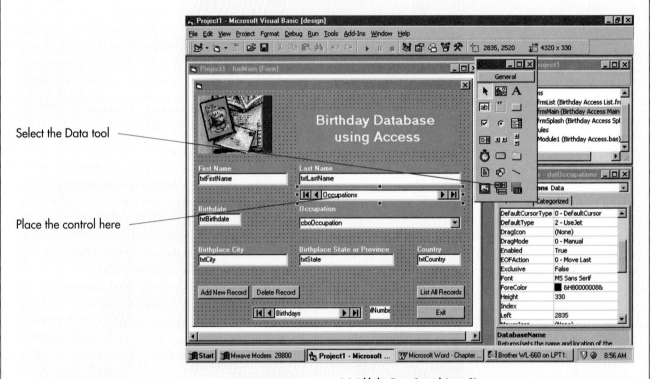

Select the Data tool

Place the control here

(e) Add the Data Control (step 8)

FIGURE 8.3   Hands-on Exercise 1 (continued)

➤ Set the following properties for this data control:

Property	Setting
Name	datOccupations
Caption	Occupations
Connect	Access
DatabaseName	Select the disk and folder for your data disk (*Exploring Visual Basic 6*) and the *Birthday Access.mdb* file
ReadOnly	False
RecordsetType	1 - Dynaset
RecordSource	Select **Occupations** from the list
Visible	False

STEP 9: Add the Data-bound Combo Box

➤ The other data tools are not intrinsic controls, so you need to add them to the Toolbox. Pull down the **Project menu** and select **Components**. Select the **Controls tab**.

➤ Click the check box beside **Microsoft Data Bound List Controls 6.0** (or **5.0**). Click the **Apply button**. Click the **OK button**.

➤ The DBList and DBCombo tools will be added to your Toolbox. You may need to resize the Toolbox to see the new tools.

➤ We'll replace the combo box with a DBCombo box. It will display the list of occupations stored in the Occupations table in the database. Delete the current **combo box** from the form.

➤ In the Toolbox, select the **DBCombo tool**. Draw the data-bound combo control in the same location as shown in Figure 8.3f.

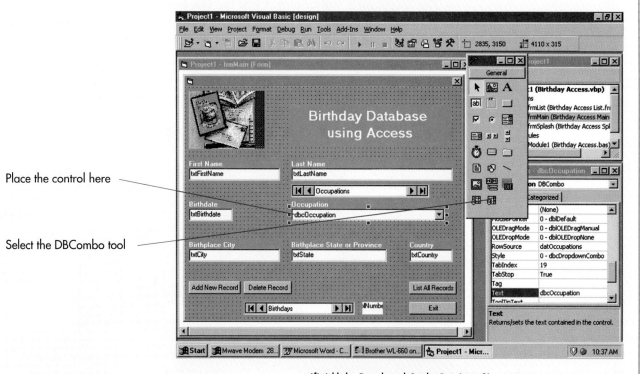

Place the control here

Select the DBCombo tool

(f) Add the Data-bound Combo Box (step 9)

FIGURE 8.3   Hands-on Exercise 1 (continued)

➤ Set the following properties for the data-bound combo control to automatically fill the list:

Property	Setting
Name	dbcOccupation
RowSource	Select **datOccupations**
ListField	Select **Occupation**
Text	dbcOccupation

➤ Set the following properties for the data-bound combo control to modify and manage the database records.

Property	Setting
DataSource	Select **datBirthdays**
DataField	Select **OccCode**
BoundColumn	Select **OccCode**

STEP 10: Test the Data-bound Combo Control

➤ Close the Toolbox and the Form Designer windows.

➤ Click the toolbar's **Start button**. Click the **Yes button** to save your form changes.

➤ The Splash form will display. Click the **OK button** to continue.

➤ The first record stored is Mel Gibson, and now his occupation of Actor/Actress is displayed in the data-bound combo box as shown in Figure 8.3g.

➤ Click the **Last button**. Donald Fagen is stored as the last record, with the occupation of Musician.

➤ Navigate through more records and examine the data-bound combo box as it changes for each record.

➤ Click the **Exit button**. Click the **Yes button** to confirm.

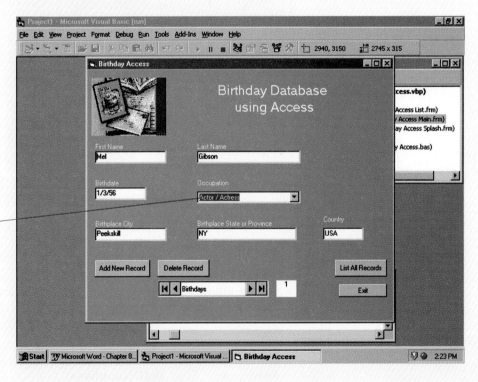

Occupation displays here

(g) Test the Data-bound Combo Box (step 10)

FIGURE 8.3   Hands-on Exercise 1 (continued)

Now we understand how to display fields in ActiveX database controls and the intrinsic data-aware controls. Next, we need to manage and update records, and search and display an appropriate record from the database. Visual Basic provides recordsets to do this work for us. A *recordset* is simply a record or set of records selected from a table or tables in a database. There are three types of recordsets available, so we need to decide which is the most appropriate for our project. In the Birthday Access database example, we want to use two tables (Birthdays and Occupations) and we want to be able to add and modify records. If we know what we want to do, choosing the correct type of recordset is easy.

Types of Recordsets

- *Table* recordsets are limited to a single table, and can add, modify, and delete records.

- *Dynaset* recordsets can be used for several tables, and can add, modify, and delete records.

- *Snapshot* recordsets can display fields from several tables, but cannot modify the records.

For our purposes, the Dynaset recordset type matches our needs. We cannot create new recordset objects using code in the Learning Edition of Visual Basic, but we can select and modify existing records, and add records.

Navigating Records with Data Control Methods

As we saw earlier in the hands-on exercises, the data control has buttons to navigate through the database. We can also write code to navigate the database using the matching data control methods. The general syntax is shown below:

Name.**Recordset**.*Method*
where
    Name is the name of the data control
    Method is one of the following:
        MoveFirst moves to the first record
        MovePrevious moves to the previous record
        MoveNext moves to the next record
        MoveLast moves to the last record

Example:
        `datBirthdays.Recordset.MoveFirst`

Finding Records with the Data Control

At times, we may want to search the database for a specific record. We could simply go through the records one at a time using the navigation buttons, but this would be a slow process if we had hundreds of records stored. Visual Basic provides methods for finding specific records. The syntax is shown below:

Name.**Recordset**.*Method*
where
    Name is the name of the data control
    Method is one of the following:
        FindFirst finds the first record satisfying the search criteria
        FindLast finds the last record satisfying the search criteria
        FindNext finds the next record satisfying the search criteria
        FindPrevious finds the previous record satisfying the search criteria

Example:
```
datBirthdays.Recordset.FindFirst "LastName = Dion"
```

Adding and Deleting Records with the Data Control

Finally, we will want to add and delete records from the database. There are methods for these operations as well.

Name.**Recordset**.*Method*
where
    Name is the name of the data control
    Method is one of the following:
        AddNew adds a new record to the end of the database
        Refresh redisplays the current record
        Update modifies the fields in the current record
        Delete deletes the current record from the database
        Close closes the recordset, and frees the memory allocated for storage

Example:
```
datBirthdays.Recordset.AddNew
```

Now we have enough information to manage and update the records for the Birthday Access project. You will also display the entire database three different ways: (1) using a data-bound list control; (2) using a data-bound grid control, where you can modify the database; (3) using a FlexGrid control, where you cannot modify the database but can easily sort the records.

Finish the Birthday Access Project

Objective: Add code to add a new record, delete an existing record, and to search for a record. Add code to display the database using the data-bound list box, data-bound grid, and the MS FlexGrid. Use Figure 8.4 as a guide for the exercise.

STEP 1: Edit the Module Code

➤ If you did not continue from the previous exercise, start **Visual Basic**. Click the New Project dialog box's **Recent tab**. Select the **Birthday Access** project. Click the **Open button** to open the project from the previous exercise.

➤ Click the toolbar's **Project Explorer button** to display the window.

➤ Open the Modules folder and select **Module1**. Click the **View Code button** to open the Code Editor window.

➤ Edit the **AddRecord procedure** as shown below:

```
'*****************************************************************
Public Sub AddRecord()
' Purpose:      Add a new record to the database
'               Add New Record command button was clicked
        With frmMain
                'data control automatically clears record
                'Set the focus to the first text box
                .txtFirstName.SetFocus
                'add record using data control
                .datBirthdays.Recordset.AddNew
        End With
End Sub
```

➤ Edit the **DeleteRecord procedure** as shown below:

```
'*****************************************************************
Public Sub DeleteRecord()
'Purpose: Delete current record
        With frmMain
                .datBirthdays.Recordset.Delete
                .datBirthdays.Recordset.MoveNext
        End With
End Sub
```

STEP 2: Test the Add Record Code

➤ Close the Code Editor window. Click the toolbar's **Start button** to test your code.

➤ Click the **Yes button** to save your changes.

➤ The Splash form will display. Click the **OK button** to continue.

➤ The Main form will display with the record for Mel Gibson.

➤ Click the **Add New Record button**. Add **Celine Dion, 03/30/1968**.

➤ Click the data-bound combo box's **down arrow** and select **Musician/Singer** for the occupation, as shown in Figure 8.4a.

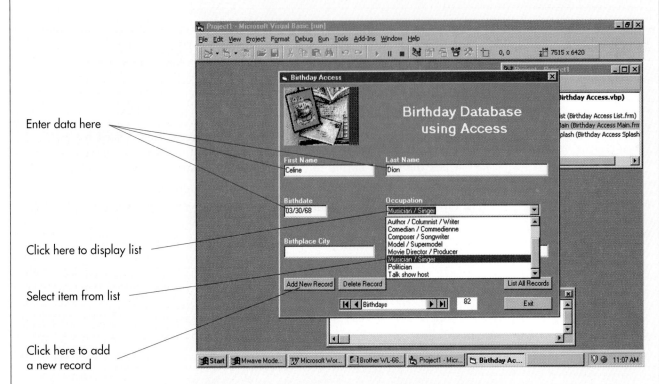

(a) Test the Add Record Code (step 2)

FIGURE 8.4 Hands-on Exercise 2

➤ Continue entering data with **Charlemagne**, **Quebec**, **Canada**.

➤ Click any of the navigation buttons to save the record and move to another record.

➤ Click the **Last button** to display Celine Dion stored as record number 83.

STEP 3: Test the Delete Record Code

➤ Click the **First button** to display Mel Gibson.

➤ Click the **Next button** to display Nicholas Cage. Click the **Delete Record button** to delete Nicholas.

➤ Click the **No button** in the confirmation dialog box as shown in Figure 8.4b.

➤ Nicholas Cage's record should remain displayed.

➤ Click the **Next button** to display Clint Black. Click the **Delete Record button** to delete Clint. Click the dialog box's **Yes button** to confirm the deletion.

➤ Click the **First button** again to display Mel's record. Click the **Next button** to display the record for Nicholas. Click the **Next button** again and notice that the deleted record for Clint Black is skipped, and Natalie Cole's record is displayed.

➤ Click the **Exit button**. Click the dialog box's **Yes button** to confirm.

STEP 4: Add the Find Record Button

➤ In the Project Explorer window, double click the **Main form**.

➤ Click the toolbar's **Toolbox button**.

➤ In the Toolbox, select the **Command Button tool** and draw the control to the right of the Delete Record button as shown in Figure 8.4c.

Click here to confirm deletion

Click here to cancel deletion

Click here to delete current record

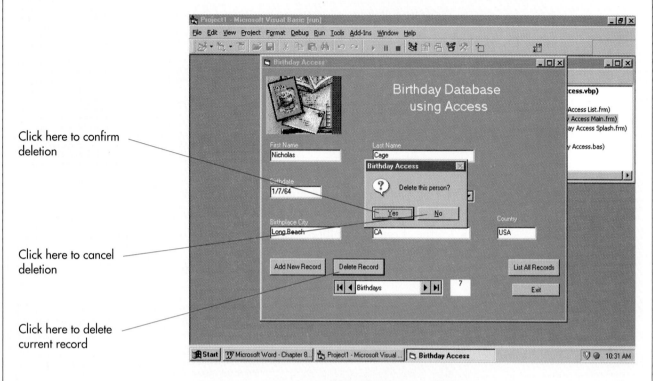

(b) Test the Delete Record Code (step 3)

Set properties here

Add command button here

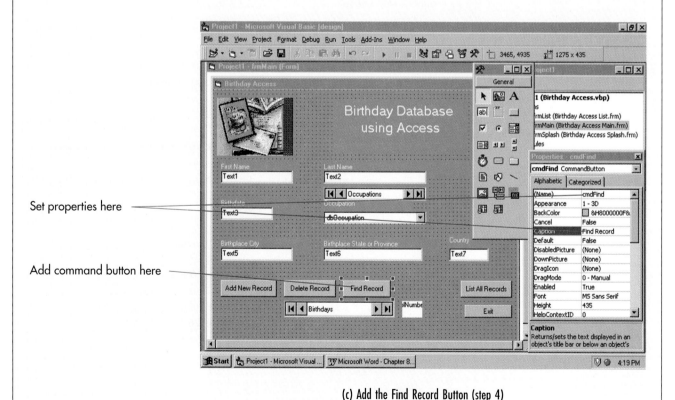

(c) Add the Find Record Button (step 4)

FIGURE 8.4 Hands-on Exercise 2 (continued)

- Set the button's Name property to **cmdFind** and the Caption property to **Find Record**.
- Double click the button to display the Code Editor window.
- Add the following code to the cmdFind Click event procedure:

```
'****************************************************
Private Sub cmdFind_Click()
'Purpose: Call the procedure to find and display a record
        Call FindRecord
End Sub
```

STEP 5: Add Code for the FindRecord Procedure
- Close the Toolbox, the Code Editor, and Form Designer windows.
- In the Project Explorer window, select Module1 and click the **View Code button**.
- Add the following code to the bottom of the module:

```
'********************************************************************
Public Sub FindRecord()
'Purpose: Find a record in the database
Dim SearchRecord As String    'record searching for
Dim OriginalRecord As String  'save current record
Dim Quotes As String          'double quotes ASCII code
'Const FindMsg = "Find whom? Enter last name: "
'Const NoMsg = "No match found."


        Quotes = Chr$(34) 'ANSI code for double quotes
        SearchRecord = InputBox(FindMsg, "Find Record")
        'Check for user selecting Cancel button
        If SearchRecord = "" Then Exit Sub

        With frmMain  'use Main form to display record
                'Save the original record key
                OriginalRecord = .datBirthdays.Recordset.Bookmark
                'Set up the Search dialog box
                SearchRecord = "[LastName]= " & Quotes & _
                SearchRecord & Quotes
                'Start search at the first record
                .datBirthdays.Recordset.MoveFirst
                .datBirthdays.Recordset.FindNext SearchRecord
                'If no match found, reset and display message
                If .datBirthdays.Recordset.NoMatch Then
                        .datBirthdays.Recordset.Bookmark = _
                        OriginalRecord
                        MsgBox(NoMsg)
                End If
        End With
End Sub
```

STEP 6: Test the Find Record Code

➤ Close the Code Editor window.

➤ Click the toolbar's **Start button**. Click the **Yes button** to save your project changes.

➤ The Splash form will display. Click the **OK button** to continue.

➤ The first record, for Mel Gibson, is displayed.

➤ Click the **Find Record button**.

➤ The input box shown in Figure 8.4d will display. Enter **Carvey** in the text box and click the **OK button**.

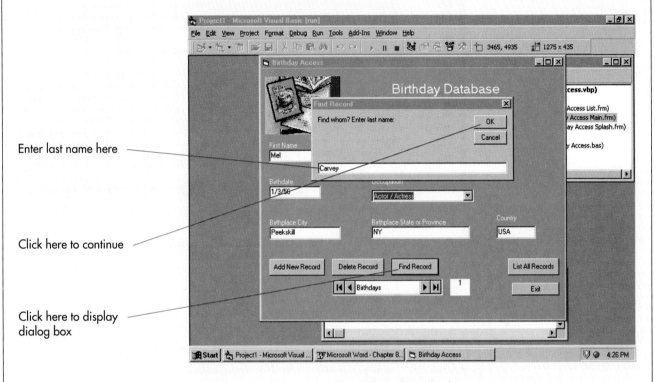

Enter last name here

Click here to continue

Click here to display dialog box

(d) Test the Find Record Code (step 6)

FIGURE 8.4   Hands-on Exercise 2 (continued)

➤ Dana Carvey's record will display in the Main form. Notice that it is stored as record number 21.

➤ Click the **Find Record button**. Enter **Black** in the input box's text box.

➤ "No match found" will display in the message box.

➤ Try to find other records in the database for your favorite celebrities.

➤ Click the **Exit button**. Click the **Yes button** to confirm.

STEP 7: Modify the List Form

➤ Double click the **List form** in the Project Explorer window.

➤ Grab the form by a corner and stretch it to the approximate size shown in Figure 8.4e (on the next page). Also, use the figure as a guide to place the controls on the form.

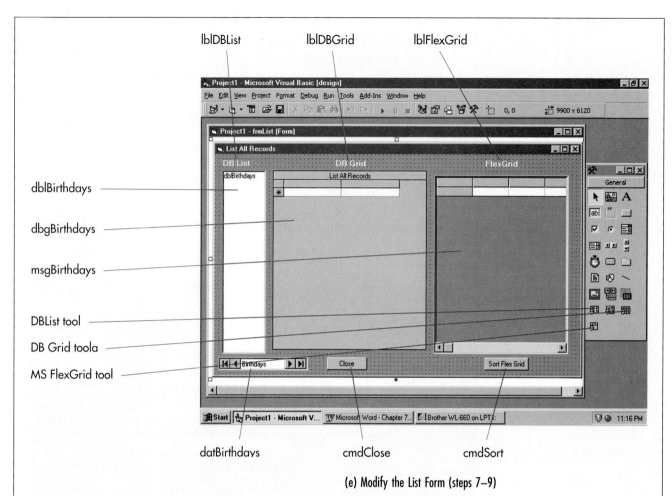

lblDBList   lblDBGrid   lblFlexGrid

dblBirthdays

dbgBirthdays

msgBirthdays

DBList tool

DB Grid toola

MS FlexGrid tool

datBirthdays   cmdClose   cmdSort

(e) Modify the List Form (steps 7–9)

FIGURE 8.4   Hands-on Exercise 2 (continued)

➤ In the Properties window, select the **List form**. Set the BackColor property to **teal** and the Caption property to **List All Records**.

➤ Click the toolbar's **Toolbox button**. Select the Label tool. Draw three labels as shown in the figure. Select the first label, hold down the Ctrl key while you select the other two, then release the Ctrl key. Change the following common properties for the selection:

Property	Setting
Alignment	2 - Center
BackColor	Teal
Font	MS Sans Serif, Bold, Size 10
ForeColor	White

➤ Select each label individually and set other properties as shown below:

Label Number	Name Property	Caption Property
1	lblDBList	DB List
2	lblDBGrid	DB Grid
3	lblFlexGrid	FlexGrid

➤ You added the Microsoft Data Bound List tools to your Toolbox in Hands-on Exercise 1. Now you need to add the others. Pull down the Project menu and select **Components**. Select the **Controls tab**.

➤ Click the check boxes beside **Microsoft Data Bound Grid Control** and **Microsoft FlexGrid Control 6.0** (or **5.0**). Click the **OK button**.

➤ The additional tools will be added to your Toolbox. (You may need to resize the Toolbox to see them.)

STEP 8: Continue Modifying the List Form

➤ Select the **Data tool** and place a control at the bottom left of the form. Set the following properties for the control:

Property	Setting
Name	datBirthdays
Caption	Birthdays
Connect	Access
Database Name	Select the disk and folder where your data disk is stored (*Exploring Visual Basic 6*) and the filename *Birthday Access.mdb*
ReadOnly	False
RecordsetType	1 - Dynaset
RecordSource	Select **Birthdays**
Visible	False

➤ Select the **DBList tool** and place the control at the left side of the form. Set the following properties for the data-bound list control:

Property	Setting
Name	dblBirthdays
RowSource	Select **datBirthdays**
ListField	Select **LastName**
DataSource	Select **datBirthdays**
DataField	Select **LastName**
BoundColumn	Select **LastName**

STEP 9: Add the Grid Controls to the List Form

➤ Select the **DBGrid tool** and place the control in the middle of the form. Set the following properties for the data-bound grid control:

Property	Setting
Name	dbgBirthdays
Caption	List All Records
DataSource	datBirthdays

➤ Select the **MSFlexGrid tool** and place the control at the right side of the form. Set the following properties for the FlexGrid control:

Property	Setting
Name	msgBirthdays
AllowUserResizing	1 - flexResizeColumns
Cols	8
DataSource	datBirthdays

➤ Select the **Command Button tool** and place a control immediately below the data-bound grid. Place a second command button control below the FlexGrid as shown in previous Figure 8.4e.

➤ For the first command button, set the Name property to **cmdClose** and the Caption property to **Close**.

➤ For the second command button, set the Name property to **cmdSort** and the Caption property to **Sort FlexGrid**.

STEP 10: Add Code for the List Form

➤ Double click the **Close button** to display the Code Editor window.

➤ Add the following code for the cmdClose click event procedure at the top of the window:

```
Option Explicit
'*****************************************************************
Private Sub cmdClose_Click()
'Purpose: Close the List form
        Unload Me
End Sub
```

➤ Select the **cmdSort object** and the **Click procedure**. Add the following code for the event procedure:

```
'*****************************************************************
Private Sub cmdSort_Click()
'Purpose: Sort FlexGrid by last name
        With Me.msgBirthdays
                .ColSel = 3  'sort by LastName in col 3
                .Col = 3
                .Sort = 5    'sort text in ascending order
                .Refresh
        End With
End Sub
```

➤ Select the **Form object** and the **Load procedure**. Add the following code for the event procedure:

```
'*********************************************************************
Private Sub Form_Load()
'Purpose:      Display the list of all records in the database
'              using the DBList, DBGrid and FlexGrid control
Dim Inch As Integer
        Inch = 1440      'logical inch in twips
        With Me
                'set column widths for DBGrid
                .dbgBirthdays.Columns(1).Width = 0.2 * Inch
                .dbgBirthdays.Refresh
                'set column widths for FlexGrid
                .msgBirthdays.Cols = 8
                .msgBirthdays.ColWidth(0) = 0.2 * Inch
                .msgBirthdays.ColWidth(1) = 0.2 * Inch
                'center form
                Move (Screen.Width - .Width) / 2, _
                        (Screen.Height - .Height) / 2
                .Refresh
        End With
End Sub
```

STEP 11: Test the List Form

➤ Close the Code Editor, Form Designer, and Toolbox windows.

➤ Click the toolbar's **Run button**. Click the **Yes button** to save your project changes.

➤ Click the **OK button** on the Splash form to continue.

➤ The Main form will display. Click the **List All Records button**.

➤ The List form will display as shown in Figure 8.4f.

➤ The DBList displays a single field of the database, in this case the LastName field.

➤ The DBGrid displays the entire database table. You can edit the records directly in the grid. **Try it**. Additional code would need to be added to actually save the modifications back to the database.

➤ The FlexGrid displays the entire database table, but you cannot edit the records. **Try it**.

➤ Click the **Sort FlexGrid button**. The records will now be displayed in alphabetical order by last name.

➤ Click the **Close button**.

➤ Click the **Exit button**. Click the **Yes button** to confirm.

➤ Congratulations, you have now completed a database front-end application for an Access database.

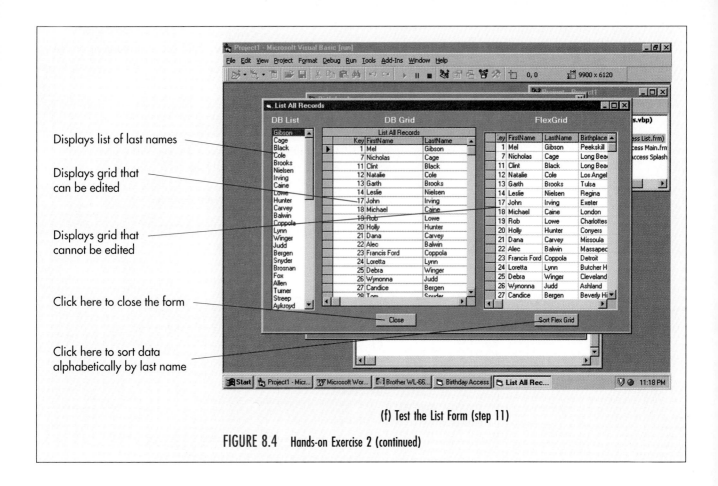

Displays list of last names

Displays grid that can be edited

Displays grid that cannot be edited

Click here to close the form

Click here to sort data alphabetically by last name

(f) Test the List Form (step 11)

FIGURE 8.4 Hands-on Exercise 2 (continued)

MORE DATABASE TOOLS

So far, we have created two applications for databases. In the previous chapter, we created a database program the "old-fashioned way" using ordinary flat files and a lot of code. Many times, we really need the power of a database application, and sometimes just a single table using a flat file will do the job. Remember to match the tool to the job. The advantage of the flat file is that the end user does not have to have the Access database application installed to use your project. If we create an executable file for the database project, Visual Basic is not required either.

In this chapter, we created a front-end application for an existing Access database. In these exercises, a major portion of the work had been finished using Access. Access provides all the capabilities of our Visual Basic project and more. This is precisely the reason we created the front-end application. Our front-end application shields the end user from the complexities of Access.

As we have seen, Visual Basic provides several tools to work with databases. There are three different ways to access data with Visual Basic 6.0: **ActiveX Data Objects** (ADO), **Remote Data Objects** (RDO), and **Data Access Objects** (DAO). The newest data access technology, ADO, is easier and more flexible than the previous technologies. Data access technology is constantly changing, and each of the three ways represents a different state of the art. For more information on database tools, browse the *Data Access Guide* and the *Microsoft DAO 3.51* books in the Visual Basic online documentation. If using Visual Basic 5.0, see the *Guide to Data Access Objects* book. The following describes some of the newest database tools currently available.

Learning Edition Tools

The Learning Edition provides a limited subset of database tools. These tools include the data control, the data-bound list and grid controls, the Microsoft Flexgrid control, and the intrinsic data-aware controls. The Learning Edition also includes the new ADO data control. You can get access to existing databases but cannot create new databases with these tools. The *Visual Data Manager* add-in can be used to create simple databases. This add-in will be discussed in the next section, and is accessible with the Learning Edition.

Professional Edition and Enterprise Edition Tools

The Professional Edition and Enterprise editions contain more database tools. You can use the new **Data View window** to browse the tables, views, and more for all of your local and remote databases. The new *Data Environment designer* provides an interactive, design-time environment for creating ADO objects. The new *Data Report* feature allows you to use drag and drop to quickly create custom reports, lists, and form letters from any database recordset. The former report feature was called **Crystal Reports** in Visual Basic 5. For more information, see the Writing *Reports with the Microsoft Data Report Designer* topic. Open the Visual Basic online documentation, then open the *Using Visual Basic* and the *Data Access Guide* books.

Enterprise Edition Tools

With Visual Basic 6.0, the Enterprise Edition integrates new visual database tools called the **Query Designer** and the **Database Designer**. You can visually create and modify database tables, views, column data types, and queries using these new tools.

ADD-INS

Add-ins are tools that are programs that customize and extend the Visual Basic environment. Add-ins can be thought of as a "snap-on" to the Visual Basic integrated development environment (IDE). Adds-ins are labor-saving tools that help programmers automate difficult, tedious or time-consuming tasks. There are four types of add-ins: (1) Add-ins, (2) Builders, (3) Wizards, and (4) Utilities. An *add-in* is the generic term for a program that performs a task within the IDE. A *wizard* is a type of add-in that leads a user step-by-step through a task, often a task that requires several steps. The VB Application Wizard, shown in Figure 8.5, is an example of a wizard. A *builder* is an add-in that helps a user view or set properties of a control. Builders were more popular in previous versions of Visual Basic. A utility is an add-in that may run without Visual Basic. Utilities are often compiled as an ActiveX executable that are also available as an add-in to the Visual Basic IDE. Visual Data Manager is an example of a utility. For more information about add-ins, open the *Component Tools Guide* book, then the *Extending the Visual Basic Environment with Add-Ins* book, and then the *Add-Ins Overview* book in Visual Basic Documentation.

Click here to continue
to next step

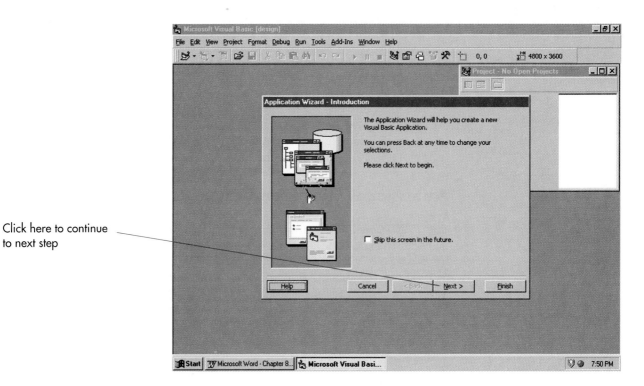

FIGURE 8.5   VB Application Wizard

Visual Data Manager

All three editions of Visual Basic include the ***Visual Data Manager*** add-in utility, which permits us to define and create new databases. This is a benefit if we do not have a database application such as Access installed on our computer. It is also available as a sample application named ***VisData***. This sample application is placed in the Vb\Samples\Pguide\Visdata folder during installation of the Visual Basic sample programs. We will use the Visual Data Manager utility, shown in Figure 8.6, to create a new database in the next hands-on exercise. To access the Visual Data Manager add-in, pull down the Add-Ins menu and select Visual Data Manager.

Learn by Doing

Now you are ready to complete your last hands-on exercise for this book. You will create a database within Visual Basic using the Visual Data Manager utility add-in and a sample record. Next, you will use the Application Wizard to create an input form for the new database. To finish up, you will add more records to the new database.

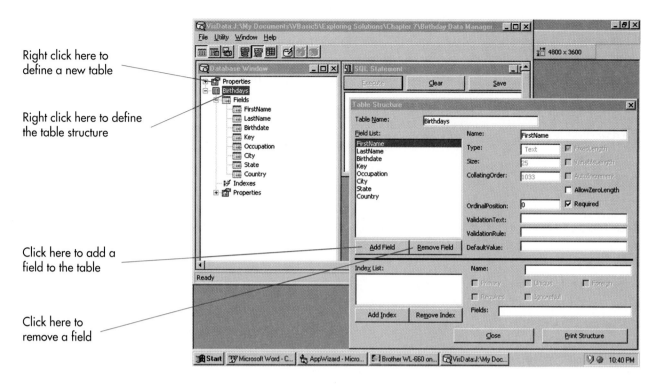

Right click here to define a new table

Right click here to define the table structure

Click here to add a field to the table

Click here to remove a field

FIGURE 8.6 Visual Data Manager

HANDS-ON EXERCISE 3

Visual Data Manager and the Birthday Database

Objective: Use the Visual Data Manager to create and define a new database. Use the Visual Basic Application Wizard to create an input form for the new database. Use Figure 8.7 as a guide for the exercise.

STEP 1: Create a New Project

➤ Start **Visual Basic**. Click the New Project dialog box's **New tab**.

➤ Select the **Standard EXE icon** and click the **Open button**.

➤ Pull down the **File menu** and select **Save Project** to display the Save File As dialog box.

➤ Select the disk and folder where your data disk is stored (*Exploring Visual Basic 6*). Enter **Birthday Data Manager** in the File name text box. Click the **Save button** to save the form.

➤ The Save Project As dialog box will display. Verify that *Exploring Visual Basic 6* folder is selected.

➤ Enter **Birthday Data Manager** in the File name text box. Click the **Save button** to save the project.

STEP 2: Create a New Database File

➤ Pull down the **Add-Ins menu** and select **Visual Data Manager**.

➤ If you get a VisData message box stating "Add SYSTEM.MD? (Microsoft Access Security File) to INI File?" select the **No button**.

➤ The Visual Data Manager window (VisData) will open.

➤ Pull down the **File menu** and select **New**, then **Microsoft Access**, then **Version 7.0 MDB** as shown in Figure 8.7a.

Pull down the File menu

Select New

Select Microsoft Access

Select Version 7.0

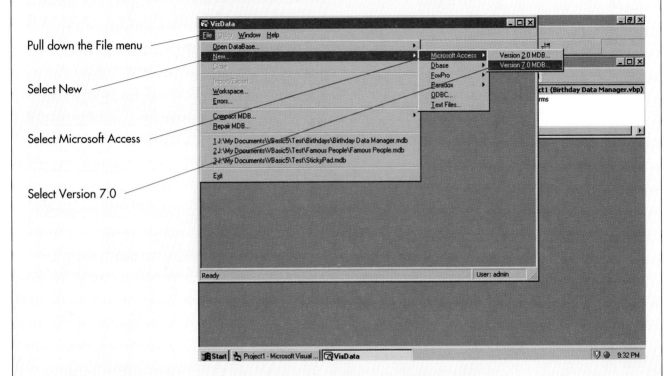

(a) Create a New Database File (step 2)

FIGURE 8.7   Hands-on Exercise 3

➤ The Select Microsoft Access Database to Create dialog box will display. Select the disk and folder where your data disk is stored (*Exploring Visual Basic 6*). Enter **Birthday Data Manager** in the File name text box. Click the **Save button** to create the database.

➤ Wait a moment for the Visual Data Manager to create the new database.

➤ Maximize the Visual Data Manager window. This window contains two other windows. The Database window will contain a single entry, "Properties," with a plus sign to indicate that it can be expanded. The SQL Statement window will be empty.

STEP 3: Create a New Table

➤ Right click **Properties** in the Database window, and select **New Table** from the menu.

➤ The Table Structure dialog box will display as shown in Figure 8.7b.

➤ Enter **Birthdays** in the Table Name text box.

STEP 4: Add Fields to the Table

➤ Click the **Add Field button**. The Add Field dialog box will display as shown in Figure 8.7c.

➤ Enter **FirstName** in the Name text box.

➤ Leave **Text** selected as the Type.

➤ Enter **25** in the Size text box.

➤ Select the **FixedField option button**.

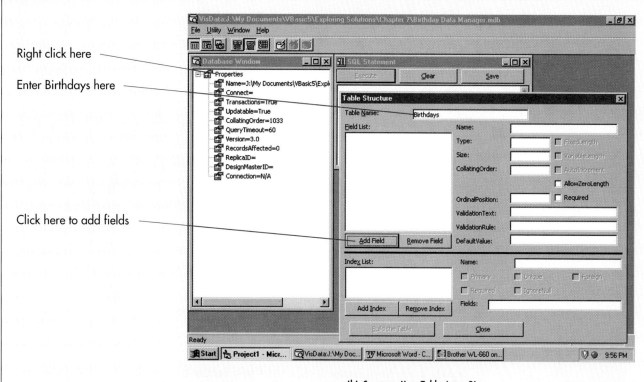

Right click here

Enter Birthdays here

Click here to add fields

(b) Create a New Table (step 3)

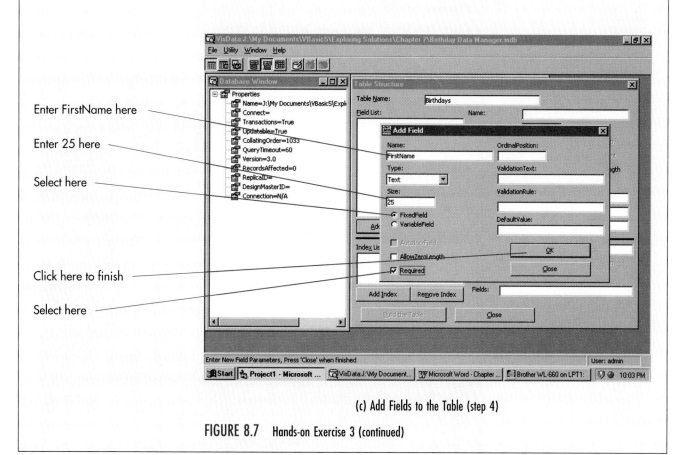

Enter FirstName here

Enter 25 here

Select here

Click here to finish

Select here

(c) Add Fields to the Table (step 4)

FIGURE 8.7   Hands-on Exercise 3 (continued)

➤ Uncheck the **AllowZeroLength check box**.

➤ Check the **Required check box**.

➤ Leave all other text box options blank.

➤ Click the **OK button** to finish.

STEP 5: Add More Fields to the Table

➤ Repeat this process for the 7 remaining fields as shown in the following table:

Field Name	Type	Size	Options	Check Boxes
LastName	Text	50	FixedField	Required
Birthdate	Date/Time	8 (cannot change)	N/A	Required
Key	Long	4 (cannot change)	N/A	AutoIncrField Required
Occupation	Text	30	FixedField	Required
City	Text	25	FixedField	Required
State	Text	25	FixedField	AllowZeroLength
Country	Text	25	FixedField	Required

➤ When you have finished, click the **Close button** to close the Add Field window.

➤ The Table Structure dialog box will show all the added fields as shown in Figure 8.7d.

➤ Click the **Build the Table button** to create the database table and close the window.

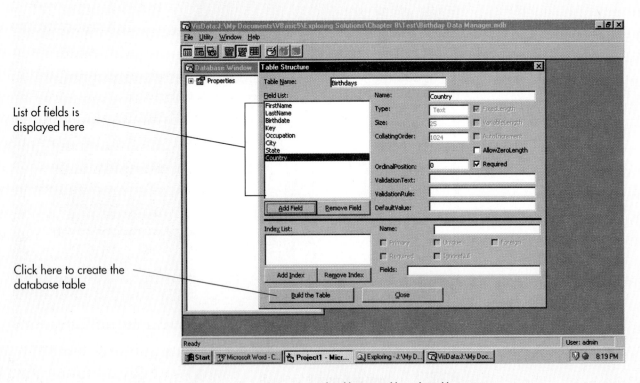

List of fields is displayed here

Click here to create the database table

(d) Add More Fields to the Table (step 5)

FIGURE 8.7   Hands-on Exercise 3 (continued)

STEP 6: Add a Record to the Database

➤ Double click the **Birthdays icon** in the Database window to open the Birthdays table.

➤ The database is empty, so go ahead and add a new record.

➤ Click the **Add button** to display the Birthdays Table window.

➤ Add the data for your birthday as shown in Figure 8.7e. Leave the Key field blank so that it can be automatically generated later.

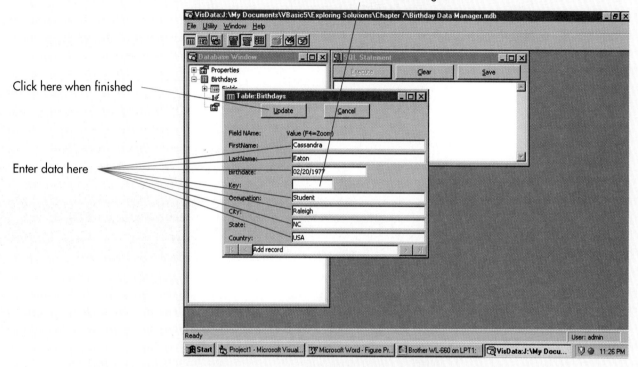

(e) Add a Record to the Database (step 6)

FIGURE 8.7   Hands-on Exercise 3 (continued)

➤ When you have finished entering your data, click the **Update button**.

➤ Notice the Key field will be automatically numbered as record 1.

➤ Click the **Close button** to close the Birthdays table.

➤ Pull down the **File menu** and select **Close**.

➤ If you see the "Data has been changed, commit it?" message box, click the **Yes button**.

➤ Close the Visual Data Manager window.

STEP 7: Start Another Project Using the Application Wizard

➤ Pull down the **File menu** and select **Add Project**.

➤ Click the Add Project dialog box's **New tab**. Select the **VB Application Wizard** icon and click the **Open button**.

➤ On the Introduction screen, do not select a profile, and click the **Next button**.

➤ On the Interface Type screen, click the **Single Document Interface (SDI)**. Enter **AppWizard** in the text box to name the project. Click the **Next button**.

- On the Menus screen, select **&File check box** to check it. Clear the other menu check boxes. Select **&File** in the left pane. In the right pane, uncheck all the submenu items except **E&xit**. You will need to scroll the list to view all the items. Click the **Next button**.
- On the Customize Toolbar screen, click the double arrow button to delete all the buttons from the toolbar. Click the **Next button**.
- On the Resources screen, select the **No option**, then click the **Next button**.
- If you get an Internet Connectivity screen, click the **No option** and then the **Next button**.
- On the Standard Forms screen, leave all the check boxes blank, and then click the **Next button**.
- On the Data Access Forms screen, click the **Create New Form button**.

THE APPLICATION WIZARD USING VISUAL BASIC 5

The Data Form Wizard is new to Visual Basic 6, so the screens in steps 8 and 9 will not be displayed. The screens for the Application Wizard have been changed, so follow the instructions for Step 7 except for the following screens:

Interface Type Screen: Click the **Single Document Interface (SDI) Option button**. Click the **Next button**.
Menus Screen: Click the **Clear All button**, then select the **File check box**. Click the **Next button**.
Data Access Forms Screen: Select the "**Yes, Create forms from my database**" option. Leave the Database Format as **Access**, and then click the **Browse button**, and select the disk and folder for your data disk (*Exploring Visual Basic 6*). Select the **Birthday Data Manager file** and click the **Open button**.
Select Tables Screen: Click the **Tables option button**. Select **Birthdays** from the Available list box, and click the **Move button** (looks like >) to move the table to the Selected list box. Click the **Next button** to continue.

STEP 8: Use the Data Form Wizard to Create the Update Form

- The Data Form Wizard will start. On the Introduction screen as shown in Figure 8.7f, do not select a profile. Click the **Next button**.
- On the Database Type screen, select **Access** from the list.
- On the Database screen, click the **Browse button**, and select the disk and folder for your data disk (*Exploring Visual Basic 6*). Select the **Birthday Data Manager file** and click the **Open button**. Click the **Next button** to continue with the wizard.
- On the Form screen, enter **Update** in the text box to name the form. Select **Single Record** from the list, and select the **ADO Data Control option button**. Click the **Next button** to continue.
- On the Record Source screen, click the **list box arrow** and select **Birthdays**. The fields will be displayed in the left pane. Click the **double arrow button** to select all the fields. Select the **Key field** in the right pane, and click the **left arrow button** to deselect the key field. Select **Key** as the column to sort by. Click the **Next button** to continue.

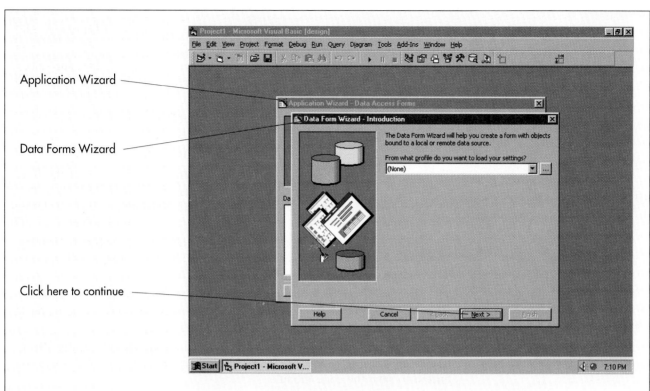

Application Wizard

Data Forms Wizard

Click here to continue

(f) Use the Data Form Wizard to Create the Update Form (step 8)

FIGURE 8.7   Hands-on Exercise 3 (continued)

➤ On the Control Selections screen, click the **Select All button**. Click the **Next button** to continue.

➤ On the Finished screen, do not save a profile. Click the **Finish button**. Wait a moment for the wizard to create the form and code.

STEP 9: Use the Data Form Wizard to Create the Grid Form

➤ Click the **Yes button** for the Create another form dialog box.

➤ On the Form screen, enter **Grid** in the text box to name the form. Select **Grid (Datasheet)** from the list, and select the **ADO Data Control option button**. Click the **Next button** to continue.

➤ On the Record Source screen, click the **list box arrow** and select **Birthdays**. The fields will be displayed in the left pane. Click the **double arrow button** to select all the fields. Select the **Key field** in the right pane, and click **the left arrow button** to deselect the key field. Select **LastName** as the column to sort by. Click the **Next button** to continue.

➤ On the Control Selections screen, click the **Update Button, Refresh button**, and **Close button check boxes**. Clear the other check boxes. Click the **Next button** to continue.

➤ On the Finished screen, do not save a profile. Click the **Finish button**. Wait a moment for the wizard to create the form and code.

➤ The Data Form wizard will close, and you will continue with the Application Wizard.

STEP 10: Finish the Application Wizard

➤ On the Data Access Forms screen, click the **Next button** to continue.

➤ On the Finished screen, do not save a profile. Click the **Finish button** to continue.

- ➤ The forms will be created and briefly display on the screen. Click the Application Created dialog box's **OK button**.
- ➤ Right click the **AppWizard project** in the Project Explorer window, and select **AppWizard properties**. Select **frmMain** for the Startup object. Click the **OK button**.
- ➤ Right click the **AppWizard project** in the Project Explorer window, and select **Set As Startup**.
- ➤ Pull down the **File menu** and select **Save AppWizard**.
- ➤ The Save File As dialog box will display for the first form. Select the disk and folder where your data disk is stored (*Exploring Visual Basic 6*). Enter **Birthday Data Manager Grid** (was Grid) in the File name text box. Click the **Save button** to save the first form.
- ➤ The Save File As dialog box will display for the next form. Enter **Birthday Data Manager Update** (was Update) in the File name text box. Click the **Save button** to save the second form.
- ➤ The Save File As dialog box will display for the third form. Enter **Birthday Data Manager Main** (was frmMain) in the File name text box. Click the **Save button** to save the third form.
- ➤ The Save File As dialog box will display for the code module. Enter **Birthday Data Manager** (was Module1) in the File name text box. Click the **Save button** to save the code module.
- ➤ The Save Project As dialog box will display for the project. Enter **Birthday Data Manager AppWizard** (was AppWizard) in the File name text box. Click the **Save button** to save the project.
- ➤ Pull down the **File menu** and select **Save Project Group**. The folder where your data disk is stored (*Exploring Visual Basic 6*) will be displayed. Enter **Birthday Data Manager Group** in the File name text box. Click the **Save button** to save the project group.
- ➤ If the AppWizard's forms are not still displayed, open them. If the Project Manager window is not still open, open it.
- ➤ Pull down the **Window menu** and select **Tile Horizontally** to display the forms as shown in Figure 8.7g.

STEP 11: Test the Update Form
- ➤ Click the toolbar's **Start button**. Click the **Yes button** to save your project changes.
- ➤ The AppWizard Main form will display. Pull down the **Data menu** and select **Update**.
- ➤ The Update form will display as shown in Figure 8.7h.
- ➤ The Application Wizard generated this form for the database. It is a simple form with a gray background, and it is a good place to start when designing database forms.
- ➤ Examine the form and change something in the current data record.
- ➤ Click the **Update button** to save the changes you made.
- ➤ Click the **Add button**, and add data for a celebrity from the previous exercise or a friend or relative's data. Click the **Update button**.
- ➤ Enter the data for at least **four more records** for a minimum of six records. If you change any fields, you will need to delete the field's previous data before entering any modifications.
- ➤ Click the Update form's **Close button**.

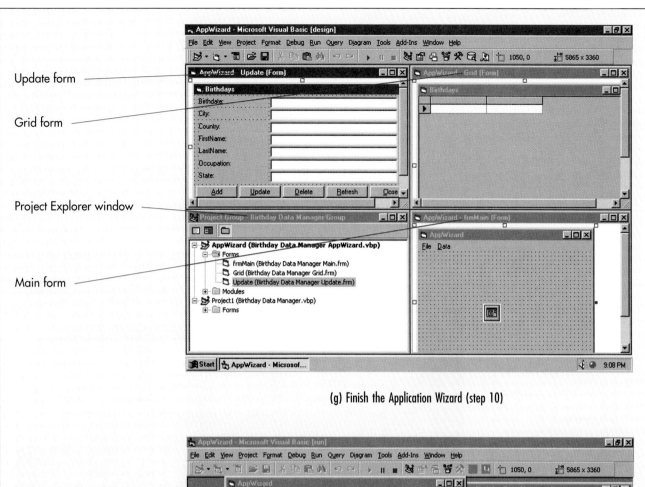

Update form

Grid form

Project Explorer window

Main form

(g) Finish the Application Wizard (step 10)

Pull down and select Update

Click here to add a new record

Click here after modifying record

(h) Test the Update Form (step 11)

FIGURE 8.7   Hands-on Exercise 3 (continued)

STEP 12: Test the Grid Form
➤ Pull down the **Data Menu** and select **frmGrid** to display the grid containing the six or more records.
➤ Grab the window by the right edge, and expand the window as shown in Figure 8.7i.

Pull down and select Grid

Click here after modifying record

Click here to close form

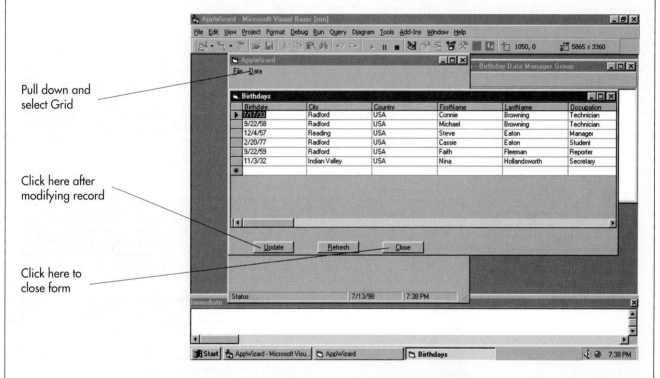

(i) Test the Grid Form (step 12)

FIGURE 8.7   Hands-on Exercise 3 (continued)

➤ Click the **Close button** to close the Grid form.
➤ Pull down Main form's **File menu** and select **Exit** to stop execution.
➤ Pull down the **File menu** and select **Exit** to exit Visual Basic.

Access is the database application included within Microsoft Office. Access is a relational database. Relational databases are composed of several tables and relationships. A table consists of rows and columns where each column is a field and each row is a record. A relationship is an association established between fields in two tables using a foreign key.

ActiveX Database controls include the data-bound list, the data-bound combo box, and the data-bound grid control. The data-bound list and data-bound combo controls are similar to the intrinsic controls but are always bound to a database. The data-bound grid control is similar to the Microsoft FlexGrid control but must be bound to a database.

A data control is used for each table that we want to access in a database. The data control uses the Microsoft Jet database engine that also powers Microsoft Access. To navigate the database using the data control, we use recordsets. A recordset is simply a record or set of records selected from a table or tables in a database. There are three types of recordsets. A Table type is used with a single table from a database. A Dynaset type is used to work with several tables when we need to add, modify, and delete records. The Snapshot type is used to display but not edit records.

Visual Data Manager is an add-in utility included in all three editions of Visual Basic. We can define and create new databases using the Visual Data Manager (VisData). The new Data Form Wizard helps us to create forms for our database tables. The Application Wizard automatically creates general forms such as Splash forms and About forms for applications.

KEY WORDS AND CONCEPTS

ActiveX database controls	DBGrid	RecordSource property
Data control	DBList box	Relational database
Database	Dynaset recordset	Relationship
DatabaseName property	Front end application	Snapshot recordset
DataField property	Microsoft Access	Table recordset
DataSource property	Microsoft Jet database engine	Visual Data Manager (VisData)
DBCombo box	Recordset	

MULTIPLE CHOICE

1. If you want to display data from a database in a grid format but do not want the user to be able to modify the data, which of the following controls is more appropriate?
   (a) MS FlexGrid
   (b) DBGrid
   (c) Either (a) or (b) would do the job
   (d) Neither (a) nor (b) would work

2. Which of the following controls is not a ActiveX database control?
   (a) Microsoft FlexGrid
   (b) Data-bound grid
   (c) Data
   (d) Data-bound combo box

3. Access is an example of which of the following database models?

(a) Hierarchical

(b) Network

(c) Object

(d) Relational

4. What defines relationships in the Access database?

(a) Primary keys

(b) Foreign keys

(c) Fields

(d) Records

5. Which control is needed for each table in a database referenced on a form?

(a) Data-bound combo

(b) Data-bound grid

(c) Data

(d) Data-bound list

6. Which type of recordset is appropriate if you only need to modify a single table in a database?

(a) Table

(b) Dynaset

(c) Snapshot

(d) Any of the above is equally appropriate

7. Which of the following methods is not available for the data control?

(a) MoveFirst

(b) MoveLast

(c) MovePrevious

(d) AddNew

8. An advantage to creating a front end application using Visual Basic for an Access database for the end user is

(a) The user can easily change the design of the database tables

(b) The user can see easily see all the forms, modules, tables, and queries associated with the database

(c) The user is shielded from the complexity of the database, and cannot easily change the design of the database tables

(d) The end user can easily create a new form

9. Which of the following is not a specialized data bound control provided with Visual Basic?

(a) Data-bound list box

(b) Data-bound combo box

(c) Data-bound grid

(d) Data-bound command button

10. Which of the following statements is false about Visual Data Manager?

(a) It is available to the Learning Edition as a sample application called VisData

(b) It is not available in the Enterprise Edition

(c) It is available as an Add-In

(d) It is used to design and create new databases

11. The Application Wizard is useful when working with existing Access databases because
    (a) It creates the entire application for you
    (b) It creates input forms for you
    (c) It creates input forms and a minimal application for you
    (d) It doesn't work with databases

12. An association established between fields in different tables is called a
    (a) Primary key
    (b) Relationship
    (c) Foreign key
    (d) Record

13. An advantage to using an Access database over flat-flat databases is
    (a) The database can contain many tables
    (b) Tools are available to help you create forms and reports
    (c) The code for accessing the data is written for you
    (d) All of the above

14. The recordset method ___ creates a new record in a recordset.
    (a) AddNew
    (b) Insert
    (c) InsertNew
    (d) Update

15. Which of the following controls allows you to quickly display data in a spreadsheet format?
    (a) Data-bound spreadsheet
    (b) Data-bound grid
    (c) Data-bound table
    (d) Data-bound list

ANSWERS

1. a	**6.** a	**11.** c
2. c	**7.** d	**12.** b
3. d	**8.** c	**13.** d
4. b	**9.** d	**14.** a
5. c	**10.** b	**15.** b

PRACTICE WITH VISUAL BASIC

VIDEO CLIP

1. **Demonstration: Data Browser Program (Learning Edition Only).** This exercise requires that you be using the Learning Edition of Visual Basic and that you have installed the Learn Visual Basic Now book on your hard drive or have access to it from the CD-ROM. This program demonstrates another front end application to the Biblio sample database program included with Visual Basic. Watch and learn.

To start the demonstration:

a. Start Learn Visual Basic Now.

b. Open the *Chapter 10* book, then the *Opening Databases* book, then the "Demonstration Data Browser" topic, as shown in Figure 8.8.

c. In the Topic pane, scroll down and click the Video demonstration icon.

d. View the entire demonstration.

Click here to start the demonstration

Open the Chapter 10 book

Open the Demonstration topic

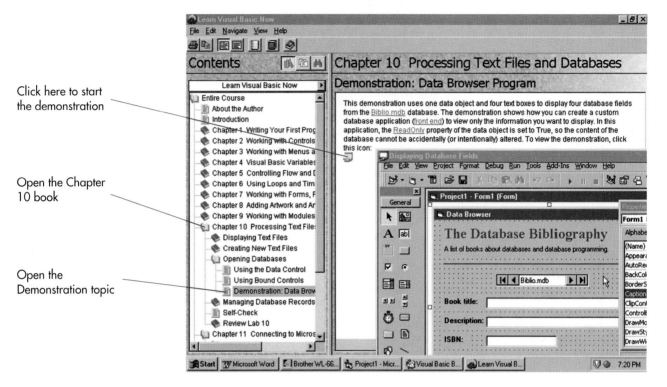

FIGURE 8.8   Screen for Practice Exercise 1: Data Browser Program Demonstration

2. Sample Program: Bibliography Database Browser. This sample application is included with Visual Basic. It should be installed in the *Biblio* folder under the *Pguide* folder in the *Samples* folder. The database stores books on the subject of databases. The database is composed of three tables that are used in the application: (1) Titles, (2) Authors, and (3) Publishers, as shown in Figure 8.9. Run the project, pull down the Help menu for considerable information about the program. Examine the sample program and the database.

ZTHE BIBLIO DATABASE AND VISUAL BASIC 5

Note that the *Biblio database* may not be distributed with Visual Basic 6. This database file was distributed with Visual Basis 5.

VIDEO CLIP

3. Demonstration: Music Review Notepad (Learning Edition Only). This exercise requires that you be using the Learning Edition of Visual Basic, and that you have installed the Learn Visual Basic Now book on your hard drive or have access to it from the CD-ROM. This program demonstrates a front end

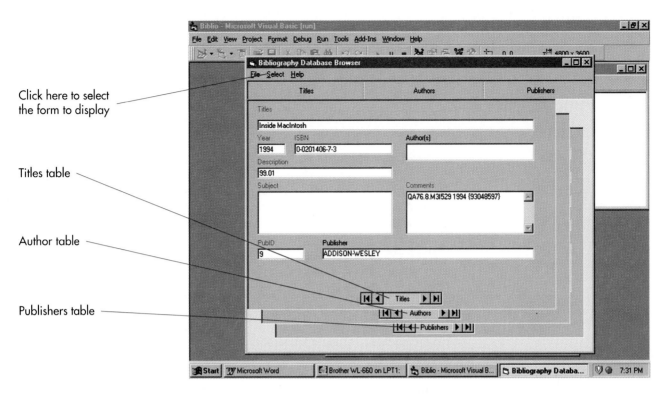

Click here to select
the form to display

Titles table

Author table

Publishers table

FIGURE 8.9   Screen for Practice Exercise 2: Bibliography Database Browser

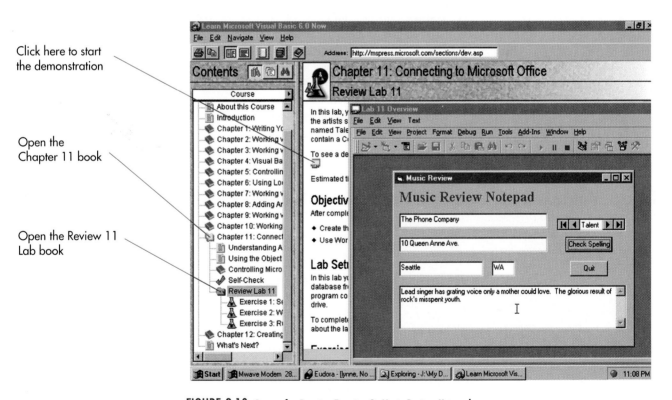

Click here to start
the demonstration

Open the
Chapter 11 book

Open the Review 11
Lab book

FIGURE 8.10 Screen for Practice Exercise 3: Music Review Notepad

application to the Music Review database included with the CD. Read the Review Lab 11 book topics for the specification of the program, and how to steps. To start the demonstration:

    a. Start Learn Visual Basic Now.

    b. Open the *Chapter 11* book, and *Review Lab 11* as shown in Figure 8.10.

    c. In the Topic pane, scroll down and click the Video demonstration icon.

    d. View the entire demonstration.

4. **Personal Address Book.** Create a new database to store addresses using the Visual Data Manager. Use the database created in Hands-on Exercise 3 as a model for this exercise. The table should contain fields such as LastName, FirstName, Address, City, State, Country, ZipCode, HomePhone, Business-Phone, Email, and Birthday. You may also include other fields as appropriate for your needs. Name the database, project, and form file **Personal Address Book**. Make a printout of your form and code, or project files on disk, and submit to your instructor.

5. **Access Demo.** If you have previous experience with Access, create a new database using the Database Wizard included with Access. Choose from such pre-designed databases as Address Book, Book Collection, Contact Management, Music Collection, Video Collection, and many more. Name your database **Access Demo**. Select the option to include sample data on the Wizard screen. Add 6 more records to the new database with appropriate valid data. Print out a report from the database with the added records, or database file on disk, and submit to your instructor.

6. **Access Demo Front End.** This is a continuation of exercise 5. Using Visual Basic and the database created in exercise 5, create a front end application to your new database. Create a Splash screen and a form for at least one table in the database. Save the project as **Access Demo Front End**, and name the forms appropriately. Use the front end application created in Hands-on Exercises 1 and 2 as a model for this exercise. Delete the sample data from the database. Add 6 more records with appropriate valid data. Print out the forms and code from your application, or the project files on disk, and submit to your instructor.

CASE STUDIES

Relational Database Design

Design a relational database that would be useful to you. Select something other than names and address or contacts. Sketch on paper the tables that would be appropriate for your database along with the fields for each table. Decide on a name, data type, and size for each field. Your database should contain at least two different tables. One of these tables can be a lookup table. Draw the input form on paper for your database. Also, design at least two other forms. These forms could be a Splash screen, List screen, Help screen, or About screen. Submit your design sketches to your instructor.

Database Design Implementation

Design and implement a database that would be useful to you. Select something other than names and address or contacts. You can start with the design from the first case study, or design an entirely new database. Create the tables for database using the Visual Data Manager or Access. Decide and create fields with appropriate names, data types, and sizes. Your database should contain at least two different tables. One of these tables can be a lookup table. Create at least two forms in your project. These forms could be a Splash screen, List screen, Help screen, or About screen. Save your database and project files as **Database Design**. Print out the forms and code from your application, or the project files on disk, and submit to your instructor.

Access Office VB Advisor

The online magazine called *Access Office VB Advisor* specializes in advice for programming with Visual Basic and Office applications. The site can be found at ***www.advisor.com***. The company publishes several magazines, so click on the Access Office VB Advisor logo from the company's home page. New articles are published every month, and a sample is shown in Figure 8.11. Go to the site and read an article of interest to you. Write a half-page summary of your reading, and submit it to your instructor.

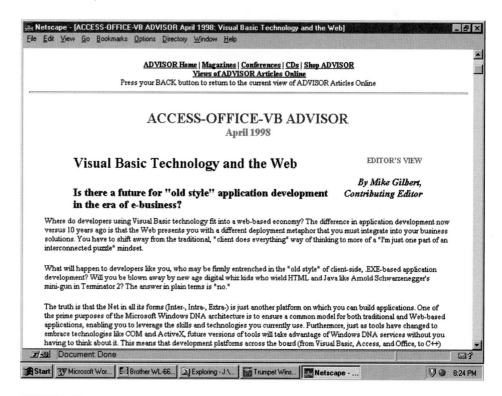

FIGURE 8.11 Access Office VB Advisor Case Study

Universal Access Web Site

Microsoft has created a site dedicated to information about database projects. This site is available at **www.microsoft.com/data** and the home page is shown in Figure 8.12. Universal Data Access is Microsoft's solution to help companies building database solutions. Microsoft Data Access Components consists of ActiveX Data Objects (ADO), OLE DB, and Open Database Connectivity (ODBC). Go to the site and learn more about one of these topics, or choose another topic of interest to you. Write a one-page summary of an article or information you read from the Web site. Submit your summary and a hard copy of your Web page references to your instructor. Remember to save the Web address of your reference and document it your summary.

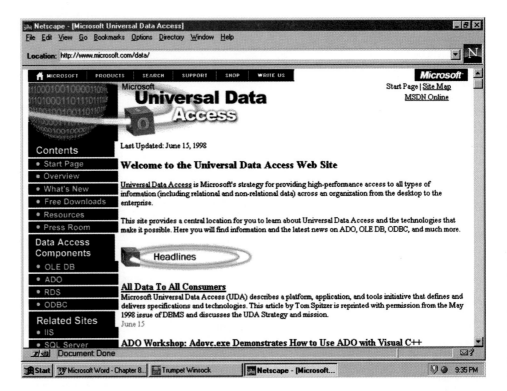

FIGURE 8.12 Universal Access Web Site Case Study

VISUAL BASIC RESERVED WORDS

OVERVIEW

Keywords are words reserved by Visual Basic that should not be used as variable or constant names in your code. A keyword is a word or symbol recognized by Visual Basic as part of the programming language—for example, a statement, function name, or operator. When creating names for your constants and variables, avoiding these words will save you a lot of debugging time.

These keywords can be found by clicking the Search tab in the online documentation and searching for **keywords**. Select the *Keywords by Task* topic to display most of the keywords. The keywords are listed in the following categories: Arrays, Collection, Compiler Directives, Control Flow, Conversion, Data Types, Dates and Times, Directories and Files, Financial, Errors, Input and Output, Math, Miscellaneous, Operators, Registry, String Manipulation, and finally Variables and Constants. The keywords are listed alphabetically below:

#Const	AppActivate	Chr
#If...Then...#Else	Array	CInt
&	Asc	Clear
*	Atn	CLng
/	Beep	Close
\	Boolean	Collection
^	Byte	Command
+	Call	Const
<	CBool	Cos
<=	CByte	CreateObject
<>	CCur	CSng
=	CDate	CStr
>	CDbl	CurDir
>=	Cdec	Currency
Abs	ChDir	CVar
Add	ChDrive	CVErr
And	Choose	Date
		(continued)

DateAdd	IsMissing	Randomize
DateDiff	IsNull	Rate
DatePart	IsNumeric	RGB
DateSerial	IsObject	ReDim
DateValue	Item	Remove
Day	Kill	Reset
DDB	LBound	Resume
Deftype	LCase	Right
DeleteSetting	Left	RmDir
Dim	Len	Rnd
Dir	Let	RSet
Do...Loop	Like	RTrim
DoEvents	Line Input #	SaveSetting
Double	Loc	Second
End	Lock	Seek
Environ	LOF	Select Case
EOF	Log	SendKeys
Eqv	Long	SetAttr
Erase	LSet	Sgn
Err	LTrim	Shell
Error	Me	Sin
Exit	Mid	Single
Exp	Minute	SLN
FileAttr	MIRR	Space
FileCopy	MkDir	Spc
FileDateTime	Mod	Sqr
FileLen	Month	Static
Fix	Name	Stop
For Each...Next	New	Str
For...Next	Not	StrComp
Format	Now	StrConv
FreeFile	NPer	String
Function	NPV	Sub
FV	Object	Switch
Get	Oct	SYD
GetAllSettings	On Error	Tab
GetAttr	On...GoSub	Tan
GetObject	On...GoTo	Time
GetSetting	Open	Timer
GoSub...Return	Option Base	TimeSerial
GoTo	Option Compare	TimeValue
Hex	Option Explicit	Trim
Hour	Option Private Module	TypeName
If...Then...Else	Or	UBound
Imp	Pmt	UCase
Input	PPmt	Unlock
Input #	Print	Val
InStr	Print #	Variant
Int	Private	VarType
Integer	Property Get	Weekday
IPmt	Property Let	While...Wend
IRR	Property Set	Width #
Is	Public	With
IsArray	Put	Write #
IsDate	PV	Xor
IsEmpty	QBColor	Year
IsError	Raise	

OBJECT-NAMING CONVENTIONS FOR VISUAL BASIC

DEFINITIONS

An *object* is a combination of code and data that can be treated as a unit—for example, a control, form, or application component. Each object is defined by a class. Here are some common terms and definitions (reprinted directly from the Visual Basic online documentation) that may be helpful in understanding this appendix.

A *class* is the formal definition of an object. The class acts as the template from which an instance of an object is created at run time. The class defines the properties of the object and the methods used to control the object's behavior.

A *method* is a procedure that acts on an object.

An *instance* is any one of a set of objects sharing the same class. For example, multiple instances of a Form class share the same code and are loaded with the same controls with which the Form class was designed. During run time, the individual properties of controls on each instance can be set to different values.

NAMING OBJECTS

It is much easier to work with objects if you give them names that help remind you of their function. Visual Basic will assign default names for your objects as you create them. The default names will work, but they are not descriptive. The first command button you create will be called Command1, for example. This can be very confusing if you have several forms, and a Command1 button on all of them.

The following rules must be followed when naming your objects and forms:

- The name must begin with a letter (not a number).
- The name must contain only letters, numbers, and the underscore (_) character.
- Neither punctuation marks nor spaces are allowed.
- The name can contain a maximum of 40 characters.

To make it easier for humans to remember the objects, the following naming conventions are suggested by Microsoft and used by many professional Visual Basic programmers. Table B.1 lists the suggested prefixes for intrinsic controls and primary objects such as forms. Table B.2 lists the prefixes suggested for many ActiveX controls. The objects are listed in alphabetical order. These tables are taken directly from the Visual Basic help files. For more information on the naming conventions recommended by Microsoft, open the Visual Basic online documentation, and select the Contents tab. Open the *Using Visual Basic* book (Visual Basic 6 only), the *Programmer's Guide*, and *Visual Basic Coding Conventions* books.

TABLE B.1 Suggested Prefixes for Intrinsic Controls and Primary Objects

Object	Prefix	Example
Check box	chk	chkReadOnly
Combo box, Drop-down list box	cbo	cboLanguages
Command button	cmd	cmdExit
Data control	dat	datAddresses
Directory list box	dir	dirPictureFiles
Drive list box	drv	drvPictureFiles
File list box	fil	filPictureFiles
Form	frm	frmWelcome
Frame	fra	fraFileLocation
Horizontal scroll bar	hsb	hsbRate
Image	img	imgWorld
Key status	key	keyCaps
Label	lbl	lblAdd
Line	lin	linBlueRule
List box	lst	lstDescription
MCI (Media Control Interface)	mci	mciVideo
MDI (Multiple-Document Interface) child form	mdi	mdiNote
Menu	mnu	mnuFile
OLE container	ole	oleWorksheet
Option button	opt	optSex
Picture box	pic	picBoySmiling
Shape	shp	shpSquare
Text box	txt	txtName
Timer	tmr	tmrAlarm
Vertical scroll bar	vsb	vsbRate

TABLE B.2 Suggested Prefixes for ActiveX Controls

Object	Prefix	Example
3D panel	pnl	pnlGroup
Animated button	ani	aniMailBox
Common dialog	dlg	dlgFileOpen
Communications	com	comFax
Control (when specific type is unknown)	ctr	ctrCurrent
Data-bound combo box	dbcbo	dbcboState
Data-bound grid	dbgrd	dbgrdListAll
Data-bound list box	dblst	dblstJobType
Gauge	gau	gauStatus
Graph	gra	graRevenue
Grid	grd	grdPrices
Hierarchical FlexGrid (not available prior to version 6)	flex	flexOrders
MAPI (Messaging Application Programming Interface) message	mpm	mpmSentMessage
MAPI session	mps	mpsSession
Microsoft FlexGrid	msg	msgBirthdays
Microsoft Tab	mst	mstFirst
Outline	out	outOrgChart
Pen Bedit	bed	bedFirstName
Pen Hedit	hed	hedSignature
Pen ink	ink	inkMap
Picture clip	clp	clpToolbar
Report	rpt	rptQtr1Earnings
Spin	spn	spnPages
UpDown	upd	updDirection
Slider	sld	sldScale
ImageList	ils	ilsIcons
TreeView	tre	treOrganization
TabStrip	tab	tabOptions
StatusBar	sta	staDateTime
ListView	lvw	lvwHeadings
Progress Bar	prg	prgLoadFile
Rich Text Box	rtf	rtfReport

Applications that are more complex generally use several menu controls, and it is useful to have a unique set of naming conventions for these controls. The prefix "mnu" should be used to indicate a menu. Each control should be named with the menu title and the menu item as demonstrated in Table B.3.

TABLE B.3 Menu-Naming Conventions

Menu caption sequence	Menu name
File...Open	mnuFileOpen
File...Send...Email	mnuFileSendEmail
Format...Character	mnuFormatCharacter
View...Toolbars...Standard	mnuViewToolbarsStandard
Help...Contents	mnuHelpContents

NAMING CONSTANTS AND VARIABLES

Constants and variables can also be named using naming conventions. This is especially useful for projects with immense amounts of code. You should also require your variables to be declared to save yourself debugging time. To do this, pull down the Tools menu, and select Options. Check the Variable Declaration option on the Editor tab of the Options dialog box.

Constants and variables should also be descriptive of the information that they are storing. You may also want to use standard abbreviations for very long words to keep your names down to a manageable length. Table B.4 lists the suggested prefixes for variables and constants. This table, too, is reprinted directly from the Visual Basic online documentation. For more information on the naming conventions recommended by Microsoft, open the Visual Basic online documentation and select the Contents tab. Open the *Using Visual Basic* book (Visual Basic 6 only), the *Programmer's Guide,* and *Visual Basic Coding Conventions* books, and browse the *Constant- and Variable-Naming Conventions* topic.

TABLE B.4 Variable-Naming Conventions

Data type	Prefix	Example
Boolean	bln	blnFound
Byte	byt	bytRasterData
Collection object	col	colWidgets
Currency	cur	curRevenue
Date (Time)	dtm	dtmStart
Double	dbl	dblTolerance
Error	err	errOrderNum
Integer	int	intQuantity
Long	lng	lngDistance
Object	obj	objCurrent
Single	sng	sngAverage
String	str	strFirstName
User-defined type	udt	udtEmployee
Variant	vnt	vntCheckSum

THE TOOLBOX, TOOLBARS, AND CONTROLS

OVERVIEW

The Visual Basic Integrated Development Environment (IDE) has a standard toolbar, three optional toolbars, and a Toolbox. The Toolbox contains the tools you use to draw controls on your forms. The toolbar buttons and Toolbox buttons are intended to be indicative of their function. Thus the Open button looks like a file folder being opened, and the Check Box tool looks like the check box control that it draws on a form. If you point to any tool or button, a ToolTip will appear that displays its name.

THE TOOLBARS

There are four toolbars available in Visual Basic: Standard toolbar, Form Editor toolbar, Edit toolbar, and Debug toolbar. The **Standard Toolbar** provides access to the most commonly used commands. The Data View button is new with Visual Basic 6.0. When you first start Visual Basic, the Standard toolbar is displayed immediately below the menu bar. Click a toolbar button once to carry out the action represented by that button. When compiling, the right area of the toolbar displays a status bar that visually indicates how the compilation is progressing. The Standard toolbar must be visible for the status area to be displayed. Table C.1 displays the Standard toolbar buttons and the command represented. The toolbars can be docked along any edge or float anywhere on the screen.

TABLE C.1 STANDARD TOOLBAR BUTTONS

Toolbar button	Button name	Action or command	Alternative using Menu bar
	Add Project	Adds a project to current project group	File, then Add Project
	Add Form	Creates a new form	Project, then Add Form
	Menu Editor	Displays the Menu Editor	Tools, then Menu Editor
	Open Project	Opens an existing project	File, then Open Project
	Save Project	Saves the current project	File, then Save Project
	Cut	Cuts the selected object and sends a copy to the Clipboard	Edit, then Cut
	Copy	Copies the selected objects to the Clipboard	Edit, then Copy
	Paste	Pastes the object on the Clipboard to the current selection area	Edit, then Paste
	Find	Displays the Find window	Edit, then Find
	Undo	Undoes the last command	Edit, then Undo
	Redo	Redoes the last command undone	Edit, then Redo
	Start	Starts executing the current project	Run, then Start
	Break	Used for debugging; Stops the execution of a program while it's running	Run, then Break
	End	Stops execution of an application and returns to design mode	Run, then End
	Project Explorer	Displays the Project Explorer	View, then Project Explorer
	Properties	Displays the Properties window	View, then Properties window
	Form Layout	Displays the Form Layout window	View, then Form Layout window
	Object Browser	Displays the Object Browser	View, then Object Browser
	Toolbox	Displays the Toolbox	View, then Toolbox
	Data View (new VB 6, not available in Learning Edition)	Displays the Data View window	View, then Data View

(a) Standard Toolbar

(b) Debug Toolbar

(c) Edit Toolbar

(d) Form Editor Toolbar

FIGURE C.1   Visual Basic Toolbars

Displaying the Toolbars

To display a toolbar, pull down the View menu and select Toolbars to display the Toolbars menu. Next select (or deselect) the appropriate toolbar: Debug, Edit, Form Editor, or Standard. The toolbars are displayed in Figure C.1. The Standard toolbar displays by default when Visual Basic is started. The **Edit toolbar** contains commands used with the Edit Code window. The **Form Editor toolbar** contains commands used with the Form Designer window. The **Debug toolbar** contains buttons for commonly used commands when running and debugging your project. The debug commands are an intermediate level feature and beyond the scope of this textbook. The three optional toolbars do not display automatically with the appropriate windows. However, the buttons on the toolbars are dimmed when the corresponding window is not open.

The Standard Toolbar's Measurement Indicators

The forms designed in this book are sized to fit in the 640-by-480-pixel outline in the Form Layout window. Here we will see the reason for doing this. Windows is device-independent, so your application is likely to be run on a variety of computers, monitors, and printers. You need to size your forms so that they will display accurately even at low resolutions.

Visual Basic by default does not change the size of your forms when you change screen resolutions. Common screen resolutions are 640 by 480, 800 by 600, and 1024 by 768 pixels, as shown in the Form Layout window. If your form is located within the 640 by 480 outline in the Form Layout window, then your application will be visible when displayed at any of the resolutions. If your form goes outside this boundary, it will display properly at the higher resolution, but will extend past the edges of a 640 by 480 screen.

When you run your application, Visual Basic places your form on the screen based on its position in the Form Layout window. If your form is located beyond the dotted lines for the 640 by 480 pixel resolution, the entire screen will not be displayed at that resolution. To avoid all of these problems, it is best to design forms that fit within the 640 by 480 border in the Form Layout window and to be sure to place them within the border.

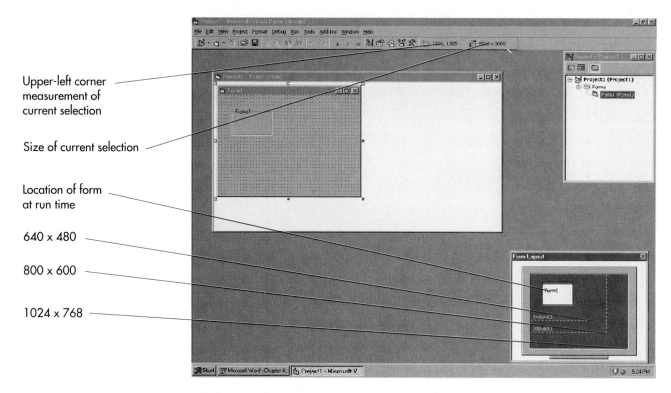

Upper-left corner
measurement of
current selection

Size of current selection

Location of form
at run time

640 x 480

800 x 600

1024 x 768

FIGURE C.2   Form Layout

Look at the Standard toolbar as shown in Figure C.2. The two indicators at the right end display the position and size of a selected form or control. These are the ***measurement indicators***. The unit of measurement in the form is called a ***twip***. When you draw and resize controls in the Form Designer window, you can look to these measurements for sizing help. You may remember coordinate system graphs from high school algebra class, and using a measurement system with x and y *coordinates*. If you do, these measurement indicators should be helpful. The first measurement describes the upper-left corner measurement of the selected control. The second indicator describes the size of the control. Any form you design in the Form Designer window is displayed as a gray grid of dots. In Chapter 2's Hands-on Exercise 1, we set the distance between the dots at 100 twips. The grid has an x and y-axes, and any object placed on it is located on them. The top left of the form has the coordinates 0,0. When you size your form in the Form Designer window, its total size is shown at the top of the window. When you click in the form, the position of the pointer is also indicated in the window. As you draw a control on a form, its size in twips is shown in a ToolTip.

See "Understanding the Coordinate System" and "Designing for Different Display Types" topics in the Visual Basic online documentation for more information on setting these options and using twip measurements. Select the Index tab (or icon), enter **twips** in the text box, and select the desired topic.

THE TOOLBOX

The Toolbox contains the tools you use to draw controls on your forms. It displays the entire set of intrinsic controls plus any ActiveX controls and Insertable Objects you have added to your project.

To display the Toolbox, click the Standard toolbar's Toolbox button, which looks like a hammer and wrench. Alternatively, pull down the View menu and select (deselect) the Toolbox command. The Toolbox will be displayed in the same position as when last displayed. To close the Toolbox, click the Close button for the window. The Toolbox can be docked along any edge or float anywhere on the screen.

You can display ToolTips for the Toolbox and toolbar buttons by selecting the Show ToolTips option in the General tab of the Options dialog box. Pull down the Tools menu, and select Options to display the Options dialog box.

Intrinsic Controls

Intrinsic controls are the controls contained inside the Visual Basic executable file. The 21 Intrinsic controls are always included in the Toolbox, as shown in Figure C.3. The two other broad categories of controls can be added and removed from the Toolbox. The Toolbox contains the tools needed to create a form. When referring to the Toolbox, the terms *controls* and *tools* are used interchangeably. The 21 intrinsic controls included in the default toolbox are listed below:

- **Pointer.** This is the only tool in the Toolbox that doesn't draw a control. Use the pointer to move or change the size of a control after it has been drawn on a form.

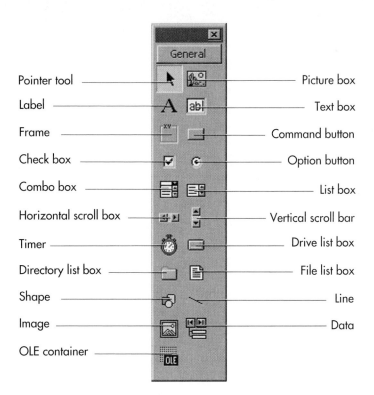

FIGURE C.3   The Toolbox

- **Picture box.** Use to display pictures, images, or graphics.
- **Label.** Use for text that you don't want the user to change.
- **Text box.** Use for text that the user can enter or change.
- **Frame.** Use to group controls together. To group controls, draw the frame first, and then draw controls inside the frame.
- **Command button.** Use to create a button the user can click on to carry out a command.
- **Check box.** Use to create a check box where the user can choose from multiple choices, and more than one choice is allowed.
- **Option button.** Use in a group of option buttons to display multiple choices, where only one choice is allowed.
- **Combo box.** Use to draw a combination list box and text box. The user can either choose an item from the list or enter a value in the text box.
- **List box.** Use to display a list of items, where only one choice is allowed. The list can be scrolled if it has more items than can be displayed at one time.
- **Horizontal Scroll Bar.** Use to provide a horizontal scroll bar. This is a handy tool for quickly navigating through a long horizontal list of items or a large amount of information.
- **Vertical Scroll Bar.** Use to provide a vertical scroll. This is a handy tool for quickly navigating through a long vertical list of items or a large amount of information.
- **Timer.** Use like a stopwatch. You can use the timer to trigger simple animation, and other events that happen at set intervals. The timer control is invisible at run time.
- **Drive List box.** Use to display valid disk drives.
- **Directory List box.** Use to display directories (folders) and paths.
- **File List box.** Use to display a list of files.
- **Shape.** Use to draw shapes. You can choose a rectangle, rounded rectangle, square, rounded square, oval, or circle.
- **Line.** Use to draw a variety of line styles.
- **Image.** Use to display a picture, image, or graphic. Images displayed in an Image control can only be decorative and use fewer resources than a Picture box.
- **OLE Container.** Use to link and embed objects from other applications in your Visual Basic application. *Object Linking and Embedding (OLE)* is a technology that enables you to create an application that can display objects from many different Windows applications. OLE enables the end user to edit the object from within the application in which it was created. In some cases, the user can even edit the object from within your Visual Basic application.
- **Data.** Use to create applications to display, edit, and update information from many types of existing databases.

ActiveX Controls

ActiveX Controls (called Custom Controls in previous Visual Basic editions) are controls that are separate files. They have a file extension of *.ocx* (*.vbx* for previous editions). ActiveX controls include such controls as data-bound list box, toolbars, and the tabbed dialog.

One way to create an object not included in the intrinsic controls is to add the ActiveX or Insertable Object to the Toolbox. Then draw the object directly on a form. This technique embeds the object within a form in your Visual Basic project.

To add an ActiveX control to your Toolbox, pull down the Project menu and select Components. Locate and select the desired control in the Controls tabbed dialog as shown in Figure C.4a, then click OK.

To remove an ActiveX control from the Toolbox, pull down the Project menu and select Components. Locate and select the desired control and clear the check box next to the name of the ActiveX control you want to delete, and then choose OK. You cannot delete an ActiveX control that is used in the current project. Instead, an error message will appear indicating that you are using the control in your current project.

Insertable Objects

Insertable Objects are objects from another application, such as an Excel worksheet, that can be embedded or linked to your application. These objects are created by another Windows application such as Word, PowerPoint, or Excel. Examples of Insertable Objects that are created by Excel include a worksheet, chart, cell, or a range of cells.

To add an Insertable Object to your Toolbox, pull down the Project menu and select Components. Locate and select the desired object in the Insertable Objects tabbed dialog (as shown in Figure C.4b) then click OK. Once you add a control to the Toolbox, you can add it to a form just as you would an intrinsic control.

To remove an Insertable Object from the Toolbox, pull down the Project menu and select Components. Locate and select the desired control and clear the check box next to the name of the Insertable Object you want to delete, and then choose OK. You cannot delete an Insertable Object that is used in the current project. Instead, an error message will appear indicating that you are using the object in your current project.

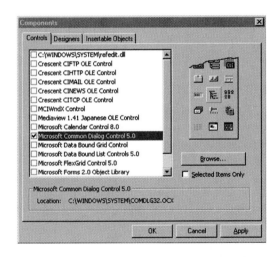

(a) ActiveX Controls

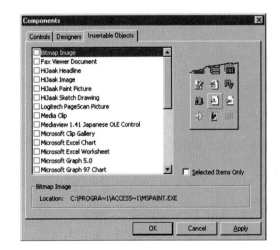

(b) Insertable Objects

FIGURE C.4   Adding Tools to the Toolbox

STANDARD MENUS FOR WINDOWS APPLICATIONS

D

OVERVIEW

The standard menu bar for all Microsoft Office 97 applications is identical in Excel, Word, and PowerPoint except for the application-specific menu item (sixth item) for each application. Table D.1 shows the position of the menu titles on the standard menu bar.

TABLE D.1 Standard Menu Titles for Office Applications

File Edit View Format Tools App-Specific Window Help

When designing your menus, use the Microsoft standard menu positions. The menu items for Office 97 applications are shown in Table D.2. For example, the Open, Close, and Print commands are always under the File menu, and Exit is the last command. The menu title is shown in boldface font in the table below, and the menu items are immediately under each.

TABLE D.2 Standard Menu Items for Office Applications

File	**Edit**	**View**	**Window**
New	Undo	Toolbars	New Window
Open	Repeat	Ruler	Arrange
Close	Cut	Zoom	Arrange All
Save	Copy		List of open windows
Save As	Paste	**Insert**	
Save As HTML	Paste Special	Picture	**Help**
Page Setup	Paste As Hyperlink	Object	Help Topics
Print	Clear		About
Send To	Select All	**Tools**	
Properties	Find	Spelling	
Most-recently used list	Replace	Macro	
Exit	Go To	Customize	
	Links	Options	
	Object		

For more information, open the Visual Basic online documentation and select the Contents tab or icon. Open the *Using Visual Basic* book (version 6 only), then the *Programmer's Guide*, then the *(Part 2) What Can You Do With Visual Basic?*, then the *Creating a User Interface*, and finally the *Using Menus in Your Applications* book. See the topic "Menu Title and Naming Guidelines."

PH/CBT SYSTEMS
CD-ROM TUTORIAL

OVERVIEW

Prentice Hall is pleased to announce a strategic partnership with CBT Systems, a leading developer of interactive computer-based products for client/server technologies. CBT has developed a complete set of CD-based tutorials that are available to colleges and universities exclusively through Prentice Hall and the Grauer/Barber (Eaton) Exploring Windows series. The tutorials and text cover many of the same topics, albeit in different sequence. Additional topics of a supplementary nature, however, may be found in one place but not the other. Students using both the text and the CD tutorials in tandem are provided with a well-rounded presentation.

To help you locate the appropriate topic, this appendix provides a series of tables, each of which displays the topics in different sequence. The first table lists the topics in alphabetic order. The second table lists the topics in the order presented on the CD. Finally, the third table lists the topics according to the chapters in this textbook.

Once you have perused the list of topics, it's time to get to work with the textbook or the CD. And, of course, you are welcome to visit the Prentice Hall and CBT Web sites at *http://www.prenhall.com/grauer* and *http://www.cbtsys.com*. At the time this text was published, the CBT Tutorials were available only for Visual Basic 5.0. Check the author's textbook Web site at *http://www.swva.net/ceaton* for more up-to-date information.

Topic	CBT Tutorial: Microsoft Visual Basic 5.0 Fundamentals: Basic Concepts	Textbook Chapter: Essentials/Exploring Microsoft Visual Basic
Access keys	Unit 3: Screen 11	Chapter 4
ActiveX Controls	—	Chapter 8, Appendix C
Add code	Unit 1: Screen 11	Chapters 2, 3
Application control	—	Chapter 3
Applications	Unit 1: Screen 1	Chapter 1
Automation	—	Chapter 6
BackColor property	Unit 2: Screen 5	Chapter 2
Books Online	Unit 1: Screen 14	Chapter 1
Borderstyle property	Unit 3: Screen 2	—
Change properties using code	Unit 2: Screen 6	Chapter 4
Class	Unit 2: Screen 1	Chapter 5, Appendix B
Code Editor window	Unit 1: Screens 2–3 Unit 2: Screen 11	Chapters 2, 3
Command button	Unit 3: Screen 9	Chapter 4
Common dialog control	—	Chapter 5
Compilers and interpreters	—	Chapter 2
Constants	—	Chapter 3
Context-sensitive help	Unit 1: Screen 13	Chapter 1
Create a Visual Basic application	Unit 1: Screens 9–12; Unit 4: Screen 1	Chapter 2
Create executable files	Unit 1: Screen 8	Chapter 2
Database basics	—	Chapter 7
Debugging	—	Chapter 2
Document an application	—	Chapter 2
Error handling	—	Chapter 5
Event procedures	Unit 2: Screen 10	Chapter 3
Event-driven languages	Unit 2: Screen 11	Chapter 1
Executable files	Unit 1: Screen 8	Chapter 2
Exploring Visual Basic data disk	—	Chapter 1
File access	—	Chapter 5
File input / output	—	Chapter 5
File menu	Unit 1: Screen 7	Chapter 2
File type	—	Chapter 5
Font property	Unit 2: Screen 4	Chapter 2
Form methods	Unit 3: Screen 3	—
Functions	—	Chapter 3

(continued)

Topic	CBT Tutorial	Textbook Chapter
GUI design	—	Chapter 4
Hands-on exercises	Unit 4: Screens 1–4	Chapters 1–8 (3 per chapter)
History of Visual Basic	Unit 1: Screen 1	Chapter 1
Insertable Objects	Unit 2: Screen 12	Chapter 6, Appendix C
Instance	—	Chapter 5, Appendix B
Integrated Development Environment	Unit 1: Screens 2–3	Chapter 1
Intrinsic controls	Unit 1: Screens 2–3 Unit 3: Screens 6–9	Chapter 4, Appendix C
Label control	Unit 3: Screen 6	Chapter 4
LostFocus event	Unit 3: Screen 8	—
MDI forms	Unit 3: Screen 4	Chapter 4
Menu editor	—	Chapter 4
Methods	Unit 2: Screen 8	Appendix B
Microsoft on the Web	Unit 1: Screen 15	Chapter 1
Modules	—	Chapter 3
Multiple forms	Unit 3: Screen 1	Chapter 4
Naming conventions	Unit 2: Screen 2	Appendix B
Object Browser	Unit 2: Screen 12	Chapter 1
Object Linking and Embedding (OLE)	—	Chapter 6
Object naming conventions	Unit 2: Screen 2	Appendix B
Objects, methods, events	Unit 1: Screen 4	Chapter 2, Appendix B
OLE Container control	—	Chapter 5
OLE objects	—	Chapter 6
Online Help	Unit 1: Screens 13–15 Unit 2: Screens 9, 13	Chapter 1
Print dialog box	—	Chapter 5
Printer object	—	Chapter 5
Procedures	Unit 2: Screen 10	Chapter 3
Programming languages	Unit 2: Screen 11	Chapter 1
Project files	Unit 1: Screens 5–6	Chapter 2
Recordsets	—	Chapter 8
Refresh method, LostFocus event	Unit 3: Screen 8	—
Set properties	Unit 1: Screen 10 Unit 2: Screen 3	Chapter 2
Set properties with code	Unit 2: Screen 6	Chapter 4

(continued)

Topic	CBT Tutorial	Textbook Chapter
Set properties with Properties window	Unit 2: Screen 3	Chapter 1
Standard menus	—	Appendix D
Steps to creating an application	Unit 4: Screen 1	Chapter 2
Strings	—	Chapter 5
Sub statement	Unit 2: Screen 10	Chapter 3
Tab order, Tab Index property	Unit 3: Screen 10	—
Technical support	Unit 1: Screen 15	Chapter 1
Test code	Unit 1: Screen 12	Chapter 2
Text box control	Unit 3: Screen 7	Chapter 4
Toolbars	Unit 1: Screens 2–3	Chapter 1, Appendix C
Toolbox	Unit 1: Screens 2–3 Unit 3: Screen 5	Chapters 1, 3, 4, Appendix C
Variables	Unit 3: Screen 3	Chapter 3
Visual Basic 6.0 features	—	Entire book and Appendix F
Visual Basic and Office 97	—	Chapter 1
Visual Basic Editions	Unit 1: Screen 1	Chapter 1
Visual Basic reserved words	—	Appendix A
Visual Data Manager	—	Chapter 8
Windows 95 dialog boxes	—	Chapter 5
With statement	Unit 2: Screen 7	—

TABLE E.2 TOPICS IN CBT TUTORIAL ORDER

Topic	CBT Tutorial	Textbook Chapter
Visual Basic Editions	**The Visual Basic Development Environment** Unit 1: Screen 1	Chapter 1
Integrated Development Environment	Unit 1: Screens 2–3	Chapter 1
Objects, methods, events	Unit 1: Screen 4	Chapter 2
Project files, beginner and advanced	**Project and Executable Files** Unit 1: Screens 5–6	Chapter 2
File menu	Unit 1: Screen 7	Chapter 2
Executable files	Unit 1: Screen 8	Chapter 2
Create a Visual Basic application	**Creating a Simple Application** Unit 1: Screens 9–12	Chapter 2
Set properties	Unit 1: Screen 10	Chapter 2

(continued)

Topic	CBT Tutorial	Textbook Chapter
Add code	Unit 1: Screen 11	Chapter 2
Test code	Unit 1: Screen 12	Chapter 2
Online Help	**Using Online Help** Unit 1: Screen 13	Chapter 1
Context-sensitive help	Unit 1: Screen 13	Chapter 1
Books Online	Unit 1: Screen 14	Chapter 1
Technical support	Unit 1: Screen 15	Chapter 1
Microsoft on the Web	Unit 1: Screen 15	Chapter 1
Class	**Naming objects** Unit 2: Screen 1	Chapter 5, Appendix B
Naming conventions	Unit 2: Screen 2	Appendix B
Set properties	**Working with Properties** Unit 2: Screen 3	Chapter 1
Font property	Unit 2: Screen 4	—
BackColor property	Unit 2: Screen 5	Chapter 2
Set properties with code	Unit 2: Screen 6	Chapter 4
With statement	Unit 2: Screen 7	—
Methods	**Methods** Unit 2: Screen 8	Appendix B
Online help for methods	Unit 2: Screen 9	Chapter 1
Event procedures	**Events** Unit 2: Screen 10	Chapter 3
Event-driven languages	Unit 2: Screen 11	Chapters 1, 3
Programming languages	Unit 2: Screen 11	Chapter 1
Object Browser	**The Object Browser** Unit 2: Screen 12	Chapters 1, 6
Online help for Object Browser	Unit 2: Screen 13	Chapter 1
Multiple forms	**Forms** Unit 3: Screen 1	Chapter 4
Borderstyle property	Unit 3: Screen 2	—
Form methods	Unit 3: Screen 3	—
MDI forms	Unit 3: Screen 4	Chapter 4
Toolbox	**Basic Controls** Unit 3: Screen 5	Chapters 1, 3, Appendix C
Label control	Unit 3: Screen 6	Chapter 4
Text box control	Unit 3: Screen 7	Chapter 4
Refresh method, LostFocus event	Unit 3: Screen 8	—
Command button	Unit 3: Screen 9	Chapter 4
Tab order, Tab Index property	**Control Accessibility** Unit 3: Screen 10	—
Access keys	Unit 3: Screen 11	Chapter 4

(continued)

Topic	CBT Tutorial	Textbook Chapter
Hands-on exercise and demo	**Live Application Tutorial** Unit 4: Screen 1	Chapters 1–8
Hands-on exercise and demo	**Creating a Logon Screen** Unit 4: Screen 2	Chapters 1–8
Hands-on exercise and demo	**Setting Object Properties** Unit 4: Screen 3	Chapters 1–8
Hands-on exercise and demo	**Adding Functionality** Unit 4: Screen 4	Chapters 1–8

TABLE E.3. TOPICS IN TEXTBOOK ORDER

Topic	CBT Tutorial	Textbook Chapter
Applications	Unit 1: Screen 1	**Chapter 1: Introduction to Visual Basic**
Programming languages	—	Chapter 1
History of Visual Basic	Unit 1: Screen 1	Chapter 1
Visual Basic Editions	Unit 1: Screen 1	Chapter 1
Integrated Development Environment	Unit 1: Screens 2–3	Chapter 1
Exploring Visual Basic data disk	—	Chapter 1
Online Help	Unit 1: Screens 13–15	Chapter 1
Visual Basic and Office 97	—	Chapter 1
Hands-on exercises	Unit 4: Screens 1–4	Chapter 1
Compilers and Interpreters	—	**Chapter 2: Build Your First Project**
Steps to creating an application	Unit 4: Screen 1	Chapter 2
Create a Visual Basic application	Unit 4: Screen 1	Chapter 2
Project files	Unit 1: Screen 5	Chapter 2
File menu	Unit 1: Screen 7	Chapter 2
Code Editor window	Unit 1: Screens 2–3	Chapter 2
Debugging	—	Chapter 2
Document an application	—	Chapter 2
Executable files	Unit 1: Screen 8	Chapter 2
Hands-on exercises	Unit 4: Screens 1–4	Chapter 2
Procedures	Unit 2: Screen 10	**Chapter 3: Programming Fundamentals**
Modules	—	Chapter 3
Code Editor window	Unit 2: Screen 11	Chapter 3

(continued)

Topic	CBT Tutorial	Textbook Chapter
Sub statement	Unit 2: Screen 10	Chapter 3
Constants	—	Chapter 3
Variables	Unit 3: Screen 3	Chapter 3
Functions	—	Chapter 3
Application control	—	Chapter 3
Hands-on exercise	—	Chapter 3
GUI design	—	**Chapter 4: Enhancing the Graphical User Interface**
Toolbox	Unit 3: Screen 5	Chapter 4
Intrinsic controls	Unit 3: Screens 6–9	Chapter 4
Set properties with code	Unit 2: Screen 6	Chapter 4
Menu editor	—	Chapter 4
Hands-on exercises	—	Chapter 4
Windows 95 dialog boxes	—	**Chapter 5: Basics of File Input and Output**
Common dialog control	—	Chapter 5
Instance	—	Chapter 5
Class	Unit 2: Screen 1	Chapter 5
File type	—	Chapter 5
File access	—	Chapter 5
File input/output	—	Chapter 5
Error handling	—	Chapter 5
Strings	—	Chapter 5
Printer object	—	Chapter 5
Print dialog box	—	Chapter 5
Hands-on exercises	—	Chapter 5
Object Linking and Embedding (OLE)	Unit 1: Screen 1	**Chapter 6: Programming with Office 97**
OLE container control	—	Chapter 6
Automation	—	Chapter 6
OLE objects	—	Chapter 6
Hands-on exercises	—	Chapter 6
Database basics	—	**Chapter 7: Database Basics**
Microsoft Flexgrid control	—	Chapter 7
Hands-on exercises	—	Chapter 7
ActiveX Database Controls	—	**Chapter 8: Relational Databases**

(continued)

Topic	CBT Tutorial	Textbook Chapter
Database controls	—	Chapter 8
Recordsets	—	Chapter 8
Visual Data Manager	—	Chapter 8
Hands-on exercises	—	Chapter 8
Visual Basic Reserved Words	—	**Appendix A: Visual Basic Reserved Words**
Object Naming Conventions	Unit 2: Screen 2	**Appendix B: Object- Naming Conventions**
Toolbox	Unit 1: Screens 2–3 Unit 3: Screen 5	**Appendix C: The Toolbox, Toolbars, and Controls**
Toolbars	Unit 1: Screens 2–3	Appendix C
Intrinsic Controls	Unit 1: Screens 2–3	Appendix C
ActiveX Controls	—	Appendix C
Insertable Objects	Unit 2: Screen 12	Appendix C
Standard Menus	—	Appendix D: Standard Menus for Windows Applications
CBT Tutorial	Entire CD-ROM	Appendix E: PH/CBT Systems CD-ROM Tutorial
Visual Basic 6.0 features	—	Appendix F: What's New in Visual Basic 6.0

WHAT'S NEW WITH VISUAL BASIC 6.0

OVERVIEW

Visual Basic 6.0 is the sixth major release of the Visual Basic programming language. This appendix is written for those migrating from Visual Basic 5.0, or using both Visual Basic 6.0 and 5.0 in the lab or at home. One of the advantages of this textbook is that it can be used with both Visual Basic 5.0 and Visual Basic 6.0. If you are using the previous version of Visual Basic, most of the exercise instructions will be exactly the same. Where they are different, alternate instructions are given in tip boxes.

Microsoft introduced the first version of Visual Basic for Windows 3 and the DOS operating system in 1992 and has released a new version of the language each year. BASIC (Beginner's All-purpose Symbolic Instruction Code) is the ancestor of the Visual Basic programming language. In the 1970s and 1980s, numerous software vendors, especially Microsoft, added features to BASIC. Today BASIC is one of the most popular and complex programming languages. However, it is still easy for beginners to use. Microsoft created Visual Basic for end users, and it remains true to its roots today. ***Visual Basic 4.0*** is designed for the Windows 95 32-bit operating system, and an edition of it is built into the Microsoft Office 95 applications. ***Visual Basic 5.0*** is designed for the Windows 95 operating system and Office 97 applications.

How significant is the upgrade to Visual Basic 6.0? The answer depends on your current installation. If you are upgrading from a version prior to Visual Basic 5.0, the change is dramatic because the default integrated development environment (IDE) is completely different. The new version is also easier to use and much more powerful. If, on the other hand, you are migrating from Visual Basic 5.0, the change is less noticeable. Visual Basic 6.0 has a number of new features, and the ones following are just a few. See Visual Basic 6.0's ***What's New*** online book for a listing of all the many new and updated features of Visual Basic 6.0.

One of the new features of Visual Basic 6.0 is the MSDN (Microsoft Developer Network) Library. Visual Basic 6.0 utilizes **Internet Explorer 4.1** to view the new **MSDN Library**. The help files and online reference books for all the development products in the Visual Studio 6.0 suite are included in the Library. The Visual Studio 6.0 suite includes Visual Basic, Visual C++, Visual FoxPro, Visual Inter-Dev, Visual J++, the MSDN Library, and other tools for developing applications. The Visual Basic 6.0 documentation includes a Documentation Map, What's New, Programmer's Guide, Samples, and Reference Guidebooks for all editions of Visual Basic. The Professional Edition and Enterprise editions include additional books such as the Component Tools Guide and the Data Access Guide. Figure F.1 shows the MSDN Library's entire table of contents.

Notice that the MSDN Library window is displayed like a browser, and divided into three panes. The left pane is the **navigation pane**. Double click a book to open it, and then double click the chapter and topic. The navigation pane contains the Contents, Index, Search, and Favorites tabs. Click the appropriate tab to change the displayed mode. The right pane is the **topic pane**. The page you select is displayed in the topic pane. The top pane contains the **toolbar**, with Hide, Locate, Previous, Next, Back, Forward, Stop, Refresh, Home, and Print buttons. If you have an Internet connection, you can also view Web pages in this window. Pull down the Go menu and select URL. Type the URL (Web address) in the dialog box. The Web page will be displayed in the right pane.

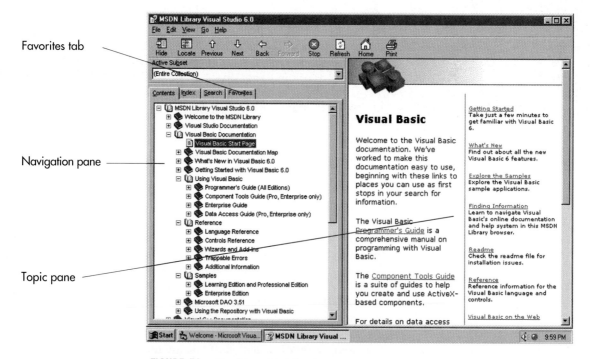

FIGURE F.1   Visual Basic 6.0 Online Documentation

Visual Basic 6.0 Alternatives to 5.0 Help Tools

One of the frequently accessed help tools available with Visual Basic 5.0 is the **Glossary**, opened by clicking the toolbar's Glossary button. There are several glossaries available in the MSDN Library. To locate the glossaries, click the Search tab, enter the word **glossary** in the text box, and check the Search Titles Only check box. Click the List Topics command button to list the glossaries. To search for a specific term, enter the specific **term + definition** in the Search text box.

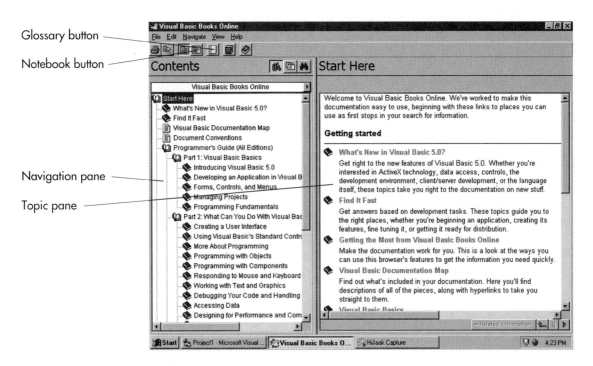

Glossary button

Notebook button

Navigation pane

Topic pane

FIGURE F.2 Visual Basic 5.0 Online Documentation

Another handy help feature with Visual Basic 5.0 is the *Notebook*. You can take notes in your online notebook as you read a section, and refer back to it later. Click the toolbar's Notebook button to display and edit the Notebook. Visual Basic 6.0 has a *Favorites tab* that displays a list of previously marked topics. This is similar to creating Favorites with Internet Explorer or bookmarks with Netscape Navigator. You can add topics to and delete topics from the Favorites list and access the previous list here. However, you cannot add your own notes to the Favorites list as you could with the Notebook.

NEW AND IMPROVED WIZARDS

Package and Deployment Wizard

The *Package and Deployment Wizard* replaces Visual Basic 5.0's *Setup Wizard*. Both wizards allow you to easily package and distribute your applications to others. The Package and Deployment Wizard automates many of the steps involved in distributing your applications. You can practice using this wizard in Chapter 2 Practice Exercise 3.

Distributing your application to others requires two basic steps: packaging and then deployment. The first step is to package the application. The *package* step compresses the application files into one or more files to fit on diskettes, CDs, network drives, or an Internet server machine. The new wizard allows you to create two types of packages: standard package or Internet package. A *standard package* is used to distribute applications to a disk or to a local or network drive. An *Internet package* is used to distribute applications over an intranet or the Internet. The *deployment* step involves decompressing and installing your application's files to the final destination disk or network drive.

To start the Package and Deployment Wizard from the Windows desktop, click the Start button and the Programs menu. Then select Microsoft Visual Basic 6.0 (alternatively Microsoft Visual Studio 6.0) and finally Package & Deployment Wizard. To start the process, select the application to package, and the type of package you wish to create. To finish, select the Deploy button and follow the instructions. For more information on the wizard, see the *Distributing Your Applications* book in the MSDN Library. To locate this topic, open the *Programmer's Guide*, and then the *Part 2* book. Alternatively, the **Setup Toolkit** lets you customize some of the installation process, and is still available with Visual Basic 6.0.

Application Wizard

In addition to the new Package and Deployment Wizard, other wizards have been improved. All editions of Visual Basic include the **Application Wizard**. The improved wizard allows you to save your settings in profiles for later use. Refer to Hands-on Exercise 1 in Chapter 4 for detailed instructions for using this wizard.

The Toolbar Wizard

You can more easily create customized tools with the **Toolbar Wizard**. This wizard automatically starts when you add a toolbar to a form when using the Application Wizard. Many more new and improved wizards are incorporated into Visual Basic 6.0. Refer to the "What's New in Wizards" topic in the *What's New in Visual Basic 6.0* online book for more information.

FILE SYSTEM OBJECT (FSO) MODEL

The **File System Object (FSO) model**, a new feature in Visual Basic 6.0, provides an object-based tool for working with drives, folders, and files. The model also makes processing sequential access to text files easier. Refer to Chapter 5 for syntax and more details for implementing sequential access to text files using FSO.

A drawback to the FSO model is that it does not yet support random or binary file access. For these, you can continue to use the older file processing statements such as Open, Input, Print, and Close.

The File System Object model has 5 objects: Drive, Folder, Files, FileSystemObject, and TextStream. The **Drive object** allows you to get information about a drive, such as available space. The **Folder object** gives you the ability to create, change, move, and delete folders, and gain information about folders, such as their name. The **Files object** allows you to create, delete, move files, and gain information about files, such as their names and paths. The **FileSystem object** is the primary object of the model, and contains methods that allow you to manipulate drives, folders, and files. The **TextStream object** enables you to read and write text files.

Before we can use any of the FSO objects, we must first create an object using the **CreateObject function**. This function has been enhanced in Visual Basic 6.0, to support FSO objects. The CreateObject function creates and returns a reference to a File System Object and other ActiveX objects. After we create a file system object, we use it to open a specified text file for sequential access using the **OpenTextFile method**. After we have opened the file, we can read, write, or close the file. The **TextStream object** is used for sequential processing of a file.

DATA AND DATABASE ENHANCEMENTS

Visual Basic 6.0 includes several enhancements to work with data and databases. The most noticeable enhancement is the Standard toolbar's new **Data View button**, as shown in Figure F.3. The Data View button displays the Data View Window. The Data View window is not available with the Learning Edition. You can access, view connections, and change the structure of a database in the Data View window.

Data view button

FIGURE F.3 The Toolbar with the Data View button

All editions of Visual Basic 6.0 incorporate the new **Data Grid control**, **Data List control**, and the **Data Combo control**. These controls are OLE database versions of the data controls contained in Visual Basic 5.0. **ADO (ActiveX Data Objects)** is a new data access technology to work with Microsoft and non-Microsoft data. For more information on database tools, refer to the *More Database Tools* topic in Chapter 8 of this text.

An updated version of the **Microsoft FlexGrid** (MSFlexGrid) is available with Visual Basic 6.0, numbered 6.0. The previous version, available in Visual Basic 5.0, was numbered 5.0. A new control, called the **Hierarchical FlexGrid**, is also available. The MSHFlexGrid provides advanced features for displaying data in a grid format. For more information on using the FlexGrid control, see the *Microsoft FlexGrid* topic in Chapter 7 of this text.

The Professional and Enterprise editions of Visual Basic 6.0 incorporate a new **Data Environment Designer** and **Visual Database Tools**. You can view, query, and design database elements such as tables, diagrams, and views. You can also visually create reusable data objects. For more information on the data and database enhancements see the *What's New in Data Access* topic in the MSDN Library. To locate this topic, first open the *What's New in Visual Basic* book.

SUMMARY

This appendix summarizes some of the major improvements of Visual Basic 6.0, for those migrating from Visual Basic 5.0, or using both Visual Basic 6.0 and 5.0 in the lab or at home. One of the advantages of this textbook is that it can be used with both Visual Basic 5.0 and Visual Basic 6.0. If you are using the previous version of Visual Basic, most of the exercise instructions will be exactly the same. Where they are different, alternate instructions are given in tip boxes.

The significance of the upgrade to Visual Basic 6.0 depends on your current installation. If you are upgrading from Visual Basic 4.0 or previous versions, the change is dramatic because the default Integrated Development Environment (IDE) is completely different. If you are migrating from Visual Basic 5.0, the change is less noticeable because version 5 already incorporates many of the more visible changes. Visual Basic 6.0 utilizes Internet Explorer 4.1 to view the new MSDN Library. The MSDN Library enables you to browse and search the Visual Basic online documentation, and gives immediate access to Web pages as well. There are several new and improved wizards that are easier to use and more powerful. The Package and Deployment wizard replaces the older Setup Wizard. The Application Wizard has been improved and automatically starts the new Toolbar Wizard when you add a toolbar to a form.

The File System Object (FSO) model simplifies file system management and offers an alternative for processing files sequentially. A drawback to the FSO model is that it does not support the random or binary file access. You can continue to use the older file processing statements for these files.

Visual Basic 6.0 includes several enhancements to work with data and databases. The Standard toolbar's new **Data View button** displays the Data View window, available with the Professional and Enterprise editions. The improved Data Grid control, Data List control, and Data Combo controls are incorporated in all three editions. ActiveX Data Objects (ADO) is a new data access technology that works with Microsoft and non-Microsoft databases. An updated version of the Microsoft FlexGrid, and a new control called the Hierarchical FlexGrid, are available to display data in grid formats. The new Data Environment Designer and Visual Database Tools are available in the Professional and Enterprise editions.

KEY WORDS AND CONCEPTS

ActiveX Data Objects (ADO)
Application Wizard
CreateObject function
Data Combo control
Data Environment Designer
Data Grid control

Data List control
Data Object Wizard
Data View button
Drive object
File System Object (FSO) model
FileSystem object
Folder object

Hierarchical FlexGrid
Microsoft FlexGrid
MSDN Library
OpenTextFile method
Package and Deployment Wizard
TextStream object
Toolbar Wizard

INDEX